International Human Rights Law Beyond State Territorial Control

Can international human rights law be applied and enforced in a part of a State's territory outside its effective control? This study provides a step-by-step analysis to show how it can. International human rights law can normalise an imperfect, defective situation through pragmatic interpretation; it imposes obligations both on the territorial State on account of its sovereign title and residual effectiveness on the one hand, and on any subject of international law exercising territorial control over the area on account of its effective control on the other. By considering effectiveness beyond formal normative sources and titles of the subjects implicated in the territorial situation, international human rights law is interpreted and applied in a manner which renders human rights practical and effective. The book provides a comprehensive analysis of State practice regarding various subjects implicated in the territorial situation, applicable legal sources and major geographic areas.

ANTAL BERKES is a lecturer in law at Brunel University London. He conducts research in public international law, especially international human rights law and international humanitarian law. He held postdoctoral positions at the University of Manchester, Manchester International Law Centre and the University of Pretoria.

CAMBRIDGE STUDIES IN INTERNATIONAL AND COMPARATIVE LAW: 156

Established in 1946, this series produces high quality, reflective and innovative scholarship in the field of public international law. It publishes works on international law that are of a theoretical, historical, cross-disciplinary or doctrinal nature. The series also welcomes books providing insights from private international law, comparative law and transnational studies which inform international legal thought and practice more generally.

The series seeks to publish views from diverse legal traditions and perspectives, and of any geographical origin. In this respect it invites studies offering regional perspectives on core *problématiques* of international law, and in the same vein, it appreciates contrasts and debates between diverging approaches. Accordingly, books offering new or less orthodox perspectives are very much welcome. Works of a generalist character are greatly valued and the series is also open to studies on specific areas, institutions or problems. Translations of the most outstanding works published in other languages are also considered.

After seventy years, Cambridge Studies in International and Comparative Law sets the standard for international legal scholarship and will continue to define the discipline as it evolves in the years to come.

A list of books in the series can be found at the end of this volume.

International Human Rights Law Beyond State Territorial Control

Antal Berkes
Brunel University London

CAMBRIDGE
UNIVERSITY PRESS

CAMBRIDGE
UNIVERSITY PRESS

University Printing House, Cambridge CB2 8BS, United Kingdom

One Liberty Plaza, 20th Floor, New York, NY 10006, USA

477 Williamstown Road, Port Melbourne, VIC 3207, Australia

314–321, 3rd Floor, Plot 3, Splendor Forum, Jasola District Centre, New Delhi – 110025, India

79 Anson Road, #06–04/06, Singapore 079906

Cambridge University Press is part of the University of Cambridge.

It furthers the University's mission by disseminating knowledge in the pursuit of education, learning, and research at the highest international levels of excellence.

www.cambridge.org
Information on this title: www.cambridge.org/9781108840620
DOI: 10.1017/9781108886543

First published 2021

A catalogue record for this publication is available from the British Library.

Library of Congress Cataloging-in-Publication Data
Names: Berkes, Antal, author.
Title: International human rights law beyond state territorial control / Antal Berkes, Brunel University.
Description: Cambridge, United Kingdom ; New York, NY : Cambridge University Press, 2021. | Series: Cambridge studies in international and comparative law ; 156 | Includes index.
Identifiers: LCCN 2020056189 (print) | LCCN 2020056190 (ebook) | ISBN 9781108840620 (hardback) | ISBN 9781108814324 (paperback) | ISBN 9781108886543 (epub)
Subjects: LCSH: Humanitarian law | Military occupation. | De facto doctrine. | Non-state actors (International relations)
Classification: LCC KZ6471 .B469 2021 (print) | LCC KZ6471 (ebook) | DDC 341.6/7–dc23
LC record available at https://lccn.loc.gov/2020056189
LC ebook record available at https://lccn.loc.gov/2020056190

ISBN 978-1-108-84062-0 Hardback

Contents

Foreword

The title of this highly informative and brilliantly researched book is *International Human Rights Law beyond State Territorial Control*. The photograph of urban wreckage and destruction on its cover gives us perhaps a better clue as to what it is about. It is a book about the practical application of International Human Rights Law (IHRL) (and general international law) in often dire situations where the rule of law of the natural sovereign has been supplanted by that of another state or an organised armed group or by a UN multinational peacekeeping force. It thus addresses the intellectually challenging subject of the application of IHRL (as well as public international law (PIL) and international humanitarian law (IHL)) to areas where the international writ appears to be excluded. These 'no-go' areas are often referred to in the literature as 'grey zones', *de facto* regimes, 'legal vacuums' or, more graphically, 'black holes'. Sometimes they also concern so-called frozen conflicts relating to disputed territories where the underlying political problems have become so intractable that the 'forgotten' conflict eludes political resolution amid apparent international indifference and lack of media coverage until the inevitable eruption occurs and takes everyone by surprise, apart, of course, from the local population and the disputing states. The disputes in Transnistria, Nagorno-Karabakh, northern Cyprus, Crimea, South Ossetia and Abkhazia are prime examples. Those in Kosovo, Iraq, Afghanistan and Colombia, to name but a few troubled regions, where armed conflict flares up at regular intervals or has never stopped, are more active conflicts in need of a political resolution.

Some of the pertinent questions that arise are – how are the rights of the local populations protected in these areas and what are the international human rights obligations of the states involved on both sides of the dispute or of the factions that exercise control over the region or of any peacekeeping forces that may be stationed there? What is the content of these obligations and can they be enforced judicially? What principles govern the extraterritorial reach of human rights treaties? Must the states derogate from their obligations under human rights treaties when they perform a policing role in such conflicts? Is there scope for the deployment of non-judicial mechanisms of promotion and protection of human rights? How do international organisations such as the UN or the Council of Europe assert their concerns for the human rights issues that arise and what judicial and non-judicial remedies, both national and international, exist for those whose rights are infringed? How does the European Court of Human Rights (ECtHR) examine complaints that inevitably emerge from these areas, often brought by individuals against both states and/or by one state against another under Article 33, ECHR?

On 25 September 1995, the renowned international lawyer and advocate, Ian Brownlie, addressed the former ECtHR in the hearing on the merits in the landmark *Loizidou* v. *Turkey* case (GC, judgment of 18 December 1996). The issue at stake was whether Turkey was responsible as a matter of international law for the acts and policies of the 'Turkish Republic of Northern Cyprus' (TRNC). Turkey's main submission – a familiar one for states that occupy territory that is not their own – was that the TRNC was a state in its own right, with all the trappings of statehood and laws enforceable before its own courts. Mrs Loizidou's lack of access to her property was to be laid at the door of the TRNC, not Turkey. The fact that Turkey was the only state that recognised the TRNC should make no difference to the Court's appreciation of Turkey's lack of responsibility for the acts of the entity. Brownlie and his team argued that international law, especially IHRL, deplored a vacuum in legal arrangements and that Turkey exercised 'effective control' over the TRNC and its territory through its large military presence and continuing financial support. It was tantamount to a 'puppet state' set up and controlled by Turkey. He added that in such a situation the Court's interpretation of the threshold requirement of 'jurisdiction' (Article 1, ECHR) must recognise that reality and find that the acts of the TRNC

All judgments and admissibility decisions of the ECtHR referred to herein can be found in Hudoc (https:// hudoc.echr.coe.int).

were attributable to Turkey and gave rise to Turkey's international responsibility.

Up until the *Loizidou* judgments, the former European Commission of Human Rights held, in the third *Cyprus* v. *Turkey* case (Dec, 25 May 1975), that 'jurisdiction' under Article 1, ECHR existed where Turkish armed forces exercised physical control and responsibility over persons. It was not limited to the national territory. In line with this approach, to establish 'jurisdiction' in *Loizidou* the applicant would have to demonstrate some form of link between the actions of Turkish officials or security forces and the acts or policies in question. However, in its judgment on the merits, the former Court accepted Brownlie's principled approach that it should reject those arguments that would have the effect of leaving the inhabitants of northern Cyprus unprotected by the provisions of the ECHR. The Court went an important step further and held that once it was established that Turkey exercised 'effective control' over the TRNC then all of its actions and policies were imputable to Turkey *ipso facto* without any need to examine the extent to which Turkey endorsed, approved or was linked to the acts under scrutiny. The acts of the entity were all capable of giving rise to the international responsibility of Turkey.

Thus was born the concept of jurisdiction under Article 1, ECHR, based on the notion of 'effective control' of territory outside the state's natural borders. As Antal Berkes's book well illustrates, the Court has since been confronted with a wide variety of extraterritorial jurisdiction cases, based on the doctrine of effective control, concerning issues arising in Transnistria; northern Cyprus, including the buffer zone; Nagorno-Karabakh and, most recently, the situation in the Crimea (*Ukraine* v. *Russia,* GC dec, 16 December 2020) and the war between Georgia and Russia (*Georgia* v. *Russia (II)*, GC judgment of 21 January 2021). Indeed, the question of whether the requirement of 'jurisdiction' was satisfied in respect of extraterritorial acts and policies, be it on the basis of effective control of territory or on the basis of control of persons, has led to the development of a rich and often complex vein of ECHR caselaw involving such landmark decisions and judgments as *Banković* (GC dec, 12 December 2001), *Ilaşcu* (GC judgment of 8 July 2004), *Behrami and Behrami* (GC dec, 2 May 2007), *Al-Skeini* (GC judgment of 7 July 2011), *Al-Jedda* (GC judgment of 7 July 2011), *Jaloud* (GC judgment of 29 November 2014), *Hassan* (GC judgment of 16 September 2014) and, recently, *Hanan* (GC judgment of 16 February 2021). If *Banković* indicated that 'jurisdiction' under Article 1, ECHR primarily refers to acts that occur in the national territory, the cases that followed sought to delineate the circumstances where there may, nevertheless, be jurisdiction in respect of extraterritorial acts. It is a fair question to ask how much of the *Banković* decision has survived the onslaught of subsequent cases which encroach considerably on its basic territorial premise? The enlightened student of these jurisprudential developments may well wonder whether the Court has not marched its troops to the top of the hill and then marched them back again!

It is a paradox known to international human rights lawyers, and well elucidated in the following pages, that it is often where human rights protection is most needed ('grey zones', war zones, *de facto* regimes, regimes governed by emergency laws) that the protection of human rights is most lacking and, worse, that the degree of scrutiny by international courts such as the ECtHR is weaker. As Antal Berkes points out, national remedies are likely to be ineffective and recourse to international courts lengthy, costly, fraught with political difficulties and perhaps ultimately ineffective. Those living in such regions have effectively become second-class or even third-class citizens whose rights exist, if they exist at all, on a very precarious footing compared to their counterparts living in more peaceful and stable countries.

The author sets out to explore in detail what general international law and IHRL has to say about the protection of rights and freedoms in such 'grey zones' for, as becomes clear in his book, much has been said on the subject by a wide variety of international human rights courts, UN bodies, the ICJ and human rights commissioners. He explores not just the legal obligations of the states that exercise effective control but also the residual obligations of the territorial state. He shows that international obligations vary in accordance with the legal status of the subject. He also examines the law and practice under IHRL and IHL applicable to organised armed groups in control of territory as well as the substantive human rights obligations applicable to the different international peacekeeping operations where effective control may be exercised by the UN (as in the case of UNMIK) or where it might reside in the troop contributing nations as in some UN mandated operations. He argues forcefully that the Court was right in *Behrami* and *Saramati* (GC dec, 2 May 2007) to find that the UN was responsible for the acts of UNMIK but applied the wrong test ('ultimate authority and control' as opposed to 'effective control') in finding that the UN was also responsible for the acts and omissions of KFOR. He demonstrates the vital importance of the various initiatives taken by bodies like the Council of Europe's CPT who have been able to visit places of detention in

Transnistria on various occasions and also in Abkhazia until authorisation was withdrawn. In a similar vein he highlights the effective and groundbreaking work carried out by Thomas Hammarberg during his many visits to Transnistria on behalf of the UN, culminating in an detailed report with multiple observations and recommendations. He observes astutely that non-judicial monitoring bodies such as human rights commissioners or bodies like the CPT may in the end be more effective in influencing states or non-state actors controlling 'grey zones' and the international community than judicial or quasi-judicial mechanisms since they are able to adopt a more holistic approach and have more flexible persuasive capabilities. An important insight is that, by pursuing pragmatic and workable modes of interaction on the fringes of formal normative sources of law, international monitoring bodies interpret and apply IHRL in a manner that renders human rights practical and effective. However, the general thrust of the book is to demonstrate that binding obligations of international law are generated not only by the formal sources of law (treaties, legal title to territory or treaty provisions expressly governing *de facto* situations) but also through the exercise of power and authority by those seeking to control territory, entities and persons.

This is a timely and important study of an area that, apart perhaps from issues concerning 'jurisdiction', is not well covered by human rights scholars and where human rights judgments are frequently derided as amounting to 'mission creep'. He gives very clear and persuasive answers to such critics. His book is, however, considerably wider in scope than a study of extraterritorial jurisdiction by international courts. It has much to recommend it to a wide readership since it covers so many areas of interest – IHRL, IHL, PIL and the law of international organisations. Mr Berkes deploys considerable scholarship in drawing together a vast array of national and international sources in a comprehensive and analytical manner while not losing sight of his main theme. There is little doubt from the multiple authorities that he surveys that the problems of accountability for human rights violations in 'grey zones' or 'black holes' will be with us for a considerable time until political solutions can be brokered. The work of judicial and non-judicial mechanisms in promoting and protecting human rights will undoubtedly have an important role to play in the construction of such solutions by political actors.

Michael O'Boyle

Deputy Registrar of the European Court of Human Rights (2006–2015)

Acknowledgements

In memory of my aunt, Valéria Czirbus (1947–2012)

This book could not have been completed without the assistance and contributions of a vast number of people. The earliest version of this book was my co-supervised PhD dissertation that I defended at Université Paris 1 Panthéon-Sorbonne and Eötvös Loránd University (ELTE) in November 2015. I am grateful to my two supervisors, Laurence Burgorgue-Larsen and Gábor Kardos, for having guided me throughout my doctoral research. I particularly thank Laurence Burgorgue-Larsen for her immense confidence as she accepted my research project without any previous academic relationship between us. I benefitted greatly from her comparative and contextual regard of regional human rights mechanisms. I am grateful for all the thought-provoking conversations and invaluable feedback that I received from Gábor Kardos throughout my doctoral research and afterwards. I also thank the members of the PhD evaluation committee for their most helpful comments that largely contributed to the later versions of the manuscript: Gérard Cahin, Olivier de Frouville, Ioannis Prezas and Pál Sonnevend.

During my doctoral research, several professors, colleagues and friends provided comments and advice for which I am truly grateful: Florian Couveinhes-Matsumoto, Giovanni Distefano, Patrick Jacob, Gábor Kajtár, Henry Torres Vásquez and Christopher Waters. Thanks to the generous funding of the French Foreign Ministry and the Centre for Franco-Russian Studies in Moscow, I was able to conduct two field trips to Colombia and the Republic of Moldova, respectively. During the visits, various interviews with legal practitioners, domestic judges, advocates, agents of NGOs and international organisations broadened my understanding about the context of areas outside the effective control of the State. During a junior research fellowship year at the University of Geneva, a high number of UN experts, members of treaty monitoring bodies and university professors shared with me their thoughts about various aspects of my research, to whom I am indebted. I also benefitted greatly from conversations with two judges of the European Court of Human Rights, Judge Iulia Motoc and András Baka, former judge of the Court.

Even though I had developed some of the ideas in my doctoral dissertation, the argument developed here has been nurtured during two postdoctoral research fellowships at the Manchester International Law Centre (MILC), University of Manchester (2016–2018) and the SARChI Professorship on International Constitutional Law, University of Pretoria (2019). I am extremely grateful to the co-directors of MILC, Jean d'Aspremont and Iain Scobbie, for having integrated me into their vibrant academic community and having shaped my international law thinking through this lifelong experience. During my years at MILC, I was fortunate enough to discuss certain aspects of the argument made here with the co-directors, together with my cherished colleagues and friends to whom I am very grateful: Işıl Aral, Martin Brown, Cecilia Juliana Flores Elizondo, John Haskell, Thibault Moulin and Maria Smirnova.

Although my reflections continued at Manchester, it was especially in 2019 that the manuscript of this book took shape and became a reality, thanks to the generous research fellowship of the SARChI Professorship on International Constitutional Law, University of Pretoria. I cannot thank enough Jean d'Aspremont and the then incumbent of the SARChI Professorship, Erika de Wet, for having tremendously supported me over many years and for having encouraged this book project. The generous research fellowship at the University of Pretoria has allowed me to make great headways in the manuscript and finish most chapters.

I am truly grateful to Erika de Wet for her invaluable guidance in successfully accomplishing the book proposal and the book writing. A special note of thanks must be extended to all her team, my close colleagues at SARChI: Lukman Adebisi Abdulrauf, Rani Pillay, Gertrude Mafoa Quan, and Marko Svicevic. Further, discussions with various professors of the University of Pretoria, especially Christof Heyns, Magnus Killander, Dire Tladi and Frans Viljoen on the African human rights mechanisms, UN treaty bodies and general international law were extremely useful in developing my argument. I am grateful to Annelize Nienaber for her invitation to a luncheon meeting of the Department of Public Law where the comments received from her colleagues helped me further sharpen my thoughts.

Beyond my departments, of which stimulating environment allowed me to carry out my research, I have an especially big debt to two persons who have provided copious intellectual support of various kinds. Their stimulating international legal thinking and friendship have been the most influential on my work. First, Vassilis Tzevelekos has been all over my career a true mentor; he kindly integrated me into various collaborative research projects that have inspired my reflections on due diligence. Second, Valentina Azarova has been a true comrade who triggered my interest in further scrutinising the simultaneous application of special regimes of international law and invited me to collaborate on two fascinating research projects on prolonged military occupation and third-party responsibility.

I would like to express my gratitude to Cambridge University Press's two anonymous reviewers, who provided constructive and very valuable comments that largely contributed to the final version of this book. I am also thankful to Isabeau de Meyer, who meticulously reviewed the final version of the manuscript. Thanks also to the team at Cambridge University Press for their efficient and precise work on the book. I am particularly grateful for their openness to update the final version by integrating the very recent case law. The closing date of the manuscript was 31 January 2021.

I cannot close my acknowledgments without extending a final word of gratitude to my friends and family. The support and community of my friends in Budapest, Paris, Geneva, Manchester and Pretoria were instrumental in striking a good balance between research and life. Without a comprehensive list, I am especially indebted to Mohamed Abdo, Ariane Bachelet, Piroska Baráti-Lak and Péter Baráti, Tibor Bartók, Péter Bischof and Petra Göndöcs, Zsuzsanna Borbély-Albu, Djurdja and Dusan Bukvic, Nassima Chariet, Bernadett Egyházi, Magdolna Egyházi, Gyöngyi Farkas-Karay and Dániel Farkas, Irén and Simon Forstner, Anna and Jean Gonthier, Myriam Hernandez, Zsuzsanna and Mátyás Ivicsics, Orsolya and Gábor Kapás, Dorottya Komáromi, Diána and Balázs Kovács, Miklós Lindmayer, János Lindmayer, Gabriella Lindmayer and Sámuel Markolt, Viktor Lőrincz, Ágota and Tamás Megyeri, Orsolya Mikola and Ábel Kaszián, Viktória Ozsváth and Gellért Lak, Ferenc Muck, György Müller, Miguel Pacheco, Pierre Philocles, Tamás Rados, Francia Rios Ramirez, Máté Rigó, Lajos Siska, Gabriel Stollsteiner, Alla Tymofeyeva, Adrienn Való and Boróka Vizy.

Finally, I would like to thank my parents, Borbála and Ferenc, my brother, Márton, my aunt, Katalin, my uncle, Miklós, and my cousins, Lőrinc and his wife Melissa, Kristóf, Tamás and his wife Orsolya, and Péter, for their constant support and patience.

Abbreviations

ACERWC	African Committee of Experts on the Rights and Welfare of the Child
ACHPR	African Charter on Human and Peoples' Rights
ACHR	American Convention on Human Rights
ACommHPR	African Commission on Human and Peoples' Rights
ACRWC	African Charter on the Rights and Welfare of the Child
ACtHPR	African Court on Human and Peoples' Rights
AOG	armed opposition group
AP I	Protocol Additional to the Geneva Conventions of 12 August 1949, and relating to the Protection of Victims of International Armed Conflicts (Protocol I), 8 June 1977
AP II	Protocol Additional to the Geneva Conventions of 12 August 1949, and relating to the Protection of Victims of Non-International Armed Conflicts (Protocol II), 8 June 1977
ARSIWA	Draft Articles on Responsibility of States for Internationally Wrongful Acts, 2001, dans : *YbILC*, 2001, vol. II, Part Two, UN Doc. A/CN.4/SER.A/2001/Add.1 (Part 2), pp. 26–30, of which the General Assembly took note [Resolution 56/83. Responsibility of States for internationally wrongful acts, UN Doc. A/RES/56/83 (28 January 2002)]
AU	African Union
CAT	Committee against Torture, under the Convention against Torture and Other Cruel, Inhuman or

	Degrading Treatment or Punishment, New York, 10 December 1984
CEDAW	Committee on the Elimination of Discrimination against Women, under the Convention on the Elimination of All Forms of Discrimination against Women, New York, 18 December 1979
CERD	Committee on the Elimination of Racial Discrimination, under the International Convention on the Elimination of All Forms of Racial Discrimination, New York, 7 March 1966
CESCR	Committee on Economic, Social and Cultural Rights
CJEU	Court of Justice of the European Union
CoE	Council of Europe
CPPED	International Convention for the Protection of All Persons from Enforced Disappearance, New York, 20 December 2006
CPT	European Committee for the Prevention of Torture and Inhuman or Degrading Treatment or Punishment
CRC	Committee on the Rights of the Child, under the Convention on the Rights of the Child, New York, 20 November 1989
CRPD	Committee on the Rights of Persons with Disabilities, under the Convention on the Rights of Persons with Disabilities, New York, 13 December 2006
DARIO	Text of the draft articles on the responsibility of international organizations, in: UN Doc. A/66/10 (2011), pp. 54–68, § 87, of which the General Assembly took note [Resolution 66/100. Responsibility of international organizations, UN Doc. A/RES/66/100 (9 December 2011)]
DRC	Democratic Republic of the Congo
ECHR	European Convention on Human Rights and Fundamental Freedoms
ECommHR	European Commission of Human Rights
ECPT	European Convention for the Prevention of Torture and Inhuman or Degrading Treatment or Punishment, Strasbourg, 26 November 1987
ECRI	European Commission against Racism and Intolerance

ECRML	European Charter for Regional or Minority Languages, Strasbourg, 5 November 1992
ECtHR	European Court of Human Rights
EU	European Union
FARC	Fuerzas armadas revolucionarias de Colombia / Revolutionary Armed Forces of Colombia
FCPNM	Framework Convention for the Protection of National Minorities, Strasbourg, 1 February 1995
FRY	Federal Republic of Yugoslavia
GC IV	Convention (IV) Relative to the Protection of Civilian Persons in Time of War, Geneva, 12 August 1949, United Nations, *Treaty Series*, vol. 75, no. 973, pp. 288–417
GRETA	Group of Experts on Action against Trafficking in Human Beings, Council of Europe
The Hague Regulations	Convention (IV) respecting the Laws and Customs of War on Land and its annex: Regulations concerning the Laws and Customs of War on Land, The Hague, 18 October 1907
HRAP	Human Rights Advisory Panel (Kosovo)
HRC	Human Rights Committee under the International Covenant on Civil and Political Rights, New York, 16 December 1966
HRRP	Human Rights Review Panel (Kosovo)
HVO	Croatian Defence Council
IACHR	Inter-American Commission on Human Rights
IACtHR	Inter-American Court of Human Rights
ICC	International Criminal Court
ICCPR	International Covenant on Civil and Political Rights, New York, 16 December 1966
ICESCR	International Covenant on Economic, Social and Cultural Rights, New York, 16 December 1966
ICJ	International Court of Justice
ICMW	International Convention on the Protection of the Rights of All Migrant Workers and Members of their Families, New York, 18 December 1990
ICRC	International Committee of the Red Cross
ICSID	International Centre for Settlement of Investment Disputes
ICTR	International Criminal Tribunal for Rwanda

ICTY	International Criminal Tribunal for the Former Yugoslavia
IHL	international humanitarian law
IHRL	international human rights law
ILA	International Law Association / *Association de droit international*
ILC	International Law Commission
IO	international organisation
IPC	Immovable Property Commission ('Turkish Republic of Northern Cyprus')
JNA	Yugoslav People's Army
KFOR	Kosovo Force
LTTE	Liberation Tigers of Tamil Eelam
MNF	Multi-National Force (Iraq)
MPEPIL	*Max Planck Encyclopedia of Public International Law*
'MRT'	'Moldovan Republic of Transnistria'
NATO	North Atlantic Treaty Organization
NGO	non-governmental organisation
'NKR'	'Nagorno-Karabakh Republic'
OAS	Organization of American States
OIK	Ombudsperson Institution in Kosovo
OP-CAT	Optional Protocol to the Convention against Torture and Other Cruel, Inhuman or Degrading Treatment or Punishment, New York, 18 December 2002
OP-CEDAW	Optional Protocol to the Convention on the Elimination of All Forms of Discrimination against Women, New York, 6 October 1999, UN Doc. A/RES/54/4 (6 October 1999)
OP-CRPD	Optional Protocol to the Convention on the Rights of Persons with Disabilities, New York, 13 December 2006
OP-ICCPR	Optional Protocol to the International Covenant on Civil and Political Rights, New York, 16 December 1966
OP 2-ICCPR	Second Optional Protocol to the International Covenant on Civil and Political Rights, aiming at the abolition of the death penalty, New York, 15 December 1989
OP-ICESCR	Optional Protocol to the International Covenant on Economic, Social and Cultural Rights, New York, 10 December 2008

OPAC-CRC	Optional Protocol to the Convention on the Rights of the Child on the Involvement of Children in Armed Conflict, New York, 25 May 2000
OPSC-CRC	Optional Protocol to the Convention on the Rights of the Child on the Sale of Children, Child Prostitution and Child Pornography, New York, 25 May 2000
PCIJ	Permanent Court of International Justice
PISG	Provisional Institutions of Self-Government (of Kosovo)
SCSL	Special Court for Sierra Leone
SFOR	Force de stabilisation (Bosnie-Herzégovine)
SRSG	Special Representative of the Secretary-General (Kosovo)
TD	territorial declarations
'TRNC'	'Turkish Republic of Northern Cyprus'
UDHR	Universal Declaration of Human Rights, Resolution 217 (III). International Bill of Human Rights (10 December 1948)
UN	United Nations
UNFICYP	United Nations Peacekeeping Force in Cyprus
UNGA	United Nations General Assembly
UNHCHR	(Office of the) United Nations High Commissioner for Human Rights
UNJYB	*United Nations Juridical Yearbook*
UNMIK	United Nations Interim Administration Mission in Kosovo
UNPROFOR	United Nations Protection Force
UNRIAA	*United Nations Reports of International Arbitral Awards*
UNSC	United Nations Security Council
UNTAET	United Nations Transitional Administration in East Timor
USSR	Union of Soviet Socialist Republics
VCLT	Vienna Convention on the law of treaties (with annex), Vienna, 23 May 1969
VRS	Army of the *Republika Srpska*
YbILC	*Yearbook of the International Law Commission*

1 Introduction

1.1 Summary and Main Argument

This book grapples with the applicability and application of international human rights law in geographic areas where the State that is recognised as the sovereign of the territory (territorial State) has lost effective control over a part of its territory. Such a situation raises difficult questions in terms of the applicability of international law and international human rights law, especially since the latter traditionally imposes obligations on the territorial State, presumed as exercising effective control over its entire territory, while it does not foresee express provisions in situations where the territorial State has lost control over part of its territory. This does not mean that these situations bring about an international regulatory vacuum. In fact, other actors exercise effective control over the territory of which obligations are not expressly addressed by international human rights law instruments. These actors include other States (outside States) controlling the territory in an invasion phase; situations of belligerent occupation; territorial lease; international organisations in peace operations, especially within the framework of an international territorial administration; and non-state *de facto* regimes, issued from an armed group consolidating its effective territorial control.

The book conceptualises whether and to what extent international human rights law is applicable and enforced in a part of the State's territory outside its effective control. It claims that international human rights law can normalise an imperfect, defective situation through pragmatic interpretation, as it imposes obligations both on the territorial State on account of its sovereign title and residual effectiveness, on the one hand, and on any subject of international law exercising territorial control over the area, on account of its effective control, on the other. These obligations vary according to the legal status of the subject (a state, a *de facto* regime or an international organisation) under international law and international human rights law, and the factual circumstances that determine its effectiveness in the specific area. These factors require a comprehensive analysis of general international law and international human rights law with regard to various subjects susceptible to exercising effective control over a part of the State's territory. In doing so, the book puts forward a new framework for international obligations: the applicability of international human rights norms no longer is exclusively determined by formal sources of law because legal bindingness, it is argued, can be generated by effectiveness. By considering effectiveness beyond formal normative sources and titles of the subjects implicated in the territorial situation, international human rights law is interpreted and applied in a manner that renders human rights practical and effective in matters of the applicability and scope of international human rights obligations, international responsibility for their breaches and international monitoring mechanisms.

1.2 The International Law Problem

In 2003, the Council of Europe Parliamentary Assembly issued a report on the 'areas where the European Convention on Human Rights cannot be applied',[1] which aimed to identify the difficulties that hinder the effective application of the European Convention on Human Rights and Fundamental Freedoms (ECHR) in certain geographic regions. The report presented a panorama on territorial situations 'where the application of the Convention comes up against insurmountable obstacles … either because of internal conflicts or as a result of the occupation of part of a member state's territory by another state'[2] and where the State is unable to fully implement the international obligations under the Convention. Although the report focused on the application of the ECHR, the problem is global as there are regions around the world where the territorial State is unable to exercise governmental authority.

The problem of the loss of effective control by the State over a part of its territory is not new but has galvanised discussion since the birth of

[1] CoE, Parliamentary Assembly, Areas where the European Convention on Human Rights cannot be implemented, Report, Doc. 9730 (11 March 2003).

[2] Ibid., Summary.

modern international law. Since Hugo Grotius, international lawyers have accepted that 'the rights of a king ... remain unimpaired, during the temporary loss of his throne'.[3] In other words, the State's sovereign title is continuous, notwithstanding the loss of territorial control over part of its territory,[4] unless an internationally-recognised case of State succession occurs. Despite its continuous sovereign title, the State's lack of territorial control over an area decreases or entirely excludes its capacity to comply with its international obligations and its international responsibility for internationally wrongful acts occurring in the area.[5] The lack of territorial control of the State erodes the fulfilment of its mission as the centralised guarantor of peace, justice and international law,[6] including international human rights law (IHRL). From the point of view of individuals, it also frustrates 'an international social function of a psychological character'[7] as some considered the shelter that the people expect from the sovereign's territorial integrity.[8]

Areas outside the effective control of the territorial State are often characterised by massive human rights violations such as, for instance, the non-respect of the right to property; internal displacement; barriers to the freedom of movement due to the non-settled political status of the area; or non-access to identity documents. Individuals have hardly any access to local and international human rights mechanisms because of the weakness of the region's administrative structure: the most common examples include the difficulty of having access to court; the lack of independent and impartial tribunals; and the obstacles to establishing the facts and determining who is responsible for violations. As international human rights mechanisms suppose the cooperation of the

[3] Hugo Grotius, *The Rights of War and Peace: Including the Law of Nature and Nations* (A. C. Campbell tr, MW Dunne 1901) 186.

[4] Thomas Baty, 'Can an Anarchy Be a State' (1934) 28 *American Journal of International Law* 444; Hans Kelsen, *Principles of International Law* (Rinehart 1952) 289.

[5] Clyde Eagleton, *The Responsibility of States in International Law* (New York University Press 1928) 28, 31.

[6] *Island of Palmas case (Netherlands, USA)*, 4 April 1928, *UNRIAA*, vol. II, 839; E. Brusa, 'Responsabilité Des Etats à Raison Des Dommages Soufferts Par Des Étrangers En Cas d'emeute Ou de Guerre Civile' (1898) XVIII *Annuaire de l'Institut de Droit international* 96, 103; Martin Kuijer and Wouter G. Werner, 'The Paradoxical Place of Territory in International Law' (2016) *Netherlands Yearbook of International Law* 3, 4.

[7] *Corfu Channel case*, judgment of 9 April 1949, *I.C.J. Reports* 1949, 43 (Separate opinion by Judge Alvarez).

[8] Charles De Visscher, *Theory and Reality in Public International Law* (Percy Ellwood Corbett tr, Princeton University Press 1957) 197–198; Jean Gottmann, *The Significance of Territory* (University Press of Virginia 1973) 14–15.

observed State, they have difficulties to operate in those areas. Moreover, the territorial situation produces a spill-over effect beyond the area: individuals' human rights in the government-controlled area might be restricted because of their non-access to their livelihood, evidence or court files in the area beyond the territorial State's effective control.

The interest to cover areas outside the effective control of the State by IHRL results from the object and purpose of human rights treaties: they tend to guarantee human rights in the entire territory of the contracting States either universally (under the treaty principle of the 'universal respect for, and observance of, human rights and freedoms'[9]) or regionally (for example, under the concept of the *espace juridique européenne*[10]). The principle of universality is the postulate inspiring the logic of the present book: it requires the broadest possible application of IHRL *ratione personae*, in favour of all persons, and *ratione loci*, everywhere around the world.[11] Expressed for the first time in the Charter of the United Nations and in the Universal Declaration of Human Rights (UDHR)[12] and later reiterated in regional conventions,[13] the universality of human rights is regarded by the international community as 'beyond question'.[14] Universality foresees the applicability of human rights to everyone independently of the territory, which *stricto sensu* seems to make the geographical criterion superfluous. Nonetheless, in practice territoriality plays an important role in the enjoyment of human rights, as individuals in areas beyond State territorial control are in a state of vulnerability on account of the territorial State's difficulty to comply with its international law obligations.[15] Human rights monitoring experts observed this problem and reiterated the principle that every

[9] E.g. ICCPR, Preamble, para 4; ICESCR, Preamble, para 4; CAT, Preamble, para 3.

[10] E.g. ECtHR, *Sargsyan* v. *Azerbaijan (Merits)* [GC], Appl. no. 40167/06, judgment of 16 June 2015, paras 147–148; see the 'vacuum' argument in the European and Inter-American case law; *infra*, Chapter 2.

[11] In general international law: André Nollkaemper, 'Universality', *MPEPIL* (Oxford University Press 2011) para 1; in IHRL: Eva Brems, *Human Rights: Universality and Diversity*, vol. 66 (Martinus Nijhoff Publishers 2001) 4.

[12] UN Charter, Article 55(3); UDHR, Preamble, 6.

[13] E.g. ECHR, Preamble, paras 1–2, 5; ACHR, Preamble, paras 3–4; ACHPR, Preamble, paras 3, 7 and Article 60 (the UDHR as a source of inspiration).

[14] Vienna Declaration and Programme of Action, UN Doc. A/CONF.157/23 (25 June 1993), para I/1.

[15] E.g. Report of the United Nations High Commissioner for Human Rights on the activities of her office in Guatemala, UN Doc. A/HRC/19/21/Add.1 (30 January 2012), para 16.

human being must be able to enjoy human rights, irrespective of where they live.[16]

As such regions vary both as to the manner in which the territorial State has lost its territorial control (Section 1.3) and as to the subject that has taken over territorial control over the area (Section 1.4), the next sections will classify and delimit the geographic areas on which the book focuses (Section 1.5), before presenting its conceptual framework (Section 1.6).

1.3 Loss of 'Effective Control' by the Territorial State

State practice and case law in IHRL has used the notion of 'effective control' over territory as a synonym of 'actual authority',[17] the main requirement of belligerent occupation within the meaning of the 1907 Hague Regulations.[18] 'Actual authority' has two factual criteria: the occupying State has to take physical possession of a land area, making the territorial State incapable of exerting its powers,[19] and must be in a position to exercise its authority.[20] Its beginning and end are

[16] Opening Statement by Ms. Navi Pillay, United Nations High Commissioner for Human Rights at the 18th session of the Human Rights Council, Geneva, 12 September 2011; Report on Human Rights in the Transnistrian Region of the Republic of Moldova, by Thomas Hammarberg, Senior Expert, 14 February 2013, 4.

[17] *Chiragov and Others* v. *Armenia (Merits)* [GC], Appl. no. 13216/05, judgment of 16 June 201, para 96; *Sargsyan (Merits)* (n 10), paras 94, 144; Human Rights Council, Situation of human rights in Crimea Sevastopol, UN Doc. A/HRC/36/CRP.3 (25 September 2017), para 38, note 30; IACHR, Report No. 121/18, Case 10.573, *Jose Isabel Salas Galindo and others* v. *United States*, Merits, 5 October 2018, paras 318–319; In the *Georgia* v. *Russia (II)* judgment, the ECtHR concluded that belligerent occupation automatically entails 'effective control' within the meaning of the Court's case-law, although the term 'effective control' is broader and also covers situations other than belligerent occupation. *Georgia* v. *Russia (II) (Merits)* [GC], Appl. no. 38263/08, judgment of 21 January 2021, para 196; for those situations, see *infra*, Section 2.1.1; Yoram Dinstein, *The International Law of Belligerent Occupation* (Cambridge University Press 2009) 40, 42; Marko Milanovic, *Extraterritorial Application of Human Rights Treaties: Law, Principles, and Policy* (Oxford University Press 2011) 142; Gerd Oberleitner, *Human Rights in Armed Conflict: Law, Practice, Policy* (Cambridge University Press 2015) 168.

[18] Hague Convention (IV) respecting the Laws and Customs of War on Land and its annex: Regulation concerning the Laws and Customs of War on Land, Martens Nouveau Recueil (ser 3) 461 (entered into force 26 January 1910), art. 42.

[19] United States Military Tribunal, *The Hostages Trial – Trial of Wilhelm List and Others*, *Law Reports of Trials of War Criminals*, 1949, vol. 8, 55; 2016 Commentary of Geneva Convention I, Article 2, para 304; *Chiragov (Merits)* (n 17), para 96; *Sargsyan (Merits)* (n 10), paras 94, 144.

[20] *Wilhelm List and Others* (n 19), 56; 2016 Commentary of GCI (n 19), para 304; ICTY, *The Prosecutor* v. *MladenNaletilić*, IT-98-34, judgment, Trial Chamber, 31 March 2003, para 217.

questions of fact: as long as the occupying State took physical possession of the area and has the potential to deploy its forces in the area, 'actual authority' persists.[21] Consequently, 'lack of effective control' or 'outside the territorial control' means that the State, that is, the official, *de jure* organs (central government and decentralised, regional or local *de jure* authorities) of the State have no actual authority over a part of the national territory.

While the State is presumed to have effective control over its entire territory,[22] various scenarios could lead to the loss of its territorial control when another subject of international law takes control over the area. This is usually public knowledge but, where it is disputed, courts will examine whether there is evidence on the presence of troops of another entity on the ground.[23] In the negative, difficulties in exercising its authority do not amount to the loss of the State's territorial control over the area.[24]

The State can lose territorial control either because it is unable or because it is unwilling to exercise effective control over the area. While most of the case law in IHRL concerns situations where the territorial State is unable to extend its effective control to the area, Chapter 2 will illustrate that unwillingness has the same legal consequences in IHRL. As far as unwillingness is concerned, examples are territories leased by the territorial State to another State through treaty,[25] or the 'demilitarised enclave' of Colombia between 1998 and 2002 (an area of 42 000 square kilometres from where the Colombian armed forces withdrew[26] and where the Revolutionary Armed Forces of Colombia (FARC) had become the *de facto* authority).[27] In IHRL, inability and unwillingness do not

[21] E.g. Marco Sassòli, 'Legislation and Maintenance of Public Order and Civil Life by Occupying Powers' (2005) 16 *European Journal of International Law* 661, 683–685; Vaios Koutroulis, *Le début et la fin de l'application du droit de l'occupation* (Pedone 2010) 48–49.

[22] Eagleton (n 5) 27.

[23] *Sargsyan (Merits)* (n 10), paras 140, 142, 144.

[24] E.g. an area on the frontline but still under the effective control of the State, ibid.; difficulties in ensuring law enforcement by local authorities: *Assanidze* v. *Georgia* [GC], Appl. no. 71503/01, judgment of 8 April 2004, paras 140–145.

[25] *Infra*.

[26] Colombia, Resolución n° 85, 14 October 1998, Departamento Administrativo de la Presidencia de la República y los Ministerios del Interior, Justicia y Defensa; Report of the United Nations High Commissioner for Human Rights on the Human Rights Situation in Colombia, UN Doc E/CN.4/2001/15 (8 February 2001), paras 126–127.

[27] Ibid., para 127; Report of the United Nations High Commissioner for Human Rights on the Office in Colombia, UN Doc E/CN.4/2000/11 (9 March 2000), para 106; Report of the United Nations High Commissioner for Human Rights on the Human Rights Situation in Colombia, UN Doc E/CN.4/2002/17 (28 February 2002), para 197.

correspond to the highly-contested 'unwilling or unable' terminology in *jus contra bellum*, concerning the State's ability or willingness to prevent terrorist attacks stemming from its territory, where the two notions might in practice overlap and entail different legal consequences as to the self-defence of other States.[28] In IHRL, however, the legal consequences of the two factual scenarios are assessed objectively, irrespectively of the State's subjective will: the effectiveness of the territorial State, that is, its actual authority or capabilities, determines the scope of its human rights obligations.

1.4 Administration of the Area by Another Subject

The loss of effective control over the area by the territorial State typically occurs simultaneously with a subject of international law substituting its authority for that of the territorial State.[29] Irrespective of the subject undertaking the territorial control, the case law required 'actual authority', that is, the legal subject's presence on the ground and the ability to substitute for the authority of the territorial State. The subject taking effective control over the area can be a (outside) State or a non-state actor, namely, a *de facto* regime or an international organisation (IO).

First, a State can take over the territorial control of the area without the consent of the territorial State in an armed conflict, on the one hand, or with the consent of the territorial State, on the other. During armed conflicts a State can exercise territorial control over foreign territory as an occupying power alone or in a multinational operation, understood as armed forces of States operating with the authorisation or a delegation of the UN Security Council with a view to using armed force for specific objectives. In invasion short of occupation, when the outside State physically penetrates the territory, it is a question of fact whether the invading State exercises sufficient effectiveness to constitute 'actual authority'.[30] Some human rights bodies were ready to accept such a scenario.[31]

[28] Theresa Reinold, 'State Weakness, Irregular Warfare, and the Right to Self-Defense Post-9/11' (2011) 105 *American Journal of International Law* 244, 268, 272, 286.

[29] For the exception when a vacuum of authority is created, see Eritrea-Ethiopia Claims Commission, *Partial Award: Central Front – Eritrea's Claims 2, 4, 6, 7, 8 & 22*, 28 April 2004, *UNRIAA*, Vol. XXVI, paras 67, 71, 83–84.

[30] Both for and against: Marten Zwanenburg, Michael Bothe and Marco Sassòli, 'Is the Law of Occupation Applicable to the Invasion Phase?' (2012) 94 *International Review of the Red Cross* 29.

[31] *Infra*, Chapter 2.

A State can also control foreign territory through a proxy if it establishes and/or supports on foreign soil a subordinate local administration whose conduct is attributable to it.[32] In other words, if an *a priori* non-state entity exercises the territorial control directly and its conduct can be attributed to an outside State, the latter exercises the (indirect) effective control over the area.

Second, an outside State can control foreign territory with the consent of the territorial State, for instance under a territorial lease agreement. Territorial lease is a treaty by which a State grants another State 'the right to use and exercise control over part of the former's territory'.[33] Another hypothesis is the stationing of foreign troops on the territorial State's soil with the latter's consent provided that the foreign forces substitute the territorial State, and exercise authority over the area and the local population in an autonomous manner and not on behalf of the territorial State.[34]

Among non-state actors only a limited number of armed opposition groups (AOGs)[35] are able to substitute the State's authority over an area, namely, those that satisfy the threshold of the applicability of Additional Protocol II (AP II) to the Geneva Convention. Those AOGs must 'under responsible command, exercise such control over a part of its territory as to enable them to carry out sustained and concerted military operations and to implement this Protocol'.[36] The degree of their control 'must be sufficient to allow sustained and concerted military operations to be

[32] *Armed Activities on the Territory of the Congo (Democratic Republic of the Congo* v. *Uganda)*, judgment, *I.C.J. Reports* 2005, 228, para 168, 177 and 230–231; Separate opinion of Judge Kooijmans, ibid., 319, para 49; *Application of the Convention on the Prevention and Punishment of the Crime of Genocide (Bosnia and Herzegovina* v. *Serbia and Montenegro)*, judgment, *I.C.J. Reports* 2007, 202–206, paras 385–395; *Loizidou* v. *Turkey (Merits)* [GC], Appl. no. 15318/89, judgment of 18 December 1996, para 52; *Cyprus* v. *Turkey* [GC], Appl. no. 25781/94, judgment of 10 May 2001, para 77.

[33] Yaël Ronen, 'Territory, Lease', *MPEPIL* (Oxford University Press 2008) para 1. A contemporary precedent for leased territory is the Bay of Guantánamo under Cuban sovereignty but under US control. Agreement for the lease to the United States of lands in Cuba for coaling and naval stations, Havana, 16 February 1903 and Washington, 23 February 1903, *Bevans*, Vol. 6, 1113–1115, Article III.

[34] The latter case would be attributable to the territorial State: Eyal Benvenisti, 'Occupation, Pacific', *MPEPIL* (Oxford University Press 2009) para 7.

[35] Defined as a non-state party to a non-international armed conflict.

[36] Protocol Additional to the Geneva Conventions of 12 August 1949, and relating to the Protection of Victims of Non-International Armed Conflicts (Protocol II), 8 June 1977 (AP II), Article 1(1).

carried out'.[37] A guerrilla group satisfies this threshold if it is present and disposes of certain premises in a remote area, generally in or close to a town of military importance from which it can conduct military operations.[38] The extent of territory the AOG 'can claim to control will be that which escapes the control of the government armed forces'.[39] Since AOGs as understood by AP II must have 'some degree of stability in the control of the territory',[40] this allows them to maintain administration over the area and the population. Beyond the ability to establish a civil or military administration, territorial control by AOGs is interpreted more flexibly than that by States under the law of occupation.[41] This book calls AOGs satisfying Article 1(1) of AP II '*de facto* regimes' (or '*de facto* administration'/'*de facto* authorities') as they are issued from a non-international armed conflict without a final peace agreement.[42] A *de facto* regime is understood as an entity that 'exercises at least some effective political authority over a territory within a state', 'without being recognised as independent State or government of an already existing state'.[43]

Finally, IOs can also exercise territorial control in peace operations, defined as '[f]ield operations deployed to prevent, manage, and/or resolve violent conflicts or reduce the risk of their recurrence'.[44] The book considers two types of peace operations led by IOs: peacekeeping

[37] Yves Sandoz, Christophe Swinarski and Bruno Zimmermann (eds), *Commentary on the Additional Protocols of 8 June 1977 to the Geneva Conventions of 12 August 1949* (International Committee of the Red Cross / Martinus Nijhoff Publishers 1987) 1352, para 4466; ICTR, *Prosecutor* v. *Jean-Paul Akayesu*, ICTR-96-4-T, judgment, Chamber I, 2 September 1998, para 626.

[38] Report of the United Nations High Commissioner for Human Rights on the human rights situation in Colombia, UN Doc. E/CN.4/2003/13 (24 February 2003), para 29; Report of the independent expert on minority issues, Gay McDougall, Mission to Colombia, UN Doc. A/HRC/16/45/Add.1 (25 January 2011), para 24.

[39] Sandoz, Swinarski and Zimmermann (n 37) 1352–1353, para 4467.

[40] Ibid., 1352–1353, para 4467.

[41] Ibid., 1352–1353, para 4467; Constitutional Court of Colombia, No. C-225/95, *Derecho internacional humanitario-Naturaleza imperativa/Ius cogens*, 18 May 1995, part 4.

[42] This is so even if there are no ongoing hostilities, as IHL 'extends beyond the cessation of hostilities until a general conclusion of peace is reached'. ICTY, *Prosecutor* v. *Tadić*, IT-94-1-AR72, Decision on the Defence Motion for Interlocutory Appeal on Jurisdiction, 2 October 1995, para 70.

[43] Michael Schoiswohl, 'De Facto Regimes and Human Rights Obligations – The Twilight Zone of Public International Law' (2001) 6 *Austrian Review of International and European Law* 45, 50–51; Jochen A. Frowein, 'De Facto Regime', *MPEPIL* (Oxford University Press 2013) paras 1–3; It is to be distinguished from a '*de facto* organ', a category of attribution; *infra*, Chapter 5.

[44] United Nations Peacekeeping Operations: Principles and Guidelines, 2008, 98.

operations and international territorial administrations. A peacekeeping operation is understood as a consent-based military action used for the defence of collective security to maintain or preserve peace with no or only a minimal use of force.[45] International territorial administrations, however, are mandated to exercise all public powers of a given territory while substituting for the territorial State.[46] The difference between the two is a degree of authority: an international administration substitutes for the State's authority, while a peacekeeping operation only exceptionally does so and usually has limited public powers.[47] Unlike those two peace operations, initiated and conducted under the auspices of an IO, a multinational operation, sometimes equally classified among peace operations, acts under the control of troop-contributing States without the operational control of an IO.

The common feature of all the above-mentioned actors is that they substitute their authority for that of the territorial State. Furthermore, they are all subjects of international law with international legal personality, that is, entities having the capacity to be addressees of international rights and obligations, with the capacity to maintain their rights by bringing international claims.[48] IOs have that capacity and possess actual rights and obligations attributed by their founding member States,[49] whereas the legal personality of AOGs has been traditionally recognised in international humanitarian law.[50] In IHRL, States

[45] Michael Bothe, 'Peacekeeping Forces', *MPEPIL* (Oxford University Press 2016) para 1.

[46] Markus Benzing, 'International Administration of Territories', *MPEPIL* (Oxford University Press 2010) para 1. Two undisputed precedents are East Timor (United Nations Transitional Administration in East Timor, 1999–2002) and Kosovo (fully governed by the civilian mission, the United Nations Interim Administration Mission in Kosovo between 1999–2008, significantly reduced following the declaration of independence by the Kosovo authorities).

[47] E.g. the buffer zone between the government controlled and the occupied areas of Cyprus, protected by UNFICYP, where the latter is obliged 'to contribute to law and order', and encourage a 'return to normal conditions' of civilian life. Note to the Assistant Secretary-General for Peacekeeping Operations, 17 August 2007, *UNJYb*, 2007, 451.

[48] *Reparation for injuries suffered in the service of the United Nations*, Advisory Opinion, *I.C.J. Reports* 1949, 179.

[49] Ibid.; *Legality of the Use by a State of Nuclear Weapons in Armed Conflict*, Advisory Opinion, *I.C.J. Reports* 1996, 81–82, para 27.

[50] Antonio Cassese, 'The Status of Rebels under the 1977 Geneva Protocol on Non-International Armed Conflicts' (1981) 30 *International & Comparative Law Quarterly* 416, 429; Daragh Murray, *Human Rights Obligations of Non-State Armed Groups* (Hart Publishing 2016) 34–41; Special Tribunal for Lebanon, Appeals Chamber, *Interlocutory decision on the applicable law: terrorism, conspiracy, homicide, perpetration, cumulative charging*, 16 February 2011, STL-11-01/I, para 105.

are the traditional addressees of obligations, while there has been an increasing tendency to impose human rights obligations on both *de facto* regimes and IOs controlling territory.[51]

It is also true that a third type of non-state actors, namely, transnational corporations, increasingly exercise governmental powers and control territories, potentially affecting human rights in those areas.[52] Nevertheless, the book does not examine the territorial control exercised by transnational corporations as it considers them internal subjects of a State, deprived of an international legal personality.[53] Yet, the conclusions on the obligations of the territorial State (Chapters 2 and 3) also apply *mutatis mutandis* to such areas controlled by transnational corporations.

1.5 Delimitation of Study

This book examines IHRL in geographic areas where the sovereign State of the territory does not exercise its effective control. While it is common to refer in scholarship to 'ungoverned spaces',[54] it is more accurate to

[51] *Infra*, Chapter 4.

[52] In this regard, the Special Representative of the Secretary-General on the Issue of Human Rights and Transnational Corporations and Other Business Enterprises (SRSG-BHR) recognised the risk of their territorial control in areas which he called 'weak governance zones', defined as 'areas where the territorial State is 'unable or unwilling' to exercise its authority'. However, the Special Representative finally renounced to apply the concept in his works. Report of the Special Representative of the Secretary-General on the Issue of Human Rights and Transnational Corporations and Other Business Enterprises, Addendum, UN Doc A/HRC/4/35/Add.2 (15 February 2007), paras 22–23.

[53] It suffices to note that States have not adopted the proposals of the SRSG-BHR on the definition of human rights obligations of transnational enterprises. The Special Representative himself limited his conclusions to impose on transnational societies an 'expectation' of the society *vis-à-vis* business enterprises to respect human rights. It is doubtful whether it reflects positive international law. Protect, Respect and Remedy: A Framework for Business and Human Rights: Report of the Special Representative of the Secretary-General on the Issue of Human Rights and Transnational Corporations and Other Business Enterprises, UN Doc A/HRC/8/5 (7 April 2008), para 9; in contrast, holding that multinational enterprises are a 'candidate for functionally limited international legal personality': Christian Walter, 'Subjects of International Law', *MPEPIL* (Oxford University Press 2007) paras 19–20.

[54] Angel Rabasa, Steven Boraz and Peter Chalk, *Ungoverned Territories: Understanding and Reducing Terrorism Risks* (RAND 2007); Robert D. Lamb, *Ungoverned Areas and Threats from Safe Havens: Final Report of the Ungoverned Areas Project* (Office of the Under Secretary of Defense for Policy (OUSD(P)) 2008); Anne L. Clunan and Harold A. Trinkunas (eds), *Ungoverned Spaces: Alternatives to State Authority in an Era of Softened Sovereignty* (Stanford Security Studies 2010); Nicholas Tsagourias, 'Non-State Actors, Ungoverned Spaces and International Responsibility for Cyber Acts' (2016) 21 *Journal of Conflict and Security Law* 455.

recognise that various actors, often States other than the territorial State and non-state actors, exercise effective control over the area. This means that several States might control the same area of the territorial State (for instance, through a multinational operation) or that the conduct of a non-state actor directly controlling the territory is attributed to an outside State.

Referring to the defective application of IHRL in a given geographic area, several official documents and scholarly works have used the metaphoric notions of 'lawless area', 'grey zone', 'vacuum', 'legal loophole' or 'black hole'. These notions have also been used to express the risk that there might be no State in the area that is responsible for the violations of IHRL. Instead of these notions that erroneously imply the lack of responsible State or applicable international norms, this book uses the more elastic notion of 'grey zone' as this has no fallacious connotations with regard to the applicability of human rights norms. Accordingly, the book understands the notion of 'grey zone' as a geographic area where the sovereign State of the territory is unable or unwilling to exercise its effective control.

There are various highly different situations leading to the birth of a 'grey zone': it could be lawful (for instance international territorial administration, territorial lease) or unlawful (that is, the illegal use of force); it could be peaceful or violent (involving armed conflict); it could be short-lived or long-term; it could involve States and/or non-state entities controlling territory. As explained in Section 1.4, the most well-known hypotheses of 'grey zones' are areas controlled through military occupation; military invasion by a foreign state; territorial lease; by a *de facto* regime; or by an international administration or another type of peacekeeping operation of an IO.

The definition of 'grey zones' also delimitates the study geographically: the territorial State lacks effective control over a part of its territory but not over its entire territory. Consequently, the book does not examine the hypothesis where the State's entire territory is beyond its effective control. This could be the result of the military occupation of the entire State, such as in the case of Denmark or Hungary under German occupation during a certain period of World War II, the Baltic States during the Cold War, or actually Palestine, if one considers it a State.[55]

[55] On the statehood of Palestine, the resolution adopted by the General Assembly on the observer State status of Palestine did not have any doubt. See Res. 67/19, UN Doc A/RES/67/19 (4 December 2012).

In contrast to the situation where a part of the State's territory remains under the control of the territorial State, States occupied entirely by another State have a much more limited margin for manœuvre to act. Such a situation has been addressed by the case law on so-called puppet states. Several judgments attributed the conduct of the occupied State to the occupying state,[56] whereas in certain exceptional situations the facts proved that the occupied State retained a given margin for manœuvre without the interference of the occupying State, in which case tribunals attributed the conduct of the occupied authorities to the occupied State itself.[57] This complexity demonstrates that a State entirely occupied requires a cautious analysis and cannot be equated with States whose central government functions independently of the interference of the occupying power.

For similar reasons, the book does not examine situations where the State has lost effective control over its entire territory as a consequence of the control exercised by non-state armed groups, which has been called the hypothesis of the 'failed state'. The only case involving the practice of a *par excellence* 'failed state' is that of Somalia. For at least two decades this State had no central government and for a lengthy period it had only a transitional government, while all its territory was controlled by non-state armed groups, warlords and unrecognised *de facto* authorities. Somalia's unique situation complicates any comparison with States of which territory is only partially controlled by similar non-state entities and which retain certain effectiveness due to their capabilities in the government-controlled area.

An often-raised counterargument against considering 'grey zones' controlled by a *de facto* regime as part of the territory of the territorial State is their alleged statehood. This argument does not influence the book's analysis as long as the overwhelming majority of States recognise the territorial State as the sovereign of the area. However, the present book agrees with the dominant scholarly view according to which

[56] E.g. *In re G.*, Greece, Criminal Court of Heraklion, judgment No. 107 of 1945, *ILR*, 1949, Vol. 12, 439 (the Greek government und.er German and Italian occupation); *Carl Zeiss Stiftung Appellants* v. *Rayner & Keeler Ltd. and Others Respondents (Original Appeal)*, House of Lords, 18 May 1966, [1967] 1 A.C. 853, 860–861 (the German Democratic Republic created by the USSR in its occupation zone); *Socony Vacuum Oil Co. Claim*, United States International Claims Commission, *ILR*, 1954, Vol. 21, 55–63 (Slovakia or the Croatian Kingdom created by the German Reich during the Second World War), etc.

[57] E.g. no responsibility arose from the unlawful conduct of Hungarian authorities during Hungary's occupation by Germany during World War II; Oberlandsgericht Berlin, 2 July 1965, *ILR*, Vol. 44, 340.

statehood is a question of fact of which the criteria are determined by law.[58] Without taking position in the debate on the question of whether the *de facto* regimes analysed in the book fulfil the factual criteria of statehood, it suffices to note that the final decision is incumbent upon the community of States through the act of recognition. By contrast, *de facto* regimes are either not recognised by any State, or only by a negligible number of States.[59] The book considers entities recognised as States by a considerable number of States – Palestine with approximately 137 recognitions; Kosovo with approximately 107 recognitions – as States *in statu nascendi* and not as 'grey zones', provided that they are allowed to ratify human rights treaties.[60] Whereas at the level of effectiveness the difference between a *de facto* regime and a State *in statu nascendi* is only one of degree and the human rights problems are similar (for instance Kosovo), an essential change occurs once the entity is allowed to enter into human rights treaties. From that moment, human rights treaty bodies consider the State *in statu nascendi* the sovereign of the territory and the addressee of obligations under IHRL and, therefore, the basic hypothesis of the book does not apply.[61]

1.6 Conceptual Framework

As mentioned in Section 1.1, the book claims that international human rights law can normalise an imperfect, defective situation through pragmatic interpretation, as it imposes obligations both on the territorial State on account of its sovereign title and residual effectiveness, on the one hand, and on any subject of international law exercising territorial

[58] See the definition of the 'State' by the ICTY: 'A State Member or non-Member of the United Nations or a self-proclaimed entity *de facto* exercising governmental functions, whether recognised as a State or not'. See ICTY, Rules of Procedure and Evidence, Version 49, IT/32/Rev 49, 22 May 2013, Article 2; Anthony Cullen and Steven Wheatley, 'The Human Rights of Individuals in De Facto Regimes under the European Convention on Human Rights' (2013) 13 *Human Rights Law Review* 691, 696.

[59] E.g. the 'Turkish Republic of Northern Cyprus' is only recognised by Turkey, whereas South Ossetia and Abkhazia are recognised by Russia, Nicaragua, Venezuela and Nauru. Vanuatu and Tuvalu recognised Abkhazia and South Ossetia as independent but subsequently withdrew their recognition.

[60] Kosovo under international administration (2000–2008) as part of Serbia is examined in detail as a case study (e.g. Chapters 4 and 6), while the book will occasionally mention where the conclusions are *mutatis mutandis* applicable to the post-2008 Kosovo, which has not been permitted to ratify any human rights treaty.

[61] See the practice of UN treaty bodies with regard to the State of Palestine after it ratified, between April 2014 and March 2019, the main UN human rights treaties. E.g. CEDAW, Concluding Observations: State of Palestine, UN Doc CEDAW/C/PSE/CO/1 (25 July 2018).

control over the area, on account of its effective control, on the other. This main claim is articulated around the following conceptual and methodological choices.

1.6.1 *Conceptual Questions*

The book aims to conceptualise whether and to what extent IHRL is applicable and enforced in a part of the State's territory outside its effective control ('grey zone'), especially with regard to the territorial State and the international law subject(s) controlling the area. This problem raises several sub-questions, in two major domains: in the field of the applicability of IHRL, on the one hand, and in the matter of the enforcement of the applicable norms, on the other. The applicability of IHRL answers the question of whether the rules of substantive law are intended to govern a given situation, whereas the enforcement of the applicable norms is understood as the effective realisation of the substantive law obligations in international law.

As for the applicability of IHRL, the major questions are the following: Does the notion 'effective control' over territory have a specific meaning in the field of IHRL? What are the consequences of the lack or exercise of effective control over a territory in general international law, especially in the law of treaties, on the one hand, and in IHRL, on the other? More generally, what is the legal relevance of territoriality in IHRL? Who are the addressees of IHRL and what are their obligations? Do non-state actors controlling territory (namely, as discussed separately, *de facto* regimes and IOs) have certain obligations under IHRL and, if so, to what extent do such duties differ from those of States? To what extent do the human rights obligations of *de facto* regimes and IOs differ from one another when they exercise effective control over an area? Do the obligations of the State controlling a foreign territory differ from those in its own territory and what specific norms, if any, oblige the State of which the territory is controlled by other subjects? What are the lawful limitations that subjects controlling a territory/the territorial State can apply in IHRL?

In the field of the enforcement/application of IHRL, 'grey zones' provoke similarly complicated questions: which State(s) can incur responsibility for the violations of human rights and are there specific circumstances in 'grey zones' excluding such a responsibility? Is it pertinent to invoke the responsibility of non-state actors, and is it at all regulated by international law (beyond individual liability in international criminal law)? Once the law of international responsibility has been clarified, which mechanisms allow for international human rights monitoring bodies to implement this responsibility or, in other words, to monitor the conduct of States (and non-state actors)? Which factors hinder the availability and effectiveness of domestic and international remedies in 'grey zones'? What are the challenges faced by international monitoring mechanisms in 'grey zones' and what practical solutions have they elaborated?

1.6.2 *Methodological Choices*

The research underlying the book has been conducted based on a thorough analysis of the case law from various international, universal and regional courts and other non-judicial human rights control bodies. The book conceptualises the substantive law and procedural law from all relevant case law available in the specific scenario of the territorial State's lack of effective control over a part of its territory. From this empirically-gained knowledge a comprehensive analytical framework was drawn, which in turn was used to examine and conceptualise the applicable law.

The cases analysed stem from international, regional and domestic courts applying international law, in general, and IHRL, in particular. While taking into account the specificities of IHRL, the book's underlying rationale is that this special regime is to be interpreted in light of general international law. Therefore, for most of the questions that international human rights monitoring bodies confronted while addressing human rights violations occurring in 'grey zones', general international law is taken into account, especially the case law of the world courts (the Permanent Court of International Justice (PCIJ), the International Court of Justice (ICJ)), arbitral tribunals and the practice of the International Law Commission (ILC).

This methodological caveat is crucial as the book cannot commend the overall tendency of IHRL to normalise 'grey zones' without stressing the limits of human rights imposed by State practice and general international law. As opposed to certain conclusions drawn by international human rights monitoring bodies announcing separateness from general international law (especially general rules of treaty law),[62] IHRL can neither expand the application of human rights at all costs, nor regulate

[62] E.g. the unconditional formulation of automatic State succession with regard to human rights treaties ('as evidenced by its longstanding practice'): HRC, General Comment 26: Continuity of Obligations, 8 December 1997, CCPR/C/21/Rev.1/Add.8/Rev.1, para 4; or the unconditional formulation that armed groups shall respect all provisions of a human

all non-state conduct falling outside its material scope. While criticising such voices, the book claims that the firm attachment to general international law allows the applicability and enforcement of IHRL in a manner that renders human rights practical and effective, especially by focusing on the primary role of (the outside and territorial) States.

Unlike most other studies, the present book does not focus on a specific international human rights convention but compares all the universal and regional human rights treaties with regard to a specific territorial situation. Furthermore, it does not limit the focus on the judicial case law but takes into account the practice of non-judicial treaty-monitoring bodies as the authoritative interpreters of the relevant treaties and other human rights bodies of IOs (for instance, Charter-based UN human rights bodies). Finally, based on the international obligations addressed by monitoring bodies to territorial States, the book takes into account the State practice and domestic case law of various territorial States (such as Columbia, the Republic of Cyprus, Moldova, Bosnia and Herzegovina) as a confirmation of *opinio juris*. While there are certain specificities according to regional human rights treaty systems, their case law converges in imposing concurrent obligations on both the State *de facto* controlling the territory and the territorial State, while universal treaty-monitoring bodies have also followed this approach.

Taking into account the divergences and convergences of the practice of international monitoring bodies, the book develops a comprehensive interpretation of IHRL that guarantees the effective protection of individuals' human rights in an imperfect situation where the territorial State has lost effective control over part of its territory.

1.7 Structure

The book analyses the applicability and implementation of IHRL in areas outside the effective control of the State. Chapters 2–4 discuss the question of the applicability of IHRL, answering the questions of its applicability *ratione loci* (Chapter 2), *ratione materiae* and *ratione personae* with regard to States (Chapter 3) and non-state actors (Chapter 4) directly implicated in the territorial situation. The conclusions clarify whether this branch of law continues to apply in an area outside the effective control of the territorial State and what obligations IHRL imposes, with

rights treaty: General Recommendation 30 on women in conflict prevention, conflict and post-conflict situations, UN Doc CEDAW/C/GC/30 (1 November 2013), para 18(a).

the supplementary question to which subjects such obligations are opposable. Chapters 5–8 review questions related to the implementation of IHRL, that is, the more theoretic and strategic question of international responsibility for human rights violations (Chapter 5: Responsibility of States; Chapter 6: Responsibility of non-state actors) and the rather practical challenge of the functioning of international human rights monitoring mechanisms with regard to 'grey zones' (Chapter 7: Judicial control mechanisms; Chapter 8: Non-judicial control mechanisms). The book's structure follows the main conceptual framework, while taking into account the differences in the law applying to the international law subjects involved in the situation (States/non-state actors) and in the control mechanisms (judicial/non-judicial control mechanisms).

2 The Legal Effect of Effective Control over Territory

International human rights law (IHRL) is applicable principally under multilateral treaties that oblige State parties. The present chapter answers the question of whether such treaties equally apply to the conduct of States in a 'grey zone'. One must note that beyond human rights treaties, all States are bound by customary international law and norms of *jus cogens*. Consequently, several elementary obligations such as the prohibition of torture bind even States that are not parties to human rights conventions.[1]

General international law, namely the law of treaties, does not precisely clarify the territorial scope of application of human rights treaties. Article 29 of the Vienna Convention on the Law of Treaties (VCLT) provides that '[u]nless a different intention appears from the treaty or is otherwise established, a treaty is binding upon each party in respect of its entire territory'. For the International Law Commission (ILC) '[t]he term "the entire territory of each party" is a comprehensive term designed to embrace all the land and appartenant territorial waters and air space which constitute the territory of the State'.[2] Commentators consider this provision a minimum rule of customary character that presumes the treaty's application over the State party's entire territory and allows for the restriction of the territorial scope of application to certain parts of the national territory but mentions nothing about its extension beyond it.[3] In fact, the ILC deliberately avoided

[1] E.g. an open list in: HRC, General comment No. 24 (52), UN Doc. CCPR/C/21/Rev.1/Add.6 (11 November 1994), para 8; *infra*, Chapter 3.

[2] Draft articles on the law of treaties with commentaries, *YbILC*, 1966, vol. II, 213, para 3.

[3] Oma Ben-Naftali and Yuval Shany, 'Living in Denial: The Application of Human Rights in the Occupied Territories' (2004) 1 *Israel Law Review* 17, 66–67; Marko Milanovic, 'The Spatial Dimension: Treaties and Territory' in Christian J. Tams, Antonios Tzanakopoulos

treating under this article the question of the extraterritorial applicability of treaties, that is, outside the national territory of the State party.[4] While Russia argued in the *Georgia* v. *Russia* case that Article 29 of the VCLT establishes a presumption against the extraterritorial applicability of treaties,[5] the International Court of Justice (ICJ) did not accept this argument,[6] and Article 29 does not establish such a presumption.[7] It also does not specify whether the treaty applies in an area over which the territorial State has lost its effective control. Because of the lack of guidance on those points in general international law, it is the autonomous interpretation of human rights conventions that can determine their territorial and extraterritorial applicability.[8]

In IHRL, 'jurisdiction' is the principal criterion of the scope of application *ratione loci* of conventions. This is not to be confused with jurisdiction under general international law, which refers to the State's 'lawful power to act and hence to its power to decide whether and, if so, how to act, whether by legislative, executive, or judicial means'.[9] In other words, the term 'jurisdiction' in general international law expresses 'the limits imposed under international law on the ability of a state to exercise prescriptive (or legislative) and enforcement jurisdiction', that is, the circumstances where the State is entitled to exercise its legal authority.[10] IHRL, however, bases jurisdiction (mainly, but not exclusively) on a factual situation, that is, effectiveness. Jurisdiction is the main criterion for the applicability of international human rights treat-

and Andreas Zimmermann (eds), *Research Handbook on the Law of Treaties* (Edward Elgar Publishing 2014) 191.

4 Draft articles on the law of treaties and commentaries, *YbILC*, 1966, vol. II, 213–214, para 5.

5 ICJ, *Georgia* v. *Russian Federation*, 8 September 2008, CR 2008/23, 40, paras 4–5 (Mr. Zimmermann).

6 *Georgia* v. *Russian Federation*, Provisional Measures, Order of 15 October 2008, *I.C.J. Reports* 2008, 386, para 109; the same argument of Israel, rejected by the HRC: UN Doc. CCPR/C/SR.2117 (9 October 2003), paras 32, 49.

7 Tobias Thienel, 'Georgian Conflict, Racial Discrimination and the ICJ: The Order on Provisional Measures of 15 October 2008' (2009) 9 *Human Rights Law Review* 465, 470; Ben-Naftali and Shany (n 3) 66–68.

8 Milanovic (n 3) 191.

9 Bernard H. Oxman, 'Jurisdiction of States', *MPEPIL* (Oxford University Press 2007) para 1.

10 Olivier De Schutter, Asbjørn Eide, Ashfaq Khalfan, Marcos Orellana, Margot Salomon and Ian Seiderman, 'Commentary to the Maastricht Principles on Extraterritorial Obligations of States in the Area of Economic, Social and Cultural Rights' (2012) 34 *Human Rights Quarterly* 1084, 1102 para 3.

ies, the nexus between the State and the individual's human rights, that is, factual control, power, or authority that the state exercises over a given individual, territory, or situation.[11] Briefly, jurisdiction establishes a link between the individual and the State. Most recently, the practice of States and treaty-monitoring bodies enlarged this understanding by establishing the territorial State's jurisdiction on its sovereign title rather than effective control over its national territory.

The present chapter explains that the jurisdiction of the outside State, based on factual power, and that of the territorial State, based on its sovereign title over territory and effectiveness, has a normalising impact on the policies of the outside State and the territorial State regarding the 'grey zone'. The dynamic interpretation of jurisdiction in IHRL expects from both States a proactive conduct regarding human rights that they shall protect within the limits of their factual power. States and monitoring bodies have interpreted the notion of jurisdiction *ratione loci* first in cases related to the conduct of States beyond their borders (outside State) (Section 2.1), and later with regard to the territorial State in a part of its own territory outside its effective control (Section 2.2). The last section explains that the two States' jurisdictions are concurrent (Section 2.3).

2.1 The Jurisdiction of the Outside State

Most conventions contain a specific clause that establishes jurisdiction either on places or territories (Convention against Torture and Other Cruel, Inhuman, or Degrading Treatment or Punishment (CAT); European Convention for the Prevention of Torture and Inhuman or Degrading Treatment or Punishment (ECPT))[12] or on persons (American Convention on Human Rights (ACHR); European Convention on Human Rights and Fundamental Freedoms (ECHR); Optional Protocol to the International Covenant on Civil and Political Rights (OP-ICCPR); Convention on the Rights of the Child (CRC); Optional Protocol to the Convention on the Rights of the Child on the Involvement of Children in Armed Conflict (OPAC-CRC))[13] subject to the jurisdiction of the State

[11] Ibid., 1102, para 3; Marko Milanovic, *Extraterritorial Application of Human Rights Treaties: Law, Principles, and Policy* (Oxford University Press 2011) 39.

[12] CAT, Article 2(1) ('in any territory under its jurisdiction'); ECPT, Article 2 ('to any place within its jurisdiction').

[13] ACHR, Article 1(1) ('to all persons subject to their jurisdiction'); ECHR, Article 1 ('to everyone within their jurisdiction'); OP-ICCPR, Article 1 ('individuals subject to its

party, or on both (International Covenant on Civil and Political Rights (ICCPR); International Convention on the Protection of the Rights of All Migrant Workers and Members of their Families (ICMW)).[14] Certain international human rights instruments do not provide on their jurisdiction,[15] but may include provisions that determine whether the concerned obligation applies to territories[16] or persons[17] under the jurisdiction of the State party. Despite the different provisions, several common principles may be identified in the State practice and case law.

Generally, human rights have been elaborated in a territorialised manner, applicable principally in the territory of the State party.[18] Although some States[19] and authors[20] have claimed that human rights

jurisdiction'); CRC, Article 2 para 1 ('each child within their jurisdiction'); OPAC-CRC, Articles 6(1), 6(3) ('within its jurisdiction', 'persons within their jurisdiction').

14 ICCPR, Article 2(1) ('to all individuals within its territory and subject to its jurisdiction'); ICMW, Article 7 ('within their territory or subject to their jurisdiction'), but see Article 77(1) ('individuals subject to its jurisdiction').

15 ICESCR, CEDAW, CERD, American Declaration of the Rights and Duties of Man, ACHPR, OPSC-CRC, CPPED, FCPNM.

16 ICESCR, Article 14 ('in its metropolitan territory or other territories under its jurisdiction'); CPPED, Articles 9(1)(a), 9(2), 11(1) ('The State Party in the territory under whose jurisdiction'), 34 ('in the territory under the jurisdiction of a State Party'); CERD, Article 3 ('in territories under their jurisdiction').

17 CERD, Articles 6 ('to everyone within their jurisdiction'), 14(1) ('from individuals or groups of individuals within its jurisdiction'); CPPED, Article 31(1) ('from or on behalf of individuals subject to its jurisdiction').

18 *Legal Consequences of the Construction of a Wall in the Occupied Palestinian Territory*, Advisory Opinion, *I.C.J. Reports* 2004, 179, para 109, 180, para 112; *Banković and Others* v. *Belgium and 16 other States* [GC], Appl. no. 52207/99, decision of 12 December 2001 on the admissibility, para 63; IACHR, Report No. 112/10, Inter-State petition IP-02, *Franklin Guillermo Aisalla Molina (Ecuador* v. *Colombia)*, Admissibility, 21 October 2010, OEA/Ser.L/V/II.140, Doc. 10, para 91; IACHR, Report No. 121/18, Case 10.573, *Jose Isabel Salas Galindo and others* v. *United States*, Merits, 5 October 2018, para 308.

19 Concluding observations: USA, UN Doc. CCPR/C/USA/CO/4 (23 April 2014), para 4; UN Doc. CCPR/C/SR.2717 (20 January 2011), para 19 (Israel); UN Doc. CCPR/C/GBR/CO/6/Add.1 (3 November 2009), para 24 (UK); UN Doc. CCPR/CO/72/NET/Add.1 (29 April 2003), para 19 (the Netherlands); Concluding observations: Belgium, UN Doc. CCPR/CO/81/BEL (12 August 2004), para 6.

20 See the debate on the disjunctive or conjunctive reading of the jurisdictional clause of the ICCPR: Dietrich Schindler, 'Human Rights and Humanitarian Law' (1981) 31 *American University Law Review* 935, 939; Egon Schwelb, 'Civil and Political Rights: The International Measures of Implementation' (1968) 62 *American Journal of International Law* 827, 863; Michael J. Dennis, 'Application of Human Rights Treaties Extraterritorially in Times of Armed Conflict and Military Occupation' (2005) 99 *American Journal of International Law* 119, 127.

conventions are not applicable outside the territory of the State party, the practice of the ICJ and monitoring bodies has clearly refuted this view. Currently it is accepted that human rights treaties are applicable to persons and territories over which the State exercises its control outside its borders. Even in cases of treaties containing a jurisdictional clause of which the wording suggests an application limited exclusively to the territory of the State party (such as the ICCPR, 'to all individuals within its territory and subject to its jurisdiction') and treaties without jurisdictional clause, the case law has accepted extraterritorial jurisdiction. Such an interpretation is often justified by the argument that it would be excessive to interpret the given convention as allowing a State party to commit in the territory of another State human rights violations which it would not be permitted to commit in its own territory.[21]

Extraterritorial jurisdiction under IHRL may have at least two alternative preconditions, based on effectiveness over territory (spatial model) (Section 2.1.1) or over persons (personal model) (Section 2.1.2). The basic difference is that, unlike the personal model, the spatial model does not require a detailed analysis of the State's factual power over the challenged conduct, while it presumes this over the given territory. The recent practice of treaty bodies establishes the State's extraterritorial jurisdiction on the effective control over activities taking place within its territory but having an effect on human rights in other States, amounting to a third alternative basis that may be called a 'causal model'. This alternative basis will be discussed together with the personal model. Whether the alternative basis of extraterritorial jurisdiction is control over territory or persons, the result is similar: the given human rights treaty applies outside the State party's territory. The notion 'scope of the jurisdiction' is understood as the applicable rights and freedoms, whereas the 'scope of obligations', defined as the content of the expected State conduct, is scrutinised in Chapter 3.

[21] HRC, *Sergio Euben Lopez Burgos* v. *Uruguay*, Communication No. R.12/52, UN Doc. A/36/40 (1981), 189–198, para 12.3; *Lilian Celiberti de Casariego* v. *Uruguay*, Communication No. R.13/56, UN Doc. A/36/40 (1981), 199–204, para 10.3; ECtHR: *Issa and Others* v. *Turkey*, Appl. no. 31821/96, judgment of 16 November 2004, para 71; *Georgia Andreou* v. *Turkey*, Appl. no. 45653/99, decision of 3 June 2008 on the admissibility, 10.

2.1.1 *The Spatial Model*

The ICJ,[22] the European Court of Human Rights (ECtHR),[23] other regional[24] and universal[25] human rights treaty bodies, and certain political organs of international organisations (IOs)[26] recognised that the State shall fully respect and protect its human rights obligations outside its territory in an area over which it exercises 'effective control'. In other words, the State has jurisdiction under IHRL in territories over which it exercises de facto and not necessarily de jure control.[27] In the spatial model all persons situated in the territory are presumed to fall within the outside State's jurisdiction without the need to prove that the latter's agents exercised authority and control over the individual. The spatial type of jurisdictional link thus serves to simplify the establishment of the jurisdiction. Especially in cases of repetitive or massive applications from the same region, the spatial jurisdictional link facilitates the procedure of monitoring bodies. The case law has recognised the spatial model in cases of territorial control exercised by an occupying State, through its occupying forces (Section 2.1.1.1) or indirectly, through a subordinated *de facto* regime (proxy) (Section 2.1.1.2), by several States/a multinational operation (Section 2.1.1.3), or in other situations of territorial control (Section 2.1.1.4).

[22] *Wall* case (n 18), 179, para 109; *Armed Activities on the Territory of the Congo (Democratic Republic of the Congo* v. *Uganda)*, judgment, *I.C.J. Reports* 2005, 231, para 178.

[23] *Loizidou* v. *Turkey (Preliminary objections)* [GC], Appl. no. 15318/89, decision of 23 March 1995 on the admissibility, para 62; *Loizidou* v. *Turkey (Merits)* [GC], Appl. no. 15318/89, judgment of 18 December 1996, para 56; *Al-Skeini and Others* v. *United Kingdom* [GC], Appl. no. 55721/07, judgment of 7 July 2011, paras 138–140.

[24] *Franklin Guillermo* (n 18), paras 101–102; ACommHPR, *Al-Asad* v. *the Republic of Djibuti*, Communication no. 383/10, 28 April–12 May 2014, paras 134, 136; *Democratic Republic of Congo* v. *Burundi, Rwanda, Uganda*, Communication no. 227/99, 29 May 2003, paras 64–65, 76–77.

[25] HRC, General comment No. 31 (80), UN Doc. CCPR/C/21/Rev.1/Add.13 (26 May 2004), para 10; General comment No. 36 (2018) on the right to life, UN Doc. CCPR/C/GC/36 (30 October 2018), para 63; CEDAW, General recommendation No. 30 (1 November 2013) UN Doc. CEDAW/C/GC/30, para 9; CAT, General comment No. 2 (24 January 2008), UN Doc. CAT/C/GC/2, para 16.

[26] UNGA Res. 53/144, UN Doc. A/RES/53/144 (8 March 1999), paras 9(5), 14(3); CoE Parliamentary Assembly, Resolution 1633 (2008), The consequences of the war between Georgia and Russia, 2 October 2008, para 12.

[27] *Wall* case (n 18), 180, para 112; CAT, Concluding observations: USA, UN Doc. CAT/C/USA/CO/2 (25 July 2006), para 15; CESCR, Concluding observations: Israel, UN Doc. E/C.12/1/Add.27 (4 December 1998), para 8.

2.1.1.1 Military Occupation

In its advisory opinion in the *Wall* case, the ICJ recognised, on the basis of the *travaux préparatoires* of the ICCPR and the practice of the Human Rights Committee,[28] that the Covenant 'is applicable in respect of acts done by a State in the exercise of its jurisdiction outside its own territory' as an occupying power.[29] The ICJ drew the same conclusion in respect of the International Covenant on Economic, Social, and Cultural Rights (ICESCR) and the CRC.[30] Likewise, in the *DRC* v. *Uganda* case the Court concluded that international human rights conventions to which Uganda, the occupying power, was party (the ICCPR, ACHPR, CRC, and OPAC-CRC) are applicable in the occupied territory.[31] While the Court did not in any of these cases expressly refer to territorial control, it took into account the Hague Regulations of 1907 while interpreting the obligations of the occupying power under IHRL and international humanitarian law.[32]

The ECtHR for the first time applied the spatial model of jurisdictional link in the *Loizidou* v. *Turkey* case, holding that

> the responsibility of a Contracting Party may also arise when as a consequence of military action – whether lawful or unlawful – it exercises effective control of an area outside its national territory. The obligation to secure, in such an area, the rights and freedoms set out in the Convention derives from the fact of such control whether it be exercised directly, through its armed forces, or through a subordinate local administration.[33]

Among regional bodies, the African Commission on Human and Peoples' Rights (ACommHPR) without hesitation applied the African Charter on Human and Peoples' Rights (ACHPR), which does not contain a jurisdictional clause, to the conduct of the occupying States.[34] The Inter-American Commission on Human Rights (IACHR) relied on the case law of the ICJ and the ECtHR regarding the Convention's applicability in occupation.[35] More expressly, in the *Galindo* case on the US occupation of Panama, the IACHR confirmed 'the existence of "effective control", and for this the relevant standards of international humanitarian law and human rights for territory subject to occupation apply'.[36] Finally, United Nations (UN) treaty bodies also recognise the jurisdiction of the

[28] *Wall* case (n 18), 179, para 109. [29] Ibid., 180, paras 110–111.
[30] Ibid., 180–181, paras 112–113. [31] *DRC* v. *Uganda* (n 22), 243–244, para 217.
[32] Ibid., 231, para 178. [33] *Loizidou (Preliminary objections)* (n 23), para 62.
[34] *DRC* v. *Burundi, Rwanda, Uganda* (n 24), paras 63, 65.
[35] *Franklin Guillermo* (n 18), paras 93–94. [36] *Galindo* (n 18), para 318.

occupying power under the respective human rights treaties in the occupied territory.[37] As 'effective control' over territory is considered in IHRL synonymous to that of 'actual authority' in occupation law,[38] the case law has based the applicability of IHRL on the outside State's effectiveness in the area.

2.1.1.2 Occupation through Proxy

In several 'grey zones', an outside State exercises certain forms of authority over a local de facto administration, without satisfying the exercise of the 'actual authority' test through the deployment of its own armed forces. In this scenario, 'effective control' under IHRL and 'actual authority' under the law of belligerent occupation might be different, and monitoring bodies have to engage in a complex factual analysis.

During belligerent occupation, humanitarian experts recognise that once the occupying power established 'actual control' over territory through the physical presence of its forces, the establishment of a proxy administration and the withdrawal of its military forces do not change its status as occupying power if it remains in a position to exercise authority over the occupied territory.[39] In IHRL, treaty bodies likewise confirmed that it is the factual situation on the ground and not the legal qualification of the administration that is decisive in the question of jurisdiction.

As noted in Section 2.1.1.1, the ECtHR very early recognised that the State can exercise effective control over territory 'directly, through its armed forces, or through a subordinate local administration'.[40] The Court found the latter case established in Northern Cyprus, mainly on the basis of the military effective that Turkey deployed in the area that led to the establishment of a proxy administration, the so-called Turkish Republic of Northern Cyprus (TRNC). Consequently, the Court created a presumption on Turkey's responsibility for the conduct of the 'TRNC', using the notion of 'effective overall control':

[37] E.g. HRC, General comment No. 36 (n 25), para 63; CEDAW, General recommendation No. 30 (n 25), para 9; CAT, General comment No. 2 (n 25), para 16.

[38] *Supra*, Section 1.3.

[39] Tristan Ferraro, 'Determining the Beginning and End of an Occupation under International Humanitarian Law' (2012) 94 *International Review of the Red Cross* 133, 149; Yoram Dinstein, *The International Law of Belligerent Occupation* (Cambridge University Press 2009) 58.

[40] *Loizidou (Preliminary objections)* (n 23), para 62.

It is not necessary to determine whether, as the applicant and the Government of Cyprus have suggested, Turkey actually exercises detailed control over the policies and actions of the authorities of the 'TRNC'. It is obvious from the large number of troops engaged in active duties in northern Cyprus ... that her army exercises effective overall control over that part of the island. Such control, according to the relevant test and in the circumstances of the case, entails her responsibility for the policies and actions of the 'TRNC' ... Those affected by such policies or actions therefore come within the 'jurisdiction' of Turkey for the purposes of Article 1 of the Convention (art. 1). Her obligation to secure to the applicant the rights and freedoms set out in the Convention therefore extends to the northern part of Cyprus.[41]

The conclusion on an indirect effective control over territory supposes an analysis of the hierarchy between the proxy and the outside State.[42] The ECtHR held that, beyond military presence, the outside State can establish its effectiveness through other non-military means. It added in the *Cyprus* v. *Turkey* judgment that the subordinate local administration 'survives by virtue of Turkish military *and other support*'.[43] The ECtHR further explored the question of jurisdiction in its Transnistrian cases, where the emphasis has changed: jurisdiction was no longer merely about control over territory but about control over the proxy, and the effectiveness of the control was defined not only in terms of military effectiveness but in terms of different means of support.

In the first Transnistrian case, the *Ilaşcu* case, four applicants were arrested in June 1992 by the agents of the 14th Army of the Union of Soviet Socialist Republics (USSR) (the ROG) and accused of terrorist activities against the 'Moldovan Republic of Transnistria' ('MRT'), a separatist de facto administration in the territory of the Republic of Moldova. The Russian army took the three first applicants to the garrison headquarters, and later transferred them to the detention premises of the 'MRT' authorities.[44] The applicants complained about the violation of their human rights by both the Federation of Russia and the Republic of Moldova. The applicants affirmed that the facts fell within the jurisdiction of Russia by virtue of the military, economic, and political support provided by Russia to the creation of the 'MRT'; briefly, 'the *de facto*

[41] *Loizidou (Merits)* (n 23), para 56. [42] *Infra*, Section 5.1.1.2/c.

[43] *Cyprus* v. *Turkey* [GC], Appl. no. 25781/94, judgment of 10 May 2001, para 77 [emphasis added].

[44] For the particular circumstances of the case, see *Ilaşcu and Others* v. *Moldova and Russia* [GC], Appl. no. 48787/99, judgment of 8 July 2004, paras 186–289.

control exercised by the Russian Federation over Transdniestrian territory'.[45]

In its judgment, the Grand Chamber took into account the various forms of military, financial, and commercial support provided by Russia to the separatist authorities.[46] As the Court concluded,

> All of the above proves that the 'MRT', set up in 1991–92 with the support of the Russian Federation, vested with organs of power and its own administration, remains under the effective authority, or at the very least under the decisive influence, of the Russian Federation, and in any event that it survives by virtue of the military, economic, financial and political support given to it by the Russian Federation.
>
> That being so, the Court considers that there is a continuous and uninterrupted link of responsibility on the part of the Russian Federation for the applicants' fate, as the Russian Federation's policy of support for the regime and collaboration with it continued beyond 5 May 1998, and after that date the Russian Federation made no attempt to put an end to the applicants' situation brought about by its agents, and did not act to prevent the violations allegedly committed after 5 May 1998.[47]

The Court concluded that the applicants fell within the jurisdiction of Russia because the de facto administration was 'under the effective authority, or at the very least under the decisive influence' of the outside State. This conclusion is not identical to the test of 'effective overall control' applied to Northern Cyprus where Turkey deployed 30 000 troops, contrary to 2 500 soldiers stationed in Transnistria.[48] The jurisdictional link 'effective authority, or at the very least decisive influence' led to several interpretations, even to confusion.[49] According to a first possible reading it is a causal link between the conduct of the agents of the State and the individual, which may be considered a personal model of jurisdictional link[50] because the Russian agents arrested and transferred the applicants to the Transnistrian authorities. A second possible interpretation is that the jurisdictional link applied in *Ilaşcu* follows the

[45] Ibid., paras 364–370.

[46] *Ilaşcu* (n 44), paras 387–391; see those factors *infra*, Section 5.1.1.2/c.

[47] Ibid., paras 392–393. [48] Ibid., 152, Dissenting opinion of Judge Kovler.

[49] Erik Roxstrom, Mark Gibney and Terje Einarsen, 'The NATO Bombing Case (*Bankovic et al.* v. *Belgium et al.*) and the Limits of Western Human Rights Protection' (2005) 23 *Boston University International Law Journal* 55, 126; Monica Hakimi, 'State Bystander Responsibility' (2010) 21 *European Journal of International Law* 341, 378.

[50] Stefan Talmon, 'The Responsibility of Outside Powers for Acts of Secessionist Entities' (2009) 58 *International & Comparative Law Quarterly* 493, 509; *Application of the International Convention on the Elimination of All Forms of Racial Discrimination (Georgia* v. *Russian Federation)*, 10 September 2008, CR 2008/27, 12–13, para 15 (Mr. A. Zimmermann).

spatial model, similar to the 'effective overall control' applied in the Northern Cyprus cases.[51] This reading is confirmed by the reference to the principles of the *Loizidou* case[52] and the lack of conclusive evidence on the direct interference by the Russian agents.[53] Third, some authors consider the test in *Ilaşcu* a jurisdictional link that is neither spatial nor personal but a mixed model.[54] This mixed model takes into account the control or influence exercised over the proxy, similar to the attribution tests applied by the ICJ in the *Nicaragua*, *Genocide*, and *DRC* v. *Uganda* cases.[55] The third interpretation is confirmed by the wording of the judgment: it is the 'MRT' and not the territory that 'remains under the effective authority, or at the very least under the decisive influence, of the Russian Federation'.[56]

Although all three readings were defendable, the Court's later case law dispersed the uncertainty, as it classified *Ilaşcu* as a precedent for 'effective control over an area', together with the *Loizidou* case.[57] As the Court summarised the applicable principles in the *Al-Skeini* judgment:

> Another exception to the principle that jurisdiction under Article 1 is limited to a State's own territory occurs when, as a consequence of lawful or unlawful military action, a Contracting State exercises effective control of an area outside that national territory. The obligation to secure, in such an area, the rights and freedoms set out in the Convention, derives from the fact of such control, whether it be exercised directly, through the Contracting State's own armed forces, or through a subordinate local administration ... Where the fact of such domination over the territory is established, it is not necessary to determine whether the Contracting State exercises detailed control over the policies and actions of the subordinate local administration. The fact that the local administration survives as a result of the Contracting State's military and other support entails that State's responsibility for its policies and actions. The controlling State has the responsibility under Article 1 to secure, within the area under its control,

[51] E.g. Yutaka Arai, *The Law of Occupation: Continuity and Change of International Humanitarian Law, and Its Interaction with International Human Rights Law* (Martinus Nijhoff Publishers 2009) 566; Milanovic (n 11) 140.

[52] *Ilaşcu* (n 44), para 377.

[53] Ibid., para 393.

[54] E.g. Olivier De Schutter, 'Globalization and Jurisdiction: Lessons from the European Convention on Human Rights' (2006) 6 *Baltic Yearbook of International Law* 185, 213–214.

[55] On these attribution tests: *infra*, Section 5.1.1.1 and Talmon (n 50).

[56] *Ilaşcu* (n 44), para 392; However, Judge Ress considers that Russia, 'through the presence of its troops', 'exercises control over the Transdniestrian region and thus also has jurisdiction'. Partly dissenting opinion of Mr Ress, ibid., paras 1, 6.

[57] *Al-Skeini* (n 23), paras 138–139; *Georgia* v. *Russia (II)*, Appl. no. 38263/08, decision of 13 December 2011 on the admissibility, para 66; *Catan and Others* v. *Moldova and Russia* [GC], Appl. nos. 43370/04, 8252/05 and 18454/06, judgment of 19 October 2012, para 106.

the entire range of substantive rights set out in the Convention and those additional Protocols which it has ratified. It will be liable for any violations of those rights . . .

It is a question of fact whether a Contracting State exercises effective control over an area outside its own territory. In determining whether effective control exists, the Court will primarily have reference to the strength of the State's military presence in the area . . . Other indicators may also be relevant, such as the extent to which its military, economic and political support for the local subordinate administration provides it with influence and control over the region.[58]

The Court calls this type of control a 'domination over the territory',[59] which includes both cases of military occupation and occupation through proxy with an effectiveness of a lower degree. The principal factor to evaluate effective control is the military presence of the outside State, but other elements may also be taken into account, such as the military, economic and political support provided by the State for the proxy.

The subsequent Transnistrian cases have further clarified the applicable jurisdictional link. In the *Catan and Others* v. *Moldova and Russia* case, the applicants, children, and parents belonging to the Moldovan community of Transnistria complained of the effects provoked on their education and family lives by the language policy of the de facto authorities.[60] They alleged that the authorities of the 'MRT' took measures forbidding the use of the Latin alphabet in schools and required all schools to start using an 'MRT'-approved curriculum and the Cyrillic script. In the framework of these measures, pupils and teachers were forcibly evicted from their schools. The Court admitted that there was no evidence of any direct involvement of Russian agents in the action taken against the applicants' schools.[61] Nevertheless, it confirmed that the 'MRT' only survived during the period in question by virtue of Russia's economic support.[62] Although the Court drew the same conclusion as in the *Ilaşcu* judgment, confirming Russia's jurisdiction, it slightly reformulated the jurisdictional link: 'the "MRT"'s high level of dependency on Russian support provides a strong indication that Russia exercised *effective control and decisive influence* over the "MRT" administration during the period of the schools' crisis'.[63]

[58] *Al-Skeini* (n 23), paras 138–139.

[59] Reiterated in: *Georgia* v. *Russia (II)* (n 57), para 66; *Catan* (n 57), para 106; *Chiragov and Others* v. *Armenia (Merits)* [GC], Appl. no. 13216/05, judgment of 16 June 2015, paras 168–169.

[60] *Catan* (n 57). [61] Ibid., para 114. [62] Ibid., paras 117–120.

[63] Ibid., para 122 [emphasis added].

Instead of the jurisdictional link used in the *Ilaşcu* judgment ('effective authority, or at the very least under the decisive influence'), the clause 'effective control *and* decisive influence'[64] reminds us of a territorial or mixed jurisdictional link rather than a personal model, considering that the Court most often uses the term 'authority' to the jurisdiction exercised over persons (*infra*), whereas the territorial model uses the term 'control'. While changing the terminology, the Court brought the Transnistrian jurisdictional test closer to that applied in its Northern Cyprus case law. The principal difference between the two jurisdictional links is the combination of control over territory and control over a proxy in *Catan*. However, it is possible to reconcile the two: a State can exercise its jurisdiction outside its borders through its direct physical control, that is, military forces, or, indirectly, via a subordinate local administration. In the latter case the Court will examine whether the outside State provides a 'military, economic, and political' or any other support for the subordinate local administration amounting to an exercise of effective control over the territory. In other words, the Court draws its conclusion on the effective control over territory from the intensity of the influence over the proxy.

The Court assimilated the Transnistrian jurisdictional test to that applied in the Northern Cyprus cases even more in the *Chiragov* case. This was the first case on the region of Nagorno-Karabakh and the surrounding areas, in the territory of Azerbaijan, that have since 1992 been controlled by a de facto administration, the so-called 'Nagorno-Karabakh Republic' ('NKR'). The case concerned complaints by six Azerbaijani refugees who, because of the occupation of their home by the de facto authorities, were unable to return to their homes and property in the district of Lachin in Azerbaijan, from where they had been forced to flee in 1992 during the Armenian–Azerbaijani conflict over Nagorno-Karabakh. Citing the principles elaborated in *Ilaşcu*, *Al-Skeini*, and *Catan*, the Court confirmed that the assessment of Armenia's jurisdiction in Nagorno-Karabakh 'will primarily depend on military involvement, but other indicators, such as economic and political support, may also be of relevance'.[65] The Court cautiously evaluated the military involvement, political and financial support given by Armenia to the 'NKR' and concluded:

[64] See the similar interpretation of *Ilaşcu* in the *Al-Skeini* judgment: 'influence and control over the region'. *Al-Skeini* (n 23), para 139 [emphasis added].

[65] *Chiragov (Merits)* (n 59), para 169.

All of the above reveals that the Republic of Armenia, from the early days of the Nagorno-Karabakh conflict, has had a significant and decisive influence over the 'NKR', that the two entities are highly integrated in virtually all important matters and that this situation persists to this day. In other words, the 'NKR' and its administration survives by virtue of the military, political, financial and other support given to it by Armenia which, consequently, exercises effective control over Nagorno-Karabakh and the surrounding territories, including the district of Lachin.[66]

Thus, while applying a jurisdictional test similar to that in the Transnistrian case, the Court concluded on the effective control exercised by the outside State over the territory directly administered by a proxy.[67]

Critiques of this case law emphasise that the test created in *Ilaşcu* considerably extends the spatial model of jurisdictional link in the sense that the exercise of a decisive influence over a *de facto* regime, even together with certain military presence, cannot be assimilated to a full-fledged military occupation.[68] This criticism may be rebutted by the fact that even in the law of occupation, the degree of the maintenance of effective control may be lower than that required for the beginning of the occupation, that is, the deployment of the outside State's military forces.[69] In IHRL, without the pragmatic approach of accepting non-military influence as amounting to effective control over territory, any outside State could escape its human rights obligations by using proxies. Accepting a lower threshold of effectiveness in the case of non-military influence over a proxy for jurisdiction helps to eliminate a vacuum of the responsible State: the ECtHR justified this case law by the necessity to

[66] Ibid., para 186.

[67] The Court confirmed this test to establish the jurisdiction of Russia over Crimea, South Ossetia, Abkhazia and the 'buffer zone' from 12 August to 10 October 2008 in Georgia. It focused on military support, when it applied the test to a transitional period from 27 February to 18 March 2014 in Crimea when Russia disarmed the military and law enforcement agents of Ukraine and backed the local self-defence forces. *Ukraine* v. *Russia (re Crimea)* [GC], Appl. nos. 20958/14 and 38334/18, decision of 14 January 2021 on the admissibility, para 335; In Georgia, the Court recognised both the Russian military presence and the economic, military and political support from the Russian Federation to the separatist authorities. *Georgia* v. *Russia (II) (Merits)* [GC], Appl. no. 38263/08, judgment of 21 January 2021, paras 164–175, esp. 174.

[68] De Schutter (n 54) 216; Kjetil Mujezinović Larsen, *The Human Rights Treaty Obligations of Peacekeepers* (Cambridge University Press 2012) 188.

[69] Vaios Koutroulis, 'The Application of International Humanitarian Law and International Human Rights Law in Situation of Prolonged Occupation: Only a Matter of Time?' (2012) 94 *International Review of the Red Cross* 165, 188.

cover the European 'legal space' by the effective application of the ECHR[70] and to eliminate 'vacuums' at the regional level.[71]

This interpretative guidance equally applies to UN treaty bodies that have followed the logic of effective control over the proxy rather than over territory. For instance, the Human Rights Committee held that 'considerable influence' over proxy armed forces 'may amount to effective control' over the proxy's activities. Consequently, it called on Russia

> to ensure the application of the Covenant in respect of acts perpetrated by armed groups and proclaimed authorities of the self-proclaimed 'Donetsk people's republic', 'Luhansk people's republic' and 'South Ossetia', to the extent that it already exercises influence over these groups and authorities which amounts to effective control over their activities.[72]

In other words, for the Human Rights Committee, effective control over the proxy entails the outside State's jurisdiction in the sense of the ICCPR, presumably in all the territory controlled by the proxy. Other UN treaty bodies also addressed treaty obligations to the outside State in the 'grey zone' on account of its influence over the proxy forces.[73] If the outside State does not exert the threshold of 'decisive' or 'considerable' influence over the proxy that amounts to 'effective control', but only some influence over a semi-autonomous *de facto* regime, the spatial model no longer is applicable but the outside State can still have due diligence obligations under the causal model (Section 2.1.2.2).

While the ECtHR intends to cover the European 'legal space' by the effective application of the ECHR, UN treaty-monitoring bodies seek to ensure the universality of human rights with the same practice. As a sign of this cross-fertilisation, the Committee against Torture recommended to Russia to 'encourage the adoption of effective measures to promote

[70] *Sargsyan* v. *Azerbaijan (Merits)* [GC], Appl. no. 40167/06, judgment of 16 June 2015, paras 147–148 and Concurring opinion of Judge Yudkivska.

[71] *Cyprus* v. *Turkey* (n 43) paras 78, 91; *Mozer* v. *the Republic of Moldova and Russia* [GC], Appl. no. 11138/10, judgment of 23 February 2013, para 136; *Demopoulos and Others* v. *Turkey* [GC], Appl. nos. 46113/99 et al., decision of 1 March 2010 on the admissibility, para 96; It is particularly contestable that the ECtHR created such a 'vacuum' by rejecting the jurisdiction of Russia over the alleged violations of the substantive right to life during the active hostilities phase of the five-day war in the territory of Georgia – both being States parties to the ECHR. See the dissenting opinions in this sense: *Georgia* v. *Russia (II) (Merits)* (n 67), Partly dissenting opinion of Judge Grozev; ibid., Partly dissenting opinion of Judge Chanturia, paras 5, 54–55.

[72] HRC, Concluding observations: Russian Federation, UN Doc. CCPR/C/RUS/CO/7 (28 April 2015), para 6.

[73] CEDAW, Concluding observations: Russian Federation, UN Doc. CEDAW/C/RUS/CO/8 (20 November 2015), para 30(a).

the prevention and prohibition of torture and ill-treatment' in Transnistria, 'taking into account the jurisdictional vacuum in the Transnistrian region'.[74]

2.1.1.3 Occupation in a Multinational Operation

When several States participate in the occupation, they may exercise effective control over the territory collectively, constituting common organs, or separately, whereby each State may control an occupation zone. In the first case it is complicated to determine who exercises the territorial control and one might argue that the correct answer is all the occupying States: under this logic, the population of the occupied territory falls within the jurisdiction of all occupying States and all those States would be bound to respect and guarantee the given convention. However, the precedents refute this solution not for theoretical but for practical reasons.

Chronologically the first case where the jurisdiction of States participating in common organs arose was the *Hess* v. *United Kingdom* case where the applicant, convicted by the International Military Tribunal of Nuremberg, complained of violations committed by the penitentiary authorities in the allied military prison of Berlin-Spandau. The latter was created by the allied *Kommandatura* of Berlin after the Four Allied Powers had in 1945 assumed the supreme authority over Germany. The prison was co-directed by the Four Powers. As the European Commission on Human Rights could not divide the jurisdiction – and responsibility – exercised over the prison, it found the application *ratione personae* inadmissible.[75] The same practical difficulty, the eventual division of jurisdiction, was raised in the *Saddam Hussein* v. *Albania and 20 Other States* case, where the former head of State of the occupied Iraq complained of human rights violations concerning his arrest, detention and transfer to the Iraqi authorities in the territory of Iraq by the States participating in the military occupation. However, the ECtHR found the application inadmissible for lack of evidence on the jurisdictional link between the respondent States and the applicant.[76] In other words, the

[74] CAT, Concluding observations: Russian Federation, UN Doc. CAT/C/RUS/CO/6 (28 August 2018), para 51.

[75] *Hess* v. *United Kingdom*, Appl. no. 6231/73, decision of the Commission of 28 May 1975 on the admissibility, 74; However, an extraterritorial prison should be treated, like embassies and consulates, within the personal model (*infra*).

[76] *Saddam Hussein* v. *Albania, and 20 other States*, Appl. no. 23276/04, Decision of 14 March 2006 on the admissibility.

applicants failed to prove how individual State parties contributed to the human rights violations in a situation where they exercised joint authority over the area.

A recent example for joint organs is the occupation by the multinational force in Iraq: the coalition of armed forces under unified command, led by the US, with a large force from the UK and small contingents from Australia, Denmark and Poland, occupied the country and established a transitional government, the Coalition Provisional Authority (CPA). The CPA administration was divided into regional areas, each of them placed under the responsibility and control of an occupying State (US, UK and Poland). While it is contested when the occupation ended, at least during the uncontested operation of the CPA (April 2003 to June 2004), the States controlling the zones acted as occupying powers. Whether each of these States could be regarded as having effective control over the entirety of Iraq depends on the case-by-case analysis of attribution, that is, the practical question of how far the State influenced the particular conduct of the joint organ.[77] If successfully proven, the jurisdiction – as in the case of effective control – can be exercised by several States over the same territory.[78]

In the second scenario, the exercise of effective control over areas separately by national contingents, during the operation of the CPA each of the occupying States responsible for an occupation zone could be considered as having jurisdiction over the same zone in the sense of human rights treaties. Likewise, in a peace operation under unified command, if the troop-contributing States exercise effective control in separated zones, one may suppose that each State exercises its jurisdiction over the given area in the sense of human rights conventions.[79] Such a hypothesis requires a preliminary analysis of attribution – what the ECtHR did in an unsatisfactory manner in the *Saramati* case on Kosovo, where the States participating in the operation of the Kosovo Force (KFOR) did exercise effective control over their national sectors.[80] Whereas jurisdiction in multinational and peace operations is closely linked to the analysis of attribution and command structure,[81] it suffices to conclude here that the military presence on the spot may *a priori*

[77] Larsen (n 68) 192–193; *infra*, Section 5.1.

[78] Milanovic (n 11) 148–149.

[79] Larsen (n 68) 192–193.

[80] *Behrami* v. *France and Saramati* v. *France, Germany and Norway* [GC], Appl. nos. 71412/01 and 78166/01, decision of 2 May 2007 on the admissibility, para 3; *infra*, Section 6.1.1.2.

[81] Ibid.

establish the jurisdiction of the State participating in the operation to the extent that it controls an occupation zone.

2.1.1.4 Other Situations of Territorial Control

Among situations of effective control over territory, human rights monitoring bodies have established the extraterritorial jurisdiction of the outside State in (i) territorial leases; (ii) peace operations; (iii) fragile occupations; and (iv) invasions/military incursions on foreign soil. This order reflects the decreasing level of the effectiveness of the outside State's control over territory. However, human rights monitoring bodies did not always have recourse to the spatial link but in certain cases prefered the personal model.

First, as explained in Section 1.4, the lessee State exercises effective control and governmental powers over the leased territory.[82] The IACHR has recognised that the Guantánamo Bay in its entirety falls within the jurisdiction of the US,[83] even though in numerous resolutions it had recourse to the personal jurisdictional link.[84] The case law thus is inconsistent: for instance, the UN Working Group on Arbitrary Detention, while confirming the extraterritorial jurisdiction of the US over human rights violations occurring in Guantánamo Bay, inaccurately held that 'only the United States of America currently exercises sovereignty over Guantánamo Bay', confusing sovereignty and effective control.[85] Be it as it may, the stable and usually long-term character of a territorial lease makes the application of the spatial test particularly straightforward. Based on effective control over territory, the outside State has jurisdiction under human rights treaties even if its legal title over territory, that is, the lease agreement is disputed.

Second, peace operations conducted under the auspices of an IO can exceptionally exert 'effective control' over territory in the sense of human rights treaties if they establish their presence on the ground and are able to substitute for the authority of the territorial State. In practice this has been the case of peacekeeping forces controlling a

[82] *Supra*, Chapter 1.

[83] IACHR, Report No. 17/12, Case P-900-08, *Djamel Ameziane* v. *United States*, Admissibility, 20 March 2012, para 34.

[84] Decision on request for precautionary measures (detainees at Guanatanamo Bay, Cuba), 12 March 2002; *ILM*, 2002, vol. 45, 532–535; Reiterated regularly, e.g. Extension of PM 259/13 (2013), 23 July 2013.

[85] UN Working Group on Arbitrary Detention, Opinion No. 50/2014 (*Mustafa al Hawsawi* v. *United States of America and Cuba*), UN Doc. A/HRC/WGAD/2014/50 (13 February 2015), para 54.

buffer zone and international territorial administrations. Mandates establishing 'safe areas', 'security zones' or other places of protection have not led to the exercise of actual authority by peace operations over territory on the ground, although one cannot exclude such a scenario in the future.[86]

Peacekeeping operations without a civilian administration mandate might exceptionally control territory, but human rights treaty bodies only confirmed this with regard to the United Nations Peacekeeping Force in Cyprus (UNFICYP), charged to supervise the respect of the ceasefire agreement of 1974 in Cyprus. As neither of the two sides can exercise its authority or extend its jurisdiction beyond its own military lines, UNFICYP controls the buffer zone called Green Line between the two.[87] The ECtHR recognised that it is the UNFICYP, thus the UN, that controls the area.[88] In the *Stephens* v. *Cyprus, Turkey and the United Nations* case, the owner of a house located in the buffer zone complained about the denial of her access to her property without compensation. The Court did not consider whether UNFICYP had jurisdiction in the sense of the ECHR in the buffer zone, as the UN is not party to the Convention, and, therefore, rejected this part of the application as inadmissible *ratione personae*. Considering that UNFICYP does not provide all governmental powers in the area but supervises the movement of persons and the military situation, certain State functions in the buffer zone may be provided by either Turkey or Cyprus. The Court found the complaint inadmissible with regard to Cyprus and Turkey as the 'applicant has not challenged a particular action or inaction by these States'.[89] In other words, even if the two conflicting parties did not have effective control over the area, the Court did not exclude that they might have jurisdiction over certain acts under the personal model.[90]

International territorial administrations exercise all governmental powers of a given territory while substituting for the territorial State, and thus differ from state-building peace operations that only support

[86] Larsen (n 68) 194–198.

[87] Report of the Secretary-General on the United Nations operation in Cyprus, UN Doc. S/12253 (9 December 1976), para 19.

[88] *Andreas Iannou* v. *Turkey*, Appl. no. 18364/91, decision of 28 March 2000 on the admissibility; *Kyriakoula Stephens* v. *Cyprus, Turkey and the United Nations*, Appl. no. 45267/06, decision of 11 December 2008 on the admissibility.

[89] *Stephens* (n 88).

[90] Under the 'authority and/or effective control' test (*infra*): *Maria Isaak and Others* v. *Turkey*, Appl. no. 44587/98, decision of 28 September 2006 on the admissibility; *Solomou and Others* v. *Turkey*, Appl. no. 36832/97, judgment of 24 June 2008, para 51.

but do not replace the administration of the territorial State. As both the United Nations Interim Administration Mission in Kosovo (UNMIK) (1999–2008, at least until the declaration of independence in Kosovo) with its civilian and military components and the United Nations Transitional Administration in East Timor (UNTAET) (1999–2002) exercised all governmental powers, treaty-monitoring bodies confirmed that the UN had effective control over the territory.[91] Even if treaty-monitoring bodies recognised the territorial control exercised by peace operations as a matter of fact, they rarely recognised their jurisdiction in the sense of human rights treaties, as IOs are not parties to those treaties. When seized by applications where the challenged conducts were attributable to the IO, the ECtHR held those applications inadmissible *ratione personae*.[92]

Third, a fragile occupation may be defined as a military occupation where the effectiveness of the occupying State's control is weakened by sporadic local resistance. In the law of occupation, occupation persists even if the rebel forces gain temporary effective control as long as the occupying power keeps its position to re-establish the control over the entire territory.[93] In IHRL, the question when the outside State is deprived of actual means to control the territory is likewise a question of fact that requires a case-by-case analysis. For example, in Iraq, the sporadic and temporary control of rebel forces over certain areas of Falujah or Najaf did not challenge the occupation of these localities by the allies,[94] as the rebels did not succeed in chasing the allied forces from those areas. Nevertheless, when facing the issue of the control exercised by the UK in those areas in *Al-Skeini*, the ECtHR decided to establish the UK's jurisdiction not on effective control over territory but on the

[91] E.g. HRC, Concluding observations: Serbia and Montenegro, UN Doc. CCPR/CO/81/SEMO (12 August 2004), para 3; CAT, Concluding observations: Republic of Serbia, UN Doc. CAT/C/SRB/CO/2 (2015), para 4; CESCR, Concluding observations: Serbia and Montenegro, UN Doc. E/C.12/1/Add.108 (23 June 2005), para 9.

[92] *Stephens* (n 88); *Behrami/Saramati* (n 80), paras 140–143; *Slavisa Gajic* v. *Germany*, Appl. no. 31446/02, decision of 28 August 2007 on the admissibility; *Ilaz Kazumaj* v. *Greece*, Appl. no. 6974/05, decision of 5 July 2007 on the admissibility; *Ali Azemi* v. *Serbia*, Appl. no. 11209/09, decision of 5 November 2013 on the admissibility, para 44; on attribution: *infra*, Section 6.1.

[93] ICTY, *The Prosecutor* v. *Mladen Naletilić*, IT-98-34, judgment, Trial Chamber, 31 March 2003, 73–74, para 217; *The Hostages Trial – Trial of Wilhelm List and Others*, United States Military Tribunal, Nuremberg, 19 February 1948, Case No. 47, *LRWTC*, vol. 8, 56.

[94] *Al-Skeini* (n 23), para 143; Kenneth Watkin, 'Use of Force during Occupation: Law Enforcement and Conduct of Hostilities' (2012) 94 *International Review of the Red Cross* 267, 299.

personal model, that is, authority and control exercised over persons.[95] However, the wording used in *Al-Skeini* suggests that the spatial link had some relevance: the UK was charged with assuring the security and supporting the civilian administration in the province of Bassorah, where the applicants' relatives died,[96] and it '(together with the United States) assumed in Iraq the exercise of some of the public powers normally to be exercised by a sovereign government'.[97] Certain commentators considered this formulation a combination of spatial and personal links in *Al-Skeini*.[98]

Whereas the applicants convincingly argued in *Al-Skeini* that under the ICJ's *DRC* v. *Uganda* judgment, belligerent occupation should lead to the recognition of the occupying State's extraterritorial human rights jurisdiction,[99] the ECtHR has left the question open, arguably because of the volatility of the control. As in the case of the applicants, Judge Bonello proposed in his separate opinion to establish a rebuttable presumption of the jurisdiction that the occupying power exercises over the occupied territory.[100] The Grand Chamber recognised this principle only in the 'Convention legal space',[101] that is, in the territory of State parties to the ECHR. Such a presumption of jurisdiction makes complete sense in any situation of stabilised effective control over territory by an outside State as it provides applicants with legal certainty. However, this presumption must be rebuttable:[102] if the outside State demonstrates that it lost effective control over territory, treaty-monitoring bodies might consider applying the personal model.

Fourth, in cases of temporary control over a foreign territory such as invasion/military incursion short of occupation, monitoring bodies have been reluctant to apply the spatial link but preferred the personal link, that is, authority and control over individuals. Such a solution spares the treaty-monitoring body the factual analysis including the spatial extension and effectiveness of the State's control over the given territory, while it exclusively evaluates the temporary link between the State's

95 *Al-Skeini* (n 23), para 149. 96 Ibid., para 147. 97 Ibid., para 149.

98 Max Schaefer, 'Al-Skeini and the Elusive Parameters of Extraterritorial Jurisdiction' (2011) 5 *European Human Rights Law Review* 566, 578–579; Paolo Ronchi, 'The Borders of Human Rights' (2012) 128 *Law Quarterly Review* 20, 22.

99 *Al-Skeini* (n 23), para 127; Schaefer (n 98) 579.

100 *Al-Skeini* (n 23), Concurring opinion of Judge Bonello, paras 24–28.

101 *Al-Skeini* (n 23), para 142; reiterated also in: *Hassan* v. *United Kingdom* [GC], Appl. no. 29750/09, judgment of 16 September 2014, para 74; on the notion of 'legal space of the Convention', *infra*.

102 *Al-Skeini* (n 23), Concurring opinion of Judge Bonello, para 24.

conduct and the individual victim. This was the practice of the IACHR in the case of the US invasion of Grenada[103] or of Panama.[104] Nevertheless, the ECtHR indicated in the *Issa* decision that it is ready to establish the spatial model of jurisdiction of the invading State where there is evidence that its forces are present in the area.[105] This requires a lower threshold of effectiveness than that of 'actual authority' in military occupation, namely, the mere military presence in the area. The IACHR seemed to follow the *Issa* decision in the *Franklin Guillermo* case where it held that the Colombian forces for a few hours exercised extraterritorial jurisdiction over an invaded Ecuadorean area.[106] Consequently, invasion can establish the spatial model of jurisdiction, even though its often short-lived character and the uncertainty about the effectiveness justify rather the recourse to the personal link. This may be the reason why the ICJ in its *Georgia* v. *Russia* order on provisional measures drew no conclusion on the effective control exercised by Russia in the invaded Georgian territory but concluded that the provisions of the International Convention on the Elimination of All Forms of Racial Discrimination (CERD) (without any jurisdictional clause) 'generally appear to apply, like other provisions of instruments of that nature, to the actions of a State party when it acts beyond its territory'.[107]

As opposed to this trend of extraterritorial jurisdiction in a phase of military incursion or invasion, in the *Georgia* v. *Russia (II) (Merits)* case the ECtHR held that Russia did not have jurisdiction over the events which occurred in the active phase of hostilities during the five-day war (from 8 to 12 August 2008) in the territory of Georgia. In a strongly divided vote (eleven votes to six), the Grand Chamber found Georgia's claim regarding the violations of the right to life allegedly committed during the five-day war inadmissible. Among various reasons, the majority attached 'decisive weight to the fact that the very reality of armed confrontation and fighting between enemy military forces seeking to establish control over an area in a context of chaos' excludes not only 'effective control' over an area but also any form of 'State agent authority and control' over individuals.[108] The refusal of the Court to examine either the outside

[103] IACHR, Report No. 109/99, Case 10.951, *Coard et al.* v. *United States*, 29 September 1999, para 37.

[104] IACHR, Report No. 31/93, Case 10.573, *Salas* v. *United States*, 14 October 1993.

[105] *Issa* (n 21), paras 73–78.

[106] *Franklin Guillermo* (n 18), para 102.

[107] *Georgia* v. *Russian Federation*, Order of 15 October 2008 (n 6), 386, para 109.

[108] *Georgia* v. *Russia (II) (Merits)* (n 67), paras 126, 137; as for the other reasons invoked by the majority, see *infra*, Section 2.1.2.2 (alleged compatibility with the earlier case-law,

State's effectiveness over the area or the temporary link between the State's conduct and individual victims contradicts the above-mentioned dominant practice. Accordingly, the Court should have engaged in a meticulous analysis to examine whether the outside State had established its effective control over a given operation area. Alternatively, it should have found that the process of deciding about large-scale military operations and carrying out the decisions taken necessarily creates a jurisdictional link and places the persons affected under the control of the belligerent State.[109]

If broadly interpreted, the *Georgia* v. *Russia (II) (Merits)* might lead to the absurd result that the ECHR is inapplicable in active hostilities in international armed conflicts, which would be in clear contradiction with the international case law.[110] The majority view should, however, not be read as a categorical exclusion of extraterritorial jurisdiction, but as the Court's evasion in the specific case to rule on the substantive aspect of the right to life during the active phase of an inter-State conflict. The majority seemed to rely in fact on a difficulty associated with evidence-gathering as an excuse for the Court not to administer justice in a large-scale inter-State war and on the belief to legitimately use different approaches to inter-State cases and individual applications.[111] Contrary to a categorical conclusion on non-jurisdiction, the Court did find unanimously that Russia had jurisdiction over the alleged violations of the rights of individuals who were detained and subjected to ill-treatment, even during the active hostilities phase, on the one hand, and over the violations of the procedural aspect of the right to life to investigate the events which occurred, even during the active hostilities, on the other.[112] Furthermore, while the majority adopted the decision in July 2020, a few months later the Court decided to grant interim measures during the active military phase of the international armed conflict of

notably the *Banković* case), Section 3.3.1 (non-derogation under Article 15 of the Convention should be interpreted as an indication of the non-existence of extraterritorial jurisdiction during an armed international conflict) and Section 3.3.2 (the events complained of were predominantly regulated by international humanitarian law).

[109] Ibid., Partly dissenting opinion of Judge Lemmens, para 2; Joint partly dissenting opinions of Judges Yudkivska, Wojtyczek and Chanturia, paras 3, 5, 9; Partly dissenting opinion of Judge Pinto de Albuquerque, para 27.

[110] The ECtHR previously rejected the same argument: *Hassan* (n 101), para 77; see more *infra*, Section 3.3.2.

[111] *Georgia* v. *Russia (II) (Merits)* (n 67), paras 61, 141; ibid., Concurring opinion of Judge Keller, paras 9–13.

[112] Ibid., paras 238–239, 268–269, 330–331; dispositive part, paras 4, 7, 12.

Nagorno-Karabakh.[113] This competence supposes the existence of at least *prima facie* jurisdiction of the States involved – in clear contradiction to the conclusion reached by the majority in the *Georgia* v. *Russia (II)* case.[114]

In sum, human rights conventions apply extraterritorially when the outside State exercises effective control over an area outside its borders. Treaty-monitoring bodies have a certain discretion in assessing the required effectiveness of control, varying from 'actual authority' in the sense of The Hague Regulations to mere military presence in the area. In the above-mentioned situations, other than occupation (territorial lease, peace operations, invasions/military incursions, fragile or ineffective occupations), treaty-monitoring bodies relied not necessarily on the spatial but the personal link. It certainly is more feasible to establish the extraterritorial jurisdiction on territorial control in stabilised situations such as a prolonged occupation or a territorial lease than in unstable, short-lived situations such as fragile occupations or military invasions/incursions.

2.1.1.5 The Scope of the Spatial Model

The question of which rights the State is obliged to respect, protect and fulfil in the 'grey zone', that is, the scope of the jurisdiction, is closely related to the choice between spatial link and personal link. The case law has determined the scope of the rights the State is required to protect in accordance with the stability, that is, the effectiveness of its control over territory.

In stable situations of control, treaty-monitoring bodies assimilate the foreign territory, from the point of view of the outside State's obligations, to the latter's national territory.[115] The legal consequence of such assimilation, as the ECtHR[116] and universal monitoring bodies[117] have

[113] Press release, ECHR 265 (2020), 30 September 2020; Press release, ECHR 276 (2020), 6 October 2020.

[114] *Georgia* v. *Russia (II) (Merits)* (n 67), Joint partly dissenting opinions of Judges Yudkivska, Wojtyczek and Chanturia, para 12.

[115] *Cyprus* v. *Turkey* [GC] (n 43), para 77; confirmed e.g. in: *Isaak and Others* v. *Turkey* (admissibility), Appl. no. 44587/98, Decision of 28 September 2006 on the admissibility, 20.

[116] *Cyprus* v. *Turkey* [GC] (n 43), para 77; *Banković* (n 18), para 70; *Al-Skeini* (n 23), para 138; *Catan* (n 57), para 106 etc.

[117] ICCPR: Concluding observations: Israel, UN Doc. CCPR/C/79/Add.93 (18 August 1998), para 10; CERD: Concluding observations: Turkey, UN Doc. CERD/C/TUR/CO/3 (24 March 2009), para 8; CEDAW, General recommendation No. 28 on the core obligations of States parties under Article 2, UN Doc. CEDAW/C/GC/28 (16 December 2010), para 39; CEDAW, General recommendation No. 30 (n 25), para 12(c).

stressed, is the 'full application' of all the human rights guaranteed by the given convention in the area. In other words, the population of the area under the State's control must enjoy the full range of human rights guaranteed by international conventions such as the population living within the outside State's borders.[118]

The ECtHR does not limit the applicability of the integrity of rights and freedoms enshrined in the Convention and its additional Protocols to occupation but extends it to any type of effective control over territory, including occupation through proxies. However, in unstable situations where the outside State's effectiveness is lower, such as a short-term military operation or an occupation zone where the occupying State lost its effective control, it would be irrealistic to require the outside State to guarantee the entire range of rights and freedoms.[119] To the extent that the monitoring bodies established the outside State's extraterritorial jurisdiction in an unstable territorial context on the basis of the personal link, they imposed certain obligations on the State in respect of rights and liberties that were relevant in the given context.[120] For example, in the *Franklin Guillermo* case the IACHR found that the trans-border incursion of a few hours entailed the applicability of only some rights and freedoms which are relevant in the context:

> What has been stated above does not necessarily mean that a duty to guarantee the catalogue of substantive rights established in the American Convention may necessarily be derived from a State's territorial activities, including all the range of obligations with respect to persons who are under its jurisdiction for the (entire) time the control by its agents lasted. Instead, the obligation does arise in the period of time that agents of a State interfere in the lives of persons who are on the territory of the other State, for those agents to respect their rights, in particular, their right to life and humane treatment.[121]

In other words, even if some treaty bodies were willing to apply the spatial model to invasions/military incursions or fragile occupations, the situation would not normally allow the applicability of the entire range of substantive rights but only those that are realistically relevant in the context. For instance, the right to life, freedom from torture and

[118] CERD, Concluding observations: Israel, UN Doc. A/37/18 (1982), 97–98, para 334; Concluding observations: Israel, UN Doc. CERD/C/ISR/CO/14–16 (3 April 2012), para 20; HRC, Concluding observations: Israel, UN Doc. CCPR/C/79/Add.93 (18 August 1998), paras 13, 21.

[119] *The Queen (On the Application of Al-Skeini and Others)* v. *The Secretary of State for Defence*, 21 December 2005 [2005] EWCA Civ 1609, para 197 (Lord Sedley).

[120] *Al-Skeini* (n 23), para 137.

[121] *Franklin Guillermo* (n 18), para 100.

the right to liberty and security certainly are relevant in an invasion phase, whereas the right to marry, the right to education and the right to free elections are not.

The spatial jurisdictional link reconciles the normative requirements of universality and effectiveness: a State is only required to apply a human rights convention if in fact it is able to implement it by reason of its effective control over a territory.[122] The advantage of this alternative basis of jurisdiction is the presumption that it establishes that all persons situated in the area are presumed to come within the jurisdiction of the outside State, without the need to search for a specific link between the State's conduct and the person concerned. In their procedure the monitoring bodies can establish *quasi*-automatically the State's jurisdiction *ratione loci*. Due to the assimilation of the area to the outside State's national territory, the spatial model has a normalising effect on the human rights situation in territories controlled by an outside State in a stable and long-term manner. For example, after the Northern Cyprus decisions of the Grand Chamber, the Court has consistently applied the spatial jurisdictional link to establish Turkey's jurisdiction over Northern Cyprus.[123] Despite the long contestation of this case law, Turkey nowadays is less inclined to raise the preliminary exception of its lack of jurisdiction *ratione loci* and accepts it implicitly.[124]

2.1.2 *The Personal Model*

The spatial link has the disadvantage that it does not cover a series of situations where the State acts beyond its borders in violation of human rights without exercising territorial control. The criterion of effective control over territory sets a high threshold that numerous operations do not reach (drone operations, the abduction of persons on foreign territory, and so forth). In such situations, alternative jurisdictional links are necessary for the applicability of human rights conventions. In the personal model, applicants must prove the State's control over the individual abroad, that is, a link between the human rights violation and the

[122] *Al-Skeini*, Court of Appeal (n 119), para 125 (Lord Justice Brooke); *R. (on the application of Al-Skeini)* v. *Secretary of State for Defence*, House of Lords, 13 June 2007, [2007] UKHL 26, para 129 (Lord Brown); Milanovic (n 11) 128.

[123] E.g. *Savvas Gavriel* v. *Turkey*, Appl. no. 41355/98, decision of 1 February 2000 on the admissibility, 9; *ChrisoKakoulli and Others* v. *Turkey*, Appl. no. 38595/97, decision of 4 September 2001 on the admissibility, 7–8.

[124] No contestation of the jurisdiction *ratione loci*, e.g. in *Michael Solomonides and 28 Others* v. *Turkey*, Appl. no. 16682/90, decision of 18 May 1999 on the admissibility; *Elawa* v. *Turkey*, Appl. no. 36772/02, judgment of 25 January 2011.

conduct of the State's agents and not the effectiveness that the State exerts over territory. The personal model might be based on two alternative preconditions: a physical link called 'State agent authority and control' (Section 2.1.2.1) or a non-physical, rather causal link (Section 2.1.2.2) between the human rights violation and the conduct of the outside State. As in the spatial model, this part also explains the scope of human rights affected by the personal model (Section 2.1.2.3).

2.1.2.1 State Agent Authority and Control

The jurisdictional link between the outside State and a person subject to the authority and control of the State's agents serves as a basis to extraterritorial jurisdiction. In case law that predates the use of the spatial model, universal[125] and regional monitoring bodies of the African,[126] Inter-American[127] and European systems[128] recognised the 'State agent and control' ('authority and control') test. In the context of 'grey zones', this jurisdictional link played an important role in the case of short-lived military operations by 'TRNC' forces in the buffer zone in Cyprus;[129] in peace operations such as the international administration of Kosovo with regard to a given troop-contributing State;[130] and in objects in foreign territory[131] such as the British prisons in Iraq or the

125 HRC: *Lopez Burgos* (n 21), paras 12.1–12.3; *Celiberti* (n 21), paras 10.1–10.3; General comment No. 31 (n 25), para 10; CAT: *P.K. and Others* v. *Spain*, Communication No. 323/2007, UN Doc. CAT/C/41/D/323/2007 (11 November 2008), para 8.2; Conclusions: USA, UN Doc. CAT/C/USA/CO/2 (25 July 2006), para 15.

126 *Al-Asad* (n 24), paras 134, 136.

127 E.g. IACHR, Report No. 38/99, Case 11.654, *Saldaño* v. *Argentina*, Admissibility, 11 March 1999, para 21; Report No. 86/99, Case 11.589, *Alejandre* v. *Cuba*, 29 September 1999, paras 23, 25; Report No. 51/01, Case 9903, *Rafael Ferrer-Mazorra* v. *United States*, Merits, 4 April 2001, paras 179–183; Report No. 153/11, Petition 189-03, *Danny Honorio Bastidas Meneses and Others* v. *Ecuador*, Admissibility, 2 November 2011, para 21.

128 E.g. ECtHR, *Öcalan* v. *Turkey*, Appl. no. 46221/99, decision of 14 December 2000 on the admissibility; *Öcalan* v. *Turkey*, Appl. no. 46221/99, judgment of 12 March 2003, para 93; *Issa and Others* v. *Turkey*, Appl. no. 31821/96, decision of 30 May 2000 on the admissibility; *Issa* (n 21), para 74; *Öcalan* v. *Turkey* [GC], Appl. no. 46221/99, judgment of 12 May 2005, para 91.

129 *Isaak* (admissibility) (n 115), 21; *Solomou and Others* v. *Turkey*, Appl. no. 36832/97, judgment of 24 June 2008, paras 48–51.

130 General comment No. 31 (n 25), para 10; HRC, *Kurbogaj* v. *Spain*, Communication No. 1374/2005, in: UN Doc. A/61/40 (Vol. II) (2006), 626–632; CAT, Conclusions: Austria, UN Doc. CAT/C/AUT/CO/3 (15 December 2005), para 18; HRC, Concluding observations: Belgium, UN Doc. CCPR/CO/81/BEL (12 August 2004), para 6; Concluding observations: Norway, UN Doc. CCPR/C/NOR/CO/5 (21 April 2006), para 6.

131 *Banković* (n 18), para 73; *Hirsi Jamaa and Others* v. *Italy* [GC], Appl. no. 27765/09, judgment of 23 February 2012, para 75; HRC, General comment No. 36 (n 25), para 63; CAT,

detention camp of Guantánamo, where the outside State exercises 'physical power and control over the person in question'.[132] Briefly, what matters is that any exercise of authority and control by State agents over a person abroad implies a certain effectiveness that some authors consider 'effective control' over persons.[133]

2.1.2.2 Causal Nexus

Several situations satisfy neither the test of effective control over territory nor the principal criterion of 'authority and control'. For example, an aerial bombardment or the gunfire shot by State agents abroad, a refusal to renew the passport of a citizen by the embassy abroad or an attack by an armed drone in a foreign territory constitute examples where there is no direct physical but rather a remote, causal link between the State and the human rights violation.

The first case where the ECtHR seemed to recognise that a situation can fall within the jurisdiction of the State when the conduct of its agents produced some effects beyond its borders is the *Drozd* v. *France and Spain* case.[134] Examples for such a nexus are the violation of fair trial rights in procedures of the State's diplomatic mission towards nationals and the violation of one's right to privacy by a foreign State on the internet.[135] In the *Banković* case the applicants argued that this model of jurisdictional link applied to an air strike in Belgrade during the Kosovo conflict by seventeen NATO Member States which were also Contracting States to the ECHR. Nonetheless, the Court accepted the respondent State's argument under which establishing the jurisdiction of the State parties participating in the aerial bombardment 'amounts to a "cause-and-effect" notion of jurisdiction not contemplated by or

General comment No. 2 (n 25), para 16; CAT, *J.H.A.* v. *Spain*, Communication No. 323/2007, Decision of 10 November 2008, UN Doc. CAT/C/41/D/323/2007 (21 November 2008), para 8.2.

132 *Al-Skeini* (n 23), para 136.

133 Vassilis P. Tzevelekos, 'Reconstructing the Effective Control Criterion in Extraterritorial Human Rights Breaches: Direct Attribution of Wrongfulness, Due Diligence, and Concurrent Responsibility' (2014) 36 *Michigan Journal of International Law* 129, 151.

134 *Drozd and Janousek* v. *France and Spain* [Plenary], Appl. no. 12747/87, judgment of 26 June 1992, para 91.

135 However, cases of extradition and expulsion constitute a false case of extraterritoriality because both the individual and the effect of the act are situated in the acting State's territory. *A contario*: Sarah Miller, 'Revisiting Extraterritorial Jurisdiction: A Territorial Justification for Extraterritorial Jurisdiction under the European Convention' (2009) 20 *European Journal of International Law* 1223, 1242–1245.

appropriate to article 1 of the Convention'.[136] In 2010, the Grand Chamber again in the *Medvedyev* case categorically excluded the extraterritorial jurisdiction 'where – as in the *Banković* case – what was at issue was an instantaneous extraterritorial act, as the provisions of Article 1 did not admit of a "cause-and-effect" notion of "jurisdiction"'.[137] Likewise, in 2020, the Grand Chamber did not find such a nexus in a humanitarian visa application submitted to a State's diplomatic mission with which the applicant had 'no connecting tie'.[138] In the *Georgia* v. *Russia (II) (Merits)* case, the Court resuscitated the *Banković* dictum by limiting the 'State agent authority and control' link to 'isolated and specific acts involving an element of proximity', while excluding its applicability to bombing and artillery shelling in the active phase of hostilities of international armed conflicts.[139]

However, in several other cases the ECtHR did use the causal model. In cases where an outside State shot individuals on foreign soil, the Court established the outside State's jurisdiction on the causal link between its conduct and the human rights violation.[140] The Inter-American bodies have likewise applied the causal model to aerial bombardment[141] and established the extraterritorial jurisdiction where there is a causal link between the State's conduct and the alleged human rights violation.[142] Beyond regional bodies, universal human rights bodies accept that the State has jurisdiction when its conduct directly causes a violation of

136 *Banković* (n 18), para 75.

137 *Medvedyev and Others* v. *France* [GC], Appl. no. 3394/03, judgment of 29 March 2010, para 64.

138 *M.N. and Others* v. *Belgium* [GC], Appl. no. 3599/18, Decision of 5 May 2020 on the admissibility, paras 123–125.

139 *Georgia* v. *Russia (II) (Merits)* (n 67), paras 132–133.

140 *Mansur Pad and Others* v. *Turkey*, Appl. no. 60167/00, decision of 28 June 2007 on the admissibility, paras 54–55; *Georgia Andreou* v. *Turkey* (n 21), 10–11 ('the opening of fire on the crowd from close range, which was the direct and immediate cause of those injuries, was such that the applicant must be regarded as 'within [the] jurisdiction' of Turkey'); In the *Al-Skeini* case, the husband of the third applicant was killed by a sudden burst of machine-gunfire shot from outside the building, while it was unclear which of the two camps was responsible for the fatal shot. The Court established the jurisdiction of the UK without detailing the model of the jurisdictional link. *Al-Skeini* (n 23), para 150.

141 IACHR, Application No. 9213, Case 9213, *Disabled Peoples' International et al.* v. *United States*, Admissibility, 22 September 1987 (under the American Declaration of the Rights and Duties of Man!).

142 E.g. *Franklin Guillermo* (n 18), para 99; *Saldaño* (n 127), para 20; IACtHR, *Caso Familia Pacheco Tineo* v. *Estado Plurinacional de Bolivia*, 25 November 2013, paras 31 (view of the IACHR) and 38 (IACtHR).

human rights beyond its borders.[143] Briefly, the international case law clearly went beyond the restrictive interpretation of jurisdiction in *Banković*.

In all the above-mentioned scenarios the State had control over the victim and/or the perpetrator, that is, State agents remotely committed the human rights violation abroad. However, one might ask whether extraterritorial jurisdiction would cover cases where the State has control neither over the victim nor over the perpetrators nor over foreign territory but over activities within its own territory that lead to foreseeable harm being caused abroad. One might think of the home State's control over its corporate nationals that violate human rights abroad or of the State of nationality's conduct with respect to its nationals seeking diplomatic or consular assistance against human rights violations abroad. In those cases, it is a third party (a third State or a non-state actor) and not the State's agents that directly violates human rights abroad, and one may ask how far such breaches may fall within the jurisdiction of the State. Human rights monitoring bodies have gradually adapted the causal model to those scenarios.[144] Most recently, the Human Rights Committee provided in its General Comment 36 (2018) on the right to life that States parties

> must also take appropriate legislative and other measures to ensure that all activities taking place in whole or in part within their territory and in other places subject to their jurisdiction, but having a direct and reasonably foreseeable impact on the right to life of individuals outside their territory [. . .] are consistent with article 6.[145]

This marks the recognition of the causality-based jurisdictional link by the most universal treaty body.

[143] E.g. CEDAW, General recommendation No. 28 (n 117), para 12; HRC, *Samuel Lichtensztejn* v. *Uruguay*, Communication No. 77/1980, UN Doc. A/38/40 (15 September 1983), 179–185, para 6.1; *Mohammad Munaf* v. *Romania*, Communication No. 1539/2006, UN Doc. CCPR/C/96/DR/1539/2006 (13 July 2009), para 14.2.

[144] UN Human Rights Council, 'Guiding Principles on Business and Human Rights: Implementing the United Nations 'Protect, Respect and Remedy' Framework', UN Doc. A/HRC/17/31 (21 March 2011), Principle 2; CEDAW, General recommendation No. 30 (n 25), paras 10, 12(b); CESCR, General comment No. 24 (2017) on State obligations under the ICESCR in the context of business activities, UN Doc. E/C.12/GC/24 (10 August 2017), paras 25–35; CRC, General comment No. 16 (2013) on State obligations regarding the impact of the business sector on children's rights, UN Doc. CRC/C/GC/16 (17 April 2013), paras 43, 45, 50.

[145] HRC, General comment No. 36 (n 25), para 63.

In its Advisory Opinion on *The Environment and Human Rights*, the Inter-American Court of Human Rights (IACtHR) is the first human rights court to recognise a new extraterritorial jurisdictional link based on effective control over domestic conducts. The Court accepted a jurisdictional link 'when the State of origin exercises effective control over the activities that caused the damage and the consequent human rights violation'.[146] In the *Issa Yassin and Others* v. *Canada* case (2017), the Human Rights Committee also confirmed that 'there are situations where a State party has an obligation to ensure that rights under the Covenant are not impaired by extraterritorial activities conducted by enterprises under its jurisdiction'.[147]

The strongest argument in favour of the causal nexus is the standard of due diligence in general international law.[148] While due diligence traditionally is conceived to protect the interests of other States within a State's territory, IHRL has enlarged its content: the State is required to take all measures within its power to prevent and repress certain wrongful acts occurring even beyond its borders whenever it has the knowledge about foreseeable wrongful acts and the capacity to prevent them. In short, treaty-monitoring bodies recognise the causal jurisdictional link in various scenarios where the State is factually linked to extraterritorial situations, where it has the knowledge on the risk of wrongful acts and the capacity to protect due to its effective control over activities within its territory.

In 'grey zones' some applicants have addressed their claim not only against the territorial State and the outside State controlling the territory or deploying its agents in the area but also against a third State that might have had an influence on the perpetrators. Regarding Transnistria, certain Ukrainian applicants complained about their State of nationality, in that Ukraine breached the ECHR by not complying with its positive obligations towards its nationals.[149] In one such case the ECtHR rejected this complaint as regards the State of nationality, holding

[146] IACtHR, The Environment and Human Rights (State obligations in relation to the environment in the context of the protection and guarantee of the rights to life and to personal integrity – interpretation and scope of Articles 4(1) and 5(1) of the American Convention on Human Rights), Advisory Opinion OC-23/17, 15 November 2017, para 104(h).

[147] HRC, *Basem Ahmed Issa Yassin et al.* v. *Canada*, Communication No. 2285/2013, Views of 26 July 2017, UN Doc. CCPR/C/120/D/2285/2013 (7 December 2017), para 6.5.

[148] *Infra*, Section 3.1.2.

[149] E.g. *Totchi and Others* v. *the Republic of Moldova, Russia and Ukraine*, Appl. no. 8833/10, lodged on 29 January 2010; *Kolobychko* v. *Republic of Moldova, Russia and Ukraine*, Appl.

that the applicants did not adduce any evidence in support of the allegation that Ukraine had jurisdiction in the case.[150] Generally speaking, the mere fact that the respondent State is the State of nationality of the victim is not sufficient evidence for the Court to establish a causal jurisdictional link, as the Convention does not require State parties to exercise diplomatic protection,[151] nor to investigate their citizens' death abroad.[152] However, the causal model may apply provided that the applicant manages to establish that the causality between the activities taking place in whole or in part within the State's territory and the human rights violation in the 'grey zone' was direct and reasonably foreseeable and that the third State had the capacity to protect against the harm. Such a causality can be based, for example, on the beginning of a continuous cross-border human rights violation (human trafficking[153] or asylum transfer[154]) in the respondent State; on the State's custody procedure to restore the bond between a parent and a child being in another country;[155] or on the institution of a criminal investigation by the State of origin in a cross-border incident leading to loss of life.[156]

The advantage of the personal model (the State agent authority and control or the causal link) is that it provides for an auxiliary means to render international human rights conventions applicable in 'grey zones': control over territory raises much difficulties of evidence and evaluation, whereas the threshold of effectiveness is lower in the case of authority and control or a causal link between the State and the person. In both cases the applicant must demonstrate only that there is a factual link, that is, certain effectiveness or the failure to exercise effectiveness between the conduct of the State and the human rights violation.

2.1.2.3 The Scope of the Personal Model

Contrary to the spatial link, the personal model of extraterritorial jurisdiction does not impose the application of the entirety of rights and

no. 36724/10, judgment of 18 September 2018; *Soyma* v. *the Republic of Moldova, Russia and Ukraine*, Appl. no. 1203/05, judgment of 30 May 2017.

150 *Soyma* (n 149), para 16.

151 *Suzana Orel and others* v. *Croatia*, Appl. no. 51506/13, decision of 7 June 2016 on the admissibility, para 73.

152 *Rantsev* v. *Cyprus and Russia*, Appl. no. 25965/04, judgment of 7 January 2010, para 244.

153 Ibid.

154 *M.S.S.* v. *Belgium and Greece* [GC], Appl. no. 30696/09, judgment of 21 January 2011.

155 *Monory* v. *Hungary and Romania*, Appl. no. 71099/01, judgment of 5 April 2005.

156 *Güzelyurtlu and Others* v. *Cyprus and Turkey* [GC], Appl. no. 36925/07, judgment of 29 January 2019, paras 192–197.

freedoms enshrined in the given convention but only the rights that are relevant in the context. This difference results from the impossibility of a State to guarantee all the rights and freedoms abroad without controlling the territory.[157] Using this argument, the applicants claimed in *Banković* that the notions of 'effective control' and 'jurisdiction' must be flexible enough to take account of the degree of authority exercised through an aerial bombardment.[158] However, the ECtHR held that such an approach

> is tantamount to arguing that anyone adversely affected by an act imputable to a Contracting State, wherever in the world that act may have been committed or its consequences felt, is thereby brought within the jurisdiction of that State for the purpose of Article 1 of the Convention.[159]

In the *Al-Skeini* case, however, the ECtHR expressly decided in favour of the divisibility of rights enshrined in the Convention that *Banković* had rejected ten years earlier:

> It is clear that, whenever the State through its agents exercises control and authority over an individual, and thus jurisdiction, the State is under an obligation under Article 1 to secure to that individual the rights and freedoms under Section 1 of the Convention that are relevant to the situation of that individual. In this sense, therefore, the Convention rights can be 'divided and tailored' (compare *Banković*, . . .).[160]

This conclusion, reaffirmed in later cases,[161] shows that it is effectiveness, that is, the extent of the authority exercised over the person, that determines the scope of the rights to be protected in the personal model. This also justifies the spatial model: as effective control over territory exercised in a stable manner supposes a high degree of effectiveness similar to that exercised by the State within its national territory, it is logical to impose on the State the full scope of human rights that such an effectiveness allows.

While the ECtHR's 'divided and tailored' test covers human rights affected by the exercise of State authority and control abroad, it hardly applies to the State's omission to prevent activities within its own territory causing foreseeable human rights violations abroad. The ECtHR, as

157 Evelyne Lagrange, 'L'application de La Convention de Rome à Des Actes Accomplis Par Les Etats Parties En Dehors Du Territoire National' (2008) 112 *Revue générale de droit international public* 521, 539–540.

158 *Banković* (n 18), para 53. 159 Ibid., para 75. 160 *Al-Skeini* (n 23), para 137.

161 *Hirsi* (n 131), para 74; *Jaloud* v. *the Netherlands* [GC], Appl. no. 47708/08, judgment of 20 November 2014, para 154; *Mirzoyan* v. *Armenia*, Appl. no. 57129/10, judgment of 23 May 2019, para 55.

mentioned in Section 2.1.2.2, has not generally recognised the causal jurisdictional link. To provide a coherent test for the scope of the rights to be protected, the approach that the present book proposes is the 'functional approach'.

It was Judge Bonello in the *Al-Skeini* judgment who proposed the so-called functional approach of jurisdiction: in his view, the outside State is obliged to assume its functions concerning all the rights and freedoms enshrined in the ECHR 'which *it is in a position to ensure*'.[162] As he explained, an occupying power is expected to ensure to all persons those human rights that its authority and control allows; in a given case this might not include, for instance, the right to education or the right to free and fair elections.[163] Judge Loucaides, in his partially dissenting opinion in the *Ilaşcu* case,[164] Lord Sedley, in the *Al-Skeini* case before the British Court of Appeal,[165] and several authors also recommend that the outside State shall guarantee human rights as far as it has the power in the given extraterritorial situation, or in other terms according to the authority and control exercised.[166] This theory takes into account not only the effectiveness exercised but also the authority that the State could have exercised, thus covering omissions. The functional approach is defendable since it promotes the universal respect of human rights, legal certainty and effectiveness, that is, the effective use of the State's capabilities to protect those human rights that it can influence abroad.

This interpretation by far defines most broadly the notion of jurisdiction, because all alleged human rights violations attributable to the State would fall within its jurisdiction,[167] which thus is in conformity with general international law.[168] One of the possible reasons for the *Banković*

[162] *Al-Skeini* (n 23), Concurring opinion of Judge Bonello, para 32. [163] Ibid.

[164] *Ilaşcu* (n 44), Partly dissenting opinion of Mr Loucaides, 143–144.

[165] *Al-Skeini*, Court of Appeal (n 119), para 197 (Lord Justice Sedely).

[166] Anna Cowan, 'A New Watershed? Re-Evaluating Banković in Light of Al-Skeini' (2012) 1 *Cambridge Journal of International and Comparative Law* 213, 225–226; Hugh King, 'The Extraterritorial Human Rights Obligations of States' (2009) 9 *Human Rights Law Review* 521, 547; Maastricht Principles on Extraterritorial Obligations of States in the Area of Economic, Social and Cultural Rights, 28 September 2011, meeting of the Maastricht University and the International Commission of Jurists, Principle 9(b)–(c).

[167] *Assanidze* v. *Georgia* [GC], Appl. no. 71503/01, judgment of 8 April 2004, Concurrent opinion of Judge Loucaides, 52; *Ilaşcu* (n 44), Partly dissenting opinion of Mr Loucaides, 143; Pierre-François Laval, 'A Propos de La Juridiction Extraterritoriale de l'Etat. Observations Sur l'arrêt Al-Skeini de La Cour Européenne Des Droits de l'homme Du 7 Juillet 2011' (2012) 116 *Revue générale de droit international public* 61, 79.

[168] In this sense: Tzevelekos (n 133) 141–142; the ECtHR case law reflects this trend progressively: *Pisari* v. *the Republic of Moldova and Russia*, Appl. no. 42139/12, judgment of 21 April 2015, Concurring opinion of Judge Motoc.

inadmissibility decision was the recognition that, beyond an analysis of attribution between the State and the wrongful act, there was no *stricto sensu* threshold in the causal model comparable to the threshold of 'effective control' in the spatial model, and the Court intended to limit the interpretation of the notion of jurisdiction.[169] For the ECtHR, which attempts to constantly stress the exceptionality of extraterritorial jurisdiction, such a broad interpretation certainly would go too far. Instances where the ECtHR stressed the exceptionality of extraterritorial jurisdiction were the references to the concept of the 'legal space' of the Convention,[170] the exercise of 'all or some of the public powers normally to be exercised by that Government',[171] or the 'instantaneous extraterritorial act'[172] or the 'isolated and specific acts involving an element of proximity'.[173] In its later case law none of these criteria constituted the mandatory requirement for the applicability of the Convention[174] but were supplementary arguments for the exceptionality of extraterritorial jurisdiction. While the ECtHR has an annual influx of 40 000–60 000 applications, other human rights treaty bodies are far less overcharged by petitions. This may be the reason why other regional and UN treaty bodies interpret jurisdiction more broadly than the ECtHR.

The ECtHR intends to avoid opening a Pandora's box by a too liberal interpretation of jurisdiction, which would give the green light to a massive flux of applications from regions where some European States were militarily active such as Iraq, Afghanistan, certain African States[175] or from international armed conflicts within the territory of States parties. This risk would be less pressing if the State parties accepted their extraterritorial jurisdiction in their domestic practice.[176] Furthermore, instead of introducing fluctuant and arbitrary criteria,

169 Milanovic (n 11) 207–208. 170 *Supra*, n 101.

171 *Banković* (n 18), para 71; confirmed, e.g. *Manoilescu andDobrescu* v. *Romania and Russia*, Appl. no. 60861/00, decision of 3 March 2005 on the admissibility, para 101; *Al-Skeini* (n 23), paras 135, 149.

172 *Medvedyev and Others* v. *France* [GC] (n 137), para 64.

173 *Georgia* v. *Russia (II) (Merits)* (n 67), para 132.

174 The Court confirmed extraterritorial jurisdiction even if the facts occurred outside Europe, e.g. *Öcalan* and *Issa* cases (n 128); *Al-Skeini* (n 23), para 142; The ECtHR, however, resuscitated the *Banković* dictum by excluding extraterritorial jurisdiction within the Convention's 'legal space', in the active phase of hostilities in the *Georgia* v. *Russia (II) (Merits)* case. *Supra*, Section 2.1.2.2.

175 Gérard Cohen-Jonathan, 'La Territorialisation de La Juridiction de La Cour Européenne Des Droits de l'homme' (2002) 52 *Revue trimestrielle des droits de l'homme* 1069, 1082; Milanovic (n 11) 221.

176 Miller (n 135) 1245–1246.

the ECtHR should ensure legal certainty by applying the 'functional' jurisdiction test.

In sum, jurisdiction is a question of yes or no, that is, either a jurisdictional link exists and entails the applicability of the human rights treaty or it does not exist, and the treaty is not applicable. The alternative preconditions of jurisdiction vary as to the required nexus between the State and the extraterritorial situation, and both the spatial and the personal model have their own legitimacy. In the spatial model all persons situated in the territory are presumed to fall within the outside State's jurisdiction without the need to prove the exercise of authority and control of the State's agents over the individual. In case of repetitive or massive applications concerning the same region, the spatial model facilitates the procedure of monitoring bodies. Where applicants cannot prove territorial control, they might establish the State's authority and control over the individual abroad or the causality between activities within the State's territory and their foreseeable harm being caused abroad. The scope of human rights to be protected varies according to the effectiveness that the State exercises – either while controlling the territory, or the person abroad, or the activities within its own territory.

2.2 The Jurisdiction of the Territorial State

It has been contested whether the human rights treaties concluded by the territorial State are applicable in an area beyond the territorial State's effective control. Since Article 29 of the VCLT does not require the exercise of effective control, monitoring bodies have to answer the question of whether the area falls within the jurisdiction of the territorial State under the concerned treaty or, on the contrary, 'a different intention appears from the treaty or is otherwise established'.[177] On the one hand, a number of concerned territorial States made territorial declarations at the time of the ratification of these treaties in which they confirmed their inability to apply the treaty in the area outside their effective control. On the other hand, not only the contractual will of the State but also the fact of the State's lack of territorial control may, at first sight, exclude the jurisdiction of the territorial State.[178] This section

[177] VCLT, Article 29.

[178] Symeon Karagiannis, 'Article 29' in Olivier Corten and Pierre Klein (eds), *Les Conventions de Vienne sur le droit des traités: commentaire article par article*, vol. 2 (Bruylant 2006) 756, para 66.

examines what the legal effects of the territorial declarations (Section 2.2.1) and of the loss of effective control (Section 2.2.2) are.

2.2.1 *The Effect of Territorial Declarations*

Territorial States often, at the time of a treaty ratification or signature, make a unilateral declaration aimed at excluding the application of the human rights treaty in its entirety in the region outside their control. Before analysing the legal effect of such territorial declarations (TD) on the applicability of the conventions, they must be distinguished from two similar treaty instruments: declarations made under colonial clauses and derogations.

First, several early human rights treaties include a so-called colonial clause that allows State parties to make a declaration that the rights contained in the treaty will apply (opt-in) or not apply (opt-out) 'in territories for whose international relations it is responsible'. For instance, the ECHR, the Convention on the Prevention and Punishment of the Crime of Genocide and some other Council of Europe (CoE) conventions include such an opt-in colonial extension clause,[179] while the 1926 Slavery Convention includes an opt-out clause.[180] Such colonial clauses concern the given treaty's territorial scope in colonial and (UN) Trusteeship territories[181] but not in the metropolitan territory of the State parties. This is confirmed by the CoE's model final clause, which allows State parties, at the time of signature or ratification, to 'specify the territory or territories to which' the given treaty shall apply.[182] The explanatory report of recent CoE conventions provides that the provision 'applies essentially to overseas territories as it would be contrary to the philosophy of the convention for a party to exclude parts of its metropol-

179 ECHR, Article 56; Convention on the Prevention and Punishment of the Crime of Genocide, Paris, 9 December 1948, UNTS, vol. 78, 277, Article XII; Framework Convention for the Protection of National Minorities, Strasbourg, 1 February 1995, ETS No. 157, Article 30.

180 Slavery Convention, Geneva, 25 September 1926, LNTS, vol. 60, Article 9.

181 Ralph Wilde, 'The Extraterritorial Application of International Human Rights Law on Civil and Political Rights' in Scott Sheeran and Sir Nigel Rodley (eds), *Routledge Handbook of International Human Rights Law*, 1st edition (Routedge 2013) 638.

182 CoE, Model Final Clauses for Conventions, Additional Protocols and Amending Protocols concluded within the Council of Europe (as adopted by the Ministers' Deputies of the CoE at their 1291st meeting, on 5 July 2017), Article C; European Convention for the Prevention of Torture and Inhuman or Degrading Treatment or Punishment, Strasbourg, 26 November 1987, ETS No. 126, Article 20(1).

itan territory from the application of this instrument'.[183] This practice shows that CoE member States have never applied the model territorial clause to metropolitan areas.

Second, derogation is understood as a unilateral measure authorised by a human rights convention by which the State party provisionally suspends certain obligations binding it under the convention.[184] It is provisional and exceptional, only authorised to the extent strictly required by the exigencies of the situation[185] and, especially, it is limited to 'certain obligations'.[186] In other words, derogation is not an appropriate solution for the territorial State because its lacking territorial control often is permanent and concerns the totality of human rights. However, the territorial States chose to make declarations regarding their 'grey zone' in general terms, concerning all the provisions of a given treaty. Moreover, contrary to the mandatory procedure of derogation (information of State parties through the depositary), the territorial States formulated their declarations at the time of the signature or ratification of the treaty. While it is true that some States applied derogations in a geographic area over which they have lost effective control, they did so always with respect to certain specific treaty provisions and only provisionally, for a determined period.[187] It follows that territorial declarations (TDs) are to be distinguished from derogations.

Contrary to declarations made under colonial clauses and derogations, TDs are closer to a third treaty instrument, reservation, defined as 'a unilateral statement, however phrased or named, made by a State, when signing, ratifying, accepting, approving or acceding to a treaty, whereby it purports to exclude or to modify the legal effect of certain provisions of the treaty in their application to that State'.[188] As this part will explain, TDs do not entirely correspond to reservations either as their legal effect

183 E.g. European Convention on Nationality (ETS No. 166) Explanatory report, para 146; European Convention on the Exercise of Children's Rights (ETS No. 160) Explanatory report, para 83.

184 E.g. ICCPR, Article 4, para 1; ACHR, Article 27, para 1; ECHR, Article 15, para 1.

185 E.g. HRC, General comment No. 29, State of emergency (Article 4), UN Doc. CCPR/C/21/Rev.1/Add.11 (31 August 2001), para 4.

186 Ibid., paras 1, 4, 5.

187 E.g. Notifications under Article 4(4) of the ICCPR (derogations), Guatemala (28 December 2010); Ukraine (5 June 2015, 27 November 2015 and 6 July 2016), UN Treaty Collection; *infra*, Section 3.3.1.

188 VCLT, Article 2(1)(d).

is more ambigious. As the practice of States (Section 2.2.1.1), and human rights treaty bodies (Section 2.2.1.2) reveal, TDs do not in themselves influence the applicability of human rights conventions.

2.2.1.1 State Practice

As was mentioned in the introduction of this chapter, Article 29 of the VCLT presumes a treaty's applicability to the entire State territory '[u]-nless a different intention appears from the treaty or is otherwise established'. A declaration on the territorial applicability made by the State party at the time of the ratification or signature, uncontested by other State parties, may indicate such an intention.[189]

Among the territorial States, certain European States of which territory is in part controlled by *de facto* regimes, namely Azerbaijan, Georgia and the Republic of Moldova, often had recourse to unilateral declarations by which they intended to exclude the application of the treaty in its entirety to the region beyond their control. Reviewing all the TDs of these States, the practice seems inconsistent regarding the concerned human rights treaties, the wording used and the purported legal effects.

First, the territorial States did not systematically make such declarations, rather they were made in an *ad hoc* manner and mainly at the regional level. Azerbaijan, Georgia or the Republic of Moldova did so at the time of the ratification of the ECHR, some of its Protocols, various other CoE conventions and certain universal human rights treaties (Table 2.1). The choice of the treaties to which these three States made a TD is inconsistent: in some cases they made it at the time of the ratification, whereas in most treaties they did not and referred to the loss of control in their periodic report. Cyprus, for instance, made similar declarations to treaties in matters other than human rights.[190] Sometimes the lack of declaration is due to the fact that the State lost territorial control after the ratification of the given treaty.[191] When it lost effective control over Crimea and certain areas in Eastern Ukraine, Ukraine made similar TDs both to some of its already-binding

[189] Mark Eugen Villiger, *Commentary on the 1969 Vienna Convention on the Law of Treaties* (Brill 2009) 392.

[190] United Nations Convention against illicit traffick in narcotic drugs and psychotropic substances, Vienna, 20 December 1988, UN Treaty Collection.

[191] E.g. ICCPR, Initial report of Moldova, UN Doc. CCPR/C/SR.2030 (25 July 2002), para 4.

Table 2.1 *Territorial declarations formulated at the time of the ratification/signature of human rights treaties*

	Azerbaijan (Nagorno-Karabakh)	Cyprus (Northern Cyprus)	Georgia (Abkhazia, South-Ossetia)	Moldova (Transnistria)	Ukraine (Crimea, Donetsk, Luhansk)
ICCPR	✗	✗	✗	✗	✗
OP-ICCPR	✗	✗	✗	✓	✗
OP 2-ICCPR	✗	✗	✗	✓	✗
CAT	✗	✗	✗	✗	✗
OP-CAT	✓	✗	✗	✗	✗
CRC	✗	✗	✗	✗	✗
OPSC-CRC	✗	✗	✗	✓	✗
OPCP-CRC		✗	✗		✓
CRPD	✓	✗	✗	✗	✗
OP-CRPD	✓	✗	✗	✗	✗
CPPED	✗	✗		✗	✗
ECHR	✓	✗	✗	✓	✗
Protocol 1	✓	✗	✓	✗	✗
Protocol 4	✓	✗	✗	✗	✗
Protocol 6	✓	✗	✗	✗	✗
Protocol 7	✓	✗	✗	✗	✗
Protocol 12	✗	✗	✓	✗	✗
Protocol 13	✗	✗	✓	✓	✗
Protocol 14	✗	✗	✗	✓	✗
ECPT	✓	✗	✓	✗	✗
	✓	✗	✓	✓	

CoE Convention on Action against Trafficking in Human Beings					✓ TD made after ratification
European Convention on Extradition	✓	×	✓	×	✓ TD made after ratification
European Charter for Regional or Minority Languages	✓	✓		×	×
CoE Convention on the Protection of Children against Sexual Exploitation and Sexual Abuse	×	×	×	✓	×

human rights treaties[192] and to those that it subsequently signed or ratified.[193]

Second, the wording varies from one State to another and from one treaty to another: most often the State declares that it is unable to guarantee the application of the treaty in the territory outside its control until its territorial integrity is restored[194] or that the provisions of the treaty apply only in the government-controlled territory.[195] Ukraine's notifications are different as they declare that the application and implementation of the State's obligations in the areas outside its effective control 'is limited and is not guaranteed'.[196]

Third, as for the purported legal effect, one may think that the territorial State intends either to limit its jurisdiction, that is, the applicability of the treaty in the concerned zone, or to decline all responsibility for the violations of the treaty in the area. The two interpretations do not necessarily lead to the same result: under the first, the declaration concerns a question of primary norms, that is, the content of obligations, whereas the second concerns secondary rules, that is, the law of State responsibility for the violations of primary norms.[197] The first interpretation exempts the State from its obligations in the 'grey zone', whereas the second leaves the State's jurisdiction under the treaty intact, and produces legal effects only in terms of State responsibility, limiting or entirely excluding it. This second approach preserves the obligations on the territorial State (for instance, procedural obligations such as the presentation of periodic reports regarding the 'grey zone').

Moldova represented both interpretations: it wished both to be exempted from responsibility and to exclude its primary norm

[192] Notification of declaration No. JJ8025C by Ukraine (Tr./024-115 and others), 23 October 2015, CoE Treaty Office; this chapter's conclusions on the lack of legal effect of TD on human rights treaties equally apply to those declarations of Ukraine.

[193] Optional protocol to the CRC on a communications procedure, New York, 19 December 2011 (Ukraine), UN Treaty Collection.

[194] E.g. Optional protocol No. 2 to CAT (Azerbaijan); CRPD (Azerbaijan), UN Treaty Collection.

[195] E.g. OP-ICCPR (Moldova); OPSC-CRC (Moldova), UN Treaty Collection; CoE Convention on Action against Trafficking in Human Beings (Georgia, Moldova), CoE Treaty Office.

[196] Nofitifation of declaration No. JJ8025C by Ukraine (n 192); Optional protocol to the CRC on a communications procedure, New York, 19 December 2011 (Ukraine), UN Treaty Collection.

[197] ARSIWA Commentary, 31, para 1.

obligations as a reservation under Article 57 of the ECHR.[198] In some TDs Georgia referred not to the applicability of the treaty, but to its responsibility,[199] while in others it expressly 'declined' its responsibility for violations of the treaty provisions in its separatist areas.[200] Azerbaijan, however, stressed that its declaration 'was not termed a "reservation"' but that its purpose was to remind all State parties that Azerbaijan was 'unable to guarantee the application of the Convention rights in the "territories occupied by the Republic of Armenia"'.[201]

To evaluate the legal effect of those declarations, one also has to consider the reaction of State parties. Whether it is considered a reservation under the VCLT[202] or another unilateral declaration,[203] a TD may be subject to reactions of States. However, in the practice of the 'reservations dialogue',[204] one cannot find any reaction from other States to the TD of the territorial States. The only analogy that can serve as a basis for the *opinio juris* of States is the reaction of States to the territorial declarations of Turkey. The difference is that the latter declarations foresee the non-applicability of a human rights convention not in Turkey's national territory but outside Turkey's territory in the occupied Northern Cyprus.

At the time of the ratification of the CERD in 1973, Turkey declared its intention to ratify the Convention 'exclusively with regard to the national territory where the Constitution and the legal and administrative order of the Republic of Turkey are applied'.[205] It made the same declaration when ratifying the ICCPR (2000), the ICESCR (2000) and the First Optional Protocol to the ICCPR (2004).[206] In respect of the last treaty, it formulated a reservation as such, limiting the examination of individual communications to 'alleged violations which result either

198 *Ilaşcu and Others* v. *Moldova and Russia* [GC], Appl. no. 48787/99, decision of 4 July 2001 on the admissibility, 13–14; Core document, Republic of Moldova, UN Doc. HRI/CORE/1/Add.114 (14 May 2001), paras 33–34.

199 Protocols Nos. 12 and 13 to the ECHR (Georgia); ECPT (Georgia); European Convention on Extradition (Georgia), CoE Treaty Office.

200 Protocol No. 1 to the ECHR (Georgia), CoE Treaty Office.

201 *Minas Sargsyan* v. *Azerbaijan* [GC], Appl. no. 40167/06, decision of 14 December 2011 on the admissibility, para 52.

202 VCLT, Articles 2(1)(d) and 20(4)(b).

203 VCLT, Article 78; Text of the guidelines constituting the Guide to Practice on Reservations to Treaties with commentaries thereto, in: Report of the ILC, Sixty-third session, UN Doc. A/66/10/Add.1 (2011) [Commentaries of the the Guide to Practice . . .], 238–241 paras 14–19.

204 Ibid., 239, para 16.

205 CERD: Turkey, 13 October 1972. UN Treaty Collection.

206 ICCPR: Turkey, 15 August 2000; ICESCR: Turkey, 15 August 2000; OP-ICCPR: Turkey, 3 February 2004; ibid.

from acts, omissions, developments or events that may occur within the national boundaries of the territory of the Republic of Turkey'. Likewise, at the regional level Turkey limited the recognition of the right of petition before the European Commission of Human Rights (ECommHR) and the ECtHR (the former Articles 25 and 46 of the ECHR, respectively) to allegations concerning acts or omissions of Turkish public authorities committed in Turkey.[207] State parties and the treaty bodies, however, strongly contested the legal effect of these declarations.

Cyprus, Greece and Sweden concluded that the territorial declaration of Turkey to the ICCPR or the ICESCR amounted to a reservation and is contrary to the object and purpose of those treaties.[208] Consequently, they made an objection to the above-mentioned reservations and declared that neither these reservations nor their objections are to preclude the entry into force of the treaty concerned.[209] Germany stressed its 'concern' about the Turkish declaration, without qualifying it as a reservation.[210]

As for the Turkish declaration formulated to the ECHR, Greece considered it a null and void reservation, whereas Sweden, Luxembourg, Denmark, Norway and Belgium reserved their position in view of a later decision of the ECHR monitoring bodies.[211] As in the case of universal treaties, the States commenting on the declaration represented only a minority among numerous State parties that failed to react to the Turkish declarations.[212] Strangely enough, the ECtHR nonetheless considered the Greek objection and the declaration of the five other States as 'a uniform and consistent State practice' which 'clearly rebuts the respondent Government's arguments that restrictions attaching to

[207] Before the ECommHR: Declaration of Turkey, 28 January 1987; before the ECtHR: Declaration of Turkey, 22 January 1990; both confirmed by the declaration of 21 November 1995, CoE Treaty Office, Declarations and reservations (Turkey, complete chronology).

[208] Cyprus: ICESCR, Objection, 26 November 2003; Greece: ICESCR, Objection, 11 October 2004 and ICCPR, Objection, 11 October 2004; Sweden: ICCPR, Objection, 30 June 2004. See UN Treaty Collection.

[209] Ibid.

[210] Germany: ICCPR, Declaration, 13 October 2004; ICESCR, Declaration, 13 October 2004; ibid.

[211] *Chrysostomos, Papachrysostomos and Loizidou* v. *Turkey (admissibility)*, Appl. nos. 15299/89, 15300/89 and 15318/89, Commission decision on the admissibility of 4 March 1991, Law, paras II.6–II.11, II.13.

[212] On 28 January 1987, date of the registration of the first territorial declaration of Turkey, there were twenty States parties to the ECHR apart from Turkey.

Article 25 and Article 46 (art. 25, art. 46) declarations must have been envisaged by the drafters of the Convention'.[213] If one bears in mind the codification works of the ILC on reservations according to which the reactions of State parties have only relative relevance,[214] one can at the most conclude that the Turkish declarations provoked some objections and doubts about their legal effect.[215]

2.2.1.2 The Practice of Human Rights Treaty Bodies

Among human rights treaty bodies, the ECommHR and the ECtHR examined the question of the legal effect of TDs, first of all in respect of the Turkish declarations. After Turkey affirmed that certain applications fall outside the competence of the Commission and the Court since the facts occurred in Northern Cyprus, that is, in a territory covered by its declaration,[216] both the Commission and the Court examined the declarations' conformity with the provision of the ECHR on their competence to receive individual applications (former Articles 25 and 46).[217]

In divided decisions[218] the Commission found that the territorial restriction figured in Turkey's declaration of 28 January 1987 was not authorised under Article 25 as it was incompatible with the object and purpose of the Convention, namely, the principle of *effet utile*.[219] Despite this incompatibility, the Commission found that the Turkish recognition of the individual petition procedure remained intact, under the *Belilos* judgment, which endorsed the principle under which the State is

[213] *Loizidou (Preliminary objections)* (n 23), para 82.

[214] Commentaries of the the Guide to Practice ... (n 203), 522, para 5; HRC, General comment No. 24 (n 1), para 17.

[215] The ILC qualified the declarations of States parties to the ECHR that 'reserved their position' as 'notifications of provisional "non-acceptance" associated with a waiting stance' rather than objections. Report of the ILC, UN Doc. A/60/10 (2005), 194, para 18.

[216] *Chrysostomos* (n 211), Law, para I.2.3; *Loizidou (Preliminary objections)* (n 23), para 36.

[217] *Chrysostomos* (n 211), Law, paras I.2.11–I.2.12; *Loizidou (Preliminary objections)* (n 23), para 36.

[218] Five dissenting members held that the colonial extension clause (former Article 63) could apply by analogy, excluding the right of individual petition in certain territories with which the mainland territory has looser constitutional ties. Partly concurring, partly dissenting opinion of M. M. Nørgaard, Jörundsson, Gözübüyük, Soyer and Danelius, in: *Chrysostomos and Papachrysostomos* v. *Turkey*, Appl. nos. 15299/89 and 15300/89, report of the Commission of 8 July 1993 and *Titina Loizidou* v. *Turkey*, Appl. no. 15318/89, report of the Commission of 8 July 1993.

[219] *Chrysostomos* (n 211), paras 40–42, 46.

presumed to be bound by the Convention independently of the validity of an interpretative declaration.[220]

The Court confirmed the conclusions of the Commission, referring to the Convention's character as 'a treaty for the collective enforcement of human rights and fundamental freedoms', and to the principle of *effet utile*, that is, 'the effectiveness of the Convention as a constitutional instrument of European public order (ordre public)'.[221] It equally took into consideration the nature of the Convention, the ordinary sense to be attributed to Articles 25 and 46 in their context and in the light of their object and purpose and the practice of Contracting Parties, and concluded that the restrictions *ratione loci* attached to Turkey's Article 25 and Article 46 declarations were invalid.[222]

This case law served as a basis for determining the validity of the TDs concerning regions within the State's national territory. First, in the *Ilaşcu* admissibility decision (2001), the Grand Chamber had to decide on the legal effect of the TD that Moldova invoked as a preliminary exception concerning its jurisdiction *ratione loci*. It argued that Article 29 of the VCLT affords States the possibility of restricting the territorial scope of the treaty, so that the Court should be able to broadly interpret the colonial extension clause of the Convention.[223] The Court first confirmed that Article 57(1) of the ECHR does not allow 'reservations of a general character', understood as a reservation that does 'not refer to a specific provision of the Convention or if it is worded in such a way that its scope cannot be defined'.[224] As this was the case of Moldova's TD, the Court held that

> the declaration in question is of general scope, unlimited as to the provisions of the Convention but limited in space and time, whose effect would be that persons on that 'territory' would be wholly deprived of the protection of the Convention for an indefinite period.[225]

Referring to the case law on the Turkish territorial declarations, the Court concluded that Moldova's declaration 'cannot be equated with a reservation within the meaning of the Convention, so that it must be deemed invalid' and rejected Moldova's preliminary exception.[226] The Court confirmed the refusal of territorial restrictions in the *Assanidze*

[220] *Belilos* v. *Switzerland*, Appl. no. 10328/83, judgment of 29 April 1988, para 60.

[221] *Loizidou (Preliminary objections)* (n 23), paras 70–75, 77.

[222] Ibid., para 89; The Court also confirmed the separability of the denounced restrictions: ibid., paras 90–98.

[223] *Ilaşcu (admissibility)* (n 198), 13–14. [224] Ibid., 20. [225] Ibid. [226] Ibid.

case (2004). Even though Georgia did not contest its jurisdiction *ratione loci*, the Court noted that Georgia ratified the Convention for its entire territory and that a specific reservation with regard to the Ajarian Autonomous Republic 'would in any event have been ineffective'.[227] Likewise, in the admissibility decision *Sargsyan* v. *Azerbaijan* (2011), the Court refused to grant legal effect to Azerbaijan's TD for the same reasons as in the case of Moldova's declaration.[228] While reaffirming its *Loizidou* and *Ilaşcu* admissibility decisions, the Court held that in the instant case, the Azerbaijani TD is 'not capable of restricting the territorial application of the Convention to certain parts of the internationally recognised territory of the Republic of Azerbaijan'.[229] The legal consequences were the same as in the *Ilaşcu* case: the declaration cannot be equated with a reservation complying with the requirements of Article 57 of the Convention and must therefore be deemed invalid.

It is worth noting that in the *Ilaşcu*, *Sargsyan* and *Assanidze* cases the Grand Chamber adopted its decision unanimously: without expressly qualifying the TD as 'reservation',[230] the Court concluded that such TD 'cannot be equated with a reservation within the meaning of the Convention', but it constitutes a reservation which is 'deemed invalid'.[231] While drawing this conclusion, the Court invoked the object and purpose of the Convention, the necessity to maintain equality between State parties and the principle of *effet utile*.[232]

As for the two other regional human rights systems, no State party has made a TD, neither to the ACHR nor to the ACHPR. However, in its advisory opinion on *The effect of reservations on the entry into force of the ACHR*, the IACtHR drew some conclusions comparable to those of the ECtHR.[233] For the Court, the ACHR attaches such great importance to the protection of the individual that it makes the right of individual petition mandatory as of the moment of ratification.[234] It follows that a restriction that would make the IACtHR's jurisdiction inoperative would be

[227] *Assanidze* (n 167), para 140. [228] *Sargsyan (admissibility)* (n 201), para 69.

[229] Ibid., paras 63–65.

[230] See nevertheless in this sense *Ilaşcu* (n 44), Dissenting opinion of Judge Kovler, 149 and the hypothetical case mentioned in *Assanidze* (n 167), para 140.

[231] E.g. *Sargsyan (admissibility)* (n 201), para 70.

[232] *Loizidou (Preliminary objections)* (n 23), paras 70; *Assanidze* (n 167), para 142.

[233] IACtHR, *The effect of reservations on the entry into force of the American Convention on Human Rights (Arts. 74 and 75)*, Advisory Opinion OC-2/82, 24 September 1982, e.g. paras 29 (the 'lawmaking treaty' character of human rights conventions), 34–35 (reservations shall not be incompatible with the object and purpose of the treaty).

[234] Ibid., para 34.

invalid.[235] This argumentation seems analogous to that of the ECtHR – related to the object and the purpose of the Convention and to the 'effectiveness' of the regional human rights system – and it could justify the inadmissibility of territorial exclusions.[236]

Universal bodies have also dealt with the Turkish declarations, but their conclusions did not serve as a basis for determining the validity of TDs concerning regions within the national territory. The Committee for the Elimination of Racial Discrimination encouraged Turkey to remove 'the territorial limitation to the application ofthe Convention'.[237] The Human Rights Committee, however, qualified Turkey's declaration expressly as

> a reservation limiting the effect of the Covenant to the national territory of the State party, which could result in the complete non-applicability of the Covenant to persons subject to its jurisdiction in situations where its troops or police forces operate abroad.[238]

Members of the Human Rights Committee invoked both the VCLT and the extraterritorial interpretation of the notion of 'jurisdiction' under the case law of the ECtHR and the ICJ.[239] Both universal bodies, the Committee for the Elimination of Racial Discrimination and the Human Rights Committee, drew the same conclusion: no State party can restrict its jurisdiction under the given convention to its national territory, and they recommended withdrawing Turkey's declaration.

As for the TD concerning the national territory, the Committee on the Rights of the Child recommended that Moldova 'consider withdrawing its declaration and take all possible measures to ensure' protection under the Optional Protocol in the area beyond its control 'to the extent possible'.[240] The Committee held that 'State obligations cannot be

[235] IACtHR, *Constitutional Court* v. *Peru*, judgment of 24 September 1999 (Competence), para 34; *Ivcher-Bronstein* v. *Peru*, judgment of 24 September 1999 (Competence), para 35; *Haniff Hilaire* v. *Trinidad and Tobago*, judgment of 1 September 2001 (Preliminary objections), para 82.

[236] The IACtHR, while invoking the 'lawmaking treaty' character of the ACHR, referred to the *Loizidou (Preliminary Observations)* decision. *Constitutional Court* v. *Peru* (n 235), para 46; *Ivcher-Bronstein* (n 235), para 47; *Haniff Hilaire* (n 235), paras 66–67.

[237] CERD, Concluding observations: Turkey, UN Doc. CERD/C/TUR/CO/3 (24 March 2009), para 8.

[238] HRC, Concluding observations: Turkey, UN Doc. CCPR/C/TUR/CO/1 (13 November 2012), para 5.

[239] HRC, UN Doc. CCPR/C/SR.2927 (24 October 2012), paras 33 (Ms. Chanet) and 36 (Mr. Scheinin).

[240] CRC, Concluding observations: Republic of Moldova, UN Doc. CRC/C/OPSC/MDA/CO/1 (29 October 2013), para 9.

arbitrarily and unilaterally curtailed either by excluding zones or areas from a State's territory or by defining particular zones or areas as not, or only partly, under the jurisdiction of the State'.[241] The Human Rights Committee also made it clear that it considers Moldova's jurisdiction extending to its entire national territory, including the area outside its effective control.[242] Generally, universal treaty bodies have confirmed most principles elaborated by the European and the Inter-American Courts on reservations: the 'lawmaking treaty' character of human rights conventions[243] and that a statement is considered a reservation 'where it is clear that the intent of the action is to limit the binding obligations assumed by the State party'.[244] The Human Rights Committee stressed that reservations that purport to evade essential guarantees (the right to remedy, presentation of periodic reports) which underpin the efficacy of the Covenant are incompatible with its object and purpose.[245] Likewise, widely-formulated reservations that essentially render ineffective all Covenant rights, and reservations of broad terms that do not refer to a particular provision of the Covenant and do not indicate in precise terms their scope in relation thereto, are also incompatible with its object and purpose.[246] These principles are important as the ECtHR invoked them to justify the invalidity of TDs as reservations.

Between regional and universal treaty bodies, there is an apparent convergence in matters of reservations,[247] and they would consider TDs as invalid reservations. For instance, when they confirmed Moldova's jurisdiction over its entire territory, the members of the Human Rights Committee considered the case law of the ECtHR.[248]

241 CRC, General comment No. 6: Treatment of unaccompanied and separated children outside their country of origin, UN Doc. CRC/GC/2005/6 (1 September 2005), para 12.

242 HRC, Concluding observations: Republic of Moldova, UN Doc. CCPR/C/MDA/CO/2 (4 November 2009), para 5; Concluding observations: Republic of Moldova, UN Doc. CCPR/C/MDA/CO/3 (18 November 2016), para 6; However, Moldova made its TD to the first and second Optional Protocol to the ICCPR and not to the ICCPR.

243 Report of the meeting of the Working Group on reservations, UN Doc. HRI/MC/2006/5 (4 July 2006), para 16(3); HRC, General comment No. 24 (n 1), para 17; CERD, Preliminary opinion on the issue of reservations to treaties on human rights, UN Doc. CERD/C/62/Misc.20/Rev.3 (13 March 2003), para 2.

244 The practice of human rights treaty bodies with respect to reservations to international human rights treaties, UN Doc. HRI/MC/2005/5 (13 June 2005), para 3; HRC, General comment No. 24 (n 1), para 3.

245 HRC, General comment No. 24 (n 1), para 11.

246 Ibid., paras 12, 19.

247 The practice of human rights treaty bodies with respect to reservations to international human rights treaties, UN Doc. HRI/MC/2005/5/Add.1 (30 May 2006), para 4.

248 HRC, UN Doc. CCPR/C/SR.2029 (14 January 2003), paras 19 (Mr. Scheinin), 36 (Mr. Ando).

The treaty bodies' practice is confirmed by the works of the ILC on reservations to treaties. Initially, the ILC considered TDs excluding the application of the treaty to a certain region since the beginning of its works as reservations.[249] However, in 2011 the ILC adopted Directive 1.1.3 with a slightly modified new wording that defined reservations as

> a unilateral statement by which a State purports to exclude the application of some provisions of a treaty, *or of the treaty as a whole with respect to certain specific aspects*, to a territory to which they would be applicable in the absence of such a statement constitutes a reservation [emphasis added].[250]

As opposed to the initial draft, the Commission decided not to include in the definition declarations aimed at excluding the application of a treaty in its entirety in a geographic area, which – as it explains – cannot be considered as reservations, 'but rather the expression of a "different intention" in the sense of article 29 of the Vienna Conventions'.[251] Therefore, TDs issued by territorial States would not produce any legal effect as to the treaty's applicability in 'grey zones'.

In sum, contrary to reservations, limited to specific provisions of the treaty or well-defined circumstances and constituting a clearly provisional measure, TDs are related to the treaty as a whole and a long-term situation of fact. Consequently, unlike reservations, TDs are to be regarded as notifications concerning a question of fact the purpose of which is to inform the other State parties about a situation influencing the territorial State's ability to apply the convention in a part of its territory.[252] Therefore, TDs do not in themselves influence the applicability of human rights conventions.

2.2.2 *The Effect of the Loss of Effective Control*

While Section 2.2.1 concluded that territorial declarations made at the time of the treaty signature or ratification cannot exclude the applicability of human rights treaties in respect of the 'grey zone', one may ask whether the fact of the loss of effective control over the area produces

[249] Text of the Guide to Practice on Reservations to Treaties, adopted by the Commission at its sixty-third session, in: Report of the International Law Commission, UN Doc. A/66/10 (2011) [Guide to Practice . . .], Draft Directive 1.1.3 [1.1.8].

[250] Ibid. [251] Ibid., 50, para 5.

[252] Jörg Polakiewicz, 'Collective Responsibility and Reservations in a Common European Human Rights Area' in Ineta Ziemele (ed), *Reservations to Human Rights Treaties and the Vienna Convention Regime: Conflict, Harmony or Reconciliation* (2004) 126; *Ilaşcu* (n 44), para 329.

such an effect.[253] If one accepts the jurisprudential principle under which effective control over territory entails jurisdiction,[254] one could suppose that, on the contrary, the loss of effective control over an area entails the lack of jurisdiction over this territory. Initially, the case law oscillated between jurisdiction and non-jurisdiction of the territorial State. Whereas the Inter-American and African bodies consistently confirm the State's jurisdiction over its entire territory despite the loss of territorial control as an irrebuttable presumption (Section 2.2.2.1), the early practice of European and universal bodies considered that the territorial State's loss of effective control excludes its jurisdiction over that area (Section 2.2.2.2). Since the *Ilaşcu* judgment (2004) of the ECtHR that conceptualised the territorial State's jurisdiction (Section 2.2.2.3), both European and universal treaty-monitoring bodies confirm the irrebuttable presumption of the territorial State's jurisdiction which is based on both the latter's sovereign title and effectiveness (Section 2.2.2.4). Where the sovereignty is not quasi-universally accepted by States, treaty-monitoring bodies should use the so-called functional approach based on effectiveness, which combines extraterritorial and territorial jurisdiction (Section 2.2.2.5).

2.2.2.1 Irrebuttable Presumption of Jurisdiction: Inter-American and African Case Law

A first stream of the case law accepts that the entire national territory falls within the jurisdiction of the territorial State, without exception and irrespective of the loss of effective control over an area. This is the view of the Inter-American and African human rights treaty bodies.

Despite the fact that the American Declaration of the Rights and Duties of Man does not contain any jurisdictional clause and that the ACHR refers only to the notion of jurisdiction and not to the national territory, both instruments presume that the State guarantees their application in its entire national territory. In the *travaux préparatoires* of the ACHR[255] nothing indicates that the State parties would have

[253] The ECtHR also examines the two questions separately. *Ilaşcu* (n 44), para 324; *Sargsyan (admissibility)* (n 201), paras 71–76.

[254] *Legal Consequences for States of the Continued Presence of South Africa in Namibia (South West Africa) notwithstanding Security Council Resolution 276 (1970)*, Advisory Opinion, *I.C.J. Reports* 1971, 54, para 118.

[255] The drafters of the ACHR based their work on Article 2(1) of the ICCPR, but finally avoided the reference to the territory and kept only the term 'jurisdiction'. Conferencia Especializada Interamericana sobre Derechos Humanos, San José, 7–22 November 1969, OEA/Ser.K/XVI/1.2, 145, 155–156.

accorded the term 'jurisdiction' any special sense, different from that of Article 2(1) of the ICCPR.[256] The interpretative practice of the monitoring bodies, the Inter-American Commission and Court has been consistent: the presumption of the State's jurisdiction over its entire territory is irrebuttable. Even if the State loses effective control over a part of its territory, it keeps its full jurisdiction under the ACHR and has certain obligations *vis-à-vis* individuals residing in its territory.

The IACHR confirmed the territorial State's jurisdiction in several 'massacre' cases, concerning human rights violations committed in an internal armed conflict in areas over which paramilitary groups took effective control. Before establishing whether the conduct of the non-state armed group was attributable to the State, the Commission systematically established, *prima facie*, that the facts fell within the territorial State's jurisdiction *ratione loci* as they occurred in its national territory.[257] Before the IACtHR, most procedures are initiated by the IACHR which already established the jurisdiction *ratione loci*, and the Court normally does not examine this question but accepts the Commission's conclusion. Even in cases where the facts occurred in an area controlled by a non-state armed group, the Court does not examine the jurisdiction *ratione loci* of the territorial State, partially because no State has ever challenged its jurisdiction *ratione loci* over its own territory.[258]

This presumption of the State's jurisdiction over its territory may be explained by the nature of the State's obligation of 'due diligence'. The obligation, expressed for the first time in the *Velásquez-Rodríguez* case, is broad enough to include even situations of loss of effective control over a territory:

> An illegal act which violates human rights and which is initially not directly imputable to a State (for example, because it is the act of a private person or because the person responsible has not been identified) can lead to international responsibility of the State, not because of the act itself, but because of the lack of

[256] *Franklin Guillermo* (n 18), para 89.

[257] E.g. Report No. 33/01, Case 12.250, *Mapiripán Masacre* v. *Colombia*, Admissibility, 22 February 2001, para 26 (without express reference to the competence *ratione loci*); Report No. 41/02, Petition 11.748, *José Del Carmen Álvarez Blanco et al. (Pueblo Bello)* v. *Colombia*, Admissibility, 9 October 2002, para 20.

[258] *19 Merchants* v. *Colombia*, judgment of 12 June 2002 (Preliminary objection), para 22; *Mapiripán Massacre* v. *Colombia*, judgment of 7 March 2005 (Preliminary objections), para 24; *Pueblo Bello Massacre* v. *Colombia*, judgment of 31 January 2006 (Merits, Reparations and Costs), para 4; *Afro-descendant communities displaced from the Cacarica River Basin (Operation Genesis)* v. *Colombia*, judgment of 20 November 2013 (Preliminary objections, Merits, Reparations and Costs), para 16.

due diligence to prevent the violation or to respond to it as required by the Convention.[259]

In other words, even if an actor other than a State agent commits the human rights violations, the territorial State's obligation of due diligence obliges the State to prevent and react to the wrongful act.[260] The Court confirmed this obligation in cases where non-state actors, especially paramilitary groups, controlled an area.[261]

A second, similar explanation is the State's position as 'guarantor': the territorial State is in the position to guarantee the Convention rights for all persons under its jurisdiction. The Court and the Commission have created the notion of 'guarantor' (in Spanish *garante*) initially to express the specific position of the State *vis-à-vis* persons deprived of their liberty by State authorities.[262] The Court later extended the notion to several categories of persons in a position of vulnerability,[263] and recently to any person falling within the State's jurisdiction.[264] The notion of 'guarantor' focuses on the State's horizontal obligations in relations between individuals in line with the theory of *Drittwirkung* which the Court applied to paramilitary areas[265] where the State's agents were neither present, nor directly contributed to the human rights violation. Moreover, the Court recognised the State's position of guarantor in a zone torn by an armed conflict[266] and nothing shows that the Court would change its view in cases where the State lacks effective control over the same area.

259 *Velásquez-Rodríguez* v. *Honduras*, judgment of July 29, 1988 (Merits), para 172.

260 *Infra*, Section 3.1.2.

261 *19 Merchants* v. *Colombia*, judgment of 5 July 2004 (Merits, Reparations and Costs), para 140; *Mapiripán Massacre* v. *Colombia*, judgment of 15 September 2005 (Merits, Reparations and Costs), paras 111–114 (referring to *erga omnes* obligations); *Pueblo Bello Massacre* (n 258), paras 113, 126, 139; *Ituango Massacres* v. *Colombia*, judgment of 1 July 2006 (Merits, Reparations and Costs), paras 134, 291, 315; *Afro-descendant communities ...* (n 258), paras 224, 370–373.

262 *Neira-Alegría et al.* v. *Peru*, judgment of 19 January 1995 (Merits), para 60; Provisional measures regarding the Republic of Colombia, *19 Tradesmen* v. *Colombia*, 26 June 2012, para 28; *Mapiripán Massacre* v. *Colombia* (n 261), para 111, etc.

263 E.g. *The Inter-ecclesial Commission on Justice and Peace*, Order of 22 November 2010, Request for Provisional measures, para 23 (human rights defenders); *Río Negro Massacres* v. *Guatemala*, judgment of 4 September 2012 (Preliminary objection, merits, reparations and costs), para 142 (children).

264 *19 Merchants* v. *Colombia* (Preliminary objection) (n 258), para 183 ('the State obligation to ensure the free and full exercise of the rights of all those subject to its jurisdiction'; in Spanish: '*el deber estatal de garantizar el libre y pleno ejercicio de los derechos de todas las personas bajo la jurisdicción de un Estado*').

265 *Mapiripán Massacre* v. *Colombia* (n 261), para 111; *Pueblo Bello Massacre* (n 258), para 113.

266 *Pueblo Bello Massacre* (n 258), para 139.

A third explanation for the presumption of the State's jurisdiction over its territory is the argument of a 'vacuum' of State responsibility. In a case on the Convention's extraterritorial application, the IACHR took inspiration from the argument of the risk of a 'vacuum' in the system of human-rights protection of the ECHR.[267] The IACHR concluded that such a 'legal *lacuna*' would run counter to the object and purpose of the ACHR.[268] The same argument applies *a fortiori* when a non-state armed group controls a part of the State's territory – in this case, a *lacuna* could occur if it was accepted that the territorial State has no jurisdiction over conducts occurring in the area beyond its effective control.

As for the African Charter, despite its lack of jurisdictional clause, the ACommHPR has interpreted Article 1 as requiring State parties to protect within their entire territory[269] and followed the approach of the Inter-American human rights bodies. The fact that the African Charter does not include any provision on reservations or derogations illustrates that the drafters intendeded to establish a system of human rights protection that resists interior troubles, civil wars and other violent conflicts. Consequently, both the ACommHPR[270] and the African Court on Human and Peoples' Rights (ACtHPR)[271] accept the State's jurisdiction *ratione loci* when the alleged violations took place in the territory of a State party to the African Charter, even if it lacks effective control over part of its territory. For instance, in *Commission Nationale des Droits de l'Homme et des Libertés* v. *Chad*, the government asserted 'that it had no control over violations committed by other parties, as Chad was in a state of civil war'.[272] Although the parties and the Commission did not invoke the question of territorial control, one could suppose that armed groups

[267] *Supra*, Section 2.1.1.2.

[268] *Franklin Guillermo* (n 18), para 98; *Danny Honorio Bastidas Menese and Others* v. *Ecuador* (n 127), para 21.

[269] E.g. ACommHPR, *Association of Victims of Post Electoral Violence & INTERIGHTS* v. *Cameroon*, Communication no. 272/03, 25 November 2009, paras 112, 119–120; Resolution on the human rights situation in the Federal Republic of Nigeria, ACHPR/Res.267(EXT.OS/XV) 2014, 14 March 20, para 11.

[270] E.g. ACommHPR, *Lawyers for Human Rights* v. *Swaziland*, Communication no. 251/02, 27 April–11 May 2005, para 46; *Samuel T. Muzerengwa and 110 Others (represented by Zimbabwe Lawyers for Human Rights)* v. *Zimbabwe*, Communication no. 306/05, 23 February–3 March 2011, para 58; *Dabalorivhuwa Patriotic Front* v. *République d'Afrique du Sud*, Communication no. 335/2006, 9–23 April 2013, para 72.

[271] E.g. ACtHPR, *African Commission on Human and Peoples' Rights* v. *Libya*, Appl. no. 002/2013, judgment of 3 June 2016, paras 58–59; *African Commission on Human and Peoples' Rights* v. *Republic of Kenya*, Appl. no. 006/2012, judgment of 26 May 2017, para 67.

[272] ACommHPR, *Commission nationale des droits de l'Homme et des libertés* v. *Chad*, Communication no. 74/92, 11 October 1995, para 19.

temporarily controlled areas beyond the State's control. The Commission concluded that, despite the perpetration of violent acts by non-state actors, Chad 'had a responsibility to secure the safety and the liberty of its citizens' in accordance with the principle of due diligence.[273] Likewise, in the *African Commission on Human and Peoples' Rights* v. *Libya* case concerning the applicant's illegal detention by a 'revolutionary brigade' in the Libyan civil war of 2011, the ACtHPR held that '[t]he State is indeed under the obligation to take measures to ensure, in its territory, the application of the laws guaranteed under the Charter'.[274]

These examples reveal the similarity between the Inter-American and African approach: despite the State's lack of territorial control, the presumption of the territorial State's jurisdiction is irrebuttable. This jurisprudential solution confirms the principle that the territorial State has the ultimate responsibility for the sort of the population living in its territory and for the application of its human rights treaties.

2.2.2.2 Rebuttable Presumption of Jurisdiction: Early European and Universal Practice

As in the case of the Inter-American and African bodies, European and universal monitoring bodies presume the State's jurisdiction over its entire territory. However, unlike the Inter-American and African bodies, the European and universal bodies over a lengthy period accepted that this presumption may have exceptions, namely, where the State has no effective control over its territory.

In the disputes related to Northern Cyprus, the ECommHR very early recognised that the ECHR 'continues to apply to the whole of the territory of the Republic of Cyprus' and that because of the loss of effective control over the northern part of the island, Cyprus '[have] since 1974 been prevented from exercising their jurisdiction in the north of the island'.[275] However, it was unclear whether the Commission used the term 'jurisdiction' in the sense of general international law or under Article 1 of the ECHR. In the *Ahmet Cavit AN and Others* v. *Cyprus* case the applicants, Turkish Cypriots residing in the 'TRNC', alleged the violation of their freedom of movement by the *de facto* authorities and directed

[273] Ibid., para 22.

[274] *African Commission on Human and Peoples' Rights* v. *Libya* (n 271), para 49.

[275] *Cyprus* v. *Turkey*, Appl. no. 8007/77, decision of the Commission of 10 July 1978 on the admissibility, 149-150, paras 23–25; confirmed in: *Chrysostomos* (n 211), Law, para 33; *Chrysostomos* (report) (n 218), para 98 (without reaffirming the applicability of the ECHR).

their claim against Cyprus. While reiterating that Cyprus is prevented from exercising its jurisdiction over the northern part of its territory, the Commission concluded that 'the Republic of Cyprus cannot be held responsible under Article 1 (Art. 1) of the Convention for the acts of Turkish Cypriot authorities in the north of Cyprus'.[276] Although this initial case law might reveal the lack of the territorial State's jurisdiction over an area beyond its effective control, it has little relevance as the applicants did not specify to what extent Cyprus would incur responsibility for the alleged human rights violations.

The ECtHR clarified its position on the territorial State's jurisdiction first in the *Assanidze* case. It held that the territorial State's jurisdiction over its national territory is presumed but the Court must determine 'whether there is valid evidence to rebut that presumption'.[277] The presumption of the territorial State's jurisdiction over its entire territory can be justified by Article 29 of the VCLT and the *travaux préparatoires* of Article 1 of the ECHR as subsidiary means of interpretation.[278] The *travaux* show that the Expert Intergovernmental Committee decided to replace the terms 'all persons residing within their territories' of the initial draft with a reference to persons 'within their jurisdiction' in order to extend 'the benefits of the Convention to all persons in the territories of the signatory States, even those who could not be considered as residing there in the legal sense of the word'.[279] Finally, as a third justification, the presumption of jurisdiction is confirmed by the principles underlying the Court's refusal of TDs that intend to exclude some areas of the national territory (object and purpose of the Convention, equality between State parties and the principle of *effet utile*).

While the presumption of the territorial State's jurisdiction is strongly defendable, the Court cited no precedent to justify why it considered the presumption rebuttable, except for the preconceived idea under which the term 'jurisdiction' in the sense of Article 1 is linked to the same notion under general international law.[280] Among the factors likely to rebut the presumption of the territorial State's jurisdiction over its territory, the Court mentioned that the Ajarian region had no separatist aspirations, and that no other State exercised effective overall control there, nor had the territorial State made any specific reservation under Article 57 of the Convention that 'would in any event have been

[276] *Ahmet Cavit AN and Others* v. *Cyprus*, Appl. no. 18270/91, Commission decision of 8 October 1991 on the admissibility.

[277] *Assanidze* (n 167), paras 138–139.

[278] VCLT, Article 31(2)(b).

[279] *Banković* (n 18), paras 19–21, 63.

[280] *Assanidze* (n 167), para 137.

ineffective, as the case-law precludes territorial exclusion'.[281] On the contrary, one might have assumed that any of those three factors could lead the Court to conclude that a State does not have jurisdiction in a part of its territory, but the Court did not specify the importance of each of those factors. This created the false impression of a rebuttable presumption that most universal treaty bodies seemed to follow.

In periodic reporting mechanisms, universal treaty monitoring bodies take into account the fact that an area is beyond the territorial State's effective control, but they draw diverse conclusions from this fact. Most reports concluded on the State party's inability[282] or difficulty[283] to apply the human rights treaty, without necessarily concluding on the State's jurisdiction in the given area. Among those conclusions, only a few reports expressly affirmed either the State's lacking jurisdiction[284] or the difficulty[285] to exercise its jurisdiction in the area.

Furthermore, contradictory conclusions of Charter-based monitoring bodies confirmed the inconclusiveness of the practice of UN treaty bodies: some of them held that the presumption on the territorial State's jurisdiction over its territory may be rebutted where the State is unable to exercise its territorial control,[286] while others considered this presumption irrebuttable.[287] The inconsistency of universal monitoring bodies' conclusions is problematic because ignoring the State's jurisdiction in the 'grey zone' disregards the protection offered by the monitoring mechanism and runs counter to the principle of universality, as well

[281] Ibid., para 140.

[282] E.g. HRC, Concluding observations: Lebanon, UN Doc. CCPR/C/79/Add.78 (5 May 1997), para 4; CERD, Conclusions: Azerbaijan, UN Doc. A/54/18 (29 September 1999), 48, para 484; CRC, Concluding observations: Cyprus, UN Doc. CRC/C/15/Add.59 (7 June 1996), para 9.

[283] E.g. CEDAW, Concluding observations: Azerbaijan, UN Doc. A/53/38/Rev.1 (1998), 7, para 41; CESCR, Concluding observations: Georgia, UN Doc. E/C.12/1/Add.42 (17 May 2000), para 6.

[284] HRC, Concluding observations: Cyprus, UN Doc. CCPR/C/79/Add.39 (3 August 1994), para 3; Concluding observations: Cyprus, UN Doc. CCPR/C/79/Add.88 (6 April 1998), para 3; CERD, Concluding observations: Republic of Moldova, UN Doc. CERD/C/60/CO/9 (21 May 2002), para 3.

[285] CRC, Concluding observations: Georgia, UN Doc. CRC/C/15/Add.222 (27 October 2003), para 4; HRC, Concluding observations: Georgia, UN Doc. CCPR/C/79/Add.75 (5 May 1997), para 3.

[286] Report of the Special Rapporteur on extrajudicial, summary or arbitrary executions, UN Doc. A/68/382 (13 September 2013), para 44, note 23.

[287] E.g. Situation of human rights in Yemen. Report of the UNHCHR, UN Doc. A/HRC/39/43 (17 August 2018), para 13; Human Rights Council, Situation of human rights in Crimea Sevastopol, UN Doc. A/HRC/36/CRP.3 (25 September 2017), para 41.

as to the consistent Inter-American and African case law about the irrebuttable presumption. However, the early European and universal practice has changed as a consequence of the *Ilaşcu* judgment in 2004.

2.2.2.3 Conceptualisation in *Ilaşcu*

The ECtHR for the first time faced the problem of the territorial State's jurisdiction in respect of an area outside its effective control in a case where the applicants, as opposed to the *Ahmet Cavit AN* case, specified to what extent the State could have had authority over the situation. One of the most remarkable decisions of the history of the ECtHR, the *Ilaşcu* judgment, has elucidated the dominant opinion on the territorial State's jurisdiction over a 'grey zone' and brought closer the European and universal practice to that of the Inter-American and African bodies.

The four applicants in the *Ilaşcu* case addressed their claim both against Russia and the territorial State, the Republic of Moldova: they alleged that Moldova was responsible for the violations of the Convention committed in Transnistria, part of Moldova's national territory. They claimed that, notwithstanding its lack of territorial control, Moldova was under an obligation to take sufficient measures to ensure respect for the rights guaranteed by the Convention throughout its territory.[288] Moldova submitted that the applicants did not come within its *de facto* jurisdiction since the State 'could not really exercise territorial jurisdiction' in an area outside its control.[289]

The Court reiterated its previous case law on the primarily territorial notion of jurisdiction, the presumption of jurisdiction throughout the State's territory and added some situations likely to exclude the State's territorial control:

> This presumption may be limited in exceptional circumstances, particularly where a State is prevented from exercising its authority in part of its territory. That may be as a result of military occupation by the armed forces of another State which effectively controls the territory concerned ... acts of war or rebellion, or the acts of a foreign State supporting the installation of a separatist State within the territory of the State concerned.[290]

This list, which is not exhaustive, enumerates the exceptional situations that can lead to the loss of the effective control by the territorial State. As for the first case, military occupation, the Court implicitly mentions its case law on Northern Cyprus as an example, whereas for other scenarios

[288] *Ilaşcu* (n 44), para 306. [289] Ibid., para 300. [290] Ibid., para 312.

the Court provided no example. As for 'acts of war or rebellion', it is doubtful whether the Court would establish the loss of the State's jurisdiction as a consequence of an internal armed conflict if, considering the Court's above-mentioned legal policy to prevent 'a regrettable vacuum in the system of human-rights protection' in the territory of State parties, the conduct of rebels would not fall within the jurisdiction of any other State.[291] Finally, the third scenario reflects precisely the situation of Transnistria: a separatist regime installed in the territory of the State with the support of an outside State. As explained in Section 2.1.1.2, in this case an outside State controls the proxy administration, which amounts to 'effective control' over territory, thus the territory falls at the same time under the jurisdiction of the outside State.

Compared to *Assanidze*, it is revealing that the Court speaks about circumstances 'limiting' rather than 'rebutting' the presumption of the territorial State's jurisdiction. This might illustrate a slight change towards the acceptance of the State's continued jurisdiction over facts occurring within its territory, despite its lack of territorial control. The Court confirmed this by a completely new principle:

> In order to be able to conclude that such an exceptional situation exists, the Court must examine on the one hand all the objective facts capable of limiting the effective exercise of a State's authority over its territory, and on the other the State's own conduct. The undertakings given by a Contracting State under Article 1 of the Convention include, in addition to the duty to refrain from interfering with the enjoyment of the rights and freedoms guaranteed, positive obligations to take appropriate steps to ensure respect for those rights and freedoms within its territory ... Those obligations remain even where the exercise of the State's authority is limited in part of its territory, so that it has a duty to take all the appropriate measures which it is still within its power to take.[292]

This conclusion marks a significant development in the Court's case law: even if the State has lost its effective control over a part of its territory, certain obligations continue to bind it, namely, the duty 'to take all the appropriate measures which it is still within its power to take'. One may interpret this principle as the maintenance of the State's jurisdiction with regard to the area or, more precisely, towards individuals in the area.

[291] Kjetil Mujezinovic Larsen, 'Territorial Non-application of the European Convention on Human Rights' (2009) 78 *Nordic Journal of International Law* 73, 83.

[292] *Ilaşcu* (n 44), para 313.

Applying this principle to the context of Transnistria, the Court first recognised Moldova's lacking territorial control over the area, uncontested by the parties, and explained what it understands under the continuity of positive obligations:

331. However, even in the absence of effective control over the Transdniestrian region, Moldova still has a positive obligation under Article 1 of the Convention to take the diplomatic, economic, judicial or other measures that it is in its power to take and are in accordance with international law to secure to the applicants the rights guaranteed by the Convention.

The concept of positive obligations

332. In determining the scope of a State's positive obligations, regard must be had to the fair balance that has to be struck between the general interest and the interests of the individual, the diversity of situations obtaining in Contracting States and the choices which must be made in terms of priorities and resources. Nor must these obligations be interpreted in such a way as to impose an impossible or disproportionate burden ...

333. The Court considers that where a Contracting State is prevented from exercising its authority over the whole of its territory by a constraining *de facto* situation, such as obtains when a separatist regime is set up, whether or not this is accompanied by military occupation by another State, it does not thereby cease to have jurisdiction within the meaning of Article 1 of the Convention over that part of its territory temporarily subject to a local authority sustained by rebel forces or by another State.

Nevertheless, such a factual situation reduces the scope of that jurisdiction in that the undertaking given by the State under Article 1 must be considered by the Court only in the light of the Contracting State's positive obligations towards persons within its territory. The State in question must endeavour, with all the legal and diplomatic means available to it *vis-à-vis* foreign States and international organisations, to continue to guarantee the enjoyment of the rights and freedoms defined in the Convention.

334. Although it is not for the Court to indicate which measures the authorities should take in order to comply with their obligations most effectively, it must verify that the measures actually taken were appropriate and sufficient in the present case. When faced with a partial or total failure to act, the Court's task is to determine to what extent a minimum effort was nevertheless possible and whether it should have been made. Determining that question is especially necessary in cases concerning an alleged infringement of absolute rights such as those guaranteed by Articles 2 and 3 of the Convention.

335. Consequently, the Court concludes that the applicants are within the jurisdiction of the Republic of Moldova for the purposes of Article 1 of the Convention, but that its responsibility for the acts complained of, committed in the territory of the 'MRT', over which it exercises no effective

authority, is to be assessed in the light of its positive obligations under the Convention.[293]

Under the Court's logic, the lack of the State's territorial control only 'reduces' but does not exclude the scope of its jurisdiction. The Court extends these conclusions not only to Transnistrian-type situations but also to any 'constraining *de facto* situation … whether or not this is accompanied by military occupation by another State'.[294] Consequently, both a *de facto* regime without the support of an outside State and occupation through proxy entail the continuity of the territorial State's jurisdiction. Moreover, the wording of the exemplification suggests that other 'constraining *de facto*' situations, that is, other types of loss of territorial control (such as peace operations exercising territorial control) produce the same result.

Consequently, the ECtHR adheres to the Inter-American and African case law on the irrebuttable presumption of jurisdiction, stressing that the scope of that jurisdiction is reduced. The territorial State's jurisdiction is limited in the sense that the State cannot be required to comply with its positive obligations to the same extent as in the government-controlled territory. This solution of a jurisdiction of reduced scope runs counter to the *Banković* decision, which refused to accept that jurisdiction 'can be divided and tailored' in an extraterritorial context,[295] and admits this solution within the State's territory.

As for the reduced scope of this jurisdiction, in the Court's view its holding is exclusively about the positive obligations of the State towards persons situated in the area outside its control.[296] The limitation of the jurisdiction to positive obligations is misleading, as it cannot exclude negative obligations which certainly continue to bind the territorial State (the duty not to violate the rights to life by indiscriminate attacks, the prohibition of torture by State agents sent to the area, and so forth),[297] such as outside its borders. Another weakness of the judgment is that IHRL distinguishes between positive and negative obligations in respect of concrete rights and freedoms, whereas here the Court seems to construct 'an independence of positive obligations'.[298] From this point of view it would be more accurate to speak about an obligation of due diligence derived from Article 1 of the ECHR, similarly to the Inter-

[293] Ibid., paras 331–335. [294] Ibid., para 333.

[295] *Banković* (n 18), paras 52 (argument of the applicants), 75. [296] *Infra*, Section 3.1.

[297] Even the Court recognised certain negative obligations: *Ilaşcu* (n 44), para 340.

[298] Larsen (n 291) 86.

American Court that derived this general duty from the ACHR independently of specific rights.

The Grand Chamber was relatively divided on Moldova's jurisdiction (11 votes to six). Six dissenting judges opposed Moldova's jurisdiction, holding that there was no evidence on Moldova's direct or indirect authority over or acquiescence in the commission of the human rights violations in Transnistria.[299] Likewise, some commentators considered the judgment too strict with regard to Moldova.[300] However, it seems that the Court did not set the threshold too high, considering that the judgment cited several specific examples where the measures taken by the Moldovan government produced real effects on individuals' lives in Transnistria in general or on the applicants in particular.[301] The measures taken by the territorial State that the ECtHR accepted as complying with its positive obligations consisted, for instance, of diplomatic acts such as protests or negotiation,[302] investigative or judicial measures operated in the government-controlled area,[303] the provision of certain socio-economic benefits for individuals in the area[304] and cooperation with other States or IOs in addressing the wrongful act.[305] Furthermore, even the dissenting judges defending the rebuttable character of the presumption accepted that the territorial State's inaction may exceptionally engage its responsibility under the Convention in respect of persons within its territory.[306] Despite the Court's divided vote in *Ilaşcu*, the subsequent case law shows unanimity or an overwhelming majority in

[299] *Ilaşcu* (n 44), Partly dissenting opinion of Sir Nicolas Bratza joined by Mr Rozakis, Mr Hedigan, Mrs Thomassen, and Mr Panţîru paras 8–9, 26; Partly dissenting opinion of Mr Loucaides.

[300] Thomas D. Grant, 'EJIL: Talk! – Ukraine v. Russian Federation in Light of Ilaşcu: Two Short Points' (*EJIL: Talk!*, 22 May 2014) <www.ejiltalk.org/ukraine-v-russian-federation-in-light-of-ilascu-two-short-points/> accessed 15 January 2018.

[301] *Ilaşcu* (n 44), paras 345, 347.

[302] *Ivanţoc and Others* v. *Moldova and Russia*, Appl. nos. 23687, 23687, 23687/05, 15 November 2011, para 108; *Catan* (n 57), para 153; *Eriomenco* v. *the Republic of Moldova and Russia*, Appl. no. 42224/11, 11 December 2017, para 60.

[303] *Catan* (n 57), paras 153, 214–216; *Turturica and Casian* v. *the Republic of Moldova and Russia*, Appl. nos. 28648/06 and 18832/07, 30 August 2016, para 53; *Paduret* v. *the Republic of Moldova and Russia*, Appl. no. 26626/11, 9 May 2017, para 33.

[304] *Catan* (n 57), para 147; *Vardanean* v. *the Republic of Moldova and Russia*, Appl. no. 22200/10, 30 May 2017, para 42.

[305] *Ivantoc* (n 302), para 109; *Vardanean* (n 304), para 42; *Khlebik* v. *Ukraine*, Appl. no. 2945/16, judgment of 25 July 2017, para 80 (cooperation with the ICRC).

[306] Ibid., para 9.

the judgments regarding Moldova's jurisdiction.[307] These factors show an evolving acceptance of the irrebuttable presumption of the territorial State's jurisdiction.

The novelty of *Ilaşcu* was the confirmation of the territorial State's jurisdiction over an area outside its control or, more precisely, over human rights violations occurring in the area. The Court rightly recognised that every territorial State retains certain authority, some residual effectiveness to influence third parties in the area and to take appropriate measures towards individuals in the 'grey zone'. It may be regretted that the Court did not, as opposed to its *Assanidze* judgment, declare more categorically that the presumption of the territorial State's jurisdiction is irrebuttable.

2.2.2.4 A Sovereignty and Effectiveness-based Jurisdiction

While most authors welcomed the conclusion of the Court in *Ilaşcu*,[308] others criticised it for introducing residual positive obligations grounded in sovereign title.[309] One of the counterarguments against the Court's holding is the confusion between the facts-based interpretation of jurisdiction, that the Court has traditionally followed in its extraterritorial case law (*supra*, Section 2.1), on the one hand, and the residual obligations that the Court derived from the State's sovereign title without effective control over the area, on the other.[310] A closer look at the territorial State's jurisdiction, however, shows that it is equally based on law and facts, that is, on the State's sovereign title and effectiveness.

As noted in Sections 2.2.2.2 and 2.2.2.3, the Court presumes the territorial State's jurisdiction on account of its sovereignty over its recognised territory. This is in conformity not only with the object and the purpose of human rights conventions (the 'legal space' and the elimination of the vacuums at the regional level, the principle of universality at the universal level) but also with a principle of general international law, reiterated in the concept of 'responsibility to protect', according to which theory it is the territorial State's primary responsibility to guarantee

[307] E.g. *Catan* (n 57), dispositive part, para 3 (unanimous); *Mozer* (n 71), dispositive part, paras 6, 8, 11, 13 (16-1 majority); *Braga* v. *the Republic of Moldova and Russia*, Appl. no. 76957/01, 17 October 2017, dispositive part, paras 4, 6, 8 (unanimous).

[308] De Schutter (n 54) 223; King (n 166) 546–547.

[309] Marko Milanovic and Tatjana Papić, 'The Applicability of the ECHR in Contested Territories' (2018) 67 *International and Comparative Law Quarterly* 779, 795.

[310] Ibid.

human rights in its territory.[311] Considering this presumption irrebuttable is a step further which relies on an empirical observation: every State lacking effective control over a part of its territory retains a certain degree of effectiveness in the government-controlled territory that it can use to prevent and mitigate human rights violations in the 'grey zone'. Despite the lack of its territorial control, the State can take a broad range of political, diplomatic, economic, legislative, judicial, administrative or other measures within its power to protect human rights against third parties (States or non-state actors). This capacity, also called the 'capacity to influence' effectively the action of third parties,[312] one of the preconditions of the standard of due diligence,[313] assesses the actual means in the State's power to protect human rights.

This means that the State shall satisfy, beyond its negative obligations, positive obligations through a diligent conduct, namely, as far as possible. In other words, it is a functional jurisdiction, adapted to the authority that the State can exercise towards the concerned individuals. Consequently, effectiveness – whatever its degree is *vis-à-vis* individuals in the 'grey zone' – is the basis of this jurisdiction as in the case of extraterritorial jurisdiction. Linking the territorial State's jurisdiction both to its sovereign title and residual effectiveness, therefore, does not entirely contradict the Court's previous case law and conforms to the Inter-American and African case law. Furthermore, it is normatively desirable: imposing obligations on a weak State on account of its sovereignty and residual effectiveness reflects a certain ideal of State, namely, an active State. It also ensures legal certainty as to the continued obligations of the territorial State: it is not by accident that in Latin-America and Africa, where armed conflicts have been far more frequent than in Europe, human rights treaty bodies accept no exception from the territorial State's jurisdiction.

Linking the territorial State's jurisdiction to both sovereignty and effectiveness also means that before human rights courts, applicants should specify the capacity that the State failed to use to prevent or

[311] See the first pillar of the concept: Resolution 60/1. 2005 World Summit Outcome, UN Doc. A/RES/60/1 (24 October 2005), para 138 and numerous resolutions of the Security Council confirming this obligation: UN Doc. S/RES/1653 (27 January 2006), para 10; UN Doc. S/RES/1674 (28 April 2006), preambular para 9; UN Doc. S/RES/1706 (31 August 2006), preambular para 2 etc.

[312] *Application of the Convention on the Prevention and Punishment of the Crime of Genocide (Bosnia and Herzegovina* v. *Serbia and Montenegro)*, judgment, *I.C.J. Reports* 2007, 221, para 430.

[313] *Infra*, Section 3.1.3.

mitigate the challenged human rights violation. If the applicant fails to do so, the court might find the application ill-founded in the merits, even though the territorial State has jurisdiction. This was the case in applications directed before the ECtHR against various territorial States other than Moldova. For instance, in the *Stephens* case about an applicant's non-access to her house in the buffer zone, the applicant did not challenge a particular action or inaction by Cyprus or otherwise substantiated any breach by the said States of their 'duty to take all the appropriate measures with regard to the applicant's rights which are still within their power to take'.[314] Consequently, the Court considered this part of the application manifestly ill-founded.[315]

Another possible criticism against the territorial State's sovereignty and effectiveness-based jurisdiction is that it sets a high threshold of obligations that apply only to State parties to the ECHR and, as it has been shown, to the other regional human rights treaties. However, UN Charter-based human rights bodies[316] and universal treaty-monitoring bodies[317] reiterated the same standard and addressed various positive obligations with regard to individuals in the non-governmental-controlled area.[318] For instance, the Human Rights Committee noted Moldova's 'continuing obligation to ensure respect for the rights recognised in the Covenant in relation to the population of Transdniestria within the limits of its effective power'.[319] It is telling that those reports were all adopted after *Ilaşcu* and that many of them expressly refer to the judgment.[320] Another sign of the universalisation of this case law is the *Serna and Others* v. *Colombia* case, where the Human Rights Committee presumed Colombia's territorial jurisdiction for the victim's alleged

314 *Stephens* (n 88), 5. 315 Ibid., 7. 316 *Supra*, n 287.

317 HRC, General comment No. 36 (2018) on the right to life, UN Doc. CCPR/C/GC/36 (30 October 2018), para 22; CEDAW, General recommendation No. 28 (n 117), paras 12, 39; CEDAW, General recommendation No. 30 (n 117), para 5.

318 HCR, Concluding observations: Republic of Moldova, UN Doc. CCPR/C/MDA/CO/2 (4 November 2009), para 5; HRC, Concluding observations: Georgia, UN Doc. CCPR/C/GEO/CO/3 (15 November 2007), para 6; CAT, Concluding observations: Ukraine, UN Doc. CAT/C/UKR/CO/6 (12 December 2014), para 11(a); CRC, Concluding observations: Iraq, UN Doc. CRC/C/IRQ/CO/2-4 (4 February 2015), paras 6, 45, 53(a); CESCR, Concluding observations: Central African Republic, UN Doc. E/C.12/CAF/CO/1 (4 May 2018), para 8.

319 UN Doc. CCPR/C/MDA/CO/2 (n 318), para 5.

320 Report on the situation of human rights in the temporarily occupied Autonomous Republic of Crimea and the city of Sevastopol, Ukraine, 13 September 2017 to 30 June 2018, UN Doc. A/HRC/39/CRP.4 (21 September 2018), para 84, note 98; Report of the Special Rapporteur on torture and other cruel, inhuman or degrading treatment or punishment (note 277), para 6; HRC, UN Doc. CCPR/C/SR.2483 (19 October 2007), para 38 (Mr. Kälin); CAT, UN Doc. CAT/C/SR.1661 (6 August 2018), para 48 (Mr. Touzé).

disappearance in an area outside governmental control.[321] While members of the Committee disagreed whether the disappearance was linked to non-state armed groups or paramilitary forces whose conduct was attributable to the State, they all agreed that, independently of the subject controlling the territory, Colombia was in breach of its positive obligations to investigate and to provide an effective remedy.[322]

Whereas the ECtHR based this case law on the necessity to cover the European 'legal space' by the effective application of the ECHR and to eliminate 'vacuums' at the regional level,[323] UN treaty-monitoring bodies seek to ensure the universality of human rights with the same practice. The irrebuttable presumption of the territorial State's jurisdiction in IHRL is in conformity not only with the object and the purpose of human rights treaties but also with the obligation of due diligence.

2.2.2.5 Borderline Cases of Disputed Sovereignty and the Functional Jurisdiction

The irrebuttable presumption is applicable in most cases where the territorial State's sovereign title over the area is universally or quasi-universally accepted by States and where only a small number of States dispute it. On the question of sovereignty over an area, human rights monitoring bodies should follow international law as reflected in the dominant practice of the international community.[324] However, there are borderline cases where a considerable number of States, especially State parties to the given human rights treaty, dispute the sovereignty

321 HRC, *Rosa María Serna* v. *Colombia*, Communication No. 2134/2012, Views of 9 July 2015, UN Doc. CCPR/C/114/D/2134/2012 (22 September 2015).

322 Ibid., para 9.3 (majority view); Individual opinion by Committee member Yuval Shany (partly concurring and partly dissenting).

323 *Supra*, n 70–71.

324 E.g. *Loizidou (Merits)* (n 23), para 44; *Cyprus* v. *Turkey* (n 43), paras 61, 90; *Güzelyurtlu* [GC] (n 156), para 193; *Ilaşcu* (n 44), para 330; *Catan* (n 57), para 110; *Mozer* (n 71), para 100; *Georgia* v. *Russia (II) (Merits)* (n 67), paras 83, 133, 140, 173, 194, 199, 310, 336 (references to the occupation of parts of Georgian territory by Russia); UN Doc. CCPR/C/RUS/CO/7 (n 72), para 23; In the *Ukraine* v. *Russia (re Crimea)* admissibility decision, however, the ECtHR ambiguously tried to avoid ruling on the question of sovereignty over Crimea. It nonetheless noted Ukraine's presumed jurisdiction over Crimea, the treaty practice of Ukraine and Russia, and the international community's refusal 'to accept any change to the territorial integrity of Ukraine in respect of Crimea within the meaning of international law'. Finally, the Grand Chamber held that 'no change to the sovereign territory of Ukraine having been accepted or notified by the applicant State, the Court must therefore assume that the applicant State's jurisdiction extends to the entirety of its territory, including Crimea'. *Ukraine* v. *Russia (re Crimea)* (n 67), paras 345–348, esp. 346, 348.

over the area. In this scenario, if a human rights treaty body applied the above-mentioned irrebuttable presumption, it would be in an uncomfortable position to pronounce upon the question of sovereignty. This exceptional situation might involve States in *statu nascendi* such as Palestine (at least until the UN General Assembly granted it the status of observer State), Kosovo (after its unilateral declaration of independence) or Taiwan.

An example for such a borderline case where the dispute over sovereignty excluded the application of the irrebuttable presumption is the *Ali Azemi* v. *Serbia* case which the ECtHR decided in November 2013, years after the unilateral declaration of independence in Kosovo. The applicant, living in Kosovo, complained that his employment had been unlawfully terminated by a socially-owned enterprise in February 1990, and that the judicial decisions recognising his compensation claim and his reinstatement had not been enforced. The first instance judgment, rendered by a municipal court in January 2002, at the time of the international administration of Kosovo, was confirmed by several judicial instances of Kosovo, including Kosovo's Constitutional Court.[325] The applicant submitted that the non-enforcement of the judgment of the municipal courts was contrary to his right to a fair trial, and that Serbia had jurisdiction in the instant case considering that the facts occurred between 1990 and 1999, before the establishment of the international administration in Kosovo. The Serbian government affirmed that the concerned decision had been rendered by a tribunal of Kosovo under UNMIK supervision, whereas Serbia had neither the power nor the responsibility to secure the rights enshrined in the ECHR.[326]

The Court only examined the period after the ratification of the ECHR by Serbia (2004) until the date of the decision (2013), during which period Kosovo was placed under the authority of UNMIK. Regarding this period, the Court reiterated the *Ilaşcu* test, the principle of the presumption of jurisdiction, and that jurisdiction may be 'limited' in exceptional circumstances.[327] Up to that point the Chamber had followed the Transnistrian case law and seemed to imply that the facts came within the jurisdiction *ratione loci* of Serbia.

According to the *Ilaşcu* logic, the Court then had to proceed to analyse the merits of the case, that is, the respect of positive obligations by the

[325] *Ali Azemi* v. *Serbia*, Appl. no. 11209/09, decision of 5 November 2013 on the admissibility, paras 3–11.

[326] Ibid., paras 33–36.

[327] Ibid., para 42.

State according to the possible measures that remained within its power. The Court followed this schema, but in a summary manner, in seven paragraphs. It noted the creation of the international administration, the declaration of independence of Kosovo, its recognition as independent State by at least 89 States, and the fact that Serbia did not exercise any authority in the territory of Kosovo.[328] It added that in these circumstances 'there existed objective limitations which prevented Serbia from securing the rights and freedoms in Kosovo'.[329] As to Serbia's positive obligations, the Court briefly concluded that

> the applicant has not been able to point to a particular action or inaction of the respondent State or substantiated any breach of the respondent State's duty to take all the appropriate measures with regard to his right which are still within its power to take. Having regard to the particular circumstances of this case, the Court cannot point to any positive obligations that the respondent State had towards the applicant (compare and contrast with Moldova's positive obligations in the case of *Ilaşcu* . . .)[330]

Therefore, the Court considered the application inadmissible *ratione personae*. The Chamber's analysis corresponds, *pro forma*, to the logic of the Transnistrian case law, even though the decision does not expressly confirm Serbia's jurisdiction *ratione loci*. However, on the merits, the analysis of positive obligations falls short of the detailed analysis of Moldova's powers towards Transnistria: the Chamber only refered to objective circumstances that exclude Serbia's effective control over Kosovo but mentioned nothing about Serbia's conduct except for the above-mentioned paragraph. Serbia's status is further blurred by the Court's additional conclusions on the State's control over other actors in Kosovo. It held that

> [t]here is no evidence that Serbia exercised any control over UNMIK, Kosovo's judiciary or other institutions that had been established by virtue of UNMIK regulations. Neither can it be said that the Serbian authorities supported militarily, economically, financially or politically Kosovo's institutions.[331]

This part of the decision follows the approach normally applied to outside States in an extraterritorial context.

The main reason for the Court's short and confusing decision is judicial restraint: deciding on the relations between Serbia and Kosovo in 2013, when 89 States and, among them most CoE member States, had

[328] Ibid., paras 43, 45–46. [329] Ibid., para 46. [330] Ibid., para 47.
[331] Ibid., para 45.

already recognised Kosovo, would be controversial, and the Court could be accused of interfering with interstate relations. Therefore, the Court carefully avoided to rule on Serbia's status with regard to Kosovo and examined its responsibility for the alleged human rights violation under both scenarios: as the territorial State and as an outside State. While this pragmatic approach seems defensible, it does not consistently follow the irrebuttable presumption of jurisdiction but only part of it as regards the scope of obligations based on effectiveness while leaving aside the question of sovereignty. The *Azemi* decision was criticised (i) for failing to set standards or provide lucid answers[332] and (ii) for 'watering down the residual obligation so much that Serbia could not have violated it even if the obligation had existed in the first place',[333] creating in Kosovo a vacuum in protection of ECHR rights which it desperately tried to avoid in other cases. To both criticisms, conceptualising the Court's status-neutral, pragmatic approach can provide adequate answers and conform to the existing alternative bases of jurisdiction.

If one accepts that both the scope of the territorial State's jurisdiction and that of the personal model of extraterritorial jurisdiction depend on effectiveness, that is, a factual and causal link between the State's conduct and the violation of human rights, reconciling the two into one common test is not an unreasonable step forward. First, it was told that the territorial State's positive obligations depend on the State's effectiveness, that is, that it is a functional jurisdiction, adapted to the authority that the State can exercise towards the concerned individuals. Second, according to the functional interpretation of the personal jurisdictional link, the outside State shall guarantee human rights as far as it has the power in the given extraterritorial situation, that is, according to the authority and control exercised. Both tests measure the State's effective power to influence individuals' rights in the 'grey zone', whether or not it has sovereign title over the territory. Therefore, by ignoring the question of sovereignty and the presumption of jurisdiction, treaty-monitoring bodies should answer the only question, namely, whether in the specific situation the State had the effective power to influence the human rights situation in the area and determine the scope of its positive obligations according to its effectiveness. Because this

[332] Kushtrim Istrefi, 'Azemi v Serbia: Discontinuity of Serbia's de Jure Jurisdiction over Kosovo' (2014) 4 *European Human Rights Law Review* 388, 393.

[333] Milanovic and Papić (n 309) 797.

context-based examination requires the evaluation of the facts, it needs to be analysed on the merits rather than as a preliminary issue.

Applying this functional approach to the *Azemi* case, one could argue that the Court should have engaged in a more detailed analysis of facts provided that the applicant specified to what extent Serbia could have taken appropriate measures within its power to ensure respect for his rights. The specific measures could have included, for instance, diplomatic exchanges between Serbia and Kosovo in matters of employment, mediation through UNMIK, or informal links between the Serbian authorities and the Privatisation Agency of Kosovo. A careful analysis of effectiveness is likely to have positive effects on the human rights situation in areas of disputed sovereignty and helps to eliminate a vacuum of responsibility. This has some confirmation in the Court's case law: the Court already condemned Serbia for the violation of the right to property of applicants from Kosovo who challenged the non-payment of their so-called 'Kosovo pensions', that is, social benefits acquired before 1999, the creation of the international territorial administration in Kosovo.[334] While the Serbian government suspended the social benefits of a high number of pensioners living in Kosovo, the Court held that the applicants' place of residence in general seemed 'irrelevant since the payment of their pensions was not suspended' on that basis.[335] Another example where Serbia has certain effective power to protect human rights in Kosovo is the operation, during a long period, of its parallel administrative and judicial system retaining their competence in Northern Kosovo: one could foresee situations where those authorities could have prevented or repaired human rights violations committed in Kosovo.

The functional approach provides a pragmatic tool to clarify the jurisdiction of various States that claim sovereignty and/or exercise various powers over the same area. An example is the dispute on the status of the Chagos Archipelago, currently under the administration of the UK, but over which both the UK and Mauritius claim sovereignty,[336] while the US

[334] *Grudić* v. *Serbia*, Appl. no. 31925/08, judgment of 17 April 2012, esp. paras 80–83.

[335] Ibid., para 82.

[336] The ICJ held that 'the United Kingdom is under an obligation to bring an end to its administration of the Chagos Archipelago as rapidly as possible, thereby enabling Mauritius to complete the decolonization of its territory in a manner consistent with the right of peoples to self-determination'. ICJ, *Legal Consequences of the Separation of the Chagos Archipelago from Mauritius in 1965 (Request for Advisory Opinion)*, Advisory opinion, 25 February 2019, para 178.

and the UK jointly operate a military base in the island of Diego Garcia. The situation is complicated by an incomplete process of decolonisation, where a colonial power might retain control over some areas of governance such as foreign affairs and/or defence, or over some parcels of territory. In such a scenario the functional approach enables treaty bodies to avoid questions of sovereign title and decolonisation, while it requires them to examine the effective power of the concerned State to influence the human rights situation in the area and determine its positive obligations accordingly.

If the functional approach can be applied to establish the jurisdiction of both the territorial and the outside States, one may ask what the added value of the above-mentioned irrebuttable presumption of jurisdiction is. The answer is that a jurisdiction based both on sovereignty and effectiveness reflects the above-mentioned (Section 2.2.2.4) principles: the primary responsibility of the State to protect individuals within its territory (the concept of 'responsibility to protect'); the standard of due diligence; and the ideal of an active State and legal certainty. Legal certainty is especially promoted by the irrebuttable presumption as it provides a foreseeable legal framework of human rights obligations that informs State authorities, treaty bodies and individuals.

At the end of the day, applying the *Ilaşcu*-type irrebuttable presumption of jurisdiction in areas where sovereignty is straightforward or the functional approach in borderline cases should lead to the same result: the human rights monitoring body must always evaluate 'the political realities',[337] namely, the authority available for the State, and decide on its positive obligations on that basis.

2.3 The Concurrent Jurisdiction of the Outside State and the Territorial State

The jurisdiction of the territorial State, on the one hand, and that of the outside State exercising control over the 'grey zone', persons in the area or activities within its own territory, on the other, are parallel and complementary. They are parallel as they trigger obligations

[337] Jean-Paul Costa, 'L'Etat, Le Territoire et La Convention Européenne Des Droits de l'homme', *Promoting Justice, Human Rights and Conflict Resolution through International Law: liber amicorum Lucius Caflisch = La promotion de la justice, des droits de l'homme et du règlement des conflits* (Martinus Nijhoff Publishers 2007) 189.

independently of other States' jurisdiction.[338] They furthermore are complementary because the imperfect territorial situation requires more than one State to be bound to protect human rights within its power, as far as its effectiveness allows.

In most Transnistrian cases, applicants addressed their application both against the territorial State, the Republic of Moldova, and the outside State, Russia.[339] As far as Northern Cyprus is concerned, the *Güzelyurtlu and Others* v. *Cyprus and Turkey* case involved a criminal investigation into the death of three Cypriot nationals of Turkish-Cypriot origin who were found dead with gunshot wounds in the Cypriot government-controlled area, while the suspects were present in the territory controlled by Turkey. The Chamber and the Grand Chamber of the ECtHR agreed that both respondent States had jurisdiction: Cyprus, as the territorial State, and Turkey, as the outside State, on account of the institution of a criminal investigation by the 'TRNC' authorities or, alternatively, on account of the circumstance that the suspects fled to the region that was under the effective control of Turkey.[340] In these cases concurrent jurisdiction led to concurrent obligations that helped to eliminate the risk of a vacuum of responsibility.

As noted in Section 2.1.2.2, regarding the causal link, the number of respondent States might be multiplied if the applicant identifies, beyond the territorial and the outside States, a third State that had an influence on the perpetrators. An example is the human rights violations committed against detainees in the military base of Guantánamo Bay, where beyond the territorial State (Cuba) and the outside State controlling the area (US), the States of nationality of the detainees might have an influence on the situation. This was established in the *David Hicks* v. *Australia* case before the Human Rights Committee, where the applicant, an Australian national, complained that by virtue of a bilateral prisoner transfer arrangement between the US and Australia, 'Australia participated directly in the retrospective punishment and imprisonment to which he was subjected while he was under the jurisdiction of the

338 E.g. Report of the detailed findings of the independent international Commission of inquiry on the protests in the Occupied Palestinian Territory, UN Doc. A/HRC/40/CRP.2 (18 March 2019), para 49 (the parallel jurisdiction of Israel and the State of Palestine).

339 E.g. *Ilaşcu* (n 44); *Ivantoc* (n 302); *Catan* (n 57); *Mozer* (n 71).

340 *Güzelyurtlu and Others* v. *Cyprus and Turkey*, Appl. no. 36925/07, judgment of 4 April 2017, paras 184–189; *Güzelyurtlu* [GC] (n 156), para 196.

United States, thus breaching his rights under the Covenant'.[341] Whereas the Human Rights Committee confirmed that Australia 'had some influence over the way the United States treated the author and was in a position to take positive measures to ensure that the author was treated in a manner consonant with the Covenant', it did not consider this influence sufficient to amount 'to the exercise of power or effective control over the author'.[342] While one may argue that under the causal nexus Australia's influence over the US (regular visits of Australian agents in Guantánamo, interviews with the author, their awareness about the ongoing human rights violations) should have been sufficient authority to instigate Australia's extraterritorial jurisdiction, what is important here is to notice that the same situation could have led to three concurrent jurisdictions. The US has jurisdiction by virtue of its effective control over the area (or authority and control over the detainees), while Cuba might have positive obligations provided that it was aware of the human rights violation and had any diplomatic or other means to influence the US. In the *Hicks* case this was highly unlikely in the given circumstances, as there was no evidence of Cuba's awareness on the alleged violations and its authority is limited to diplomatic actions or to the control over access roads to the camp which for a long time had been closed.[343] In other words, the concurrent jurisdiction of each State should be examined on a case-by-case basis.

Procedurally, this means that before human rights treaty bodies, individuals are encouraged to direct their complaints against all States involved in the situation, while specifying the powers that they should have used to protect human rights. Directing the complaint against only one respondent State delimits the applicant's procedural strategy and oversimplifies complex factuals situations where multiple States have various factual links to human rights violations. For instance, in the *Khlebik* v. *Ukraine* case concerning procedural files left in the separatist Luhansk Region of a detainee in the governmental-controlled area, the ECtHR noted that 'the scope of its examination of the case is delimited by the fact that the application is directed against Ukraine only'.[344] One

341 HRC, *David Hicks* v. *Australia*, Communication No. 2005/2010, Views of 5 November 2015, UN Doc. CCPR/C/115/D/2005/2010 (19 February 2016), para 1.2.

342 Ibid., paras 4.4–4.5.

343 Moreover, before the Human Rights Committee, no individual communication could have been directed against the US and Cuba as none of them is party to the Optional Protocol to the ICCPR.

344 *Khlebik* (n 305), para 66.

may reasonably speculate that Russia could also have had jurisdiction on account of its effective control over the proxy authorities of the Luhansk Region where the applicant's file was left (spatial model) or, alternatively, on account of its influence on the proxy authorities if they were aware of the case files and have instituted a criminal investigation (personal model).[345]

2.4 Concluding Remarks

Jurisdiction in IHRL mainly, but not exclusively, is based on factual power, that is, effectiveness. While establishing jurisdiction mainly on the factual situation, human rights treaty bodies intend to eliminate 'vacuums' of responsibility and the universality of human rights. The jurisdiction of the outside State, based on factual power, and that of the territorial State, based on its sovereign title over territory and effectiveness in the government-controlled area, has a normalising impact on the policies of the outside State and the territorial State with regard to the 'grey zone'. Treaty-monitoring bodies have adopted a dynamic interpretation of jurisdiction in IHRL that expects from both States a proactive conduct towards human rights in the 'grey zone'. The scope of the jurisdiction, that is, the applicable rights and freedoms, should be interpreted functionally: both the territorial State and the outside State shall protect the human rights that are relevant, that is, affected by the given State's conduct. The scope of human rights to be protected varies according to the effectiveness that the State exercises – either while controlling the territory, or the person abroad, or the activities within its government-controlled territory. The concurrent jurisdiction of all States involved in the situation leads to concurrent obligations that help to eliminate the risk of a vacuum of responsibility.

[345] *Güzelyurtlu* [GC] (n 156), para 196.

3 The Human Rights Obligations of States

IHRL imposes obligations on States that have jurisdiction over facts occurring in the 'grey zone', namely, the territorial State and the outside State. However, beyond the States directly involved in the 'grey zone', international law imposes certain obligations on all (third) States. For instance, international cooperation in ensuring the exercise of economic, social and cultural rights of the population of the 'grey zone' is an obligation incumbent upon third States.[1] The obligations not to recognise as lawful a situation created by a serious breach of a peremptory norm, nor to render aid or assistance in maintaining that situation, as enshrined in Article 41(2) of the Articles on the Responsibility of States for Internationally Wrongful Acts (ARSIWA),[2] are opposable to all States *erga omnes*.[3]

Despite certain obligations of all third States, it is the territorial State (Section 3.1) and the outside State (Section 3.2) that have the primary obligations in the 'grey zone'. Because of the territorial State's lack of territorial control, and the extraterritoriality of the outside State, their obligations have certain specialities that require careful analysis. The principal question which the present chapter answers is dual: what the scope is of the obligations binding the concerned States in respect of the 'grey zone' and what the limits are of these obligations, especially compared to the obligations binding them in a 'normal' situation where the State has effective control over its entire territory. Beyond the inherent

[1] CESCR, General comment No. 3: The nature of States parties obligations, in: UN Doc. HRI/GEN/1/Rev.7 (12 May), 18, para 14.

[2] Article 41(2) ARSIWA.

[3] *Legal consequences for States of the continued presence of South Africa in Namibia (South West Africa) notwithstanding Security Council resolution 276 (1970)*, Advisory Opinion, *I.C.J. Reports* 1971, 55, para 126.

limits of obligations that arise from the effectiveness of the territorial and outside States, they can resort to certain lawful restrictions that the chapter also analyses (Section 3.3). The chapter claims that the degree of the State's effectiveness and the lawful limitations the State introduces can decrease the modalities of the expected protection but cannot restrict the heart of the obligations under human rights conventions.

3.1 The Obligations of the Territorial State

As human rights treaty bodies recognised, the territorial State's lack of effective control over a part of its territory, even though it does not remove its jurisdiction, reduces its scope. This reduction, as was already explained, affects the scope of the State's positive obligations,[4] while the State continues to be bound by negative obligations (Section 3.1.1). In the heart of its positive obligations, the territorial State is bound by the standard of due diligence under which it shall use all the means that are reasonably at its disposal to prevent and represss, as far as possible, the violation of human rights (Section 3.1.2). The required degree of diligence depends on objective factors (Section 3.1.3). As was mentioned above, the ECtHR applies a two-step approach: the territorial State's positive obligations relate both to the measures needed to re-establish its control over its territory, 'as an expression of its jurisdiction' (Section 3.1.4) 'and to measures to ensure respect for the individual applicants' rights'[5] (Section 3.1.5). While beyond the ECtHR, other treaty-monitoring bodies have confirmed those positive obligations, their scope still has certain gaps that the principle of normality (Section 3.1.6) should fill. Answering the dual question of the chapter on the scope of obligations and their limits, this section classifies the territorial State's obligations and identifies the State's lack of territorial control as their principal limit.

3.1.1 *Negative Obligations*

As mentioned in Section 2.2.2.3, all negative obligations under IHRL bind the territorial State both in the government-controlled area and in the area outside its effective control. For instance, as far as the territorial

[4] *Ilaşcu and Others* v. *Moldova and Russia* [GC], Appl. no. 48787/99, judgment of 8 July 2004, para 333.

[5] *Ilaşcu* (n 4) para 339; *Catan and Others* v. *Moldova and Russia* [GC], Appl. Nos. 43370/04, 8252/05 and 18454/06, judgment of 19 October 2012, para 145; *Mozer* v. *the Republic of Moldova and Russia* [GC], Appl. no. 11138/10, judgment of 23 February 2016, para 151.

State's agents have an effect on individuals in the 'grey zone', they must not restrict non-derogable rights.[6]

Another noteworthy example is the freedom of movement, the right to leave the 'grey zone' and to return there or the mobility of workers travelling on a daily basis to work in the government-controlled area.[7] Some territorial States have restricted the freedom of movement and return of internally-displaced persons.[8] Criticising those laws, treaty-monitoring bodies recommended not to obstruct, through restricting measures or criminalisation, the return of internally-displaced persons and humanitarian access to the area.[9]

While certain territorial States adopted economic sanctions against the 'grey zone', they are obliged to 'refrain from adopting measures, such as embargoes or other economic sanctions, which would result in nullifying or impairing the enjoyment of economic, social and cultural rights'.[10] Moreover, 'any deliberately retrogressive measures in that

[6] On derogations, *infra*, Section 3.3.1; Human rights violations and abuses and international humanitarian law violations committed in the context of the Ilovaisk events in August 2014, UN Doc. A/HRC/39/CRP.3 (19 September 2018), para 32, note 46; OHCHR Communication, Submission to the UN High-Commissioner for Human Rights by Six Mandate-holders, Reference: OL, UKR 1/2015, 9 June 2015.

[7] E.g. Commission on Human Rights, Guiding Principles on Internal Displacement, UN Doc. E/CN.4/1998/53/Add.2 (11 February 1998), Principle 14.

[8] The law of Georgia on Occupied Territories, Venice Commission, Opinion n° 516 / 2009, 19 January 2009, CDL(2009)004, Clause 4; Law of Ukraine on 'On Ensuring Civil Rights and Freedoms, and the Legal Regime on the Temporarily Occupied Territory of Ukraine' (Abstract text of April 15, 2014), at https://zakon.rada.gov.ua/laws/anot/en/1207-18 (4 June 2019).

[9] E.g. On the Georgian law: Report of the Representative of the Secretary-General on the human rights of internally displaced persons, Walter Kälin, Follow-up mission to Georgia, UN Doc. A/HRC/10/13/Add.2 (13 February 2009), paras 55–56; Venice Commission, Law on occupied territories of Georgia, Opinion n° 516/2009, CDL(2009)015 (17 March 2009), paras 17–18, 35–36, 50; CRC, Concluding observations: Georgia, UN Doc. CRC/C/GEO/CO/4 (3 February 2017), para 4; on the Ukrainian law: UNHCR's preliminary comments on draft legislation regarding the rights and obligations of citizens on the territory of the Autonomous Republic of Crimea, 23 March 2014, at http://unhcr.org.ua (18 April 2014); CERD, Concluding observations: Ukraine, UN Doc. CERD/C/UKR/CO/22-23 (4 October 2016), para 30.

[10] Maastricht Principles on Extraterritorial Obligations of States in the Area of Economic, Social and Cultural Rights, adopted by experts convened by the Maastricht University and the International Commission of Jurists, 28 September 2011, at www.etoconsortium.org/nc/en/main-navigation/library/maastricht-principles/?tx_drblob_pi1%5BdownloadUid%5D=23 (10 May 2014), Principle 22; CESCR, General comment No. 8 (1997): The relationship between economic sanctions and respect for economic, social and cultural rights, UN Doc. E/C.12/1997/8 (12 December 1997), para 14 (obligation to take measures 'to respond to any disproportionate suffering experienced by vulnerable groups within the targeted country').

regard would require the most careful consideration and would need to be fully justified by reference to the totality of the rights' provided for in the ICESCR and 'in the context of the full use of the maximum available resources'.[11] As the territorial State is often the only source of certain elementary resources, it should at all times refrain from imposing embargoes or similar measures that prevent the supply of water, food, and healthcare on the population of the 'grey zone'.[12]

The territorial State may make certain reasonable distinctions between individuals in the 'grey zone' and those in the government-controlled area without violating the obligation of non-discrimination. For instance, the ECtHR held that requiring citizens from the 'grey zone' to travel to relocated institutions in the government-controlled area for the enjoyment of certain human rights is not discriminatory, as due to objective factors (ongoing hostilities, lack of territorial control over the area) individuals from the 'grey zone' do not find themselves in an 'analogous situation' compared to those who reside in the government-controlled area.[13] Likewise, the fact that the territorial State requires permanent residence in the government-controlled territory for the exercise of the right to vote in the legislative elections is not in itself a discriminatory or disproportionate restriction.[14]

3.1.2 *The Principle Underlying Positive Obligations: Due Diligence*

The underlying principle for the territorial State's positive obligations with regard to the 'grey zone' is the so-called due diligence standard (in French *obligation de vigilance*)[15] under which '[n]o State has the right to use or permit the use of its territory in such a manner as to cause injury by fumes in or to the territory of another or the properties or persons therein'.[16]

11 CESCR, General comment No. 3 (n 1), para 9.

12 CESCR, General comment No. 14 (2000), The right to the highest attainable standard of health, UN Doc. E/C.12/2000/4 (11 August 2000), para 41; General comment No. 12 (1999), The right to adequate food (art. 11), UN Doc. E/C.12/1999/5 (12 May 1999), para 37; General comment No. 15 (2002), The right to water, UN Doc. E/C.12/2002/11 (20 January 2003), paras 21–22.

13 ECtHR, *Tsezar and Others* v. *Ukraine*, Appl. nos. 73590/14 et al., judgment of 13 February 2018, para 77.

14 ECtHR, *Ali Erel and Mustafa Damdelen* v. *Cyprus*, Appl. no. 39973/07, decision of 14 December 2010 on the admissibility, 11.

15 E.g. ILA Study Group on Due Diligence in International Law, First Report, Duncan French (Chair) and Tim Stephens (Rapporteur), 7 March 2014, 8.

16 *Trail Smelter Case (United States, Canada)*, 16 April 1938 and 11 March 1941, *UNRIAA*, vol. III, 1965; in the same sense: *Corfu Channel Case*, judgment of 9 April 1949, *I.C.J. Reports* 1949, 22.

Consequently, the State 'on whose territory or in whose waters an act contrary to international law has occurred, may be called upon to give an explanation', and where the State knew, or ought to have known, of any unlawful act perpetrated in its territory that caused damage to another State, then the first State is obliged to take measures to prevent it or, in the case of a continuing or a terminated violation, to respond to it.[17] Considered also a customary norm[18] or general principle of law,[19] due diligence is understood in several special branches of international law as a 'standard',[20] that is, a norm that prescribes the limits of legal conduct while allowing 'a certain margin of attainment within the bounds of reason', as opposed to a 'rule', defined as 'capable of strictly logical application'.[21]

Initially established as an obligation of the State towards foreign citizens in its territory, due diligence has traditionally been conceived to protect the interests of other States within a State's territory.[22] Today, an increasing number of international instruments provide on the States' obligation of due diligence to prevent their territories from being used as a base for the commission of acts of terrorism.[23] In IHRL, however, it is perceived as a general obligation of the State to protect human rights within its jurisdiction against acts committed by third parties, defined as other States, IOs, *de facto* regimes and private persons.[24] The obligation to prevent, therefore, concerns only the conduct of

17 *Corfu Channel Case* (n 16), 18.

18 *Pulp Mills on the River Uruguay (Argentina* v. *Uruguay)* (Merits) (2010) ICJ Rep 14, 55–56, para 101.

19 *Corfu Channel Case* (n 16), 22; Timo Koivurova, 'Due Diligence', *MPEPIL* (Oxford University Press 2010) para 2.

20 The ILC usually applies this term to due diligence, see ILC, International Responsibility: Second Report by F. V. Garcia Amador, UN Doc A/CN.4/106 (15 February 1957), 122, para 3; ILC, The Law of the Non-Navigational Uses of International Watercourses, UN Doc A/49/10 (1994), 103, para 5.

21 Roscoe Pound, 'Standards in International Law' (1921) 34 *Harvard Law Review* 776.

22 Joanna Kulesza, *Due Diligence in International Law* (Brill Nijhoff 2016) 254–255.

23 E.g. Declaration on Principles of International Law concerning Friendly Relations and Cooperation among States in accordance with the Charter of the United Nations, UN Doc. A/RES/2625(XXV) (24 October 1970), Principle no. 10; International Convention against the taking of hostages, New York, 17 December 1979, Article 4; International Convention for the Suppression of the Financing of Terrorism, New York, 9 December 1999, Article 9.

24 Ashfaq Khalfan, 'Division of Responsibility amongst States' in Malcolm Langford, Wouter Vandenhole and Martin Scheinin (eds), *Global Justice, State Duties: The Extraterritorial Scope of Economic, Social, and Cultural Rights in International Law* (Cambridge University Press 2013) 304; CESCR, General comment No. 15 (n 12), para 23.

third parties (other States and non-state actors):[25] the State is bound as far as possible to prevent the unlawful acts committed by third parties, whereas in the case of persons whose conduct is attributable to the State, the responsibility for the violation of due diligence is not applicable as the State is responsible for the violation committed and not for its failure to prevent.[26] In other words, the State is automatically responsible for the human rights violations committed by its organs even if it took all appropriate measures to prevent these.[27] However, unlike the obligation to prevent, the other component of due diligence, the duty to investigate and prosecute the perpetrators applies not only to third parties but also *vis-à-vis* persons whose conduct is attributable to the State.[28]

All regional human rights systems enshrine the standard in this sense, protecting against third party violations. As the IACtHR formulated the obligation, 'the State Party is under the obligation, *erga omnes*, to protect all persons who are under its jurisdiction', 'not only with respect to the power of the State but also with respect to actions by third parties, including irregular armed groups of any type'.[29] Likewise, the English version of Article 1 of the ECHR ('shall secure to everyone within their jurisdiction') expresses the proactive role of the State in protecting against third parties. It 'does not merely oblige the higher authorities of the Contracting States to respect for their own part the rights and freedoms' guaranteed by the Convention but also to secure the enjoyment of rights and freedoms so that 'those authorities must prevent or remedy any breach at subordinate levels'.[30] The effect of the ECHR

[25] Despite a case law which uses the term for violations committed by the authorities of the State in their operations abroad, e.g. *Cyprus* v. *Turkey*, Appl. nos. 6780/74 and 6950/75, report of the Commission of 10 July 1976, para 373; Eritrea–Ethiopia Claims Commission, *Partial Award: Civilian Claims – Ethiopia's Claim 5*, 17 December 2004, *UNRIAA*, vol. XXVI, 277, para 90.

[26] *Application of the Convention on the Prevention and Punishment of the Crime of Genocide (Bosnia and Herzegovina* v. *Serbia and Montenegro)*, judgment, *I.C.J. Reports* 2007, 200–201, para 382.

[27] Marco Sassòli, 'The Approach of the Eritrea–Ethiopia Claims Commission towards the Treatment of Protected Persons in International Humanitarian Law' in Andrea De Guttry, Harry H. G. Post and Gabriella Venturini (eds), *The 1998–2000 War between Eritrea and Ethiopia. An International Law Perspective* (TMC Asser Press 2009) 348.

[28] *Genocide case (Bosnia and Herzegovina* v. *Serbia and Montenegro)* (n 26), 201, para 383; *Georgia* v. *Russian Federation*, Memorial of Georgia, vol. I, 2 September 2009, 382, para 9.83.

[29] *Peace Community of San José de Apartadó* v. *Colombia*, Order, 18 June 2002, para 11.

[30] *Ireland* v. *United Kingdom* [GC], Appl. no. 5310/71, 18 January 1978, para 239; Eirik Bjorge, 'Human Rights, Treaties, Third-Party Effect', *MPEPIL* (Oxford University Press 2011) para 5.

vis-à-vis third parties or the *Drittwirkung* results from the objective of the effectiveness in the Convention's application.[31]

Article 1 of the ACHPR provides that member States of the African Union (AU) 'shall recognise the rights, duties and freedoms enshrined in the Charter and shall undertake to adopt legislative or other measures to give effect to them'. Applying the conclusions on due diligence of the *Velásquez Rodríguez* judgment of the IACtHR, the ACommHPR recognised that the Charter imposes 'positive obligations on States to prevent and sanction private violations of human rights'.[32] It follows that the act of a third party that is not attributable to the State may generate the responsibility of the State 'not because of the act itself, but because of the lack of due diligence to prevent the violation or for not taking the necessary steps to provide the victims with reparation'.[33]

Thus, the standard of due diligence gives a positive scope to human rights 'with regard to what should be legitimately expected to be secured ... by a reasonably well-organized modern State',[34] while its content depends on the facts and circumstances of each case.

3.1.3 *Factors Determining the Required Diligence*

The standard of due diligence leads to positive obligations to prevent and respond to human rights violations in the State's territory. Therefore, the relation between the due diligence standard and positive obligations under IHRL is that of the general and the special. The standard is especially applicable to a territorial State having lost its effective control over part of its territory, as third parties control the area. The State only incurs responsibility for failing to comply with due diligence under two cumulative conditions, namely, (i) that it had the means to prevent or to repress the human rights violation, and (ii) that it knew or should have known about the risk of the human rights violation.[35]

[31] Ibid., 6.; *Airey* v. *Irlande*, Appl. no. 6289/73, judgment of 9 October 1979, para 24.

[32] ACommHPR, *Zimbabwe Human Rights NGO Forum* v. *Zimbabwe*, Communication no. 245/02, 15 May 2006, para 143; *Association of Victims of Post Electoral Violence & INTERIGHTS* v. *Cameroon*, Communication no. 272/03, 25 November 2009, paras 90–92.

[33] *Zimbabwe Human Rights NGO Forum* v. *Zimbabwe* (n 32), para 143; *Sudan Human Rights Organisation & Centre on Housing Rights and Evictions (COHRE)* v. *Sudan*, Communication no. 279/03–296/05, 27 May 2009, para 148.

[34] *Asian Agricultural Products Ltd (AAPL)* v. *Republic of Sri Lanka* (ICSID Case No. ARB/87/3) Award (27 June 1990), para 77.

[35] *Genocide case (Bosnia and Herzegovina* v. *Serbia and Montenegro)* (n 26), 221–222, paras 430–431.

The responsibility of the State is engaged if it 'manifestly failed to take all measures' reasonably available to prevent the wrongful act.[36] The question of what is 'reasonably available' or a 'manifest' failure must be assessed in an objective manner. This is a minimum threshold required from the territorial State: the State violates this standard if its conduct amounts 'to an insufficiency of governmental action so far short of international standards that every reasonable and impartial man would readily recognize its insufficiency'.[37] The objectivity of the standard of due diligence means that the subjective fault, the psychological attitude of State authorities, is unsubstantial from the point of view of the respect of the obligation.[38] Generally speaking, the minimum degree of diligence is that which could be expected from a civilised State.[39] In IHRL, treaty-monitoring bodies confirmed that due diligence obliges the State to 'organize the governmental apparatus, and in general, all the structures through which public power is exercised, so that they are capable of juridically ensuring the free and full enjoyment of human rights'.[40]

The required diligence 'calls for an assessment *in concreto*'.[41] The ICJ defined it as an obligation of States 'to employ all means reasonably available to them', so as to prevent a violation as far as possible.[42] The Seabed Disputes Chamber pointed out that 'capabilities', that is, specific factors, lead to varying degrees of due diligence.[43] The Chamber's conclusion is regarded as reflecting the standard of general international

[36] Ibid., 221, para 430.

[37] *L.F.H. Neer and Pauline Neer (U.S.A.)* v. *United Mexican States*, 15 October 1926, *UNRIAA*, vol. IV, 61–62; *Affaire des biens britanniques au Maroc espagnol (Espagne contre Royaume Uni)*, 1 May 1925, *UNRIAA*, vol. II, 644.

[38] Riccardo Pisillo-Mazzeschi, 'The Due Diligence Rule and the Nature of the International Responsibility of States' (1992) 35 *German Yearbook of International Law* 9, 42–44 (referring to the *Corfu Channel case* where the ICJ did not examine the subjective element).

[39] International responsibility. Second report by F. V. Garcia Amador, Special Rapporteur, UN Doc. A/CN.4/106 (1957), in: *YbILC*, 1957, vol. II, 122, para 6 (commentary of draft article 12) and 124, para 15 (commentary of draft article 10); '*Force majeure*' and 'fortuitous event' as circumstances precluding wrongfulness. Study prepared by the Secretariat, UN Doc. A/CN.4/315, in: *YbILC*, 1978, vol. II(1), 115–116, para 204 (*Negrete* case, 1887).

[40] IACtHR, *Velásquez-Rodríguez* v. *Honduras*, judgment of 29 July 1988 (Merits), para 166; *Zimbabwe Human Rights NGO Forum* v. *Zimbabwe* (n 32), para 147.

[41] *Genocide case (Bosnia and Herzegovina* v. *Serbia and Montenegro)* (n 26), 221, para 430.

[42] (in preventing genocide). Ibid., 221, para 430; ECtHR, *Osman* v. *United Kingdom* [GC], Appl. no. 87/1997/871/1083, judgment of 28 October 1998, para 116.

[43] *Responsibilities and obligations of states sponsoring persons and entities with respect to activities in the Area* (Advisory Opinion) ITLOS Reports 2011, Case No. 17, paras 161–162.

law.[44] International courts, IOs and international law scholarship have defined the following capacities under the due diligence standard:

- degree of influence a State has over the author of the unlawful conduct;[45]
- control over territory;[46]
- level of development of the State;[47]
- level of scientific knowledge and technical capability available to the State;[48]
- degree of harm.[49]

International human rights treaty-monitoring bodies also consider these factors when deciding about the required diligence. Each of these factors, including their relevance in 'grey zones', are examined in detail.

3.1.3.1 Degree of Influence a State Has over the Author of the Unlawful Conduct

The ICJ held that the required diligence first depends on the State's 'capacity to influence effectively the action of persons likely to commit, or already committing'[50] a wrongful act (in the instant case genocide), 'the geographical distance of the State concerned from the scene of the events, and on the strength of the political links, as well as links of all other kinds, between the authorities of that State and the main actors in

[44] ILA, Study group on due diligence in international law, First report, 7 March 2014, 26–27; ILA, Study Group on due diligence in international law, Second Report, July 2016, 7.

[45] *Genocide case (Bosnia and Herzegovina* v. *Serbia and Montenegro)* (n 26), 221, para 430; ILC, First report on crimes against humanity by Sean D. Murphy, UN Doc A/CN.4/680 (17 February 2015), para 80; ICRC, 'International humanitarian law and the challenges of contemporary armed conflicts. 32nd International Conference of the Red Cross and Red Crescent' (8–10 December 2015), 26, 55.

[46] *Leonor Buckingham (Great Britain)* v. *United Mexican States*, 3 August 1931, *UNRIAA*, vol. V, 288; *Wipperman* case, in: John Bassett Moore, *History and Digest of the International Arbitrations to which the United States Has Been a Party*, vol. 3 (Government printing office 1898) 3041–3042; *Armed Activities on the Territory of the Congo (Democratic Republic of the Congo* v. *Uganda)*, judgment, *I.C.J. Reports* 2005, 268, para 301.

[47] ILC, Text of the Draft articles on prevention of transboundary harm from hazardous activities with commentaries thereto, *YbILC*, 2001, vol. II (Part Two), 155, para 13 (Draft Article 3); ILA, Second report (n 44), 13.

[48] *Activities in the Area* AO (n 43), para 162.

[49] Draft articles on Prevention of Transboundary Harm . . . (n 47), 155, para 18 (Draft Article 3); Guiding Principles on Business and Human Rights, UN Doc A/HRC/17/31 (21 March 2011), Principle 17(b); IHL and the challenges of contemporary armed conflicts (n 45), 55.

[50] *Genocide case (Bosnia and Herzegovina* v. *Serbia and Montenegro)* (n 26), 221, para 430.

the events' of the violations committed.[51] The 'capacity to influence' cannot be defined in the abstract but depends on other above-cited criteria such as the geographical distance of the State from the amputated area and the intensity of the political and all other links between the State's authorities and the authorities *de facto* exercising territorial control. Thus, the capacity to effectively influence the action of third parties assesses the actual means in the State's power to take legal, administrative, diplomatic and other measures to protect human rights. For example, a State involved in an ongoing armed conflict with armed groups within its territory, such as Mali in 2012, could not be required to take as diverse economic, social or diplomatic measures *vis-à-vis* the *de facto* authorities as Moldova could *vis-à-vis* the 'MRT', with whom it has since 1993 conducted status negotiations. While deciding on the required degree of diligence, the ECtHR usually takes into account the existing contacts between the territorial State and the *de facto* authorities[52] or between the territorial State and the outside State,[53] on the one hand, and the likelihood of their preventive or mitigative effect,[54] on the other. The absence of cooperation on the part of the *de facto* authorities, for instance, decreases the required diligence.[55]

3.1.3.2 Control over Territory

Another factor identified is the effectiveness of the territorial control: the degree of diligence cannot be the same in a densely-populated territory controlled by the government as in a remote area or *a fortiori* in an area outside the government's control.[56] In the *DRC* v. *Uganda* case the ICJ took into account the 'mountainous terrain, its remoteness from

[51] Ibid.

[52] E.g. *Ilaşcu* (n 4), paras 346–351; *Ivanţoc and Others* v. *Moldova and Russia*, Appl. no. 23687/05, judgment of 15 November 2011, para 109; *Eriomenco* v. *the Republic of Moldova and Russia*, Appl. no. 42224/11, judgment of 9 May 2017, paras 34, 60.

[53] E.g. *Ilaşcu* (n 4), para 349; *Ivanţoc* (n 52), para 109.

[54] E.g. *Pocasovschi and Mihaila* v. *the Republic of Moldova and Russia*, Appl. no. 1089/09, judgment of 29 May 2018, paras 81–82; *Soyma* v. *the Republic of Moldova, Russia and Ukraine*, Appl. no. 1203/05, judgment of 30 May 2017, paras 38–39; *Sandu and Others* v. *the Republic of Moldova and Russia*, Appl. nos. 21034/05 and 7 others, judgment of 17 July 2018, paras 20, 99.

[55] *Draci* v. *the Republic of Moldova and Russia*, Appl. no. 5349/02, judgment of 17 October 2017, para 61.

[56] *Leonor Buckingham (Great Britain)* v. *United Mexican States*, 3 August 1931, *UNRIAA*, vol. V, 288; *J. J. Boyd (U.S.A.)* v. *United Mexican States*, 12 October 1928, *UNRIAA*, vol. IV, 380; *Wipperman* case, in: Moore, vol. III, 3040–3041; Individual opinion by Judge Alvarez, *Corfu Channel Case* (n 16), 44, para 2; Pisillo-Mazzeschi (n 38) 44.

Kinshasa (more than 1 500 km), and the almost complete absence of central government presence or authority in the region' where rebel groups operated, to conclude that the territorial State's inaction against those rebel groups did not fall short of the required degree of diligence.[57] Judge Tomka held that

> [t]he geomorphological features or size of the territory does not relieve a State of its duty of vigilance nor render it less strict. Nor does the absence of central governmental presence in certain areas of a State's territory set aside the duty of vigilance for a State in relation to those areas.[58]

This view is accurate in the sense that the loss of effective control does not affect the validity of the obligation of due diligence. Nevertheless, the measures that the territorial State is able to take are reduced, as no impossible or disproportional burden can be expected but a positive action which is reasonable.

3.1.3.3 The Technical and Material Capability Available to the State

Material capacity is another objective factor influencing the required diligence: a developing State with modest material capacity to influence the authorities controlling the area is not required to exercise the same degree of diligence as a developed State with broader means to take positive measures.[59] Briefly, it is the evaluation of the State's reduced effectiveness towards the concerned individuals that makes the required diligence flexible.

In the *DRC* v. *Uganda* case, the Democratic Republic of the Congo (DRC) was not in a position to put an end to the rebel activities in the eastern part of its territory. Consequently, the ICJ could not conclude 'that the absence of action by Zaire's Government against the rebel groups in the border area is tantamount to "tolerating" or "acquiescing" in their activities' which customary international law prohibits.[60] *A contrario*, should the DRC have been able to eliminate the rebel activities by regaining control over its territory, it would have violated its due diligence obligation by not exercising its power.

[57] *DRC* v. *Uganda* (n 46), 268, para 301; in the same sense: Ibid., Separate Opinion of Judge Parra-Aranguren, 305, para 48.
[58] *DRC* v. *Uganda* (n 46), Declaration of Judge Tomka, 352, para 4.
[59] ILA Study Group on Due Diligence in International Law (n 15), 18.
[60] *DRC* v. *Uganda* (n 46), 268, paras 300–301.

3.1.3.4 Degree of Harm

Finally, a last objective factor influencing the scope of the required diligence is the protected interest: in the matter of human rights, different rights may require different degrees of action. In other words, certain human rights norms impose on the territorial State a higher degree of diligence than others. The IACtHR took into account 'the quantitative and qualitative intensity of the human rights violations'[61] when it assessed the required diligence, while the ACommHPR held that '[i]t could well be assumed that for non-derogable human rights the positive obligations of States would go further than in other areas'.[62] Likewise, the ECtHR stressed the importance of non-derogable rights in *Ilaşcu* when it noted that determining the threshold of a minimum effort 'is especially necessary in cases concerning an alleged infringement of absolute rights such as those guaranteed by Articles 2 [rights to life] and 3 [freedom from torture or inhuman or degrading treatment or punishment] of the Convention'.[63]

3.1.3.5 Knowledge

According to the second precondition, the State is only responsible for not complying with due diligence if the human rights violation actually occurred and if the State was aware of (actual knowledge) or should normally have learned of (constructive knowledge) the risk of the violation.[64] The latter, the so-called constructive knowledge, covers the 'reasonably foreseeable',[65] 'real and imminent danger'[66] or 'a real and immediate'[67] risk of human rights violations. Generally speaking, early warning signs of the harm increase the predictability of the wrongful act

[61] IACtHR, *Pueblo Bello Massacre* v. *Colombia*, judgment of 31 January 2006 (Merits, Reparations and Costs), para 127.

[62] *Zimbabwe Human Rights NGO Forum* v. *Zimbabwe* (n 32), para 155.

[63] *Ilaşcu* (n 4), para 334.

[64] *Genocide case (Bosnia and Herzegovina* v. *Serbia and Montenegro)* (n 26), 222, para 431; *Corfu Channel Case* (n 16), 22.

[65] HRC, General comment No. 36 (2018) on article 6 of the ICCPR on the right to life, UN Doc. CCPR/C/GC/36 (30 October 2018), para 21; HRC, General comment No. 35, Article 9: Liberty and security of person, UN Doc. CCPR/C/GC/35 (16 December 2014), para 9 ('protect individuals from foreseeable threats'); *Pueblo Bello Massacre* (n 61), para 140.

[66] *Pueblo Bello Massacre* (n 61), para 123; *Valle Jaramillo et al.* v. *Colombia*, judgment of 27 November 2008 (Merits, Reparations, and Costs), para 78 ('real and imminent risk'); IACHR, Report No. 64/11, Case 12.573, *Marino López et al. (Operation Génesis)* v. *Colombia*, Merits, 31 March 2011, para 235.

[67] *Osman* (n 42), para 116.

and thus instigate the obligation of due diligence.[68] For instance, the degree of expected diligence is lower where only minor crimes had taken place in a region before a murder,[69] and higher in situations of systematic violence and grave violations of human rights, in an area declared a zone of emergency and military operations.[70] Where the territorial State has no knowledge and should not have known about a human rights violation in the 'grey zone', it incurs no responsibility for the failure to exert due diligence.[71]

In a 'grey zone' the foreseeability of the violations may refer to events related to the loss of territorial control or events having occurred after the loss of territorial control. For example, in the *Association of Victims of Post Electoral Violence & INTERIGHTS* v. *Cameroon* case, the ACommHPR held that the incidents 'would not have taken place if the State which, through its investigations knew or should have known about the planning of the said events, had taken the necessary measures to prevent their happening'.[72] It took into account that the authorities only acted four days after the explosion of the hostilities; disturbances of law and order had existed in the country since May 1990 and specifically during the elections; the threats of the opposition party sufficiently proved the existence of early warning signs and consequently the predictability of the events; finally, that

> the Respondent State had manifested its control of the territory and therefore its ability to stand up to the perpetrators of the post electoral events, by instituting a state of siege a few days after the events in question; had this state of siege been instituted earlier, the events in question would have at least been reduced in scope if not entirely quelled.[73]

In other words, individual circumstances determine which events leading to the loss of territorial control and human rights violations might be predictable and reasonably preventible by diligent conduct.

Similarly, the IACtHR examined the predictability of human rights violations committed by paramilitary groups in areas where they took

[68] *Association of Victims of Post Electoral Violence* (n 32), para 117.

[69] *J. J. Boyd (U.S.A.)* v. *United Mexican States* (n 56), 380.

[70] *Pueblo Bello Massacre* (n 61), para 134; *Ituango Massacres* v. *Colombia*, judgment of 1 July 2006 (Merits, Reparations and Costs), para 137.

[71] *Military and Paramilitary Activities in and against Nicaragua (Nicaragua* v. *United States of America)*, Merits, Judgment, *I.C.J. Reports* 1986, 85, para 158; *Apcov* v. *the Republic of Moldova and Russia*, Appl. no. 13463/07, judgment of 30 May 2017, para 46; *Soyma* (n 54), paras 38–39.

[72] *Association of Victims of Post Electoral Violence* (n 32), para 115.

[73] Ibid., paras 117–118.

effective control. In the *Pueblo Bello Massacre* v. *Colombia* case the Court recognised that the Colombian authorities had information about the activity of paramilitary groups in the zone of Pueblo Bello where the latter abducted and massacred 43 persons, and that the State authorities even adopted several preventive measures such as strengthening the military presence or the declaration of an emergency zone. However, the Court held that Colombian authorities failed to adopt 'all the necessary or sufficient measures to avoid these groups continuing to commit acts such as those of the instant case'.[74] In particular, they should have adopted measures to control the available routes in the area.[75] Even after having declared these groups unlawful, Colombia did not translate this legislation into the concrete and effective neutralisation of the danger that the State itself had helped create.[76]

The second type of prevention, that concerning events that occurred after the loss of effective control, characterises stabilised situations such as the 'frozen conflicts' in Europe. In such a situation the judge must analyse the reasonable possibilities of the territorial State to mitigate the consequences and prevent the extension of continuing violations rather than to prevent the materialisation of the danger.

Human rights monitoring bodies should evaluate all these factors realistically, so as not to impose on the State 'an impossible or disproportionate burden'.[77] The ECtHR does not indicate which the most effective measures are that the authorities shall take but verifies 'that the measures actually taken were appropriate and sufficient' in the specific case.[78] Other human rights treaty bodies also refer to the minimum effort, the so-called 'reasonableness' standard:[79] they assess whether the State, in light of the above-mentioned factors, took all steps that were reasonable, commensurate with the State's limited ability to protect human rights in the area outside its effective control.[80] In this choice, the State enjoys a certain leeway or margin of appreciation: the ECtHR found that certain measures such as judicial investigations may be ceased if they prove to be ineffective.[81] Once the territorial State

[74] *Pueblo Bello Massacre* (n 61), para 126. [75] Ibid., paras 138–140.
[76] *Ituango Massacres* (n 70), paras 134, 137.
[77] *Ilaşcu* (n 4), para 332; *Osman* (n 42), para 116.
[78] *Ilaşcu* (n 4), para 334; *Ivanţoc* (n 52), para 108; *Catan* (n 5), para 145.
[79] E.g. HRC, General comment No. 36 (n 65), para 21; *Velásquez-Rodríguez* (n 40), para 174; *Zimbabwe Human Rights NGO Forum* v. *Zimbabwe* (n 32), para 156.
[80] *Mozer* (n 5), para 216. [81] *Ilaşcu* (n 4), para 347; *Ivanţoc* (n 52), para 110.

ceases all reasonable steps within its power to ensure the respect for human rights, it violates its positive obligations.[82]

Finally, the burden of proof lies with the territorial State:[83] after the adverse party substantiated a human rights violation in the 'grey zone' and the lack of reasonable measures taken by the State,[84] it is for the territorial State to demonstrate that it made serious efforts to prevent its territory from being used for the commission of human rights violations.[85] The lack of effective control over the territory creates a situation similar to the lack of resources: in economic, social and cultural rights, if resource constraints render it impossible for a State to comply fully with its obligations, the State has the burden of justifying that it nevertheless has made every effort to use all available resources at its disposal in order to satisfy, as a matter of priority, its obligations.[86] However, once the State substantiates that it took certain measures to comply with the required diligence, the burden of proof again shifts and it is for the applicant to point to any other particular action which it would still be in the territorial State's power to take in the particular circumstances.[87]

Shortly, due diligence is flexible in the sense that it imposes an obligation of conduct and not of result: the occurrence of the harm does not in itself entail the violation of the obligation if the State complied with the required diligence.[88] This is the reason why in 'grey zones' human rights monitoring bodies examine the efforts deployed by the territorial State rather than the final result of its conduct.

[82] *Ilaşcu* (n 4), paras 350–352.

[83] *Ilaşcu* (n 4), para 348; ibid., Partly dissenting opinion of Sir Nicolas Bratza joined by Mr Rozakis, Mr Hedigan, Mrs Thomassen and Mr Panţîru, paras 24–26; *a contrario*: *Osman* (n 42), para 116.

[84] *Zimbabwe Human Rights NGO Forum* v. *Zimbabwe* (n 32), para 160; ACERWC, *Minority Rights Group International and SOS-Esclaves* v. *The Government of The Republic of Mauritania*, Communication No. 008/Com/002/2016, May 2017, para 54.

[85] *Genocide case (Bosnia and Herzegovina* v. *Serbia and Montenegro)* (n 26), 225, para 438; *DRC* v. *Uganda* (n 46), Separate Opinion of Judge Kooijmans, 325, para 82; ibid., Declaration of Judge Tomka, 352, para 4.

[86] CESCR, General comment No. 14 (n 12), para 47.

[87] ECtHR, *Ali Azemi* v. *Serbia*, Appl. no. 11209/09, decision of 5 November 2013 on the admissibility, para 47; *Khlebik* v. *Ukraine*, Appl. no. 2945/16, judgment of 25 July 2017, para 79; *Zimbabwe Human Rights NGO Forum* v. *Zimbabwe* (n 32), para 163.

[88] *DRC* v. *Uganda* (n 46), Declaration of Judge Tomka, 352, para 4; *Genocide case (Bosnia and Herzegovina* v. *Serbia and Montenegro)* (n 26), 221, para 430; IACtHR, *Godínez-Cruz* v. *Honduras*, judgment of 20 January 1989 (Merits), para 185.

3.1.4 *Obligation to Express Jurisdiction over the Territory*

The first group of positive obligations that follows from due diligence consists of general obligations to express jurisdiction over the 'grey zone'. At the very least, the territorial State is bound to refrain from supporting the *de facto* regime or the occupying power (Section 3.1.4.1), while under a progressive interpretation of IHRL it is also bound to take all the political, judicial and other measures at its disposal to re-establish its control over its territory (Section 3.1.4.2).

3.1.4.1 The Obligation Not to Support the Unlawful Situation

At the very general level, due diligence requires the territorial State not to allow its territory to be used for human rights violations. If the territorial situation is based on a wrongful act, such as the unlawful use of inter-State force or the violation of the right to self-determination of people (as opposed to lawful situations of territorial control by other international law subjects[89]), the territorial State is required not to support the unlawful situation. This also follows from the obligations of non-recognition, non-aid and non-assistance under Article 41(2) ARSIWA.[90] As the ECtHR formulated it,[91] the territorial State is required to refrain from supporting the unlawful *de facto* regime or the occupying power, which might be regarded as the special translation of the above-mentioned negative obligations of general international law. Likewise, the Inter-American bodies in several cases concluded that the territorial State committed a human rights violation by its conduct of acquiescence, tolerance or support, when the authorities consented to the commission of unlawful acts by paramilitary groups.[92] Briefly, the prohibition to support the unlawful situation results from negative obligations to refrain from violating human rights.

However, even those negative obligations cannot disproportionately restrict human rights. Under the so-called *Namibia* exception formulated by the ICJ, the obligation of non-recognition cannot result in depriving local residents from the benefits that they may obtain from international cooperation. This is the reason why the nullity of acts cannot extend to administrative acts and everyday transactions such as the registration of

[89] *Supra*, Chapter 1. [90] Article 41(2) ARSIWA.

[91] *Ilaşcu* (n 4), para 340; *Ivanţoc* (n 52), para 106; *Catan* (n 5), para 145.

[92] E.g. *Velásquez-Rodríguez* (n 40), para 173; *19 Tradesmen* v. *Colombia*, judgment of 5 July 2004 (Merits, Reparations and Costs), paras 135–138, 141; *Mapiripán Massacre* v. *Colombia*, judgment of 15 September 2005 (Merits, Reparations and Costs), paras 121–123; *Ituango Massacres* (n 70), para 133, 325; *Marino López et al.* (n 66), para 227.

births, deaths and marriages, the effects of which can only be ignored to the detriment of the inhabitants of the territory.[93] It follows that, on the one hand, the practice of some territorial States to ignore the certificates issued by *de facto* authorities or by the international administration is strongly criticised by human rights monitoring bodies.[94] On the other hand, legal mechanisms guaranteeing citizens of the 'grey zone' their constitutional rights, the acquisition of identity and civil registry documents or diplomas issued by institutions of the territorial State may reconcile the tension between the obligation of non-recognition and IHRL. For instance, the Moldovan government opened territorial offices of civil status and documentation in the government-controlled area for the population of the Transnistrian region.[95]

3.1.4.2 The Obligation to Strengthen Jurisdiction

As the ECtHR holds, the territorial State shall take 'all the political, judicial and other measures at its disposal to re-establish its control over that territory'.[96] The expected measures may consist of asserting sovereignty over the area[97] or symbolic protests,[98] 'both internally and internationally';[99] restriction of trade to and from the 'grey zone';[100] criminal proceedings against certain leaders of the *de facto* authorities;[101] diplomatic negotiations;[102] or certain forms of cooperation with the *de facto* authorities with a view to normalise the everyday lives of the people living in the area.[103]

Although the ECtHR recognised that there might be little that the territorial State could do to re-establish its authority over the area,[104]

[93] *Namibia* AO (n 3), 56, para 125; Separate opinion of Judge Dillard, ibid., 167; ECtHR, *Cyprus* v. *Turkey* [GC], Appl. no. 25781/94, judgment of 10 May 2001, para 96; *Demopoulos and Others* v. *Turkey* [GC], Appl. nos. 46113/99 et al., decision of 1 March 2010 on the admissibility, para 94.

[94] E.g. Regarding Cyprus: CESCR, UN Doc. E/C.12/2009/SR.10 (13 April 2010), para 12; the Georgian law of 23 October 2008: Special follow-up mission to the areas affected by the South Ossetia Conflict, by Thomas Hammarberg, Commissioner for Human Rights of the CoE, Doc. CommDH(2008)33 (21 October 2008), para 81; regarding Serbia, where certain diplomas obtained in Kosovo were not recognized: FCPNM, Opinion on Serbia and Montenegro (2 March 2004), ACFC/INF/OP/I(2004)002 (27 November 2003), paras 92, 157.

[95] National report: Republic of Moldova, UN Doc. A/HRC/WG.6/12/MDA/1 (19 July 2011), paras 109–110.

[96] *Ilaşcu* (n 4), para 340; *Catan* (n 5), para 145.

[97] *Ilaşcu* (n 4), para 343.

[98] *Ilaşcu* (n 4), para 341; *Ivanţoc* (n 52), para 108.

[99] *Ilaşcu* (n 4), para 341.

[100] *Ivanţoc* (n 52), paras 19, 108.

[101] *Ilaşcu* (n 4), para 342.

[102] Ibid., para 344.

[103] Ibid., para 345.

[104] Ibid., para 341.

the means at its disposal might be numerous. The territorial States have adopted a wide range of pacific measures aimed at strengthening their jurisdiction over the 'grey zone': one can mention status negotiations as a diplomatic expression of the will of reunification; the creation of a governmental body charged with the reintegration of the area;[105] the adoption of domestic laws governing the region's legal status;[106] the implementation of a long-term strategy providing for a policy of commitment towards the population living in the 'grey zone';[107] an economic rehabilitation programme;[108] the monitoring of human rights violations in the region by the diplomatic service;[109] the seizure of international dispute settlement procedures;[110] or the signature and the ratification of the Statute of Rome of the International Criminal Court.[111] Even if each of these measures in itself is hardly effective, the totality of these efforts may contribute to strengthening the State's jurisdiction.

Such measures serve as a mere expression of the territorial State's jurisdiction over the non-governmental-controlled area,[112] regardless of their ineffectiveness. While only the ECtHR has formulated a general obligation to take measures to re-establish the territorial control, other universal treaty bodies also recommend to territorial States general

105 E.g. in Georgia, the actual Office of the State Minister of Georgia for Reconciliation and civic equality, Fourth and Fifth periodic report: Georgia, UN Doc. CERD/C/GEO/4-5 (25 February 2011), para 6; in Serbia, the Coordination Center for Kosovo and Metohija, transformed into the Ministry for Kosovo and Metohija, and then into the Office for Kosovo and Metohija; In Ukraine, the Ministry of Temporarily Occupied Territories and IDPs, see Ukraine: National report, UN Doc. A/HRC/WG.6/28/UKR/1 (31 August 2017), para 6.

106 European Commission for Democracy through law (Venice Commission), Law on occupied territories of Georgia, Opinion n° 516/2009, CDL(2009)015 (17 March 2009), para 38; such legislations: Georgia, 'Law on Occupied Territories of Georgia', 23 October 2008 ; Ukraine, 'On the peculiarities of the State policy to ensure the State sovereignty of Ukraine over the temporarily occupied territories in Donetsk and Luhansk regions', 18 January 2018.

107 CEDAW, Combined 4th and 5th periodic report: Georgia, UN Doc. CEDAW/C/GEO/4-5 (30 October 2012), para 11.

108 CRC, UN Doc. CRC/C/SR.1317 (26 May 2008), para 34 (Georgia).

109 CERD, 7th periodic report: Moldova, UN Doc. CERD/C/MDA/7 (6 September 2006), para 31.

110 E.g. Common core document: Ukraine, UN Doc. HRI/CORE/UKR/2018 (30 January 2018), para 72 (seizure of the ICJ by Ukraine: *Ukraine* v. *Russian Federation*).

111 CERD, UN Doc. CERD/C/SR.1862 (5 March 2008), para 26 (Moldova); Common Core document: Ukraine (n 110), para 66.

112 *Ilaşcu* (n 4), para 339; *Catan* (n 5), para 145.

measures strengthening their jurisdiction over the 'grey zone'.[113] One might consider these measures 'to be pure political rhetoric'[114] or the mere expression of the State's desire to re-establish its territorial control, which is incapable of being subjected to judicial review.[115] Although it is difficult to derive such an obligation from IHRL, which primarily protects individuals rather than State sovereignty, it can have two justifications. First, if one accepts the territorial State's positive obligations to protect individuals in the 'grey zone' (Section 3.1.5), the question of whether it discharged its positive obligations is closely bound up with its influence over the wrongdoer, including its relations with the third party *de facto* controlling the area.[116] Therefore, specific measures protecting individuals cannot be separated from the State's general policy regarding the 'grey zone'. Second, the obligation to strengthen jurisdiction may be considered part of due diligence. The latter standard, that of the *bonus pater familias*,[117] expects from any reasonable civilised government, as a minimum, to refrain from acquiescing in the wrongful acts[118] and to reassert its responsibility for its national territory and its residents.[119] Thus, the territorial State's continued commitment to protect individuals within its territory and general international law constitute the rationale for the obligation to strengthen jurisdiction.

Beyond the legal basis in international law, the ECtHR's conclusions also raise the questions of whether the obligation to strengthen

113 E.g. HRC, Concluding observations: Cyprus, UN Doc. CCPR/C/CYP/CO/4 (30 April 2015), para 17 (recommendation to open new crossing points and facilitate greater access to the 'grey zone'); CESCR, Concluding observations: Central African Republic, UN Doc. E/C.12/CAF/CO/1 (4 May 2018), para 10 ('the rights enshrined in the Covenant must guide the strategy for restoring the State's authority').

114 Ganna Yudkivska, 'Territorial Jurisdiction and Positive Obligations of an Occupied State: Some Reflections on Evolving Issues under Article 1 of the European Convention' in Anne van Aaken and Iulia Motoc (eds), *The European Convention on Human Rights and General International Law* (Oxford University Press 2018) 143.

115 Marko Milanovic and Tatjana Papić, 'The Applicability of the ECHR in Contested Territories' (2018) 67 *International and Comparative Law Quarterly* 779, 796.

116 *Ilaşcu* (n 4), Partly dissenting opinion of Judge Casadevall joined by Judges Ress, Bîrsan, Tulkens and Fura-Sandström, para 3; ibid., Partly dissenting opinion of Judge Ress, paras 3–4; ibid., Partly dissenting opinion of Sir Nicolas Bratza joined by Mr Rozakis, Mr Hedigan, Mrs Thomassen and Mr Panţîru, para 20.

117 *Negrete* case (n 39).

118 *DRC* v. *Uganda* (n 46), 268, para 300; ibid., Declaration of Judge Tomka, 351–352, paras 2–3.

119 Even the partly dissenting judges rejecting Moldova's jurisdiction agreed that the failure to do so could amounts to acquiescence: *Ilaşcu* (n 4), Partly dissenting opinion of Sir Nicolas Bratza joined by Mr Rozakis, Mr Hedigan, Mrs Thomassen and Mr Panţîru, para 9.

jurisdiction may amount to a duty to use armed force and to what extent the Court can interfere with the State's foreign affairs, strategic and military policies. On the one hand, IHRL certainly does not require the State to recapture its amputated territory by force.[120] Human rights monitoring bodies at the most recommend the reinforcement of the State's presence in the area or its capacity to guarantee the protection of civilians in conflict areas;[121] the demobilisation of armed opposition groups and peace negotiation.[122] On the other hand, the measures aimed at strengthening the State's jurisdiction shall be taken within the limits defined by international law.[123] The recapture of the State's own territory through the use of force is not contrary to international law,[124] except arguably against stabilised *de facto* regimes that respect the same norm during a longer period.[125] The ECtHR does not impose any specific measures but only minimum State action.

If an institution maintained by the territorial State in the area outside its control can only continue to function at the cost of disproportionate

[120] Syméon Karagiannis, 'Le Territoire d'application de La Convention Européenne Des Droits de l'homme. Vetera et Nova' (2005) 61 *Revue trimestrielle des droits de l'homme* 33, 75.

[121] E.g. HRC, Concluding observations: Democratic Republic of the Congo, UN Doc. CCPR/C/COD/CO/3 (26 April 2006), para 13.

[122] E.g. ACommHPR, Concluding observations: Democratic Republic of Congo, 6–20 November 2003, para 22; Report of the High Commissioner for Human Rights on the situation of human rights in Colombia, UN Doc. A/HRC/19/21/Add.3 (31 January 2012), para 118(i); HRC, Concluding observations: Cyprus, UN Doc. CERD/C/CYP/CO/17–22 (23 September 2013), para 7.

[123] *Genocide case (Bosnia and Herzegovina* v. *Serbia and Montenegro)* (n 26), 221, para 430; *Ilaşcu* (n 4), para 331; *Ivanțoc* (n 52), para 105; *Catan* (n 5), paras 109–110; *Mozer* (n 5), paras 99–100.

[124] In non-international armed conflicts, the prohibition of the use of force under Article 2 (4) of the UN Charter does not apply. However, special (e.g. ceasefire) agreements or binding UN Security Council resolutions could still prohibit the use of force against a non-state *de facto* regime. See Olivier Corten, 'Le Rapport de La Mission d'enquête Internationale Indépendante Sur Le Conflit En Géorgie' (2010) 114 *Revue générale de droit international public* 35, 54–60; in international armed conflicts, the use of force by the territorial State against the occupying State may be lawful under the strict conditions of Article 51 of the UN Charter on self-defence, and provided that it does not violate any special agreement or binding UN Security Council resolution.

[125] Jochen A. Frowein, *Das De facto-Regime im Völkerrecht: eine Untersuchung zur Rechtsstellung nichtanerkannter Staaten und ähnlicher Gebilde* (C Heymann 1968) 67–69; Wolfgang Vitzthum and Alexander Proelß (eds), *Völkerrecht* (6. Auflage, De Gruyter Lehrbuch 2013) 586 (para 14); A precedent in favour of this principle is Resolution 82 of the UNSC, declaring that the armed attack on the Republic of Korea by forces from North Korea 'constitutes a breach of the peace'. UN Doc. S/RES/82 (25 June 1950), preambular paras 3–4; Independent International Fact-Finding Mission on the Conflict in Georgia, September 2009, vol. II, 239–242.

restrictions of human rights, the State must consider to transfer the institution in the government-controlled territory – that is what Moldova has chosen to safeguard the right to instruction of the ethnic Moldovan children of Transnistria in the *Catan* case or what the European Committee for the Prevention of Torture and Inhuman or Degrading Treatment or Punishment (CPT) recommended to protect the health of the detainees in the Bender prison, deprived by the Transnistrian authorities of running water and connection to the electricity supply.[126] The evaluation of the proportionality of human rights restrictive measures may lead the territorial State to renounce its continued presence in the amputated area in order to better guarantee human rights, and in this case the objective of strengthening its jurisdiction takes a step backward.

The State's obligation to take the measures with a view to re-establish its control over the 'grey zone' is all the more ambiguous that it could run against the international settlement of the territorial dispute, including the territorial State's choice to renounce a part of its territory in order to obtain other benefits in exchange. It is difficult to imagine that such a diplomatic action would engage the State's international responsibility under the ECHR.[127] Generally speaking, foreign policy has not been immune from the the control of human rights treaty bodies.[128] Consequently, at least *prima facie* the ECtHR verifies whether the territorial State expressed its commitment to strengthen its jurisdiction in the 'grey zone', leaving the State broad room for manoeuvre.[129] As human rights treaty bodies are not in the position to scrutinise the pertinence or efficacy of the State's foreign policy,[130] the review of the obligation to strengthen jurisdiction necessarily is summary.

[126] CPT, Report to the Government of the Republic of Moldova on the visit to Prison Establishment No. 8 in Bender, CPT/Inf (2008) 37 (4 December 2008), para 21.

[127] Karagiannis (n 120) 81, note 137.

[128] E.g. ECtHR, *Stoll* v. *Switzerland* [GC], Appl. no. 69698/01, judgment of 10 December 2007, para 128 (review of the confidentiality of diplomatic reports); *Bosphorus* v. *Ireland* [GC], Appl. no. 45036/98, judgment of 30 June 2005, para 154 (control of policies covered by the transfer of competences to an IO); Guidelines on treaty-specific documents to be submitted by States parties under Articles 16 and 17 of the ICESCR, UN Doc. E/C.12/ 2008/2 (24 March 2009), paras 3(c), 9 (information on the respect of human rights in the framework of its foreign action).

[129] Olivier de Frouville, 'Ilaşcu et Autres c. Moldova et Russie' (2005) 109(2) *Journal du droit international* 472, 476.

[130] *Ilaşcu* (n 4), para 340; ibid., Partly dissenting opinion of Judge Casadevall joined by Judges Ress, Bîrsan, Tulkens and Fura-Sandström, para 8; ibid., Partly dissenting opinion of Judge Ress, para 4.

3.1.5 *Specific Positive Obligations*

The territorial State's special measures aimed at protecting individuals' rights include positive duties 'to take the diplomatic, economic, judicial or other measures that were both in its power to take and in accordance with international law'.[131] Likewise, in the *Velásquez-Rodríguez* v. *Honduras* case the IACtHR required 'all those means of a legal, political, administrative and cultural nature that promote the protection of human rights', without establishing an exhaustive list of positive measures, 'since they vary with the law and the conditions of each State Party'.[132] Some good practices may nonetheless be cited: the major types of measures the territorial State is required to take are preventive measures (Section 3.1.5.1); providing remedies (Section 3.1.5.2); redressing the harm caused by the human rights violation (Section 3.1.5.3);[133] and cooperation with *de facto* authorities (Section 3.1.5.4).

3.1.5.1 Preventive Measures

Once the territorial State loses its effective control over the area, it is obliged to mitigate the consequences of the situation on human rights and prevent the extension of continuing violations. It satisfies this obligation by taking measures to bring about the end of the wrongful act. For instance, in the *Catan* case the Republic of Moldova adopted socio-economic measures to enable the schools of Moldovan/Romanian-speaking children to continue operating and the children to continue learning in Moldovan/Romanian (the payment of the rent and refurbishment of new premises; the payment for all equipment of a Moldovan school; the transfer of the school to a building in the government-controlled area; and the organisation of the everyday transport of the pupils), reacting to the violations of the children's right to education by the *de facto* authorities.[134] Similar measures mitigating continuing violations may be the sending of humanitarian staff to the 'grey zone';[135] the financial assistance given to the applicants' families and their help in

[131] *Ilaşcu* (n 4), para 331; *Catan* (n 5), paras 109–110; *Mozer* (n 5), paras 99–100.

[132] *Velásquez-Rodríguez* (n 40), para 175; *Anzualdo Castro* v. *Peru*, judgment of 22 September 2009 (Preliminary Objection, Merits, Reparations and Costs), para 63; regarding all violations of human rights: *Godínez-Cruz* v. *Honduras*, judgment of 20 January 1989 (Merits), para 185.

[133] HRC, General comment No. 31 [80], UN Doc. CCPR/C/21/Rev.1/Add.13 (26 May 2004), para 8.

[134] *Catan* (n 5), paras 49, 56, 61, 147.

[135] *Ilaşcu* (n 4), paras 346–347.

arranging visits to the applicants during their detention;[136] protests and claims addressed to the *de facto* authorities[137] or the outside State;[138] or negotiations with the *de facto* authorities with a view to reaching an agreement guaranteeing respect for human rights.[139]

Another example to fulfil the obligation to prevent is the recourse to the assistance of other States and IOs.[140] To provide protection, for instance, to internally-displaced persons, 'the State has an obligation to allow others to contribute to the fulfilment of this duty, in particular international agencies and organizations'.[141] The territorial State shall consider such support in good faith and not as interference in its internal affairs. Furthermore, it shall grant and facilitate the free passage of humanitarian assistance and grant persons engaged in the provision of such assistance rapid and unimpeded access to the internally displaced.[142] Especially in the protection of economic, social and cultural rights, the territorial State has the obligation to seek international assistance and cooperation on mutually-agreed terms when it is unable, despite its best efforts, to guarantee economic, social and cultural rights within its territory.[143]

The territorial State is required to prevent even new human rights violations as far as it has the capacity to take reasonable measures. For instance, it is reasonable to expect from the territorial State to apply its existing criminal code and/or to adopt special legislation criminalising certain human rights violations in the 'grey zone', even if it is unable to

[136] Ibid., paras 346–347. [137] Ibid., paras 347, 350. [138] Ibid., paras 349–350.

[139] Ibid., para 348; Likewise, the Ukrainian authorities managed to exchange four victims of trafficking of human beings, kidnapped by separatist militia. Report concerning the implementation of the CoE Convention on Action against Trafficking in Human Beings by Ukraine, GRETA(2018)20, 13 July 2018, para 126.

[140] *Ilaşcu* (n 4), para 347; *Turturica and Casian* v. *the Republic of Moldova and Russia*, Appl. nos. 28648/06 and 18832/07, judgment of 30 August 2016, paras 53–54; *Vardanean* v. *the Republic of Moldova and Russia*, Appl. no. 22200/10, judgment of 30 May 2017, paras 42–43; CRC, Concluding observations: Cyprus, UN Doc. CRC/C/CYP/CO/3-4 (24 September 2012), para 53.

[141] Report of the Representative of the Secretary-General on the human rights of internally displaced persons, Walter Kälin, Follow-up mission to Georgia, UN Doc. A/HRC/16/43/Add.3 (23 December 2010), para 3; Guiding Principles on Internal Displacement (n 7), Principle 25(2); HRC, Concluding observations: Georgia, UN Doc. CCPR/C/GEO/CO/3 (15 November 2007), para 6.

[142] Guiding Principles on Internal Displacement (n 7), Principles 25(2)–25(3), 30.

[143] Maastricht Principles (n 10), Principle 34; CESCR, General comment No. 4: The right to adequate housing, UN Doc. HRI/GEN/1/Rev.9 (Vol. I) (27 May 2008), 14, para 10; Human Rights Council, Final draft of the guiding principles on extreme poverty and human rights, UN Doc. A/HRC/21/39 (18 July 2012), para 94.

enforce it.[144] Another reasonable measure is to control the movement of persons and goods through the administrative or cease-fire line so as to prevent human trafficking or the smuggling of illicit products from or to the 'grey zone'. Likewise, the territorial State may be expected to facilitate the monitoring of the human rights situation in the 'grey zone' through international human rights mechanisms.[145] It is also required to ensure that an information campaign on human rights instruments reaches the persons living in the area.[146] To prevent the risk of statelessness, the territorial State is expected to ensure individuals' access to personal identity documents,[147] for instance, by allowing the registration of births that occurred in the 'grey zone' by any court in the government-controlled area.[148] Furthermore, providing effective remedies for individuals in the 'grey zone' by the territorial State might have a general preventive effect on human rights violations.

3.1.5.2 Providing Remedies

Under the obligation to provide remedies, not only is the obligation to investigate, repress and repair understood but also the obligation to adopt measures aimed at the facilitation of the protection of human rights.[149] In other words, even if the territorial State is unable to prevent the commission of a violation, under due diligence it is required to mitigate its consequences.

As the territorial State is unable to have physical access to the victim, the perpetrator or the evidence of the breach in the 'grey zone', all its judicial and investigative authorities are limited to the government-controlled area. Its obligation to provide remedies should consist in enabling the victim to inform the state authorities 'of the details of his

[144] CRC, Concluding observations: Iraq, UN Doc. CRC/C/OPAC/IRQ/CO/1 (4 February 2015), para 17(b); CAT, Concluding observations: Republic of Moldova, UN Doc. CAT/C/MDA/CO/2 (29 March 2010), para 4.

[145] E.g. Government of Georgia, Human Rights Action Plan for 2018–2020, para 24.1.6.1.

[146] CRC, Concluding observations: Democratic Republic of the Congo, UN Doc. CRC/C/15/Add.153 (9 July 2001), para 19.

[147] CRC, Concluding observations: Syrian Arab Republic, UN Doc. CRC/C/SYR/CO/5 (1 February 2019), para 24(a); UNHCR, Submission by the United Nations High Commissioner for Refugees for the Office of the High Commissioner for Human Rights' Compilation Report – Universal Periodic Review: Georgia, July 2010, 4–5.

[148] E.g. the practice of Ukraine: GRETA(2018)20 (n 139), paras 75–77; Fourth periodic report: Cyprus, UN Doc. CCPR/C/CYP/4 (19 March 2013), para 259.

[149] Riccardo Pisillo Mazzeschi, 'Responsabilité de l'Etat Pour Violation Des Obligations Positives Relatives Aux Droits de l'homme' (2008) 333 *Recueil des cours de l'Académie de droit international de La Haye* 175, 414–428.

situation and to be kept informed of the various legal and diplomatic actions taken',[150] and taking 'all the measures available to it to organise its judicial system in a way that would render the rights guaranteed' under the right to a fair trial 'effective in practice'.[151] A possibility is to enable individuals to seek a remedy remotely, for instance, by allowing files to be sent electronically, providing information about remedies and allowing modern information technology solutions for individuals from the 'grey zone'.[152] Likewise, universal treaty bodies recommended States to guarantee access to a toll-free helpline for victims in all regions within their territory.[153] Another possible compliance with the obligation to provide a remedy is creating, in the government-controlled area, 'a set of judicial, investigative and civil service authorities which work in parallel' with those created by the *de facto* authorities.[154] While some applicants from the Donetsk region complained in the *Tsezar and Others* v. *Ukraine* case that they could bring no claims before the courts relocated to the government-controlled areas because of health problems, a lack of safety and a lack of funds to travel to those regions, the ECtHR held that, by relocating domestic remedies to government-controlled areas, Ukraine did not disproportionately restrict the applicants' right of access to a court.[155] In fact, the proportionality of the restriction of the right to remedy by relocating authorities in the government-controlled area is case-sensitive: it makes a difference whether the territorial State relocates them near to the ceasefire line or in distant cities, or whether it facilitates obtaining information online rather than through travel to the courts.[156] While the effects of any decisions taken by these authorities can only be felt outside the conflict area, they have the function of enabling cases to be brought before the territorial State's authorities, 'which can then initiate diplomatic and legal steps to attempt to intervene in specific cases'.[157]

[150] *Mozer* (n 5), para 214. [151] *Khlebik* (n 87), para 71; *Tsezar* (n 13), para 48.

[152] CEDAW, General recommendation No. 33 on women's access to justice, UN Doc. CEDAW/C/GC/33 (3 August 2015), para 16(a) (on remote areas); some good practices of Ukrainian relocated courts in: OSCE Special Monitoring Mission to Ukraine, Access to Justice and the Conflict in Ukraine, December 2015, 18–19.

[153] CRC, Concluding observations: Georgia, UN Doc. CRC/C/GEO/CO/4 (9 March 2017), para 24(e); UN Doc. CRC/C/CYP/CO/3–4 (n 140), para 53; State practice shows that this could reach victims of 'grey zones', e.g. UNOHCHR, Report on the human rights situation in Ukraine, 15 June 2014, para 173.

[154] *Mozer* (n 5), para 215; *Tsezar* (n 13), para 52. [155] *Tsezar* (n 13), paras 55, 70.

[156] On good practices: Access to Justice and the Conflict in Ukraine (n 152), 18–19.

[157] *Mozer* (n 5), para 215.

Even after the territorial State relocates local remedies to the government-controlled area, the right to a fair trial might still be restricted as evidence or the case file of pending applications might no longer be available as a result of their situation in the 'grey zone'. This scenario occurred in the *Khlebik* v. *Ukraine* case, where the applicant was convicted at first instance by a court of the Luhansk region for a series of armed attacks committed in the Luhansk region. The court of appeal was unable to hear his appeal as the parts of the Luhansk region where the case file was located were no longer under Ukrainian government control following the creation of the self-proclaimed 'Luhansk People's Republic'. The applicant complained that the authorities' failure to adopt rules and procedures that would allow for his appeal to be effectively examined constituted a violation of his right to a fair trial. The ECtHR examined whether Ukraine took all the measures available to it to organise its judicial system in a way that would render the right to a fair trial effective in practice by examining the applicant's appeal.[158] In the instant case the Court held that the Ukrainian authorities had duly examined the possibility of restoring the applicant's case file and done all in their power under the circumstances to address the applicant's situation. Indeed, the Court welcomed the initiatives taken by the authorities to attempt to gather evidence in the government-controlled areas, to solicit the help of the International Committee of the Red Cross in facilitating recovery of the files located in the separatist area and legislative proposals intended to facilitate similar situations.[159]

The territorial State is required to investigate and document all reported human rights violations promptly, thoroughly and impartially, and duly prosecute those responsible.[160] While the territorial State's means to control the acts occurring in the 'grey zone' are considerably limited, its authorities can always open an investigation on the basis of information and witnesses available in the government-controlled area, secondary sources and so forth. Therefore, it is not certain whether such a procedure *ab initio* is unsuccessful.

[158] *Khlebik* (n 87), paras 71–72. [159] Ibid., para 80.

[160] Committee on Enforced Disappearances, Concluding observations: Iraq, UN Doc. CED/C/IRQ/CO/1 (13 October 2015), para 23; CEDAW, Concluding observations: Syria, UN Doc. CEDAW/C/SYR/CO/2 (18 July 2014), paras 8(c), 27(a) and (c); Committee on the Protection of the Rights of All Migrant Workers and Members of Their Families, Concluding observations: Libya, UN Doc. CMW/C/LBY/CO/1 (12 April 2019), para 29(b); *Velásquez-Rodríguez* (n 40), paras 176–177; *Mapiripán Massacre* (n 92), paras 219, 223; *Pueblo Bello Massacre* (n 61), para 143.

The territorial State is obliged to carry out the investigation 'by all available legal means' with the aim of determining the circumstances of the given case[161] and, where appropriate, take action against those allegedly responsible for the human rights violations.[162] In Moldova, criminal courts quash the judicial decisions of Transnistrian *de facto* authorities if their procedure is vitiated or contrary to Article 6 of the ECHR, referring to the positive obligation under the *Ilaşcu* judgment,[163] and open criminal proceedings against the *de facto* judges who breached those human rights. The ECtHR considered those measures as satisfying Moldova's positive obligations.[164] Likewise, investigative authorities should seek various available forms of international cooperation, for example, the application to other States and IOs for their assistance in law enforcement.[165]

The territorial State's obligation to provide effective remedies applies equally to violations committed by a peace operation in its territory: the case law of the internationalised tribunals of Bosnia and Herzegovina provides some precedents. In the *Sabahudin Fijukjanin* case, as a reaction to the arrest and unlawful detention of a man by Stabilisation Force (Bosnia and Herzegovina) (SFOR), the Human Rights Chamber for Bosnia and Herzegovina ordered, as a provisional measure, that the authorities of Bosnia and Herzegovina request SFOR that the victim be placed under the jurisdiction of the Federation authorities.[166] In the *Bogdan Subotić* case, which similarly concerned the arrest and detention of a man by SFOR and the alleged omissions of Bosnia and Herzegovina, the Constitutional Court referred to *Ilaşcu*: it held that the State was bound to take adequate measures to protect the victims' rights when a

161 *Velásquez-Rodríguez* (n 40), para 181; *Pueblo Bello Massacre* (n 61), para 143.

162 HRC, General comment No. 31 (n 133), para 18; Basic Principles and Guidelines on the Right to a Remedy and Reparation for Victims of Gross Violations of International Human Rights Law and Serious Violations of International Humanitarian Law, UN Doc. A/RES/60/147 (21 March 2006), para 3(b).

163 E.g. *Petiş Mihail et al.*, No. 1re-130/12, Supreme Court of the Republic of Moldova, Criminal chamber, 10 July 2012; *Eliţov Eduard Petru*, No. 1re-486/12, Supreme Court of the Republic of Moldova, Criminal chamber, 18 December 2012.

164 *Ilaşcu* (n 4), para 346; *Ivanţoc* (n 52), para 110; *Mozer* (n 5), para 153.

165 *Ilaşcu* (n 4), para 347; *Mozer* (n 5), para 153; CRC, Concluding observations: Syrian Arab Republic, UN Doc. CRC/C/SYR/CO/5 (1 February 2019), para 21(h); CEDAW, Concluding observations: Syrian Arab Republic, UN Doc. CEDAW/C/SYR/CO/2 (18 July 2014), para 40(g).

166 Human Rights Chamber for Bosnia and Herzegovina, *Sabahudin Fijukjanin* v. *Bosnia and Herzegovina and The Federation of Bosnia and Herzegovina*, Case No. CH/02/12499, decision on admissibility and to strike out, 4 March 2003, paras 11, 35.

violation results from the action of a peace operation over which the State has no *de facto* control but which occurs in its territory.[167] In the instant case, even though the deprivation of liberty was attributable to a peace operation, the State had a positive obligation to thoroughly investigate and to address the forces of the peace operation in order to ascertain the truth about the events and persuade SFOR to release and financially compensate the appellant for the damage caused.[168] Likewise, universal treaty-monitoring bodies require territorial States to ensure remedies against human rights violations by peace operations in their territory. The Human Rights Committee recommended a territorial State to 'prevail upon' States contributing troops to a peace mission operating in its territory 'suspected of having committed acts of sexual abuse to open inquiries into the matter and take the appropriate measures'.[169] The Committee on the Rights of the Child recommended a territorial State to include in the status-of-forces agreements with troop and police-contributing countries provisions guaranteeing their unconditional national responsibility for the investigation, prosecution and trial of their security forces operating in the territorial State or allowing prosecution by the latter when the contributing country is unable or unwilling to take action.[170]

Even if obstacles prevent progress in the legal remedies of the territorial State, the prompt opening of an inquiry and criminal procedures is vital in preventing any appearance of collusion in or tolerance of unlawful acts.[171] The choice of the concrete forms of investigation depends on the context, but the State shall use all available lawful means. However, there is a risk that human rights monitoring bodies reduce the territorial State's due diligence to the mere opening of an investigation, without verifying the intensity and the diligence of the investigation, and the minimum efforts that the State should have further taken at the legal, economic, administrative or diplomatic level.[172] Beyond investigative

[167] Constitutional Court of Bosnia and Herzegovina, *Bogdan Subotić*, AP-696/04, 23 September 2005, Merits, published in *Službeni glasnik* BiH 86/05, paras 51–52.

[168] Ibid., paras 53–55.

[169] HRC, Concluding observations: Democratic Republic of the Congo, UN Doc. CCPR/C/COD/CO/3 (26 April 2006), para 13.

[170] CRC, Concluding observations: Central African Republic, UN Doc. CRC/C/CAF/CO/2 (8 March 2017), para 41(d)–(e).

[171] *Varnava and Others* v. *Turkey* [GC], Appl. nos. 16064/90 et al., judgment of 18 September 2009, para 191.

[172] In this sense, the ECtHR applying a *prima facie* view on the opening of investigation: *Mangîr and Others* v. *the Republic of Moldova and Russia*, Appl. no. 50157/06, judgment of

measures, international monitoring bodies should on a case-by-case basis examine 'the background of the efforts made by other authorities, including those at the highest level, to ensure the protection of the applicant's rights'.[173]

3.1.5.3 Reparation

The obligation of diligence plays a guiding role in the territorial State's obligation to ensure reparation. States shall make reparation to victims of human rights violations, even if committed by third parties (other States or non-state actors).[174] Beyond redressing its own omissions, the territorial State 'should endeavour to establish national programmes for reparation and other assistance to victims in the event that the parties liable for the harm suffered are unable or unwilling to meet their obligations'.[175]

Such reparation shall be offered both victims who flee the 'grey zone' to the government-controlled area[176] and those staying in the 'grey zone'.[177] The latter can benefit from reparation through compensation paid by the State, convoys sent to the area,[178] existing multilateral, bilateral or other programmes,[179] or the funding of private rehabilitation facilities, including those provided by non-governmental

17 July 2018, paras 41–42 and 16; *Paduret* v. *the Republic of Moldova and Russia*, Appl. no. 26626/11, judgment of 9 May 2017, paras 33–34 and 8.

173 *Mozer* (n 5), para 154.

174 HRC, General comment No. 31 (n 133), para 8; CAT, General comment No. 3(2012): Implementation of article 14 by States parties, UN Doc. CAT/C/GC/3 (13 December 2012), para 7; ACommHPR, General comment No. 4 on the African Charter on Human and Peoples' Rights: The Right to Redress for Victims of Torture and Other Cruel, Inhuman or Degrading Punishment or Treatment (Article 5), paras 61, 62, 64.

175 Basic Principles and Guidelines on the Right to a Remedy and Reparation for Victims . . . (n 162), para 16.

176 E.g. HRC, Concluding observations: Iraq, UN Doc. CCPR/C/IRQ/CO/5 (3 December 2015), para 20(d); CAT, Concluding observations: Iraq, UN Doc. CAT/C/IRQ/CO/1 (7 September 2015), para 13; CRC, Concluding observations: Iraq, UN Doc. CRC/C/IRQ/CO/2-4 (4 February 2015), para 24(e).

177 As States are required, under the CAT or the ACHPR, to ensure that means of reparation are accessible to victims of torture even outside their territory, the same obligation applies *a fortiori* to victims in an area of their territory outside their effective control. CAT, General comment No. 3 (n 174), para 22; ACommHPR, General comment No. 4 (n 174), para 27.

178 CRC, Concluding observations: Syrian Arab Republic, UN Doc. CRC/C/SYR/CO/5 (1 February 2019), para 37(c).

179 Optional Protocol to the Convention on the Rights of the Child on the involvement of children in armed conflict, 25 May 2000, Article 7(2).

organisations (NGOs) operating in the area.[180] The territorial State can fulfil its obligation to redress in various ways without controlling the area: for instance, the ECtHR held that through measures granting individuals compensation for losses caused by certain policies of the *de facto* authorities,[181] or by granting the victim's family financial support and the victim a free apartment,[182] the territorial State satisfied its positive obligations. Various forms of satisfaction and the right to truth, such as an official declaration or judicial decision restoring the dignity, reputation and rights of the victims, public apologies, judicial and administrative sanctions against the wrongdoers or commemorations and tributes to the victims,[183] do not necessarily require territorial control. Likewise, guarantees of non-repetition may be performed in the government-controlled area, such as the training of public officials or promoting the observance of regional and international standards by public servants.[184] Again, the extent and form of the specific measures depend on the territorial State's capabilities in the concrete circumstances: for instance, Moldova was able to establish a service in Transnistria to offer housing to mother and child victims of torture,[185] whereas the same might not be feasible in an ongoing armed conflict on the spot.

3.1.5.4 Cooperation with *De Facto* Authorities

Compliance with the obligation to protect may entail the expectation that the territorial State seek cooperation, beyond other States and IOs, even with the *de facto* authorities at least in the protection of physical integrity of persons (right to life, prohibition of torture or other inhuman or degrading treatment or punishment, freedom from slavery).[186] The territorial State is required 'to cooperate effectively and

[180] CAT, General comment No. 3 (n 174), para 15; ACommHPR, General comment No. 4 (n 174), para 43.

[181] *Sandu and Others* v. *the Republic of Moldova and Russia*, Appl. nos. 21034/05 and 7 others, judgment of 17 July 2018, paras 87, 20.

[182] *Vardanean* (n 140), paras 42–43.

[183] CAT, General comment No. 3 (n 174), para 16; ACommHPR, General comment No. 4 (n 174), para 44.

[184] CAT, General comment No. 3 (n 174), para 18; ACommHPR, General comment No. 4 (n 174), paras 46–47.

[185] CAT, UN Doc. CAT/C/SR.1575 (10 November 2017), para 26.

[186] ECtHR, *Güzelyurtlu and Others* v. *Cyprus and Turkey*, Appl. No. 36925/07, judgment of 4 April 2017, paras 291, 293–296; *Güzelyurtlu and Others* v. *Cyprus and Turkey* [GC], Appl. No. 36925/07, judgment of 29 January 2019, paras 237–238, 241–257; The difference between the Chamber's and the Grand Chamber's ruling is the extent to which the

take all reasonable steps necessary to this end in order to facilitate and realise an effective investigation into the case overall'.[187] Where the territorial State has formal diplomatic relations with the outside State *de facto* controlling the area, it shall use all the possibilities available under international treaties applicable to both States.[188] 'In the absence of formal diplomatic relations, formalised means of cooperation are more likely to fail and States may be required to use other more informal or indirect channels of cooperation, for instance through third States or international organisations'.[189] The ECtHR examines whether the State actually took appropriate and sufficient measures and whether it made the minimum effort required in the circumstances of the case.[190] In the same sense, the Human Rights Advisory Panel in Kosovo confirmed that a State having 'reduced State jurisdiction', that is not in a position to take measures that will have a direct impact on proceedings pending before the local courts, has the obligation to endeavour, with all the diplomatic means available to it *vis-à-vis* the local *de facto* authorities, to obtain assurances that the cases filed by individuals will be duly processed in accordance with the ECHR.[191]

Despite the strong contestation of this duty,[192] the ECtHR set a clear limit to the obligation to cooperate: it 'should be interpreted in the light of international treaties or agreements' applicable to the territorial State concerned, 'following as far as possible a combined and harmonious application of' IHRL and those instruments, 'which should not result in conflict or opposition between them'.[193] In line with this intention to

State is expected to take reasonable steps to cooperate. Contrary to the Chamber, the Grand Chamber held that supplying the whole investigation file to the *de facto* authorities would be unreasonable, as it 'would amount in substance to a transfer of the criminal case by Cyprus to the 'TRNC' courts, and Cyprus would thereby be waiving its criminal jurisdiction' over the crime; ibid., para 253; *a contrario*, considering the majority judgment as the rejection of the territorial State's procedural obligation to cooperate with the 'TRNC', see ibid., Partly dissenting opinion of Judges Karakaş and Pejchal, para 11.

187 *Güzelyurtlu (Chamber)* (n 186), para 285; *Güzelyurtlu* [GC] (n 186), paras 232, 235.

188 *Güzelyurtlu* [GC] (n 186), para 237.

189 Ibid.

190 *Güzelyurtlu (Chamber)* (n 186), para 289; *Güzelyurtlu* [GC](n 186), para 265.

191 The HRAP applied this duty *mutatis-mutandis* to UNMIK vis-à-vis the authorities of Kosovo and EULEX Kosovo, e.g. HRAP, *Petko Milogorić et al.* v. *UNMIK*, Cases No. 38/08 et al, 24 March 2010, para 52; *Lalić and Others*, Cases No. 30/08 et al., 13 May 2011, para 32, etc.

192 *Güzelyurtlu (Chamber)* (n 186), para 238 (Republic of Cyprus) and partly dissenting opinion of Judge Serghides, para 47(h), (o); *Güzelyurtlu* [GC] (n 186), paras 207–208 (Republic of Cyprus).

193 *Güzelyurtlu* [GC] (n 186), para 236.

reconcile IHRL with general international law, especially the rights of the State, the territorial State is required to cooperate only as far as it does not waive its criminal jurisdiction over the crime.[194] For less serious human rights violations, other than the protection of physical integrity of persons, one may argue that the territorial State should consider seeking cooperation with *de facto* authorities.[195]

The ECtHR found that certain forms of cooperation with the *de facto* authorities established to normalise the everyday lives of the people living in the area satisfy the territorial State's positive obligations.[196] The ECtHR also confirmed that acts of technical and administrative cooperation between Moldova and the 'MRT', 'given their nature and limited character ... cannot be regarded as support for the Transdniestrian regime' but, on the contrary, 'they represent affirmation by Moldova of its desire to re-establish control over the region of Transdniestria'.[197] The less the given form of cooperation affects the sovereign interests of the State, the more the State should take that positive measure.

3.1.6 Gaps in the Scope of Positive Obligations: The Principle of Normality

The case law still contains uncertainties concerning the degree of positive obligations. First, it is unclear what IHRL expects from territorial States regarding social benefits. Especially if individuals in the 'grey zone' are granted parallel social benefits by the *de facto* authorities or the outside State, can the territorial State deny providing its social benefits on this ground? Second, it is also disputed whether the territorial State is expected to recognise or take into account the performance of individuals' obligations under public law in the 'grey zone' such as the performance of military service, tax payment, or the enforcement of criminal sanctions in the unrecognised administration. Third, one may consider the tension between the human rights of the territorial State's citizens originating from the occupied territory, on the one hand, and

[194] Ibid., paras 253–255.

[195] CRC, Concluding observations: Republic of Moldova, UN Doc. CRC/C/MDA/CO/3 (20 February 2009), para 30; CEDAW, Concluding observations: Republic of Moldova, UN Doc. CEDAW/C/MDA/CO/4–5 (29 October 2013), para 12; CEDAW, Concluding observations: Georgia, 24 July 2014, UN Doc CEDAW/C/GEO/CO/4–5, para 13.

[196] *Ilaşcu* (n 4), paras 341–345; *Eriomenco* (n 52), para 61; *Soyma* (n 54), paras 38–39.

[197] *Ilaşcu* (n 4), para 345; ibid., Partly dissenting opinion of Judge Casadevall joined by Judges Ress, Bîrsan, Tulkens and Fura-Sandström, para 7.

those of settlers who have acquired rights in violation of international humanitarian law (IHL), on the other. It is submitted that for all those gaps, the so-called principle of 'normality' provides a useful guidance.

Pictet introduced the principle of 'normality' in IHL as guidance to protect victims of armed conflicts, under which 'protected persons must be able to lead as normal a life as possible'.[198] In IHRL, monitoring bodies have interpreted the obligations of the territorial State in a similar sense, so as to allow individuals residing in the area outside the State's control to normalise their quality of life.[199] While deciding on the conflict between the human rights of individuals in 'grey zones' and other international law obligations, such as the obligation of non-recognition, *ne bis in idem* or IHL, the territorial State should adopt the solution that both reconciles conflicting norms, using systemic integration under Article 31(3)(c) of the VCLT, and most favours the enjoyment of human rights.

In sum, human rights treaty-monitoring bodies do not determine a well-defined threshold of the territorial State's positive obligations but require *une certaine dose de volontarisme* ('a determined effort') and sanction the State's passivity.[200] In the heart of its positive obligations, the standard of due diligence constitutes the legal basis. As the latter requires proactive conduct, States are expected to invest in strengthening their effectiveness towards individuals in the 'grey zone'.

As a sign of the increasing authority of the international case law, several territorial States have accepted the positive obligations towards individuals in the 'grey zone'.[201] They have adopted a series of positive measures to protect the human rights in the area outside their effective

[198] (translated by the author) Jean Pictet, *Le Droit Humanitaire et La Protection Des Victimes de La Guerre* (Sijthoff 1973) 49.

[199] E.g. Report of the Representative of the Secretary-General on the human rights of internally displaced persons, Walter Kälin, Follow-up to the report on the mission to Georgia, UN Doc. A/HRC/13/21/Add.3 (14 January 2009), paras 37–41; CPT, Report on to the Government of Moldova on the ad hoc visit, CPT/Inf (2011) 8 (3 March 2011), 10, para 14; CoE Parliamentary Assembly, Legal remedies for human rights violations on the Ukrainian territories outside the control of the Ukrainian authorities, Resolution 2133 (2016), 12 October 2016, para 17.3.

[200] Karagiannis (n 120) 78.

[201] E.g. Georgia: HRC, UN Doc. CCPR/C/SR.2483 (19 October 2007), para 11; CEDAW, 4th and 5th reports: Georgia, UN Doc. CEDAW/C/GEO/4-5 (30 October 2012), para 11; CAT, Third report: Georgia, UN Doc. CAT/C/73/Add.1 (4 July 2005), para 35; HRC, Eighth report: Ukraine, UN Doc. CCPR/C/UKR/8 (30 January 2019), para 61; Ukraine: National report (n 105), para 39; Republic of Moldova: HRC, Third report: Republic of Moldova, UN Doc. CCPR/C/MDA/3 (17 March 2016), para 77.

control,[202] which may be considered the proper implementation of IHRL. Whereas Georgia went as far as to speak about its positive obligations towards its separatist regions 'imposed by the Convention and the customary international law',[203] it would be premature to speak about a customary legal regime in its entirety. Considering the evolving State practice and the gaps in the scope of positive obligations, it is sound to consider the territorial State's positive obligations as a progressive development of international law.

3.2 The Obligations of the Outside State

It is highly controversial whether the outside State's extraterritorial jurisdiction entails different obligations from those that the State has in its own territory. At first sight, numerous circumstances suggest a positive answer: first, no outside State disposes in a foreign territory of an institutional structure as elaborated as in its own territory. Second, a military operation conducted abroad may lead the outside State to limit human rights in several ways. Such differences between the outside State's conduct abroad and that in its national territory raise the question as to what the scope and the limitations of its obligations are.

This section explains that the outside State is bound by all negative obligations under IHRL in the 'grey zone' (Section 3.2.1). Under the functional approach, the State is also bound by positive obligations with which it can comply according to its effectiveness in the specific circumstances (Section 3.2.2). Section 3.2.3 demonstrates that the functional approach leads to a series of specific positive obligations in the 'grey zone'.

3.2.1 *Negative Obligations*

The outside State is obliged to respect all human rights, independently of the type of control it exercises in the given situation. In 'grey zones', outside States typically violate the freedom of movement and the right to

[202] E.g. Georgia: CERD, Sixth-eighth reports: Georgia, UN Doc. CERD/C/GEO/6–8 (31 October 2014), paras 74–90; Republic of Moldova: HRC, Third report: Republic of Moldova (n 201), 14–17; Iraq: CERD, Twenty-second–twenty-fifth reports: Iraq, UN Doc. CERD/C/IRQ/22–25 (22 November 2017), paras 25–29; Ukraine: CAT, Seventh report: Ukraine, UN Doc. CAT/C/UKR/7 (11 February 2019), paras 45–71.

[203] CRC, Written replies by Georgia to the list of issues, UN Doc. CRC/C/GEO/Q/3/Add.1 (20 May 2008), para 41.

one's home,[204] unlawfully deprive displaced persons from the enjoyment of their right to property[205] or discriminate on the basis of national or ethnic origin.[206] The massive attribution of nationality to the local population, the so-called policy of extraterritorial 'passportisation', for example, that of Russia in Transnistria, South-Ossetia, Abkhazia or Crimea, not only is presumed unlawful in international law,[207] but is also likely to violate the prohibition of discrimination based on racial or ethnic origin and lead to loss of the nationality of the territorial State.[208]

3.2.2 *The Scope of Positive Obligations: The Functional Approach*

The extent to which a State having extraterritorial jurisdiction is required to comply with positive obligations has been contested. According to a first solution, the extraterritorial jurisdiction should entail positive obligations only in the case of effective control over a territory, whereas control over persons by the State's agents abroad without spatial control should entail only negative obligations.[209] This concept, which has the advantage of establishing a system of predictable obligations, nevertheless seems simplistic: human rights cannot be rigidly divided into negative and positive obligations, because the enforcement of each human rights requires both negative and positive duties.[210] For instance, the abduction or arrest of a person by State agents abroad does entail positive obligations: beyond the respect of the right to liberty, the abducted or detained person has the right to water or adequate food during the detention, to a fair trial which requires institutional measures, and so forth.

204 *Cyprus* v. *Turkey* [GC] (n 93), paras 175, 296, 301; *Demades* v. *Turkey*, Appl. no. 16219/90, judgment of 31 July 2003, paras 36–37; *Georgia* v. *Russia (II) (Merits)* [GC], Appl. no. 38263/08, judgment of 21 January 2021, para 298.

205 *Loizidou* v. *Turkey (Merits)* [GC], Appl. no. 15318/89, judgment of 18 December 1996, paras 63–64; *Cyprus* v. *Turkey* [GC] (n 93), paras 189, 269–270.

206 *Cyprus* v. *Turkey* [GC] (n 93), para 311.

207 OSCE High Commissioner on National Minorities, The Bolzano/Bozen Recommendations on National Minorities in Inter-State Relations & Explanatory Note, June 2008, para 11; Anne Peters, 'Extraterritorial Naturalizations: Between the Human Right to Nationality, State Sovereignty and Fair Principles of Jurisdiction' (2010) 53 *German Yearbook of International Law* 623, 693, 718.

208 Ibid., 671, 702.

209 Marko Milanovic, *Extraterritorial Application of Human Rights Treaties: Law, Principles, and Policy* (Oxford University Press 2011) 210; John Cerone, 'Human Dignity in the Line of Fire: The Application of International Human Rights Law during Armed Conflict, Occupation, and Peace Operations' (2006) 39 *Vanderbilt Journal of Transnational Law* 1447, 1504–1506.

210 Pisillo Mazzeschi (n 149) 225.

A second solution is the functional approach. It has already been explained that extraterritorial jurisdiction should be functional in the sense that the outside State shall guarantee human rights as far as it has the power in the given extraterritorial situation, or in other terms according to the authority and control exercised. The functional approach determines not only the applicable rights and freedoms ('scope of the jurisdiction'),[211] but also the 'scope of obligations', that is the content of the expected State conduct. Accordingly, the State is bound by obligations with which it can comply according to its effectiveness in the specific circumstances.

In the *Wall* advisory opinion the ICJ seemed to support the functional applicability of the rights guaranteed by the ICESCR when it affirmed that '*[i]n the exercise of the powers available to it* on this basis, Israel is bound by the provisions of the International Covenant on Economic, Social and Cultural Rights' (emphasis added).[212] This interpretation is all the more defensible that the scope of socio-economic rights varies even in the national territory according to the economic capacity of the State party. Likewise, the ECtHR concluded, in the context of an unstable occupation, that 'in circumstances such as these the procedural duty under Article 2 must be applied realistically, to take account of specific problems faced by investigators'.[213] This conclusion shows that the procedural aspect of the right to life, which requires an institutional structure, must be interpreted in a flexible manner, according to the circumstances.[214]

For instance, in the *Al-Skeini* case the shooting from outside the building caused the death of the third applicant's wife and entailed the UK's obligation to investigate the circumstances of the shooting.[215] Thus, even a short-lived exercise of authority or control over a person abroad implies certain effectiveness and entails certain positive obligations of which the scope varies according to the capabilities of the State. However, for their effective implementation, some positive obligations require territorial control[216] such as the positive obligations related to

[211] *Supra*, Section 2.1.2.3.

[212] *Legal Consequences of the Construction of a Wall in the Occupied Palestinian Territory*, Advisory Opinion, *I.C.J. Reports* 2004, 181, para 112.

[213] *Al-Skeini and Others* v. *United Kingdom* [GC], Appl. no. 55721/07, judgment of 7 July 2011, para 168.

[214] Marko Milanovic, 'Al-Skeini and Al-Jedda in Strasbourg' (2012) 23 *European Journal of International Law* 121, 131.

[215] *Al-Skeini* (n 213), para 170.

[216] Milanovic (n 209) 215–216.

the right to education, the right to property or the protection against slavery and forced labour. In conclusion, the typology of negative and positive obligations is simplistic, since the outside State is bound by both types of duties abroad. Under the functional approach, it has positive obligations according to the authority or control it has in the given situation.

3.2.3 *Specific Positive Obligations*

Among its positive obligations the outside State is required to protect human rights, that is, to ensure that individuals' human rights are not violated by third parties. The general international law basis of such obligation, as in the case of the territorial State, is the standard of due diligence. As a customary international law obligation, due diligence binds the State in all territories it controls, even outside its borders.[217] Even though the traditional concept of due diligence relates to the State's national territory, the ILC[218] and the ICJ[219] interpreted it as covering State conduct beyond its national territory. In the *DRC* v. *Uganda* case the Court held that the occupying power's responsibility is engaged 'for any lack of vigilance in preventing violations of human rights and international humanitarian law by other actors present in the occupied territory, including rebel groups acting on their own account'.[220] Certain human rights monitoring bodies have also confirmed that 'due diligence may imply extraterritorial obligations for States that are exercising jurisdiction and effective control abroad'.[221] Universal

[217] *Affaire des biens britanniques au Maroc espagnol* (n 37), 699–700; regarding the obligation to prevent terrorism: James Crawford, *State Responsibility: The General Part* (Cambridge University Press 2013) 158.

[218] International liability for injurious consequences arising out of acts not prohibited by international law. Report of the Working Group, in: *YbILC*, 1996, 131, draft article 22(c).

[219] *Application of the International Convention on the Elimination of all Forms of Racial Discrimination (Georgia* v. *Russian Federation)*, Provisional Measures, Order of 15 October 2008, *I.C.J. Reports* 2008, 398, para 149(4); *Application of the Convention on the Prevention and Punishment of the Crime of Genocide*, Provisional Measures, Order of 8 April 1993, *I.C.J. Reports* 1993, 24, para 52(2); *Genocide case (Bosnia and Herzegovina* v. *Serbia and Montenegro)* (n 26), 221, para 430, while noting that it is about an obligation under the Genocide Convention.

[220] *DRC* v. *Uganda* (n 46), 231, para 179.

[221] Report of the Special Rapporteur on violence against women, its causes and consequences, Yakin Ertürk, UN Doc. E/CN.4/2006/61 (20 January 2006), para 34.

treaty-monitoring bodies[222] and regional monitoring bodies[223] have reiterated this conclusion.

Under the standard of due diligence, the outside State is expected to take preventive measures (Section 3.2.3.1), to react to the wrongful act, that is, to provide remedies and to redress the harm caused (Section 3.2.3.2), and to exercise its influence over autonomous local authorities (Section 3.2.3.3). Furthermore, in line with the generally-accepted classification of the obligations to respect, protect and fulfil human rights,[224] the outside State is bound by obligations to fulfil (Section 3.2.3.4).

3.2.3.1 Preventive Measures

Various universal treaty-monitoring bodies have formulated a general obligation to prevent third parties from violating human rights in other countries 'if they are able to influence these third parties by way of legal or political means, in accordance with the Charter of the United Nations and applicable international law'.[225] This obligation to prevent applies to all scenarios of extraterritorial jurisdiction.

In the case of *Isaak and Others* v. *Turkey* the ECtHR condemned the failure of Turkish and Turkish Cypriot soldiers to attempt to apprehend the victim in the mass or 'to prevent the counter-demonstrators from continuing their violent behaviour' in the buffer zone of Cyprus, under the control of UN peacekeeping forces.[226] The example illustrates that the obligation to prevent binds the State when an individual is within its extraterritorial jurisdiction,[227] irrespective of whether the latter is based on control over territory or persons. It follows that the obligation to

222 CAT, General comment 2, Implementation of article 2 by States parties, UN Doc. CAT/C/GC/2 (24 January 2008), paras 16–18; CEDAW, General recommendation No. 30 on women in conflict prevention, conflict and post-conflict situations, UN Doc. CEDAW/C/GC/30 (18 October 2013), paras 2–3.

223 IACHR, Access to justice for women victims of violence in the Americas, 20 January 2007, OEA/Ser.L/V/II, Doc. 68, para 48; CoE Ad hoc Committee on preventing and combating violence against women and domestic violence, The duty of due diligence, CAHVIO(2010)7, 21 May 2010, para 99.

224 E.g. ACommHPR, *Social and Economic Rights Action Center (SERAC) and Center for Economic and Social Rights (CESR)* v. *Nigeria*, Communication no. 155/96, 27 October 2001, para 44; CESCR, General comment No. 14 (n 86), para 33.

225 CESCR, General comment No. 14 (n 86), para 39.

226 *Isaak* v. *Turkey*, Appl. no. 44587/98, judgment of 24 June 2008, para 119.

227 Maarten den Heijer and Rick Lawson, 'Extraterritorial Human Rights and the Concept of "Jurisdiction"' in Malcolm Langford, Wouter Vandenhole and Martin Scheinin (eds), *Global Justice, State Duties: the Extraterritorial Scope of Economic, Social, and Cultural Rights in International Law* (Cambridge University Press 2013) 189–190.

protect also binds troop-contributing States in peace operations in the territory of another State: they shall take all reasonable measures to prevent human rights violations by third parties. In cases concerning the responsibility of The Netherlands for the genocide committed in Srebrenica, Dutch courts concluded that the State shall take preventive measures that are within its power when its agents have information about the prejudicial conduct at an appropriate time.[228]

The obligation to protect *a fortiori* applies in cases of extraterritorial jurisdiction based on control over territory, as it typically ensures the outside State more effectiveness. For instance, the ICJ in the *DRC* v. *Uganda* case condemned the occupying power for having failed to take measures to prevent ethnic conflict and the recruitment of child soldiers in the occupied territory.[229] The ECtHR also confirmed that Turkey, the occupying power in Northern Cyprus, was bound by the 'obligation to secure', in the northern part of Cyprus, the respect of all the rights and freedoms set out in the Convention.[230] This phrasing implies the duty to protect against human rights violations by third parties. Likewise, the IACHR[231] and universal treaty bodies[232] required the occupying State to prevent human rights violations committed by third parties, including private individuals, in the occupied territory. The factors determining the required diligence are the same as in the case of the territorial State (Section 3.1.3).

228 *Mehida Mustafic-Mujic et al.* v. *the State of the Netherlands*, Appeal Court in The Hague, 200.020.173/01, 5 July 2011, para 5.18; *Hasan Nuhanovic* v. *the State of the Netherlands*, Appeal Court in The Hague, 200.020.174/01, 5 July 2011, para 5.18; confirmed in: *Hasan Nuhanovic* v. *the State of the Netherlands*, Supreme Court of the Netherlands, 12/03324 LZ/TT, 6 September 2013, para 3.17.3; *Mehida Mustafic-Mujic et al.* v. *the State of the Netherlands*, Supreme Court of the Netherlands, 12/03329 LZ/TT, 6 September 2013, para 3.17.3.

229 *DRC* v. *Uganda* (n 46), 240–241, paras 209–211.

230 *Loizidou* v. *Turkey (Preliminary objections)* [GC], Appl. no. 15318/89, decision of 23 March 1995 on the admissibility, para 62; *Loizidou* v. *Turkey (Merits)* (n 205), para 52; *Cyprus* v. *Turkey* [GC] (n 93), paras 76, 78; *Banković and Others* v. *Belgium and 16 other States* [GC], Appl. no. 52207/99, decision of 12 December 2001 on the admissibility, para 70.

231 IACHR, Report No. 121/18, Case 10.573, *Jose Isabel Salas Galindo and others* v. *United States*, Merits, 5 October 2018, para 284.

232 HRC, General comment No. 36 (2018) (n 65), para 63; CEDAW, General recommendation No. 30 (n 222), para 12(c); CAT, Concluding observations: Israel, UN Doc. CAT/C/ISR/CO/5 (3 June 2016), para 39; CAT, Concluding observations: Israel, UN Doc. CAT/C/ISR/CO/4 (23 June 2009), para 32; CEDAW, Concluding observations: Israel, UN Doc. CERD/C/ISR/CO/14-16 (3 April 2012), para 28; CRC, Concluding observations: Israel, UN Doc. CRC/C/ISR/CO/2-4 (4 July 2014), paras 26(b), 60(d), 64(a).

3.2.3.2 Providing Remedies

Once a human rights violation occurs, the outside State is required to investigate, prosecute and punish the perpetrators and provide the victims remedies, with effective reparation. The duty to investigate violations of the physical integrity of persons is triggered if the outside State controls the territory where the suspected perpetrators or evidence are and it is informed of this circumstance[233] or another investigating State seizes the outside State of a cooperation request.[234] Where the investigation about the physical integrity of persons implicates more than one State, the outside State is expected to seek cooperation with other States and IOs, including both formal diplomatic and informal or *ad hoc* channels of cooperation.[235]

The State exercising effective control over a foreign territory, especially if control is stabilised, has means (including access to evidence) to conduct investigations and to repress the perpetrators, such as in its national territory. In its Concluding Observations on the report of Turkey, the Human Rights Committee confirmed the conclusions of the ECtHR related to Northern Cyprus, referring expressly to the *Cyprus* v. *Turkey* judgment:

> The State party should ensure the effective, transparent and independent investigations into all outstanding cases of alleged disappearances. In all such cases, the State party should prosecute and punish the perpetrators and grant effective reparation, including appropriate compensation, to victims or their families. Additionally, it should ensure that all mass graves are thoroughly investigated.[236]

Treaty-monitoring bodies also confirmed that the occupying power is bound to conduct an effective investigation into the whereabouts and fate of disappeared persons[237] or on killings that occurred[238] in the occupied territory.

[233] *Güzelyurtlu* [GC] (n 186), paras 191–196, 231; *Georgia* v. *Russia (II) (Merits)* (n 204), paras 330–332.

[234] *Güzelyurtlu (Chamber)* (n 186), paras 187, 189, 262; *Güzelyurtlu* [GC] (n 186), paras 194–196, 230, 233.

[235] *Güzelyurtlu* [GC] (n 186), paras 237–238.

[236] HRC, Concluding observations: Turkey, UN Doc. CCPR/C/TUR/CO/1 (13 November 2012), para 11.

[237] ECtHR, *Cyprus* v. *Turkey* [GC] (n 93), paras 136, 150; *Varnava* (n 171), para 186; UN Doc. CCPR/C/TUR/CO/1 (n 236), para 11; CAT, Concluding observations: Turkey, UN Doc. CAT/C/TUR/CO/3 (20 January 2011), para 9.

[238] *Adalı* v. *Turkey*, Appl. no. 38187/97, judgment of 10 March 2005, para 233.

The obligation to investigate binds the outside State *a fortiori* if its own agents committed the human rights violation in foreign territory. For instance, the Human Rights Committee recommended that Russia conduct an impartial investigation 'into all allegations of involvement of members of Russian forces and other armed groups under their control in violations of human rights in South Ossetia' regarding the armed conflict of August 2008.[239] This demonstrates that even in an invasion, without stabilised control, the invading State is obliged to investigate human rights violations occurring in the area.[240] In the *Al-Skeini* case, in the context of a fragile occupation, the Court also confirmed the obligation to investigate under the right to life: victims have to be questioned 'as quickly after the event as possible' and 'every effort should have been taken to identify' the eye witnesses.[241] Likewise, States contributing troops to a peace operation whose nationals are suspected of having committed sexual violence are obliged to open inquiries into the matter and to take the appropriate measures to prosecute their agents.[242]

However, the difficulties that the outside State may face on the spot influence the required diligence.[243] As with the territorial State, the outside State's limited capacities restrict the degree of the expected diligence. As the ECtHR held, where a human rights violation occurs 'in circumstances of generalised violence, armed conflict or insurgency, obstacles may be placed in the way of investigators and concrete constraints may compel the use of less effective measures of investigation or may cause an investigation to be delayed'.[244] The 'nature and degree of scrutiny which satisfies the minimum threshold of an investigation's effectiveness depends on the circumstances of the particular case',[245] such as the security circumstances, access to available evidence,

[239] HRC, Concluding observations: Russian Federation, UN Doc. CCPR/C/RUS/CO/6 (24 November 2009), para 13.

[240] CoE Commissioner for Human Rights, Monitoring of Investigations into cases of missing persons during and after the August 2008 armed conflict in Georgia, CommDH (2010)35 (29 September 2010), para 92 (Russia's obligation to investigate on the remains of missing persons died during the armed conflict); confirmed in: *Georgia* v. *Russia (II) (Merits)* (n 204), paras 331–337.

[241] *Al-Skeini* (n 213), para 170.

[242] HRC, Concluding observations: Democratic Republic of the Congo, UN Doc. CCPR/C/COD/CO/3 (26 April 2006), para 13.

[243] *Varnava* (n 171), para 191.

[244] ECtHR, *John George Miller* v. *the United Kingdom*, Appl. no. 32001/18, decision of 25 July 2019 on the admissibility, para 82.

[245] Ibid., para 90; for those factors: *supra*, Section 3.1.3.

difficulties in hearing the witnesses or the impossibility to establish the identity of the perpetrators.

3.2.3.3 Autonomous Local Authorities

One might ask how far the outside State is required to protect and fulfil human rights if local authorities operate in the area under its effective control. If its influence over those authorities amounts to attribution, the outside State shall ensure that those local authorities comply with its obligations.[246] However, if the local authorities operate in relative autonomy from the outside State, the latter shall implement its obligations under IHL and IHRL in some form of influence or cooperation with those authorities.[247] In other words, the outside State is required to make use of its influence over the local authorities to ensure the protection of human rights, to the extent that it has influence over them.[248] While in its *Wall* advisory opinion the ICJ used less mandatory wording, focusing on Israel's negative obligations ('not to raise any obstacle to the exercise of such rights in those fields where competence has been transferred to Palestinian authorities'),[249] it did not mean that the positive obligations are incumbent only upon the Palestinian authority.[250] As mentioned in Section 3.2.3.1, in the *DRC* v. *Uganda* case, rendered a year later, the ICJ used clear wording on the occupying power's positive obligations. International human rights monitoring bodies also clarified that transferring powers and functions to self-governing bodies does not exempt

[246] HRC, Concluding observations: Russian Federation, UN Doc. CCPR/C/RUS/CO/7 (28 April 2015), para 6; on attribution: *Infra*, Section 5.1.

[247] In IHL: GCIV, Articles 6(3), 47, 50, and 56; 'Expert Meeting: Occupation and Other Forms of Administration of Foreign Territory' (International Committee of the Red Cross 2012) 70 <www.icrc.org/eng/assets/files/publications/icrc-002-4094.pdf>.

[248] CEDAW, Concluding observations: Russian Federation, UN Doc. CEDAW/C/RUS/CO/8 (20 November 2015), para 30(a) (with regard to the self-proclaimed 'Donetsk people's republic' and 'Luhansk people's republic', '[t]o make use of its influence in the context of the Minsk peace agreements'); CAT, Concluding observations: Russian Federation, UN Doc. CAT/C/RUS/CO/6 (28 August 2018), para 51 (with regard to Transnistria, 'through its participation in the '5+2 talks'').

[249] *Wall* case (n 212), 181, para 112; some commentators interpreted this conclusion as imposing on the occupying power only negative obligations; Cerone (n 209) 1499.

[250] The CESCR interpreted the ICJ's conclusion as the obligation of Israel to 'take measures so as to enable the Palestinian Authority to exercise its functions and powers', with a view to ensure human rights under the ICESCR. CESCR, Concluding observations: Israel, UN Doc. E/C.12/ISR/CO/3 (16 December 2011), paras 23, 32, 35.

the outside State from its obligations to guarantee human rights to people under its territorial control.[251]

International human rights treaty bodies, especially in periodic reporting procedures, are often unable to decide on attribution of conduct, as the latter requires a detailed factual analysis on a case-by-case basis. Instead, they might confirm the outside State's positive obligation to protect human rights in accordance with its influence over the local authorities, that is, its effectiveness, without determining a sound threshold.[252] *Mutatis mutandis*, in the phase on provisional measures of the *Georgia* v. *Russia* case, where the ICJ could not engage in a detailed analysis of facts, the Court called on Russia (and Georgia) to 'do all in their power to ensure that public authorities and public institutions under their control or influence do not engage in acts of racial discrimination against persons, groups of persons or institutions'.[253] Outside States controlling a part of the territory of another State are also more willing to accept their commitment to influence the conduct of the local authorities than to admit the attribution of their conduct.[254]

3.2.3.4 Obligation to Fulfil

The obligation to fulfil or to realise obliges the State to take legislative, administrative budgetary, judicial and other measures that provide access to human rights for individuals within the State's jurisdiction. It enables individuals to effectively enjoy human rights.

In their extraterritorial application there is no fundamental difference between the positive obligations enshrined in conventions on civil and political rights and those guaranteeing socio-economic rights.[255] Any

[251] CAT, Concluding observations: Israel, UN Doc. CAT/C/ISR/CO/4 (23 June 2009), para 11; CAT, Concluding observations: Israel, UN Doc. CAT/C/ISR/CO/5 (3 June 2016), para 9; Human Rights in Palestine and in other occupied Arab territories, Report of the United Nations Fact-Finding Mission on the Gaza Conflict, UN Doc. A/HRC/12/48 (25 September 2009), para 303.

[252] UN Doc. CEDAW/C/RUS/CO/8 (n 248), para 30(a).

[253] *Application of the International Convention on the Elimination of all Forms of Racial Discrimination (Georgia* v. *Russian Federation)*, Provisional Measures, Order of 15 October 2008, *I.C.J. Reports* 2008, 398, para 149; in a similar sense: *Application of the Convention on the Prevention and Punishment of the Crime of Genocide*, Provisional Measures, Order of 8 April 1993, *I.C.J. Reports* 1993, 52, para 24(2).

[254] E.g. the FRY in the Dayton process in respect of the *Republika Srpska*: *Prosecutor* v. *Duško Tadić*, IT-94-1-A, judgment, Appeals Chamber, 15 July 1999, 70–71, para 159; or Armenia, in its request of accession to the CoE: CoE, Parliamentary Assembly, Opinion No. 221 (2000), Armenia's application for membership of the CoE, adopted by the Parliamentary Assembly on 28 June 2000, para 13.2(b).

[255] Heijer and Lawson (n 227) 182–183.

occupying power or State that otherwise exercises effective control over territory outside its national territory must respect, protect and fulfil the economic, social and cultural rights of persons within that territory.[256] Some of the economic and social rights enshrine minimum obligations of immediate effect,[257] others of a progressive nature. The former, obligations of immediate effect, oblige the outside State irrespective of its limited capabilities. For instance, any outside State shall observe certain minimum standards regarding the conditions of detention regardless of the State's level of development, such as the provision of clothing and food of nutritional value adequate for health and strength.[258] Likewise, the outside State shall ensure that persons in need of medical assistance are able to have access to and receive the necessary health care and services in a timely fashion.[259]

The latter, the obligation to progressively realise socio-economic rights, depends on the 'available resources',[260] whereas civil and political rights enshrine immediate obligations to respect and fulfil.[261] Even where the outside State has limited capabilities, under Article 2(1) of the ICESCR it is still obliged 'to take steps … to the maximum of its available resources' to achieve progressively the full realisation of the rights recognised in the Covenant. Thus, even where 'the available resources are demonstrably inadequate, the obligation remains for a State party to ensure the widest possible enjoyment of economic, social

[256] Maastricht Principles (n 10), Principle 18; Resolution on ongoing violations of human rights and fundamental freedoms in the Autonomous Republic of Crimea and the city of Sevastopol (Ukraine), paras 14, 16, in: Berlin Declaration and Resolutions adopted by the OSCE Parliamentary Assembly at the twenty-seventh annual session, Berlin, 7–11 July 2018.

[257] CESCR, General comment No. 3 (n 1), paras 2 ('to take steps' under Article 2(1) of the ICESCR), 5 (various other provisions) and 10 (the minimum core content of each socio-economic right under the ICESCR).

[258] HRC, *Albert Womah Mukong* v. *Cameroon*, Communication No. 458/1991, Views, 21 July 1994, UN Doc. CCPR/C/51/D/458/1991 (10 August 1994), para 9.3; IACHR, Report No. 49/01, Case nos. 11.826, 11.843, 11.847, *Leroy Lamey et al.* v. *Jamaica*, Decision, 4 April 2001, para 203; *Georgia* v. *Russia (II) (Merits)* (n 204), para 243.

[259] CESCR, General comment No. 14 (n 12), para 43(a); Guiding Principles on Internal Displacement (n 7), Principle 19; UN Doc. E/C.12/ISR/CO/3 (n 250), para 32; UNOHCHR, Situation of human rights in the temporarily occupied Autonomous Republic of Crimea and the city of Sevastopol (Ukraine), 2014–2017, 31–32, para 226(j), (r).

[260] ICESCR, Article 2; ACommHPR, *Kevin Mgwanga Gunme et al.* v. *Cameroon*, Communication no. 266/03, 27 May 2009, para 206.

[261] CESCR, General comment No. 3 (n 1), para 9.

and cultural rights under the prevailing circumstances'.[262] These views confirm the validity of the functional approach as to the scope of the obligations: the outside State is required to fulfil socio-economic rights within the limits of its effectiveness.

The flexibility left for the State to progressively realise socio-economic rights should not be misinterpreted as allowing the occupying State 'to wait for the most favourable circumstances before meeting its obligations' under the ICESCR.[263] While the ICESCR is a flexible treaty, it 'imposes an obligation to move as expeditiously and effectively as possible towards' the goal of 'the full realisation of the rights in question'.[264] The outside State can fulfil certain socio-economic rights without further reforms by ensuring the continuous operation of the existing social institutions. This was the case with Crimea, where Russia, after taking control over the area without armed resistence, was required to '[e]nsure the availability of education in the Ukrainian language'.[265] Other human rights might require the outside State to adopt reform measures in the 'grey zone'. For instance, an occupying State shall adopt both long-term policies to ensure the access of all children to a regular educational system in the occupied territory and, until such time, alternative educational frameworks as an interim solution.[266] In the matter of social security, it would be irrealistic to require the outside State to ensure the same contributory or insurance-based social benefits to persons in the 'grey zone' as in its own territory, especially if it does not dispose of the common fund to which those contributions were paid in the area. However, it is expected to ensure the right of access to social security on a non-discriminatory basis,[267] and to fulfil the core obligations to ensure

[262] CESCR, An evaluation of the obligation to take steps to the 'maximum of available resources' under an Optional Protocol to the Covenant. Statement, UN Doc. E/C.12/2007/1 (10 May 2007), para 4.

[263] Tristan Ferraro, 'The Law of Occupation and Human Rights Law: Some Selected Issues' in Robert Kolb and Gloria Gaggioli (eds), *Research Handbook on Human Rights and Humanitarian Law* (Edward Elgar 2013) 281.

[264] CESCR, General comment No. 3 (n 1), para 9.

[265] *Application of the International Convention for the Suppression of the Financing of Terrorism and of the International Convention on the Elimination of All Forms of Racial Discrimination (Ukraine v. Russian Federation)*, Provisional Measures, Order of 19 April 2017, *I.C.J. Reports* 2017, 140, para 106; in the same sense: CERD, Concluding observations: Russian Federation, UN Doc. CERD/C/RUS/CO/23-24 (20 September 2017), para 20; *Cyprus* v. *Turkey* [GC] (n 93), para 280.

[266] UN Doc. E/C.12/ISR/CO/3 (n 250), para 33.

[267] Ibid., para 17; CESCR, Concluding observations: Russian Federation, UN Doc. E/C.12/RUS/CO/6 (16 October 2017), para 10;

the right to social security under the ICESCR such as access to a (non-contributory) social security scheme that provides a minimum essential level of benefits to all individuals and families.[268] In a prolonged occupation, it may also be realistically required to adopt and implement a social security strategy and plan of action for the occupied territory.[269] In other words, a functional approach takes into account that the effectiveness of a stabilised situation allows the outside State for more reforms, whereas unstable or short-lived territorial control might realistically only allow for provisional, often humanitarian socio-economic services.

One of the characteristic obligations to fulfil in 'grey zones' is the obligation to contribute to the normalisation of the situation for the local population, on the model of the same obligation binding the territorial State (Section 3.1.6). The outside State is bound to secure 'normal, secure and equal conditions of life';[270] to provide for effective remedies;[271] to authorise direct contacts between the interested communities;[272] and to allow for the effective enjoyment of the freedom of movement through the issuance of passports and identity documents.[273] Likewise, the right to return of displaced persons supposes positive measures by the outside State, especially the establishment of a property claims mechanism.[274] An outside State controlling territory, if unable to fulfil human rights on its own, is required to seek assistance by other States or IOs. For instance, it is required to guarantee and facilitate the access of humanitarian organisations in support of individuals in need in the area.[275]

[268] CESCR, General comment no. 19: The right to social security (art. 9), UN Doc. E/C.12/GC/19 (4 February 2008), para 59(a).
[269] Ibid., para 59(d).
[270] UNGA Res. 62/243, UN Doc. A/RES/62/243 (25 April 2008), para 4.
[271] *Infra*, Chapter 7.
[272] Letter of the OSCE Minsk Group Co-Chairs to the OSCE Permanent Council on the OSCE Minsk Group fact-finding mission to the occupied territories of Azerbaijan surrounding Nagorno-Karabakh, in: UN Doc. A/59/747-S/2005/187 (21 March 2005), Annex I, 4.
[273] Guiding Principles on Internal Displacement (n 7), Principle 20; UNOHCHR, Situation of human rights in Crimea, 2014–2017 (n 259), 31, para 226(k).
[274] ECtHR, *Chiragov and Others* v. *Armenia (Merits)* [GC], Appl. no. 13216/05, judgment of 16 June 2015, para 199; Commission on Human Rights, Principles on housing and property restitution for refugees and displaced persons, UN Doc. E/CN.4/Sub.2/2005/17 (28 June 2005), Principles 12–13; CoE Parliamentary Assembly, Solving property issues of refugees and internally displaced persons, Resolution 1708 (2010), 28 January 2010, para 10.
[275] Guiding Principles on Internal Displacement (n 7), Principles 25(2)–25(3), 30; UN Doc. E/C.12/ISR/CO/3 (n 250), para 24; UNOHCHR, Report on the human rights situation in Ukraine, 15 May 2014, para 155(q).

3.3 The Limitations of Human Rights

Beyond their limited effectiveness, the territorial State and outside State may resort to certain lawful limitations of human rights. First, the general limitation clauses of human rights conventions ('provided by law, necessary to protect national security, public order' and so forth) provide for the criteria under which a State party may at any time restrict human rights. As they apply to normal circumstances, unrelated to the territorial situation, they will not be examined here. Second, in their practice States relied on two legal bases of limitations in 'grey zones': derogations (Section 3.3.1) and IHL (Section 3.3.2).[276] Derogation is understood as a lawful, unilateral non-application of some treaty obligations temporarily by a State party in a state of emergency. States in armed conflicts further invoked IHL as a limitation of their obligations under IHRL. As this part will demonstrate, States may in certain circumstances invoke these two lawful restrictions, while they cannot fully exempt the 'grey zone' of the protection of IHRL and must comply with the core of their obligations.

3.3.1 *Derogations*

Under several human rights conventions, the State may provisionally suspend the application of one or more human rights, to the extent strictly required by the exigencies of the situation, in time of a sufficiently grave crisis that threatens the community of the State, provided that such measures are not inconsistent with their other obligations under international law. This is the case of the ICCPR, the ECHR, the ACHR and the Arab Charter.[277] However, a certain number of rights are not derogable, either under the treaty provisions[278] or on the basis of an

[276] A third limitations that outside States oft invoked is obligations arising under Article 103 of the UN Charter. It suffices to note that international human rights treaty bodies have applied the harmonization approach (*infra*, Section 3.3.2) to reconcile obligations of UN member States under UNSC resolutions and the UN Charter as much as possible with States' obligations under IHRL. ECtHR, *Al-Jedda* v. *United Kingdom* [GC], Appl. no. 27021/08, judgment of 7 July 2011, paras 102, 109; *Nada* v. *Switzerland* [GC], Appl. no. 10593/08, judgment of 12 September 2012, para 170; HRC, *Nabil Sayadi and Patricia Vinck* v. *Belgium*, Communication No. 1472/2006, Views of 22 December 2008, UN Doc. CCPR/C/94/D/1472/2006 (29 December 2008), paras 10.3, 10.6.

[277] ECHR, Article 15(1); ICCPR, Article 4(1); ACHR, Article 27(1); Arab Charter on Human Rights, Tunis, 22 May 2004, Article 4(1).

[278] ECHR, Article 15(2); ICCPR, Article 4(2) and Second Optional Protocol, Article 6; ACHR, Article 27(2); Arab Charter on Human Rights, Article 4(c).

interpretation by the monitoring body.[279] The list of non-derogable rights differs according to the given human rights treaty (ICCPR, ECHR, ACHR, the Arab Charter) but some rights are considered non-derogable by all treaties: the prohibition of torture or cruel, inhuman or degrading treatment or punishment and the principle of legality in criminal law.[280] Furthermore, three out of four conventions consider non-derogable the right to life, the prohibition of slavery and the procedural guarantees of a fair trial or the presumption of innocence.[281] Beyond non-derogable rights, derogation cannot limit the application of fundamental guarantees of IHL either.[282] This protected scope of human rights constitutes the core of IHRL. Some human rights monitoring bodies justified non-derogable rights by their customary or *jus cogens* character,[283] which suggests that their category might evolve over time.

Article 15 of the ECHR only allows derogations '[i]n time of war or other public emergency threatening the life of the nation'. It is questionable whether State parties may derogate to rights beyond their borders, considering that an extraterritorial operation faces generally less 'public emergency threatening the life of the nation' than trouble within the State. So far, the Court has not established any clear precedent and no State has made a derogation in an extraterritorial context.[284] The fact that the ECtHR left open the possibility of derogation in some

[279] HRC, General comment No. 29: States of emergency (Article 4), UN Doc. CCPR/C/21/Rev.1/Add.11 (31 August 2001), paras 8 (certain aspects of the right to non-discrimination), 13 (acertain number of prohibitions of general international law), 15 (provisions related to procedural guarantees); HRC, General comment No. 32 Article 14: Right to equality before courts and tribunals and to a fair trial, UN Doc. CCPR/C/GC/32 (23 August 2007), para 6 (prohibition of restricting fair trial guarantees 'that would circumvent the protection of non-derogable rights'); ACtHPR, *The African Commission on Human and Peoples' Rights* v. *Libya*, App. No. 002/2013, judgment of 3 June 2016, para 77 (right to liberty and security; right to a fair trial).

[280] ECHR, Article 15(2); ICCPR, Article 4(2); ACHR, Article 27(2); Arab Charter on Human Rights, Article 4(c).

[281] Ibid. [282] HRC, General comment No. 29 (n 279), paras 9, 16.

[283] ACERWC, *Minority Rights Group International and SOS-Esclaves on behalf of Said Ould Salem and Yarg Ould Salem* v. *The Government of The Republic of Mauritania*, Communication No. 008/Com/002/2016, May 2017, para 80; Working Group on Arbitrary Detention, Opinion No. 10/2013 (USA), *Communication addressed to the Government on 6 February 2013 Concerning Mr. Obaidullah*, UN Doc. A/HRC/WGAD/2013/10 (25 July 2013), para 32.

[284] On the applicability of derogations to a colonial territory: *Greece* v. *the United Kingdom*, Appl. no. 176/56, Report of the Commission of Human Rights of 26 September 1958, 132–140.

extraterritorial cases[285] suggests that derogation may be made in situations outside the State's territory.[286] The ICJ and the Human Rights Committee also presume the applicability of Article 4 of the ICCPR in military operations abroad.[287] The main reason for this view, which seems to run *a priori* counter to the protection of human rights in extraterritorial troubles, is a realist consideration: 'applying the Convention, even seriously restricted, will be always preferable for a human rights defender to the perspective of not applying the Convention at all'.[288]

However, some human rights conventions do not allow for State parties to derogate from their treaty obligations during emergency situations. This is the case of the ACHPR,[289] which may 'be seen as an expression of the principle that the restriction of human rights is not a solution to national difficulties', 'especially for what is generally referred to as non-derogable rights', although the ACommHPR may take into account the difficulties faced in times of crisis.[290] It nonetheless foresees limitations on an *ad hoc* basis under Article 27(2) of the ACHPR, the general clause on limitations to the rights,[291] with the exception of non-derogeable rights.[292]

285 *Georgia* v. *Russia (II)*, Appl. no. 38263/08, decision of 13 December 2011 on the admissibility, para 73; *Hassan* v. *United Kingdom* [GC], Appl. no. 29750/09, judgment of 16 September 2014, para 104.

286 In the *Georgia* v. *Russia (II) (Merits)* case, however, the ECtHR noted 'the practice of the High Contracting Parties in not derogating under Article 15 of the Convention in situations where they have engaged in an international armed conflict outside their own territory'. Controversially, the Court concluded that 'this may be interpreted as the High Contracting Parties considering that in such situations, they do not exercise jurisdiction within the meaning of Article 1 of the Convention'. *Georgia* v. *Russia (II) (Merits)* (n 204), para 139.

287 *Wall* case (n 212), 178, para 106 and 192, para 136; in the same sense: HRC, Concluding observations: Israel, UN Doc. CCPR/C/79/Add.93 (18 August 1998), paras 4, 21; Concluding observations: Israel, UN Doc. CCPR/CO/78/ISR (21 August 2003), para 12; HRC, General comment No. 35 (n 65), para 65, note 185.

288 (translated by the author) Karagiannis (n 120) 62.

289 E.g. ACommHPR, *Commission nationale des droits de l'Homme et des libertés* v. *Chad* [English], Communication no. 74/92, 11 October 1995, para 21; *Constitutional Rights Project* v. *Nigeria*, Communication nos. 140/94, 141/94, 145/95, 15 November 1999, para 41.

290 ACommHPR, *Amnesty International, et al.* v. *Sudan*, Communications nos. 48/90-50/91-52/91-89/93, 15 November 1999, paras 42, 79.

291 *Media Rights Agenda, Constitutional Rights Project, Media Rights Agenda and Constitutional Rights Project* v. *Nigeria*, Communication nos. 105/93, 128/94, 130/94, 152/96, 31 October 1998, para 68.

292 *Kenneth Good* v. *Botswana*, Communication no. 313/05, 12–26 May 2010, para 175 (right to a fair trial); *Constitutional Rights Project* v. *Nigeria*, Communication nos. 140/94, 141/94, 145/95, 15 November 1999, para 38 (right to receive information).

States enjoy a wide margin of appreciation to decide both on the presence of the emergency and on the nature and scope of the derogations necessary to avert it,[293] but their discretion is not unlimited. To ensure that the measures only restrict human rights proportionately, human rights treaty bodies require States to limit the duration, geographic and material scope of the derogating measures to those strictly required by the exigencies of the situation.[294] To ensure the temporary nature and the objectivity of the derogation, the State is expected to regularly review the necessity and proportionality of derogation measures by an independent mechanism.[295] A State can derogate to certain rights in a conflict area,[296] but this must also be subject to the above-mentioned restrictions, including regular review. In summary, States can only derogate to certain rights to the extent strictly required by the exigencies of the situation and cannot exempt a region of the full scope of human rights.

3.3.2 *International Humanitarian Law*

Certain States for a long time have not ceased to contest the applicability of human rights conventions in times of armed conflict,[297] and the question of the relationship between IHL and IHRL stimulates a passionate academic debate. To the simpler question of the applicability of IHRL in times of war, international law has answered in the affirmative. Some international human rights conventions implicitly or explicitly recognise that they apply during armed conflicts.[298] The ICJ in several cases confirmed that human rights conventions continue to apply in armed

293 ECtHR, *Şahin Alpay* v. *Turkey*, Appl. no. 16538/17, judgment of 20 March 2018, para 75; *Mehmet Hasan Altan* v. *Turkey*, Appl. no. 13237/17, judgment of 20 March 2018, para 91; *Alparslan Altan* v. *Turkey*, Application no. 12778/17, judgment of 16 April 2019, para 116;

294 HRC, General comment No. 29 (n 279), paras 4–5; HRC, General comment No. 35 (n 65), para 65; *Alparslan Altan* v. *Turkey* (n 293), paras 116–119; *Mehmet Hasan Altan* v. *Turkey* (n 293), para 140; *Şahin Alpay* v. *Turkey* (n 293), para 119.

295 UNOHCHR, Report on the human rights situation in Ukraine, 16 May to 15 August 2017, para 182(l).

296 E.g. Notification: JJ7979C Tr./005-189 (10 June 2015), Ukraine. Derogation to the Convention on the Protection of Human Rights and Fundamental Freedoms (ETS No. 5).

297 E.g. Israel: HRC, Fourth periodic report: Israel, UN Doc. CCPR/C/ISR/4 (12 December 2013), paras 46–47; Russia: ECtHR, *Georgia* v. *Russia (II)*, Appl. no. 38263/08, decision of 13 December 2011 on the admissibility, para 69; Netherlands: Replies to the concluding observations, UN Doc. CCPR/CO/72/NET/Add.1 (29 April 2003), para 19; USA: HRC, Fourth periodic report: USA, UN Doc. CCPR/C/USA/4 (22 May 2012), paras 506–507.

298 CRC, Article 38; ACRWC, Article 22; CPPED, Article 43.

conflicts.[299] The ILC[300] and human rights monitoring bodies[301] have unanimously confirmed the simultaneous applicability of IHRL and IHL. In this regard, the decision of the ECtHR to find the ECHR inapplicable in the active phase of the hostilities in the *Georgia* v. *Russia (II) (Merits)* case can only be considered as an exception limited to the particular circumstances of this inter-State application.[302]

As to the second question, the relationship between IHRL and IHL, certain international lawyers invoked the principle of *lex specialis derogat legi generali* to settle the tension between IHL and IHRL, proposing the prevalence of IHL over IHRL.[303] Recent case law, however, refuted this approach: instead of a norm conflict that has to be settled by prioritising one set of norms over the other, a reconciliation of the two sets of norms at the level of the interpretation is more favourable. This is in line with the method of systemic integration under Article 31(3)(c) of the VCLT, and has been proposed as a tool to eliminate fragmentation of international law.[304] Most importantly, this is the approach that the ICJ adopted in its advisory opinion on the *Wall*:

As regards the relationship between international humanitarian law and human rights law, there are thus three possible situations: some rights may be exclusively matters of international humanitarian law; others may be exclusively matters of human rights law; yet others may be matters of both these branches of international law. In order to answer the question put to it, the Court will have

299 *Legality of the Threat or Use of Nuclear Weapons*, Advisory Opinion, *I.C.J. Reports* 1996, 240, para 25; *Wall* case (n 212), 178, para 106; *Armed Activities on the Territory of the Congo (Democratic Republic of the Congo* v. *Uganda)*, Provisional Measures, Order of 1 July 2000, *I.C.J. Reports* 2000, 129, para 47(3); *Georgia* v. *Russian Federation*, Provisional Measures (n 253), 387, para 112; *DRC* v. *Uganda* (n 46), 231, paras 178–180 and 243–244, paras 216–217.

300 ILC, Draft articles on the effects of armed conflicts on treaties, 2011, in: UN Doc. A/66/10 and Add.1 (2011), 175–178, Article 7 and Annex, (f) and its commentaries, ibid., 210–211, paras 47–51.

301 E.g. *Varnava* (n 171), para 185; *Hassan* (n 285), paras 77, 102–107; *Mapiripán Massacre* (n 92), paras 114–115; HRC, General comment No. 29 (n 279), paras 3, 9, 11, 16; HRC, General comment No. 31 (n 133), para 11; HRC, General comment No. 35 (n 65), paras 64–66.

302 *Georgia* v. *Russia (II) (Merits)* (n 204), paras 141, 143–144; *supra*, Section 2.1.1.4.

303 Michael Dennis, 'Non-Application of Civil and Political Rights Treaties Extraterritorially During Times of International Armed Conflict' (2007) 40 *Israel Law Review* 453, 482–486.

304 ILC, Fragmentation of International Law: Difficulties arising from the diversification and expansion of international law. Report of the Study Group of the International Law Commission. Finalized by Martti Koskenniemi, UN Doc. A/CN.4/L.682 (13 April 2006), paras 479–480.

to take into consideration both these branches of international law, namely human rights law and, as *lex specialis*, international humanitarian law.[305]

IHL sometimes provides on behaviours that IHRL does not govern, for example, the conduct of hostilities or the status of 'combatants' and 'prisoners of war'. In those cases there is no norm conflict in the strict sense and IHL provides for the regulatory framework. Other rights and freedoms not governed by IHL, such as the freedom of speech, the freedom of association or the right to social security, continue to be governed by IHRL.[306] As for rights and liberties that are simultaneously governed by the two branches of international law, IHL and IHRL provide for competing norms in the sense that they are 'supposed to apply to the same situations and the same recipients, leading to diverging positions'.[307] In case of such competing norms, the ICJ avoided settling the tension by prioritising one set of rules over the other, and chose a conciliatory approach, where one set of norms is interpreted in light of the other. While regarding IHL as *lex specialis* because of its scope of application (being restricted to armed conflicts) and specific object (regulation of the conduct of hostilities), the Court chose to interpret IHRL in light of IHL and not conversely.[308]

Most international human rights treaty bodies have followed this approach: they have had recourse to IHL as a source of interpretation for IHRL, in a complementary manner.[309] The African Charter even

305 *Wall* case (n 212), 178, para 106; IACtHR, *Santo Domingo Massacre* v. *Colombia*, judgment of 30 November 2012 (Preliminary Objections, Merits and Reparations), para 187; *Afro-descendant communities displaced from the Cacarica River Basin (Operation Genesis)* v. *Colombia*, judgment of 20 November 2013 (Preliminary Objections, Merits, Reparations and Costs), para 221.

306 Marco Sassòli, 'Article 43 of The Hague Regulations and Peace-Operations in the Twenty-First Century' (2004) Background Paper prepared for Informal High-Level Expert Meeting on Current Challenges to International Humanitarian Law 12 <www.hpcrresearch.org/sites/default/files/publications/sassoli.pdf> accessed 25 August 2013.

307 Jean D'Aspremont and Elodie Tranchez, 'The Quest for a Non-conflictual Coexistence of International Human Rights Law and Humanitarian Law: Which Role for the Lex Specialis Principle?' in Robert Kolb and Gloria Gaggioli (eds), *Research Handbook on Human Rights and Humanitarian Law* (Edward Elgar 2013) 233.

308 Ibid., 239–241; *Legality of the Threat or Use of Nuclear Weapons* (n 299), 240, para 25.

309 HRC, General comment No. 31 (n 133), para 11; *Varnava* (n 171), para 185; *Hassan* (n 285), para 102; *Galindo* (n 231), para 325; *Santo Domingo Massacre* (n 305), para 187; *Afro-descendant communities* … (n 305), paras 221–222, 349; ACommHPR, *Democratic Republic of Congo* v. *Burundi, Rwanda and Uganda*, Communication no. 227/99, 15–29 May 2003, paras 84, 86–89; ACommHPR, General comment No. 3 on the African Charter on Human and Peoples' Rights: The Right to Life (Article 4), 4–18 November 2015, para 13.

obliges the African human rights treaty bodies to draw inspiration from IHL that the ACommHPR considered as 'part of the general principles of law recognised by African States'.[310] While applying IHL as an interpretative source, the Inter-American bodies expressly recognise that in armed conflicts it is a *lex specialis*,[311] whereas the ECtHR implicitly, and more recently even expressly takes it into consideration.[312]

Having said that, the complementary application of IHL to interpret IHRL is not unproblematic. Even if the dominant approach is followed, the use of IHL as a guidance to interpret IHRL, it remains to be decided which sources of and to what extent IHL can shape the interpretation of IHRL. One may choose customary IHL,[313] or humanitarian treaties binding the State, or even humanitarian treaties not binding the State[314] as interpretative guidance. This interpretative process also supposes that the guiding sources of IHL are selected according to whether the relevant armed conflict is classified as international or non-international. International human rights monitoring bodies might feel uncomfortable to decide on such complex questions if the factual situation is unclear and requires an analysis of attribution. A good example of the importance of conflict classification is the *Savchenko* v. *Russia* case about the legality of the detention of the applicant, a servicewoman of the Ukrainian Air Force captured in June 2014 by *de facto* armed groups operating near Luhansk and subsequently detained by the Russian authorities.[315] Depending on whether the ECtHR considers the armed conflict in Eastern Ukraine international or non-international armed conflict, the outcome of the case could be entirely different. In an

[310] Based on Articles 60–61 of the ACHPR: *DRC* v. *Burundi, Rwanda, Uganda* (n 309), paras 70, 78; ACommHPR, General comment No. 4 (n 174), para 63 (*a contrario*: para 64, recommending the more favourable set of norms).

[311] *Coard et al.* v. *United States*, Report No. 109/99, Case 10.951, Merits, 29 September 1999, para 42; *Gregoria Herminia et al.* v. *El Salvador*, Report No. 11/05, Petition 708/03, Admissibility, 23 February 2005, para 20; *Galindo* (n 231), para 325; *Santo Domingo Massacre* (n 305), para 187; *Afro-descendant communities* . . . (n 305), para 221.

[312] E.g. the examination of the criteria 'absolutely necessary', proportionate and reasonable use of the force: *Ergi* v. *Turkey*, Appl. no. 66/1997/850/1057, judgment of 28 July 1998, para 79; *Issayeva* v. *Russia*, Appl. no. 57950/00, judgment of 24 February 2005, paras 169–171, 181; for an explicit consideration: *Hassan* (n 285); *Georgia* v. *Russia (II) (Merits)* (n 204), paras 92–95, 194–199, 234–237, 266–267, 278, 290–291, 310–311, 323–325, 331.

[313] *Galindo* (n 231), para 341.

[314] Ibid., para 346.

[315] *Nadia Savchenko* v. *Russia*, Appl. no. 50171/14, in: Press release, CEDH 055 (2015), 13 February 2015.

international armed conflict the applicant would be considered a prisoner of war, and her internment by Russia would be authorised under the rules of Geneva Convention (GC) III,[316] whereas in the contrary case her detention would be subject to the rules of non-international armed conflict which, subject to academic debates, might not contain any authorisation to intern.[317]

The other subsequent difficulty is to decide the extent to which IHL can shape the interpretation of IHRL. While the armed conflict does not exempt State parties from their obligations under IHRL, it can limit the modality of the protection guaranteed by the State. As the Special Rapporteur on Extrajudicial, Summary or Arbitrary Executions emphasised, '[o]n a case-by-case basis a State might utilise less effective measures of investigation in response to concrete constraints. For example, when hostile forces control the scene of a shooting, conducting an autopsy may prove impossible'.[318] It is in this sense that the ECtHR recognised in the *Al-Skeini* case that 'in circumstances of generalised violence, armed conflict or insurgency, obstacles may be placed in the way of investigators and ... concrete constraints may compel the use of less effective measures of investigation or may cause an investigation to be delayed'.[319] It concluded that 'the procedural duty under Article 2 must be applied realistically, to take account of specific problems faced by investigators'.[320]

In the *Hassan* v. *United Kingdom* case (2014), the ECtHR for the first time expressly recognised that, without formal derogation, a limitation of the Convention rights may result from the context of an international armed conflict, under the applicable rules of IHL.[321] Specifically regarding the limitation of the right to liberty and security (Article 5), beyond the grounds of permitted detention already set out in the Convention (Article 5(1)), the Court held that IHL can limit the right to liberty and security under the following conditions: (i) to be 'lawful' pursuant to powers under IHL, the deprivation of liberty must comply with the rules of IHL and, most importantly, it should be in keeping with the

[316] GC III, Article 21.

[317] Lawrence Hill-Cawthorne, 'Humanitarian Law, Human Rights Law and the Bifurcation of Armed Conflict' (2015) 64 *International & Comparative Law Quarterly* 293, 309.

[318] Extrajudicial, summary or arbitrary executions, Report of the Special Rapporteur, Philip Alston, UN Doc. E/CN.4/2006/53 (8 March 2006), para 36.

[319] *Al-Skeini* (n 213), para 164.

[320] Ibid., para 168.

[321] *Hassan* (n 285), paras 103–107; The dissidents call this novelty the 'method of "*accommodation*" of Convention rights'. See ibid., Partly dissenting opinion of Judge Spano, joined by Judges Nicolaou, Bianku and Kalaydjieva, para 18.

fundamental purpose of Article 5(1), which is to protect the individual from arbitrariness; (ii) as regards procedural safeguards, Articles 5(2) and (4) must also be interpreted in a manner that takes into account the context and the applicable rules of IHL and which provides sufficient guarantees of impartiality and fair procedure to protect against arbitrariness; (iii) finally, the provisions of Article 5 will be interpreted and applied in light of the relevant provisions of IHL only where this is specifically pleaded by the respondent State.[322] Since in the instant case the Court considered the challenged capture and detention consistent with the powers available to the UK under GC III and IV, and thus not arbitrary, it found no violation of Article 5.

Other treaty bodies have also followed the contextual approach of the *Hassan* case. The Human Rights Committee also recognised that '[d]uring international armed conflict, substantive and procedural rules of international humanitarian law remain applicable and limit the ability to derogate, thereby helping to mitigate the risk of arbitrary detention'.[323] Likewise, the Human Rights Committee took into account, in the context of the territorial State's duty to investigate, 'the particular difficulties that a State party may face in investigating crimes that may have been committed on its territory by the hostile forces of a foreign State'.[324]

Taking into account the existence of an armed conflict and IHL as a limitation of human rights, the approach of human rights treaty bodies is a convenient solution that accommodates, as far as possible, human rights within the context of war. It reconciles the differences between two sets of rules, IHRL and IHL, on the one hand, and the limited effectiveness that the State faces in an armed conflict, on the other. Despite the limitation, the heart of obligations such as the independence of the investigation must be respected.[325]

3.4 Concluding Remarks

The obligation of due diligence requires the State to protect human rights within its jurisdiction against acts committed by third parties to an extent that could be reasonably expected of it. The territorial State,

[322] Ibid., paras 105–107. [323] HRC, General comment No. 35 (n 65), para 66.

[324] HRC, *Emina Kožljak and Sinan Kožljak* v. *Bosnia-Herzegovina*, Communication No. 1970/2010, UN Doc. CCPR/C/112/D/1970/2010 (1 December 2014), para 9.5; *Tija Hero, Ermina Hero, Armin Hero* v. *Bosnia-Herzegovina*, Communication No. 1966/2010, UN Doc. CCPR/C/112/D/1966/2010 (27 November 2014), para 9.5.

[325] *Al-Skeini* (n 213), paras 164, 170–175.

while lacking effective control over the area, is expected to invest in strengthening its effectiveness towards individuals in the 'grey zone'. The outside State exercising effective control over the area has obligations comparable to those binding it within its national territory. These obligations may be limited in line with the functional approach, under which the burden imposed on the State is proportionate to the authority and control exercised in the area. The limitations of the States' obligations furthermore result from the context of an emergency, under a formal derogation or the application of IHL. While such limitations can restrict the modalities of the protection provided by the State, they cannot decrease the heart of the obligations under human rights conventions.

Ideally, the obligations of the territorial State and those of the outside State exercising effective control over the area complement each other and contribute to the effectiveness of human rights. On the one hand, the territorial State has a 'primary responsibility': it is responsible for human rights of individuals situated in its national territory.[326] On the other hand, it is the outside State exercising territorial control that has more effectiveness to respect, protect and fulfil human rights. Consequently, the obligations of the territorial State are complementary and always parallel to the obligations of the outside State.

[326] On the concept of 'Responsibility to protect', *supra*, Section 2.2.2.4; e.g. UNGA Res. 62/134, UN Doc. A/RES/62/134 (7 February 2008), preamble, para 13; UN Doc. S/RES/2016 (24 June 2013), para 7.

4 The Human Rights Obligations of Non-state Actors

The previous chapters have demonstrated that IHRL applies to areas outside the effective control of the State, obliging both the territorial State and the outside State controlling the territory. This chapter explains that IHRL also binds non-state actors when they exercise effective control over the territory and imposes on them positive obligations in accordance with their effectiveness. In other terms, beyond the question of the territorial applicability of IHRL in the 'grey zone', a further question is whether it is binding (or, in French, *opposable*) *vis-à-vis* non-state entities, especially peace operations and *de facto* regimes. While international human rights conventions as a main rule oblige only State parties, they might be 'opposable', that is, produce legal effects[1] towards non-parties including non-state actors. The Human Rights Committee clearly expressed this difference between the treaty's territorial applicability and its binding character (the French *opposabilité*) towards a non-state actor: it noted that, while, instead of a State party, the United Nations Interim Administration Mission in Kosovo (UNMIK) *de facto* controlled Kosovo, 'the Covenant continues to apply in Kosovo'.[2] Beyond the opposability of human rights treaties, customary international human rights law might also impose obligations on non-state actors.

Nonetheless, two features of IHRL run against its opposability towards non-state actors. First, rules of IHRL traditionally protect individuals against the arbitrary exercise of public power by the State. Second,

[1] Jean Salmon, *Dictionnaire de droit international public* (Bruylant 2001) 782; V. D. Degan, *Sources of International Law* (M Nijhoff 1997) 339–343, para 70.

[2] HRC, Concluding observations: Serbia, UN Doc. CCPR/C/SRB/CO/2 (20 May 2011), para 3; HRC, Concluding observations: Serbia and Montenegro, UN Doc. CCPR/CO/81/SEMO (12 August 2004), para 3.

human rights treaties are almost exclusively open for signature by States. However, the fact that non-state actors increasingly exercise public authority over individuals modifies both features. As this chapter explains, IHRL increasingly imposes obligations on any authority exercising power of which abuse it aims to prevent – this also results from its philosophical inspiration.

Chapter 1 explained that non-state actors discussed in the book, peace operations established by international organisations (IOs) and *de facto* regimes have international legal personality, as they have independence, they are capable to and do possess international rights and obligations. This chapter identifies various legal bases under which non-state actors can be addressees of IHRL. Among those possible legal bases, the *de facto* control theory is the most widely-accepted explanation under which territorial control irrespective of the legal title instigates certain obligations. The doctrine is already present in contemporary international law, confirmed by the famous holding of the ICJ that '[p]hysical control of a territory, and not sovereignty or legitimacy of title, is the basis of State liability for acts affecting other States'.[3] Beyond general international law, human rights monitoring bodies and political organs of IOs addressed a high number of recommendations to local authorities exercising territorial control independently of their legal status, whether States or non-state actors.[4]

An entity's ability to possess rights and obligations under international law, however, is not uniform but is determined according to factors specific to that entity.[5] Thus, even if one accepts that certain norms of IHRL bind non-state actors, some obligations of States cannot be adapted to the context of non-state actors, whereas others can be imposed on them *mutatis mutandis*. These preliminary considerations raise the question of the specificity of the obligations of non-state entities compared to those of States.

[3] *Legal consequences for States of the continued presence of South Africa in Namibia (South West Africa) notwithstanding Security Council resolution 276 (1970)*, Advisory Opinion, *I.C.J. Reports* 1971, 54, para 118.

[4] E.g. Guiding Principles on Internal Displacement, UN Doc. E/CN.4/1998/53/Add.2 (16 October 1998), Preamble para 3(c)–(d), Principle 2(1); Report of the UNOHCHR on the question of human rights in Cyprus, UN Doc. A/HRC/25/21 (22 January 2014), para 11, note 13 (see the sources cited there).

[5] *Reparation for injuries suffered in the service of the United Nations*, Advisory Opinion, *I.C.J. Reports* 1949, 178; *Legality of the Use by a State of Nuclear Weapons in Armed Conflict*, Advisory Opinion, *I.C.J. Reports* 1996, 78, para 25.

The present chapter answers two questions: first, whether IHRL has a binding effect on peace operations (Section 4.1) and *de facto* regimes (Section 4.2); and, second, in the affirmative, what the specificity of their obligations is.

4.1 The Obligations of Peace Operations

Peace operations, as organs of IOs, are bound by the international law obligations of the relevant IO unless there is a properly-established indication to the contrary.[6] Conversely, an obligation binding the peace operation should bind the entire organisation as well.[7] IHRL may bind a peace operation either on account of certain sources of international law of which elaboration the given IO did not participate in, called 'extrinsic sources' (Section 4.1.1), or on account of legal acts elaborated by the peace operation itself, called 'intrinsic sources' (Section 4.1.2). While those sources might lead to different thresholds of obligations, they all enshrine a core group of obligations in line with the *de facto* control theory. This core group relates to the obligation to ensure public order and safety which applies *mutatis mutandis* to peace operations as a customary obligation (Section 4.1.3). The obligations of peace operations under IHRL have further specificities in terms of the restrictions of human rights (Section 4.1.4).

4.1.1 Extrinsic Sources

Among extrinsic sources, customary international law and general principles of law (Section 4.1.1.1), on the one hand, and international human rights treaties (Section 4.1.1.2), on the other, may impose obligations on peace operations in IHRL. As this section argues, an evolving body of general international law imposes obligations of human rights on IOs, while the formal bindingness of human rights treaties on peace operations does not in practice play a significant role.

[6] Draft articles on the law of treaties between States and international organizations or between international organizations with commentaries, 1982, in: *YbILC*, 1982, vol. II (Part Two) [VCLT-II Commentaries], 40, para 3; Draft articles on the responsibility of international organizations, with commentaries, *YbILC*, 2011, vol. II (Part Two) [DARIO Commentaries], 55, Draft Article 6(1).

[7] VCLT-II Commentaries (n 6), 40, para 3.

4.1.1.1 Customary International Law and General Principles of Law

As a subsidiary organ of an IO, the peace operation is bound by customary international law and general principles of law.[8] The ICJ recognised that '[i]nternational organizations are subjects of international law and, as such, are bound by any obligations incumbent upon them under general rules of international law'.[9] As a derived subject of international law, an IO is automatically bound by the rules of general international law, even though not all customs may bind it. The ICJ also held that 'the rights and duties of an entity such as the Organization must depend upon its purposes and functions as specified or implied in its constituent documents and developed in practice'.[10] This 'relative binding effect'[11] of the custom not necessarily leads to the lack of binding effect of a customary norm *vis-à-vis* an IO, which is rare, but most often to an adjustment of its legal effect to the institutional requirements of the IO.[12] It must be examined whether and how this 'relative binding effect' operates in the case of customary international human rights norms.

In IHRL two remarks seem important: first, some customary norms, by reason of their content, are hardly applicable to IOs, which is the consequence of the functional legal personality of the IO.[13] The rights to a nationality and to diplomatic protection – if there is such a human rights obligation – are only relevant in the context of States which a peace operation cannot exercise.[14] However, most customary norms may be adapted to peace operations controlling territory.[15] For instance, the ICJ

[8] DARIO Commentaries (n 6), 84–85, para 3; ICC, *The Prosecutor* v. *Germain Katanga and Mathieu Ngudjolo Chui*, Decision on an Amicus Curiae application, ICC-01/04-01/07, 9 June 2011, paras 67–70 (the ICC recognised itself bound by the customary norms of non-refoulement and the right to effective remedy).

[9] *Interpretation of the Agreement of 25 March 1951 between the WHO and Egypt*, Advisory Opinion, *I.C.J. Reports* 1980, 89–90, para 37.

[10] *Reparation for injuries suffered in the service of the United Nations*, Advisory Opinion, *I.C.J. Reports* 1949, 180.

[11] Gérard Cahin, *La coutume internationale et les organisations internationales: l'incidence de la dimension institutionnelle sur le processus coutumier* (Pedone 2001) 520–527.

[12] Ibid.

[13] Mathias Forteau, 'Organisations internationales et sources du droit' in Évelyne Lagrange and Jean-Marc Sorel (eds), *Droit des organisations internationales* (LGDJ-Lextenso éditions 2013) 272; Robert Kolb, Gabriele Porretto and Sylvain Vité, *L'application du droit international humanitaire et des droits de l'homme aux organisations internationales: forces de paix et administrations civiles transitoires* (Bruylant 2005) 256–257.

[14] DARIO Commentaries (n 6), 86, para 2.

[15] UNOHCHR, *International Legal Protection of Human Rights in Armed Conflict* (United Nations 2011) 29.

held that the obligation of non-recognition and non-assistance in an unlawful situation resulting from a serious breach of *jus cogens* binds not only States but also organs of the UN.[16] The UN administrative tribunals recognised various rights under the Universal Declaration of Human Rights (UDHR) as customary international norms binding the UN, such as the right to a fair trial[17] or the principle of 'equal pay for equal work'.[18] If one accepts that IOs are bound by customary international law to the extent that they exercise certain functions that may be assimilated to the exercise of jurisdiction by the State,[19] it follows that international territorial administrations, on account of their exercise of public powers, are bound by customary norms of IHRL. The same remarks are equally applicable to general principles of law: they apply, when it is reasonable, to an IO. For example, the principle of equal access to tribunals or the right to be heard are considered general principles of law applicable to IOs.[20] Furthermore, peremptory norms oblige peace operations in the same way as States.[21] The UN itself recognised its obligations under *jus cogens* norms, such as the principle of the best interests of the child.[22]

In IHRL, non-derogable rights certainly have a customary character.[23] Another customary norm of particular importance is the obligation of the occupying power to respect, 'unless absolutely prevented, the laws in

[16] *Legal Consequences of the Construction of a Wall in the Occupied Palestinian Territory*, Advisory Opinion, *I.C.J. Reports* 2004, 200, paras 159–160.

[17] E.g. UN Dispute Tribunal, *Samoulada* v. *Secretary-General of the United Nations*, UNDT/GVA/2017/057, 30 August 2017, paras 14–15; *Chaoui, Kalotay & Richards* v. *Secretary-General of the United Nations*, UNDT/2018/097, judgment on recevability, 2 October 2018, paras 29–30.

[18] UN Appeals Tribunal, *Tabari* v. *Commissioner General of the United Nations Relief and Works Agency for Palestine Refugees*, 2010-UNAT-030, 30 March 2010, paras 17, 21.

[19] Tobias H. Irmscher, 'The Legal Framework for the Activities of the United Nations Administration Mission in Kosovo: The Charter, Human Rights, and the Law of Occupation' (2001) 44 *German Yearbook of International Law* 353, 370; Ioannis Prezas, *L'administration de collectivités territoriales par les Nations Unies: étude de la substitution de l'organisation internationale à l'État dans l'exercice des pouvoirs de gouvernement* (Anthemis 2012) 440.

[20] Forteau (n 13) 275.

[21] Fourth report on responsibility of international organizations, by Giorgio Gaja, Special Rapporteur, UN Doc. A/CN.4/564 (28 February 2006), para 47; VCLT-II Commentaries (n 6), 56, para 2.

[22] UN Dispute Tribunal, *Benamar* v. *Secretary-General of the United Nations*, UNDT/2017/025, 10 April 2017, para 91.

[23] *Supra*, Section 3.3.1.

force in the country' (Article 43 of The Hague Regulation).[24] While it is contested whether the law of occupation applies to peace operations controlling a territory,[25] at least some of its customary rules, especially the obligation to ensure public order and safety (Article 43 of The Hague Regulations) and the provisions on the protection of persons in occupied territory (Articles 47–78 of the Convention (IV) Relative to the Protection of Civilian Persons in Time of War (GC IV)) are applicable by analogy to IOs controlling territory. The basis of this analogy is that those rules aim at protecting individuals *vis-à-vis* a 'mere administrator of fact' other than the territorial State.[26] The practice of IOs confirms this analogy: the UN itself recognises that peacekeeping operations with an executive mandate that 'act as a substitute or partial substitute for, host-State police capacity' are committed to 'maintain public order and safety in adherence to the rule of law and international human rights law'.[27] The application of customary norms of the law of occupation to an IO also is not unprecedented: the UN derived from Article 52 of The Hague Regulation the right to compensation of owners whose properties were requisitioned by the forces of a peacekeeping operation.[28]

When different non-binding instruments stipulate on the requirement to respect human rights by IOs,[29] they seem to refer to general international law. While the content of customary law is controversial, the core of human rights is binding on all subjects of international law,

[24] *Armed Activities on the Territory of the Congo (Democratic Republic of the Congo* v. *Uganda)*, judgment, *I.C.J. Reports* 2005, 244, para 219.

[25] Expert meeting on multinational peace operations. Applicability of International Humanitarian Law and International Human Rights Law to UN Mandated Forces Geneva, 11–12 December 2003, ICRC/University Centre for International Humanitarian Law, Report, 2004, at www.icrc.org/en/doc/assets/files/other/icrc_002_0912.pdf (14 March 2020), 13–17.

[26] Sylvain Vité, 'L'applicabilité Du Droit International de l'occupation Militaire Aux Activités Des Organisations Internationales' (2004) 86 *International Review of the Red Cross* 9, 31–32; Marco Sassòli, 'Legislation and Maintenance of Public Order and Civil Life by Occupying Powers' (2005) 16 *European Journal of International Law* 661, 691.

[27] Report of the Secretary-General on United Nations policing, UN Doc. S/2016/952 (10 November 2016), para 8.

[28] Memorandum to the Under-Secretary-General for Peacekeeping Operations, in: *UNJYB*, 1994, Part Two, Chapter VI, 403–406, esp. paras 20–23.

[29] Opinion of the United Nations Legal Counsel, cited in: DARIO Commentaries (n 6), 66, para 6; CoE Parlimentary Assembly, Resolution 1979 (2014) and Recommendation 2037 (2014), Accountability of international organisations for human rights violations, 31 January 2014; European Commission for Democracy through Law (Venice Commission), Opinion on Human Rights in Kosovo: Possible establishment of review mechanisms, Opinion no. 280/2004, CDL-AD(2004)033-e (11 October 2004), para 78.

including IOs: non-derogable rights constitute such a legal body, at least those protected under *jus cogens* and the customary norms of IHL.

4.1.1.2 International Human Rights Treaties

While international human rights treaties traditionally are open only to States, certain treaties foresee accession by IOs. One of these exceptions is the Convention on the Rights of Persons with Disabilities (CRPD), open for signature and accession by all States and 'regional integration organisations'.[30] Actually, the only regional integration organisation having signed and ratified the Convention is the European Union (EU) which actively participated in its negotiation.[31] Other conventions open for accession by the EU include the ECHR[32] and a few Council of Europe (CoE) treaties.[33] The technical implementation of the EU's accession to the ECHR has been problematic but remains on the EU's agenda,[34] while the EU has signed but not yet ratified the CoE Convention on Preventing and Combating Violence against Women and Domestic Violence.[35]

Even without formal accession, the IO may subject itself to the legal regime of the human rights convention through an *ad hoc* arrangement concluded with the treaty supervisory body, which does have precedents in the international administration of Kosovo. That is the case of the Framework Convention for the Protection of National Minorities and the European Convention for the Prevention of Torture and Inhuman or Degrading Treatment or Punishment, which UNMIK has applied under an agreement concluded with the CoE in 2004.[36] Under the agreement,

[30] CRPD, Articles 42–43.

[31] The EU signed the Convention on 30 March 2007 and confirmed it formally on 23 December 2010. United Nations, *Treaty Series*. However, it has not signed the Optional Protocol, equally open for accession by IOs: OP-CRPD, Article 11.

[32] Protocol No. 14 to the Convention for the Protection of Human Rights and Fundamental Freedoms, amending the control system of the Convention, CETS No. 194, Strasbourg, 13 May 2004, Article 17; TEU, Article 6(2)–6(3).

[33] E.g. European Convention on the Exercise of Children's Rights, CETS No. 160, Strasbourg, 25 January 1996, Article 22(1); CoE Convention on Action against Trafficking in Human Beings, CETS No. 197, Warsaw, 16 May 2005, Article 42(1); CoE Convention on Preventing and Combating Violence against Women and Domestic Violence, CETS No. 210, Istanbul, 11 May 2011, Article 75(1).

[34] The Court of Justice of the EU held that the negotiated agreement on the accession of the EU to the ECHR was not compatible with Article 6(2) TEU or with Protocol (No 8). Opinion 2/13 (Full Court) [2014] ECLI:EU:C:2014:2454.

[35] CoE, The European Union signs the Istanbul Convention, at www.coe.int/en/web/genderequality/-/european-union-signs-the-istanbul-convention (19 June 2017).

[36] Agreement between the UNMIK and the CoE on technical arrangements related to the Framework Convention for the Protection of National Minorities, Strasbourg, 23 August

UNMIK affirmed 'on behalf of itself and the Provisional Institutions of Self-Government that their respective responsibilities will be exercised in compliance with the principles contained in the Framework Convention'.[37] The agreement related to the European anti-torture convention authorises the anti-torture Committee to visit any place within Kosovo where persons are deprived of liberty by UNMIK, under the same conditions as provided for in the Convention. In 2006, the North Atlantic Treaty Organisation (NATO) and the CoE concluded a similar agreement on the modalities of the inspections to NATO-run Kosovo Force (KFOR) detention facilities.[38] Nevertheless, these agreements provide that they do not make UNMIK a party to the given convention and that they are concluded without prejudice to the future status of Kosovo to be determined in accordance with UN Security Council (UNSC) Resolution 1244 (1999).[39] Consequently, the pragmatic solution found is not a formal accession but an acceptance of the applicability of these treaties and cooperation at the level of their implementation. The solution amounts to a *de facto* binding effect of the treaty's substantive norms because the technical agreements imposed the same obligations on the IO as the relevant conventions.

In sum, human rights treaties rarely foresee accession by IOs but their bindingness on peace operations may be based on *ad hoc* arrangements. Beyond those treaties, an evolving body of general international law imposes obligations of human rights on IOs. As has been explained, the content of customary human rights norms is limited to non-derogable rights, norms of *jus cogens* and, in the case of an armed conflict, customary IHL. Furthermore, IOs can unilaterally accept these guarantees in intrinsic sources.

4.1.2 *Intrinsic Sources*

The intrinsic sources or, in other terms, the 'rules of the organisation',[40] are of two types: rules concerning all the IOs in their entirety (Section

2004, CoE, 890th meeting (30 June 2004), Appendix 2 [Agreement on technical arrangements related to the FCPNM]; Agreement between the UNMIK and the CoE on technical arrangements related to the European Convention for the Prevention of Torture and Inhuman or Degrading Treatment or Punishment, Pristina, 23 August 2004 [Agreement on technical arrangements related to the ECPT].

37 Agreement on technical arrangements related to the FCPNM (n 36), Article 1.

38 CPT, Press Release, CoE Anti-Torture Committee gains access to NATO-run detention facilities in Kosovo, at www.cpt.coe.int/documents/srb/2006-07-19-eng.htm (3 May 2010).

39 Agreement on technical arrangements related to the FCPNM (n 36), Preamble, para 9; Agreement on technical arrangements related to the ECPT (n 36), Preamble, para 7.

40 DARIO Commentaries (n 6), Draft Article 2(b).

4.1.2.1), and those specifically concerning peace operations (Section 4.1.2.2). As this section will show, peace operations controlling territory committed themselves to guaranteeing a series of international treaties and instruments of IHRL in the area.

4.1.2.1 Rules concerning the Entire Organisation

IOs and especially the UN have adopted a variety of rules providing for their obligations to respect human rights, without specifying which norms, namely, which human rights conventions are applicable. This is the case of the constitutive acts and other internal rules adopted by the IO.

The constitutive act of the organisation, especially Articles 1(3) and 55 (c) of the UN Charter, provide for the protection of human rights among the purposes of the organisation. Several authors consider these a source of the UN's obligations to respect human rights,[41] while others regard them as programmatic and too general without a binding effect.[42] Both opinions are defendable. On the one hand, the purposes and principles of the Charter are binding on the UN.[43] On the other hand, UN peace operations cannot be expected to satisfy these requirements without further internal specification of the IHRL rules binding the UN.

The same applies *mutatis mutandis* to constitutive acts of IOs that express in similar general terms their commitment to human rights standards: that of NATO refers to the UN Charter,[44] while that of the African Union (AU) to human rights, the UDHR and the 'African Charter on Human and Peoples' Rights and other relevant human rights

[41] Geir Ulfstein, 'Les activités normatives de l'organisation internationale' in Évelyne Lagrange and Jean-Marc Sorel (eds), *Droit des organisations internationales* (LGDJ-Lextenso éditions 2013) 753–754; Mathias Forteau, 'Le droit applicable en matière des droits de l'homme aux administrations territoriales gérées par des organisations internationales' in Hervé Ascensio and Jean-François Flauss (eds), *La soumission des organisations internationales aux normes internationales relatives aux droits de l'homme* (Société française pour le droit international, Pedone 2009) 17–18.

[42] Kolb, Porretto and Vité (n 13) 258; Prezas (n 19) 440–441.

[43] UN Charter, Article 24(2); *Namibia* AO (n 3), 57, para 131; *United States Diplomatic and Consular Staff in Tehran*, judgment, *I.C.J. Reports* 1980, 42, para 91; CJEU, *Yassin Abdullah Kadi* v. *Council of the European Union and Commission of the European Communities*, case T-315/01, judgment of 21 September 2005, paras 228–229; CJEU, *Ahmed Ali Yusuf et Al Barakaat International Foundation* v. *Council of the European Union and Commission of the European Communities*, case T-306/01, judgment of 21 September 2005, paras 279–280.

[44] The North Atlantic Treaty, Washington, 4 April 1949, Preamble.

instruments'.[45] The Treaty on the EU goes well beyond those other treaties, as it declares not only in principle its commitment to human rights and fundamental freedoms but provides that the Charter of Fundamental Rights of the EU binds the institutions and bodies of the Union.[46]

Among the internal rules, numerous codes of conduct of the UN[47] and the AU[48] declare the expectation to respect human rights. For the sake of legal certainty, an express and binding undertaking by the UN is desirable.[49] Such a declaration exists in the domain of IHL, where the Secretary-General specified the IHL norms applicable to the UN forces in situations of armed conflict.[50] Regarding IHRL, the Convention on the Safety of United Nations and Associated Personnel provides for instance that '[n]othing in this Convention shall affect' the applicability of 'universally recognized standards of human rights as contained in international instruments in relation to the protection of United Nations operations and United Nations and associated personnel or the responsibility of such personnel to respect such law and standards'.[51] The UN and other IOs should replace such general clauses by an express and binding reference to the universally-ratified human rights conventions,[52] that is, the International Covenant on Civil and Political Rights (ICCPR), the International Covenant on Economic, Social and Cultural Rights (ICESCR), the International Convention on the Elimination of All Forms of Racial Discrimination

45 Constitutive Act of the African Union, Lome, 11 July 2000, Article 3(e), (h); Protocol relating to the Establishment of the Peace and Security Council of the African Union, Article 4(c) (UDHR).

46 TEU, Preamble, paragraphs nos. 2, 4, 5, Articles 2, 3(5), 6; Charter of Fundamental Rights of the European Union, Article 51(1).

47 E.g. Staff Regulations of the United Nations, UN Doc. ST/SGB/2009/6 (27 May 2009), Article 1.2(a); Ten rules: Code of personal conduct for blue helmets, para 5; United Nations Peacekeeping Operations: Principles and Guidelines, UN DPO Operations Department of Field Support, January 2008, 14–15, 27; Handbook on policing in peacekeeping operations, United Nations Department of Peacekeeping Operations, 2005 (first published in 1995), 20, para 4.4.

48 African Union policy on conduct and discipline for peace support operations, 3 December 2018 (adopted at the 813th Meeting of the Peace and Security Council of the AU), para 4.1.

49 Ray Murphy, *UN Peacekeeping in Lebanon, Somalia and Kosovo: Operational and Legal Issues in Practice* (Cambridge University Press 2007) 286; Kolb, Porretto and Vité (n 13) 245.

50 Secretary-General's Bulletin: Observance by United Nations forces of international humanitarian law, UN Doc. ST/SGB/1999/13 (6 August 1999), esp. Articles 1.1, 6.2, 8 (GC III).

51 Convention on the Safety of United Nations and Associated Personnel, New York, 9 December 1994, Article 20(a).

52 Andrew Clapham, *Human Rights Obligations of Non-State Actors* (Oxford University Press 2006) 123–124.

(CERD), the Convention on the Elimination of All Forms of Discrimination against Women (CEDAW), the Convention against Torture and Other Cruel, Inhuman or Degrading Treatment or Punishment (CAT) and the Convention on the Rights of the Child (CRC) and, eventually, three other universal human rights treaties, the Convention on the Rights of Persons with Disabilities (CRPD), the International Convention on the Protection of the Rights of All Migrant Workers and Members of their Families (ICMW) and the International Convention for the Protection of All Persons from Enforced Disappearance (CPPED) which have not yet been universally ratified. As will be explained, the rules concerning peace operations follow this tendency.

4.1.2.2 Rules concerning Peace Operations

Among the rules regarding peace operations, the mandate of the operation and the regulations adopted by international territorial administrations provided for the peace mission's obligations in IHRL.

The mandates of peace operations do not always declare the obligations of the mission to respect IHRL but they provide for the respect for human rights among the objectives of the mission.[53] While their mandates did not necessarily clarify whether they only set an objective or an obligation of the peace operation to respect IHRL, international administrations interpreted their mandate in the latter sense. The Special Representative of the Secretary-General (SRSG) in Kosovo confirmed that '[i]n assuming its responsibilities, UNMIK will be guided by internationally recognized standards of human rights as the basis for the exercise of its authority in Kosovo',[54] whereas in Eastern Timor the Secretary-General affirmed that the United Nations Transitional Administration in East Timor (UNTAET) had the objective to ensure that the local institutions to be created respect the international human rights norms and standards.[55] More expressly, the mandate of the 'Rule of law' mission conducted by the European Union Rule of Law Mission in Kosovo (EULEX Kosovo) provides that the operation shall 'ensure that all its activities respect international

[53] UNMIK: UN Doc. S/RES/1244 (10 June 1999), para 11(j) ('[p]rotecting and promoting human rights'); UNTAET: UN Doc. S/RES/1272 (25 October 1999), para 8 (obligation to develop 'an independent East Timorese human rights institution', and 'local democratic institutions').

[54] Report of the Secretary-General on the United Nations Interim Administration Mission in Kosovo, UN Doc. S/1999/779 (12 July 1999), paras 42, 49.

[55] Report of the Secretary-General on the situation in East Timor, UN Doc. S/1999/1024 (4 October 1999), para 29 (h) and (m).

standards concerning human rights and gender mainstreaming'.[56] Recently, an increasing number of UNSC resolutions establishing the mandate of peace operations refer expressly to the obligations of the deployed mission under the applicable IHL and IHRL.[57] Consequently, peace operation mandates contribute to an evolving practice of the binding effect of IHRL on peace operations.

The regulations of peace operations have to a certain extent specified the vagueness of the mandate provisions on the protection of human rights. The Handbook on United Nations Multidimensional Peacekeeping Operations affirms that seven international instruments (ICCPR, ICESCR, CERD, CAT, CEDAW, CRC and ICMW) are binding on peacekeeping operations, reiterated by other internal rules.[58] The two international territorial administrations adopted a more extended list of applicable conventions. The regulations of both UNTAET and UNMIK provided that '[i]n exercising their functions, all persons undertaking public duties or holding public office … shall observe internationally recognised human rights standards'.[59] The two regulations specify that such norms must be understood 'as reflected in particular in' the most important human rights instruments, that is the UDHR, ICCPR, ICESCR, CERD, CEDAW, CAT and the CRC. In the case of Kosovo, the ECHR and its additional protocols were further listed and a later UNMIK regulation, the Constitutional Framework of 2001, added the European Charter for Regional or Minority Languages and the Framework Convention for the Protection of National Minorities.[60] This list raised several interrogations, among others regarding the question of the binding effect of these conventions on the international administration itself. While the clause 'all persons undertaking public duties or holding public office' could be

[56] Council joint action 2008/124/PESC of 4 February 2008 on the European Union Rule of Law Mission in Kosovo, EULEX KOSOVO, *OJ*, 2008, L42, 92–98, Article 3(i).

[57] E.g. UN Doc. S/RES/1856 (22 December 2008), paras 3(g), 14 (deployment of MONUC); UN Doc. S/RES/2085 (20 December 2012), paras 9, 18 (deployment of AFISMA); UN Doc. S/RES/2124 (12 November 2013), paras 1, 12 (deployment of AMISOM); UN Doc. S/RES/2149 (10 April 2014), para 42 (deployment of MISCA, EUFOR RCA).

[58] Handbook on United Nations Multidimensional Peacekeeping Operations, Peacekeeping Best Practices Unit, Department of Peacekeeping Operations, United Nations, December 2003, 103; UNMIK/REG/2006/12 (23 March 2006) on the establishment of the Human Rights Advisory Panel, para 1.2.

[59] UNMIK/REG/1999/24 (12 December 1999) on the Law applicable in Kosovo, section 1.3; UNTAET/REG/1999/1 (27 November 1999) On the Authority of the Transitional Administration in East Timor, section 2.

[60] UNMIK/REG/2001/9 (15 May 2001) on a Constitutional Framework for Provisional Self-Government in Kosovo [Constitutional Framework], Article 3.2.

interpreted as referring exclusively to local authorities of Kosovo and Eastern Timor, excluding the international presences,[61] the practice of IOs refuted this interpretation. The Human Rights Advisory Panel (HRAP),[62] the Ombudsperson of Kosovo[63] and the OSCE Mission[64] also confirmed the binding effect on UNMIK organs of the same international instruments as those listed in the regulation on the applicable law.

Based on the experience of the two international territorial administrations, some conclusions may be drawn about their regulations. First, a significant body of the international human rights instruments listed in the UNMIK and UNTAET regulations as applicable law reflects customary international law. These are the international conventions that are the most universally ratified by States (ICCPR, ICESCR, CERD, CEDAW, CAT and CRC) and that can fill with content the general clauses of UN instruments such as 'universally recognized standards of human rights'.[65] Due to the uncertainty on the identification of customary norms, one must again refer to the core of customary human rights norms identified above: non-derogable rights, with the rights protected by *jus cogens* norms and, in the case of an armed conflict, customary IHL. These core obligations undoubtedly are binding on any peace operation.

Second, practice shows that general international law, that is, custom and general principles, undoubtedly bind IOs but, as for treaty norms, the most realistic option of their binding effect is an *ad hoc* acceptation by the organisation administering the territory. This undertaking of the IO may take various forms: it is rarely incorporated in an extrinsic source such as a formal agreement but is increasingly enshrined in intrinsic sources. The importance of intrinsic sources shows that, for IOs, effective control over territory was a decisive reason to assume obligations under IHRL.[66] This is

[61] Marcus Brand, 'Effective Human Rights Protection when the UN "Becomes the state": Lessons from UNMIK' in Nigel D. White and Dirk Klaasen (eds), *The UN, Human Rights and Post-conflict Situations* (Manchester University Press 2005) 365.

[62] E.g. UNMIK/REG/2006/12 (23 March 2006) on the establishment of the Human Rights Advisory Panel, Article 1.2; HRAP, *Snežana Zdravković* v. *UNMIK*, Case No. 46/08, 25 February 2013, para 67.

[63] OIK, Special report no. 2 on Certain Aspects of UNMIK Regulation No. 2000/59 Amending UNMIK Regulation No. 1999/24 on the Law Applicable in Kosovo (27 October 2000) para 11.

[64] OSCE Mission in Kosovo, Review 1: The Criminal Justice System in Kosovo (February–July 2000), 19.

[65] Convention on the Safety of United Nations and Associated Personnel (n 51), Article 20(a).

[66] E.g. HRC, UN Doc. CCPR/C/SR.2384 (28 July 2006), para 18 ('UNMIK, as an interim administration, felt it had a duty to assist all human rights treaty bodies in assessing the situation in Kosovo').

the reason why human rights monitoring bodies most often based their conclusions on intrinsic sources such as the mandate or regulations of the international territorial administration rather than on the fact of territorial control.[67] Territorial control continues to be crucial for the implementation of the obligations, as it is due to the territorial administration that the IO is in a position to affect the human rights of individuals in the territory.

Third, beyond the core of customary human rights as a minimum content of these obligations, when an IO administers a territory, one may legitimately require it, *de lege ferenda*, to ensure the highest levels of internationally-recognised human rights in the region.[68] The more the peace operation's regulations take into account the most recent development of IHRL and regional instruments, the more swiftly they adapt local law to its international law environment.

4.1.3 The Maintenance of Public Order and Safety

It has already been noted that IHRL applies *mutatis mutandis* to the conduct of peace operations exercising effective control over a territory, in a way similar to States. By reason of the functional legal personality of the IO, the 'relative binding effect' of the custom leads to an adjustment of its legal effect to the context of an IO. This section examines how far the obligations of peace operations under IHRL are specific compared to the obligations of States. Among specificities, one may mention the peace operation's obligation to maintain public order and safety in the area under its effective control. As was mentioned in Section 4.1.1.1, the obligation of the occupying power 'to restore, and ensure, as far as possible, public order and safety, while respecting, unless absolutely prevented, the laws in force in the country' applies *mutatis mutandis* to

[67] E.g. HRC, Concluding observations: Kosovo (Serbia), UN Doc. CCPR/C/UNK/CO/1 (14 August 2006), para 4 (the mandate, UNSC resolution 1244 and UNMIK regulations on the applicable law); CEDAW, Concluding comments: Serbia, UN Doc. CEDAW/C/SCG/CO/1 (11 June 2007), para 7 (UNSC resolution 1244); CRC, Concluding observations: Republic of Serbia, UN Doc. CRC/C/SRB/CO/1 (20 June 2008), para 6 (*idem.*); Report of the Special Representative of the Secretary-General on the Situation of Human Rights Defenders, Hina Jilani, Mission to Serbia, including Kosovo, UN Doc. A/HRC/7/28/Add.3 (4 March 2008), para 149 ('United Nations standards' and UNMIK regulations).

[68] See this formulation: Basic agreement on the region of Eastern Slavonia, Baranja and Western Sirmium, UN Doc. A/50/757-S/1995/951 (15 November 1995), Annex, Article 6; Report of the Secretary-General pursuant to Security Council resolution 1025 (1995), UN Doc. S/1995/1028 (13 December 1995), para 5 (regarding Eastern Slavonia); HRC, UN Doc. CCPR/C/SR.2384 (28 July 2006), para 8 (Mr. Kälin); UNOHCHR (n 15) 29–30.

peace operations having a territorial control as a customary obligation.[69] The obligation to maintain public order and safety may be analysed in terms of two related duties: positive obligations under IHRL arising from due diligence (Section 4.1.3.1) and the obligation to maintain the laws in force (Section 4.1.3.2).

4.1.3.1 Positive Obligations

A specificity of the obligations of a peace operation controlling territory compared to an IO not having such a function is its obligation not only to respect but also to ensure IHRL in the area under its control as a guarantor, on the model of the State.[70] As a guarantor, as in the case of the State, the IO is bound by the customary obligation of due diligence resulting from the State's territorial exclusivity:[71] it includes the obligation to prevent within the territory conduct likely to infringe the rights of other States, including the rights of their nationals.[72] Beyond this core norm in general international law, due diligence requires the peace operation to prevent foreseeable violations of IHRL and to mitigate their effects.

When an IO, typically the UN, controls a territory, it has the obligation to ensure that, beyond its agents, also subjects whose conduct is not attributable to the organisation respect IHRL.[73] Regarding non-UN security forces, the obligation of due diligence of the UN includes the obligation to ensure that '[s]upport by United Nations entities to non-United Nations security forces must be consistent with the Organization's ... obligations under international law to respect, promote and encourage respect for international humanitarian, human rights and refugee law'.[74] Even in respect of national contingents, the IO must ensure that

[69] *Supra*, Section 4.1.1.1.

[70] It is the Ombudsperson of Kosovo who 'recalls that UNMIK is a surrogate state [...] and, as such, is institutionally bound not only to observe international human rights standards, but to implement them as well'. OIK, Special report no. 2 (n 63), para 11; 'primary responsibility' of the peace operation to guarantee human rights: HRAP, *S.C.* v. *UNMIK*, Case No. 02/09, 6 December 2012, para 111; *B.A.* v. *UNMIK*, Case No. 52/09, 1 February 2013, para 94; *Milisav Gogić* v. *UNMIK*, Case No. 135/09, 31 October 2013, para 131, etc.

[71] Prezas (n 19) 373–374.

[72] *Supra*, Section 3.1.2.

[73] UN Doc. CCPR/C/UNK/CO/1 (n 67), para 17 (UNMIK 'should [...] seek the cessation of detentions under COMKFOR Detention Directive 42').

[74] Human rights due diligence policy on United Nations support to non-United Nations security forces, in: UN Doc. A/67/775-S/2013/110 (5 March 2013), Annex, para 1; regarding KFOR, UNMIK had the same obligation: UN Doc. CCPR/C/UNK/CO/1 (n 67), para 17.

their personnel respect IHRL.[75] The Human Rights Review Panel (HRRP) established by EULEX Kosovo also emphasised that EULEX Kosovo is bound to protect human rights and intervene whenever it knows or ought to have known of a real and immediate risk of a human rights violation.[76] In line with the State's standard of due diligence, the peace operation cannot bear an impossible or disproportionate burden but it is bound to take reasonable measures.[77]

In their practice, the two consultative organs mandated to control the international presences in Kosovo, the Human Rights Advisory Panel (HRAP) and the HRRP, set out various positive obligations binding the peace operation. They often concluded that the international administration violated its obligations of due diligence to prevent attacks by private persons,[78] to investigate and prosecute those responsible for human rights violations[79] or to guarantee the right to a fair trial,[80] inspired by the case law of the ECtHR. The HRAP confirmed that the international territorial administration is bound to fulfil certain positive obligations such as the requirement to set up an effective justice system to the same extent as a State.[81] Generally speaking, its positive obligations are comparable to those of the State in the sense that it is required, as far as possible, to take necessary and reasonable measures.[82]

As in the case of States, if the peace operation transfers certain functions of its authority to other persons while keeping its territorial

[75] The due diligence standard as a tool for the elimination of violence against women, Report of the Special Rapporteur on Violence against Women, Its Causes and Consequences, Yakin Ertürk, UN Doc. E/CN.4/2006/61 (20 January 2006), para 99.

[76] HRRP, *A, B, C and D* v. *EULEX*, decision of 20 June 2013, Case No. 2012-09, 2012-10, 2012-11 and 2012-12, para 50; HRRP, *H & G* v. *EULEX*, decision of 30 September 2013, Case No. 2012-19 & 2012-20, para 42; Council Joint Action 2008/124/CFSP of 4 February 2008 on the European Union Rule of Law Mission in Kosovo, EULEX KOSOVO, *OJ* L 42/92 (12 February 2008), e.g. Article 3(b), (i).

[77] HRRP, *A, B, C and D* v. *EULEX* (n 76), para 50; HRRP, *H & G* v. *EULEX* (n 76), paras 41, 44; HRAP, *Shaip Canhasi* v. *UNMIK*, Case No. 04/08, 12 November 2008, para 33; *Milisav Gogić* v. *UNMIK* (n 70), paras 92–93.

[78] HRRP, *A, B, C and D* v. *EULEX* (n 76), paras 57–65.

[79] E.g. HRAP, *Shaip Canhasi* v. *UNMIK* (n 77), paras 30–33; *Svetlana Jočić* v. *UNMIK*, Case No. 34/09, 23 April 2013, paras 90–93; HRRP, *A, B, C and D* v. *EULEX* (n 76), para 67.

[80] E.g. HRAP, *Gani Emini* v. *UNMIK*, Case No. 17/08, 18 June 2010, paras 31–32.

[81] HRAP, *Petko Milogorić and Others* v. *UNMIK*, Cases No. 38/08 et al., 24 March 2010, para 44; *Marija Lalić* v. *UNMIK*, Case No. 31/08, 14 March 2013, para 45.

[82] The HRAP rejected the argument of the SRSG under which 'the standards set by the European Court of Human Rights for an effective investigation cannot be the same for UNMIK as for a State with a functioning, well organized police apparatus': *Svetlana Jočić* v. *UNMIK* (n 79), paras 54, 74–76; *Snežana Zdravković* v. *UNMIK* (n 62), paras 108–110; *B.A.* v. *UNMIK* (n 70), paras 63–65.

control, it is bound to guarantee human rights. This was the case of the UNMIK's responsibilities in the area of justice that it effectively transferred to EULEX Kosovo on 9 December 2008. Whereas the HRAP did not have competence to examine the violations committed by the authorities under the control of EULEX Kosovo after that critical date, it did have competence in respect of continuing violations that started before the transfer. In several cases related to claims of compensation submitted by property owners for damages that occurred during the hostilities in Kosovo, the courts of Kosovo remained passive and UNMIK also failed to take reasonable measures. In particular, UNMIK failed to adopt a mechanism aimed at assisting the courts, which the HRAP considered a denial of justice.[83] In such cases the HRAP engaged the responsibility of UNMIK for the inactivity of the local tribunals, stressing that the transfer of that competence to EULEX Kosovo did not exempt UNMIK of its obligation to remedy violations for which it was responsible.[84] Referring to the *Ilaşcu* judgment of the ECtHR, the Panel recommended that

> [i]n line with the case law of the ECtHR on situations of reduced State jurisdiction, the Panel is of the opinion that UNMIK must endeavour, with all the diplomatic means available to it *vis-à-vis* the Kosovo authorities, to obtain assurances that the cases filed by the complainants will be duly processed.[85]

In some cases the HRAP expressly emphasised this positive obligation of UNMIK *vis-à-vis* the local authorities of Kosovo and EULEX Kosovo.[86] Therefore, similarly to the territorial State's obligation of diligence, an IO exercising territorial control has the obligation of diligence to guarantee the enjoyment of human rights with all the legal and diplomatic means at its disposal towards third parties, local authorities or other IOs. However, the HRAP held that this due diligence standard of the international administration with regard to violations exclusively attributable to the local Kosovo authorities ceased at the latest on 15 June 2008,

[83] *Petko Milogorić and Others* (n 81), para 43. [84] Ibid., para 52.

[85] Ibid., para 52 and Recommendation no. 4; confirmed in: *Nadica Kušić* v. *UNMIK*, Case No. 08/07, 15 May 2010, para 74; Mr. V. Z. v. UNMIK, Case No. 25/08, 18 June 2010, paras 18–19; *Nenad Mladenović and Others* v. *UNMIK*, Cases nos. 172/09 et al., 16 December 2011, para 33; *Olga Lajović and Others* v. *UNMIK*, Cases nos 09/08 et al., 9 June 2012, para 31; *Svetlana Jočić* v. *UNMIK* (n 79), para 130 and Recommandation 3(a), etc.

[86] HRAP, *S.C.* v. *UNMIK* (n 70), para 114; *B.A.* v. *UNMIK* (n 70), para 97; *Milisav Gogić* v. *UNMIK* (n 70), para 134, etc.; *a contrario*, refusing to address a recommendation on the positive obligations of UNMIK related to alleged human rights violations committed by the local tribunals: *Feti Islami* v. *UNMIK*, Case No. 13/10, 16 September 2011, paras 20–21.

the date of entry into force of the Constitution of Kosovo, as UNMIK had ceased to perform most functions of public power in Kosovo.[87]

In sum, the case law of consultative human rights bodies mandated to control the international presences in Kosovo confirms the *de facto* control theory applied to peace operations controlling territory. They are considered as guarantors of human rights, on the model of the State, and have positive obligations to protect in accordance with their effectiveness.

4.1.3.2 The Maintenance of Laws in Force in the Area

As mentioned in Section 4.1.1.1, the occupying State is obliged to respect, 'unless absolutely prevented, the laws in force in the country'. The maintenance of the territorial State's law in force has some advantages: the local law is the best known by the local population[88] and, even if it is incompatible with IHRL norms, its maintenance for a provisional period helps to avoid a legal vacuum where there would be no applicable law.

If one accepts that peace operations controlling territory have to comply with certain norms of the law of occupation by analogy, one must also apply the principle of the maintenance of the laws in force in the territory as they guarantee a continuity of public order and safety. Several international instruments establish the obligation of peace operations to respect the laws in force of the host State,[89] to the extent that the latter are not incompatible with the norms of IHRL.[90] The two international territorial administrations, UNMIK and UNTAET, declared the primacy of their regulations, administrative directives and the laws adopted by the new local institutions, while maintaining the subsidiarity of the previous local laws in force before the creation of the

[87] HRAP, *Kolë Krasniqi* v. *UNMIK*, Case No. 48/08, 13 March 2010, paras 12–15; *N.G.* v. *UNMIK*, Case No. 45/10, 13 April 2011, paras 12–15; *Dragan Stojanović and Others* v. *UNMIK*, Cases Nos. 27/10 et al., 17 February 2012, paras 10–13, etc.; However, even after that date, HRAP recommended UNMIK to take diplomatic measures towards the local authorities, to inform and encourage them so that they implement the HRAP's recommendations. Human Rights Advisory Panel Annual Report, 2010, para 119.

[88] Kolb, Porretto and Vité (n 13) 267, 307.

[89] Model status-of-force agreement for peace-keeping operations, UN Doc. A/45/594 (9 October 1990), Article 6; Convention on the Safety of United Nations and Associated Personnel (n 51), Article 6.

[90] Handbook on policing in peacekeeping operations (n 47), 20, para 4.4; Ten rules: Code of personal conduct for blue helmets, para 2; African Union policy on conduct and discipline for peace support operations (n 48), para 4.4.

administration as far as they were compatible with IHRL.[91] UNMIK then obliged its personnel and that of KFOR to 'respect the laws applicable in the territory of Kosovo and regulations issued by the Special Representative of the Secretary-General'.[92] The idea of continuity, however desirable it may be, nevertheless raised several challenges concerning the implementation of the former local laws. These challenges comprised the difficulty to establish the provisions in force at the critical date, the non-access of international judges to translated versions and the rejection of Serbian laws by the Albanian judges in Kosovo.[93] This situation led to a 'legal chaos', going against the purpose of legal certainty.

Nevertheless, the principle under Article 43 of The Hague Regulations contains certain exceptions. Whereas Article 64 of GC IV protects the *status quo* of the occupied State's criminal laws, it allows their modification or abrogation by the occupying power 'in cases where they constitute a threat to its security or an obstacle to the application' of the Geneva Convention.[94] Similarly, the occupying State can adopt legislation 'essential to enable the Occupying Power to fulfil its obligations' enshrined in GC IV, and 'to maintain the orderly government of the territory, and to ensure the security' of the occupying forces or administration.[95] State practice and scholarship have interpreted these exceptions broadly, allowing for the occupying State some legislative power beyond criminal law.[96] The law of occupation might even require

[91] UNMIK/REG/1999/1 (25 July 1999) on the Authority of the interim administration in Kosovo, Article 3 and its modification, UNMIK/REG/1999/24 (n 59), Section 1.1(b); UNTAET/REG/1999/1 (n 59), Article 3.1.

[92] UNMIK/REG/2000/47 (18 August 2000) on the status, privileges and immunities of KFOR and UNMIK and their personnel in Kosovo, Articles 2.2 (KFOR), 3.5 (MINUK).

[93] Simon Chesterman, 'Unaccountable? The United Nations, Emergency Powers, and the Rule of Law' (2009) 42 *Vanderbildt Journal of Transnational Law* 1509, 1522–1523; Jetish Jashari, 'U.N. Field Missions in the Context of Legal and Judicial Reform: The Kosovo Case' (2007) 1(1) *Columbia Journal of East European Law* 76, 95–98; Venice Commission, Opinion on Human Rights in Kosovo (n 29), para 57.

[94] CG IV, Article 64(1). [95] Ibid., Article 64(2).

[96] GC IV, Commentary of 1958, 335–336; Sassòli (n 26) 668–670; Steven R. Ratner, 'Foreign Occupation and International Territorial Administration: The Challenges of Convergence' (2005) 16 *European Journal of International Law* 695, 707; Eyal Benvenisti, 'The Laws of Occupation and Commercial Law Reform in Occupied Territories: A Reply to Jose Alejandro Carballo Leyda' (2012) 23 *European Journal of International Law* 199; *a contrario*, rejecting the applicability of Article 64(2) of GC IV to non-criminal laws: Jose Alejandro Carballo Leyda, 'The Laws of Occupation and Commercial Law Reform in Occupied Territories: Clarifying a Widespread Misunderstanding' (2012) 23 *European Journal of International Law* 179.

the occupying power to legislate to ensure the protection of civilians.[97] Incompatibility with IHRL would constitute an 'absolute prevention' to maintain and respect the legislation under Article 43 of The Hague Regulation,[98] and may require new legislation.

A peace operation controlling territory, similarly to the occupying State, may modify local laws incompatible with IHRL or adopt new legislation in order to harmonise them with human rights norms.[99] From the position of the peace operation as a guarantor of human rights in the area, it follows that it has to ensure that applicable IHRL is protected against inconsistent local law. For instance, where the local law did not provide adequate protection for human rights, international monitoring bodies recommended that the international administration legislate or advise the local authorities under its control on the need to adopt new legislation.[100] A peace operation, as in the case of the occupying power, can only introduce as many legislative modifications as are absolutely necessary to guarantee human rights in the region, in order to avoid a disproportionate interference with the territorial State's sovereignty and the right to self-determination of the people.[101] Certain regulations of the international administrations arguably violated this principle while well-functioning local laws were in force.[102]

The obligation to respect, as far as possible, the right of the people to self-determination equally entails the subsidiarity of the peace operation with respect to local institutions: for example, while the newly-established tribunals must apply the criminal laws introduced by the peace operation, the local judges must have jurisdiction in any other case.[103] Likewise, the Advisory Committee on the Framework Convention for the protection of national minorities highlighted that in each case where local authorities have proven to be not yet prepared to fulfil their tasks in the domain of the protection of minorities, the SRSG

[97] E.g. GC IV, Articles 50(3), 59, 61.
[98] Sassòli (n 26) 676–677.
[99] Ibid., 676–678; Ratner (n 96) 710.
[100] E.g. CESCR, Concluding observations: UNMIK, UN Doc. E/C.12/UNK/CO/1 (1 December 2008), paras 14, 17, 19–20, 23(a); Report of the Special Representative of the Secretary-General on the situation of human rights defenders, Hina Jilani, Mission to Serbia, including Kosovo, UN Doc. A/HRC/7/28/Add.3 (4 March 2008), paras 111, 149, 155 (addressed to the PISG).
[101] Sassòli (n 26) 677.
[102] Irmscher (n 19) 393–394 (mentioning as examples: Regulation No. 2000/68 on Contracts for the sale of goods, UNMIK/REG/2000/68 (29 December 2000) and Regulation No. 2001/5 on Pledges, UNMIK/REG/2001/5 (7 February 2001)).
[103] Sassòli (n 26) 691–692.

shall fully assume their responsibilities.[104] The mandate of international territorial administrations impliedly confirmed the subsidiarity of the peace operation as it provided for capacity building for self-government.[105] It follows that the peace operation can only provisionally set aside local laws and institutions, whereas it is obliged to transfer the assumed functions to the local authorities while promoting the right to self-determination of people. Shortly, exceptions from the obligation to maintain the laws in force in the area only allow the peace operation to legislate as far as necessary for the protection of human rights, following a subsidiary role *vis-à-vis* local law and authorities.

4.1.4 *The Limitations of Human Rights*

The IO establishing a peace operation, as addressee of obligations of IHRL, can limit human rights under strict conditions defined by international human rights treaties. However, international territorial administrations sometimes went well beyond these limits, claiming that their mandate or the circumstances of the post-conflict emergency justify human rights limitations to a larger extent than those authorised for States. Furthermore, individuals whose rights the peace operation affects face the restriction of their right to remedy on account of the jurisdictional immunity enjoyed by the peace operation. Therefore, peace operations might have certain specificities in terms of the power to derogate (Section 4.1.4.1) and the right to remedy, limited by IOs' jurisdictional immunity (Section 4.1.4.2).

4.1.4.1 The Power to Derogate

To justify the limitations of human rights, peace operations have claimed the power to derogate based on the post-conflict emergency, or on a binding UNSC resolution. First, UNMIK often invoked the numerous difficulties the international presences had to face in Kosovo.[106] While recognising the interim character of UNMIK, the difficulties encountered and its insufficient resources, the HRAP systematically concluded that in

[104] Advisory Committee on the Framework Convention for the protection of national minorities, Opinion on the implementation of the Framework Convention for the protection of national minorities in Kosovo (adopted on 25 November 2005), ACFC/OP/I (2005)004 (2 March 2006), para 18.

[105] UN Doc. S/RES/1272 (n 53), para 2(e); UN Doc. S/RES/1244 (n 53), paras 10, 11(a), (c).

[106] E.g. Letter of the SRSG of 13 November 2001, cited in OIK, Second Annual Report 2001–2002, 10 July 2002, 18; HRC, UN Doc. CCPR/C/SR.2383/Add.1 (28 August 2006), para 47; *Petko Milogorić and Others* (n 81), para 29.

no circumstances could these elements serve as an excuse for diminishing standards of respect for human rights.[107] The Panel added that the difficulties related to the gradual creation of institutions cannot be invoked from 2003, when the SRSG acknowledged the establishment of a 'well-functioning' and 'sustainable' police and judicial system.[108]

Second, another argument raised to justify derogation is based on the mandate of the peace operation, a binding UNSC resolution. KFOR[109] and UNMIK[110] often invoked that the responsibility of ensuring public safety and order under UNSC Resolution 1244, adopted under chapter VII, authorised them to arrest and detain persons without judicial control. Counter-arguments against the idea of derogation authorised by the mandate stress the contradictions of invoking Article 103 of the UN Charter to justify any kind of limitation.[111] On the one hand, the UN is not an addressee of Article 103, which relates to 'the obligations of the Members of the United Nations' rather than of the organisation. On the other hand, even if Article 103 applied to the UN, it would not be possible for the UN to invoke its own internal law against its obligations arising from extrinsic sources.[112]

Another argument against the idea of derogation authorised by the mandate focuses on the limits of such derogation. A first limit to the UNSC's action, firmly recognised in international case law,[113] is *jus cogens*, and so peremptory human rights norms. A second limit is certain

[107] *Petko Milogorić and Others* (n 81), para 44; *Olga Lajović and Others* v. *UNMIK* (n 85), para 22; *Nenad Mladenović and Others* (n 85), para 24; *B.A.* v. *UNMIK* (n 70), para 65.

[108] Report of the Secretary-General on UNMIK, UN Doc. S/2003/113 (29 January 2003), paras 28–29; HRAP, *S.C.* v. *UNMIK* (n 70), para 92; *B.A.* v. *UNMIK* (n 70), para 69; etc.

[109] UN Doc. S/RES/1244 (n 53), para 9(d); on this practice of KFOR: OSCE Mission in Kosovo, Review 1 (n 64), 19; OSCE Mission in Kosovo, Review 4: Review of the Criminal Justice System (September 2001–February 2002), 47.

[110] OSCE Mission in Kosovo, Review 3: The Criminal Justice System (March 2001–August 2001), 35; press declaration by UNMIK on 2 July 2001, cited by Carsten Stahn, 'The United Nations Transitional Administrations in Kosovo and East Timor: A First Analysis' (2001) 5 *Max Planck Yearbook of United Nations Law* 105, 166; UNMIK, 'UNMIK, Security and the Rule of Law in Kosovo', 12 January 2000, cited ibid., 163.

[111] The two reasons were elaborated in Forteau (n 41) 32.

[112] Vienna Convention on the Law of Treaties between States and International Organizations or between International Organizations, Vienna, 21 March 1986, UN Doc. A/CONF.129/15 (1986), Article 27(2).

[113] CJEU, *Kadi*, 2005 (n 43), paras 226, 230; CJEU, Yusuf (n 43), paras 277, 281; *Application of the Convention on the Prevention and Punishment of the Crime of Genocide*, Provisional Measures, Order of 13 September 1993, *I.C.J. Reports* 1993, Separate opinion of Judge ad hoc Lauterpacht, 440, paras 100–101.

customary norms,[114] especially non-derogable human rights that bind the peace operation.[115] One may conclude that the mandate of peace operations does not authorise a general power of derogation, but any derogation must expressly specify its scope of application and the affected human rights.[116] Indeed, the mandate of the international administration of Kosovo only provides that the KFOR is established 'with all necessary means to fulfil its responsibilities', such as '[e]nsuring public safety and order until the international civil presence can take responsibility for this task',[117] but does not authorise it any specific derogation.[118] This view corresponds to the human rights case law under which there is a presumption that UNSC resolutions comply with human rights treaties unless the wording of the resolution expressly obliges States to take measures capable of breaching human rights.[119]

Third, beyond the post-conflict circumstances and the peace operation's mandate, another possible basis for derogation is the conventions' derogation clauses.[120] However, those human rights treaties are formally not binding on a peace operation such as UNMIK and KFOR,[121] and UNMIK also rejected this idea.[122] Monitoring bodies excluded the applicability of derogation clauses on account of the non-fulfilment of

[114] *Questions of Interpretation and Application of the 1971 Montreal Convention arising from the Aerial Incident at Lockerbie (Libyan Arab Jamahiriya* v. *United States of America)*, Provisional Measures, Order of 14 April 1992, *I.C.J. Reports* 1992, Dissenting Opinion by Judge Bedjaoui, para 29; Prezas (n 19) 389–390.

[115] E.g. the right to challenge one's detention: OSCE Mission in Kosovo, Review 3 (n 110), 34; OSCE Mission in Kosovo, Review 4 (n 109), 49.

[116] UNOHCHR (n 15) 29; Stahn (n 110) 167; John Cerone, 'Minding the Gap: Outlining KFOR Accountability in Post-Conflict Kosovo' (2001) 12 *European Journal of International Law* 469, 478–479, n 50; *a contrario*, claiming that no general derogation must be authorised, as the procedural requirements of human rights treaties do not bind directly the UN: Prezas (n 19) 446–447.

[117] UN Doc. S/RES/1244 (n 53), paras 7, 9(d).

[118] OSCE Mission in Kosovo, Review 3 (n 110), 36.

[119] *Al-Jedda* v. *United Kingdom* [GC], Appl. no. 27021/08, judgment of 7 July 2011, paras 102, 109; *Al-Dulimi and Montana Management Inc.* v. *Switzerland* [GC], Appl. no. 5809/08, judgment of 21 June 2016, para 140; HRC, *Nabil Sayadi and Patricia Vinck* v. *Belgium*, Communication No. 1472/2006, Views of 22 December 2008, UN Doc. CCPR/C/94/D/1472/2006 (29 December 2008), paras 10.6–10.7 (the HRC implied that national implementing measures of UN member States have some leeway in enforcing binding UNSC resolutions) and Individual opinion of Sir Nigel Rodley (concurring), 36.

[120] *Supra*, Section 3.3.1.

[121] Prezas (n 19) 446–447; Federico Sperotto, 'The International Security Presence in Kosovo and the Protection of Human Rights' (2008) 48 *Human Rights & Human Welfare Working Papers* 1, 7.

[122] HRC, Report of UNMIK, Kosovo (Serbia and Montenegro), UN Doc. CCPR/C/UNK/1 (13 March 2006), 57, para 6.

their conditions, either because there no longer was a state of emergency justifying derogation,[123] or because the measures taken would not conform to the criteria of derogation, including proportionality.[124] Based on intrinsic sources, international territorial administrations can rely on the substantive norms including, arguably, the derogation clause of those treaties, but only within their strict limits.

Shortly, neither the post-conflict circumstances, nor a binding UNSC resolution, nor the conventions' derogations clauses authorise peace operations to derogate to human rights to a larger extent than States. Beyond the strict limits of derogation clauses, peace operations can only limit human rights under the general limitation clauses of human rights conventions and the harmonised interpretation regarding binding UNSC resolutions or IHL rules if applicable.[125]

4.1.4.2 Jurisdictional Immunity as a Limit of the Right to Remedy

Peace operations exercising control over territory are expected to guarantee the right to effective remedy, recognised in the main international human rights instruments:[126] they shall establish an accountability mechanism against the conduct of IOs active in the region.[127] Such a remedy by IOs is not necessarily a judicial mechanism but it must comply with procedural guarantees of the right to an effective remedy. In Kosovo, for example, the HRAP and HRRP, established by UNMIK an EULEX Kosovo, respectively, are both consultative bodies.[128]

However, the right to an effective remedy cannot be constructed against a peace operation in the same way as against a sovereign State. It is especially limited by the immunities accorded to the IO and to members of the peace operation. Among the immunities of peace operations and their agents, it is the jurisdictional immunity of the organisation which is the key issue of this section, because it is a preliminary

[123] OSCE Mission in Kosovo, Review 3 (n 110), 36.

[124] OIK, Special Report no. 1 on the compatibility with recognized international standards of UNMIK Regulation No. 2000/47 on the Status, Privileges and Immunities of KFOR and UNMIK and Their Personnel in Kosovo (18 August 2000), para 34.

[125] *Supra*, Section 3.3.2.

[126] UDHR, Article 8; ICCPR, Article 2(3); ECHR, Article 13; ACHR, Article 25; ACHPR, art. 7 (1).

[127] E.g. FCPNM, Second Opinion on Kosovo, 5 November 2009, ACFC/OP/II(2009)004 (31 May 2010), paras 14, 46; confirmed in: CoE, Committee of Ministers, Resolution CM/ResCMN (2011)14 (6 July 2011).

[128] *Infra*, Section 8.2.1.1.

question whether the IO enjoys a right not to be the subject of the given court proceedings.[129] If it is established that a judgment could be given against the organisation, immunity from enforcement and the personal immunity of agents of the IO are only secondary questions.[130]

Article 105(1) of the UN Charter provides that '[t]he Organization shall enjoy in the territory of each of its Members such privileges and immunities as are necessary for the fulfillment of its purposes'. It follows that individuals can neither challenge the acts of members of a peace operation, nor the scope of application of the jurisdictional immunity.[131] Under UNMIK Regulation 2000/47 on the status, privileges and immunities of KFOR and UNMIK and their personnel in Kosovo, personnel of KFOR not locally recruited enjoy absolute immunity from jurisdiction before the domestic courts of Kosovo, which cannot be waived.[132] UNMIK, however, enjoys a functional immunity: 'UNMIK personnel, including locally recruited personnel, shall be immune from legal process in respect of words spoken and all acts performed by them in their official capacity'.[133] UNTAET enjoyed similar immunities to those of UNMIK, without a special regulation.[134]

The only exception from the jurisdictional immunity of the officials is the decision of the UN Secretary-General: he 'shall have the right and the duty to waive the immunity of any UNMIK personnel in any case where, in his opinion, the immunity would impede the course of justice and can be waived without prejudice to the interest of UNMIK'.[135] It is the duty of the Secretary-General to evaluate whether his agents acted in their official capacity and his conclusion concerning the immunity creates a presumption 'which can only be set aside for the most compelling

[129] Venice Commission, Opinion on Human Rights in Kosovo (n 29), para 64.

[130] Ibid.; in the same sense, regarding immunities of States: *Jurisdictional Immunities of the State (Germany* v. *Italy: Greece intervening)*, judgment, *I.C.J. Reports* 2012, 146–147, para 113.

[131] ICJ, *Difference Relating to Immunity from Legal Process of a Special Rapporteur of the Commission on Human Rights*, Written statement submitted on behalf of the Secretary-General of the United Nations, 2 October 1998, para 56.

[132] UNMIK/REG/2000/47 (n 92), Article 2.4; They can only be sewed before the tribunals of the troop contributing State.

[133] Ibid., Article 3.3.

[134] Legal status of certain categories of United Nations personnel serving in peacekeeping operations, in: *UNJYB*, 2002, Part Two, Chapter VI, 467–468; Amnesty International, East Timor: Justice past, present and future, AI Index: ASA 57/001/2001, 26 July 2001, 30; Markus Benzing, 'Midwifing a New State: The United Nations in East Timor' (2005) 9 *Max Planck Yearbook of United Nations Law* 295, 338.

[135] Ibid., Article 6.1 and the analogous provision of the Convention on the Privileges and Immunities of the United Nations, New York, 13 February 1946, Article V(20).

reasons and is thus to be given the greatest weight by national courts'.[136] In practice, it is possible but unlikely that domestic tribunals of the territory under the peace operation's control consider a human rights violation as the most compelling reason and set aside the peace operation's immunity contrary to the decision of the Secretary-General.[137]

As for the claims for compensation of damages arising from acts performed by the UN, the ICJ concluded that the Organization indeed can be required to bear responsibility for the consequences of such acts but 'any such claims against the United Nations shall not be dealt with by national courts'.[138] The immunity of IOs would apply even to situations where the acts of the organisations or their agents would be distinct from the exercise of their official functions or where they would exceed them – the contrary would be a 'functional' immunity. In the context of UN peacekeeping operations, the Secretary-General,[139] the ECtHR,[140] the HRAP[141] and numerous domestic courts[142] confirmed that the jurisdictional immunity of the UN is not functional but absolute. As the ECtHR concluded, '[t]o bring such operations within the scope of domestic jurisdiction would be to allow individual States, through their courts, to interfere with the fulfilment of the key mission of the United Nations in this field including with the effective conduct of its operations'.[143] This has the consequence that, as the UN Secretary-General observes, 'insofar as the United Nations is concerned, when it has acted

[136] *Difference Relating to Immunity from Legal Process of a Special Rapporteur of the Commission on Human Rights*, Advisory Opinion, *I.C.J. Reports* 1999, 87, para 61.

[137] Lindsey Cameron, 'Human Rights Accountability of International Civil Administrations to the People Subject to Administration' (2007) 2 *Human Rights & International Legal Discourse* 267, 290.

[138] *Difference Relating to Immunity* AO (n 136), 88–89, para 66.

[139] Administrative and budgetary aspects of the financing of the United Nations peacekeeping operations, Report of the Secretary-General, UN Doc. A/51/389 (20 September 1996), para 7; ILC, Responsibility of international organizations: Comments and observations received from international organizations, UN Doc. A/CN.4/637/Add.1 (17 February 2011), 32–33, para 21(2).

[140] ECtHR, *Stichting mothers of Srebrenica and Others* v. *The Netherlands*, Appl. no. 65542/12, decision of 11 June 2013 on the admissibility, para 154.

[141] HRAP, Case No. 13/08, *Gani Thaçi* v. *UNMIK*, 12 September 2012, para 73.

[142] *Manderlier c. Organisation des Nations Unies et Etat Belge (Ministre des Affaires Etrangères)*, Tribunal Civil de Bruxelles, 11 May 1966, *Journal des Tribunaux*, 10 December 1966, no. 4553, 121 and Cour d'appel de Bruxelles, 15 September 1969, *Pasicrisie Belge*, 1969, 247, in: (1971) 25 *Revue critique de jurisprudence belge* 449–455; *Mothers of Srebrenica* v. *the State of the Netherlands*, Supreme Court of the Netherlands, 10/04437, judgment of 13 April 2012, para 4.3.6; *Delama Georges, et al.* v. *United Nations, et al.*, 9 January 2015, 2015 WL 129657 (S.D.N.Y.).

[143] *Stichting mothers of Srebrenica* (n 140), para 154.

as an interim territorial administrator, no remedies in local courts or administrative bodies were available to private persons with respect to actions taken by the Organization'.[144]

The right of access to court is not a *jus cogens* norm and the jurisdictional immunity of IOs as a legitimate aim necessarily limits the right.[145] Whether and to what extent this limitation is necessary and proportionate depends on whether individuals have access to reasonable alternative means to effectively protect their right to a remedy.[146] To comply with the right to access to court, the IO controlling the peace operation has to set up an alternative remedy.[147] While instruments granting immunity frequently provide for the IO's obligation to establish internal accountability mechanisms,[148] the latter are often not set up at all or do not provide an effective remedy.[149]

In conclusion, whereas among the extrinsic sources IOs are bound by minimal customary obligations (non-derogable rights, peremptory human rights norms and, if applicable, customary norms of IHL), human rights monitoring bodies most often invoked the obligations voluntarily assumed by the peace operation. The obligations of peace operations undoubtedly present a specificity at the level of limitations of human rights, as their jurisdictional immunity restricts the right to a remedy. However, they have no specificity as to positive obligations, as their positive obligations related to the maintenance of public order and safety are comparable to the occupying State's obligations.

4.2 The Obligations of *De Facto* Regimes

Contrary to peace operations, a *de facto* regime has no legal basis to exercise its territorial control but operates against the territorial State's will. Thus, it plays an ambigious role in matters of human rights: as an

144 UN Doc. A/CN.4/637/Add.1 (n 139), 32–33, para 21(2).

145 *Stichting mothers of Srebrenica* (n 140), paras 138, 139(c); HRC, General comment No. 32, Article 14: Right to equality before courts and tribunals and to a fair trial, UN Doc. CCPR/C/GC/32 (23 August 2007), para 18.

146 ECtHR, *Waite and Kennedy* v. *Germany* [GC], Appl. no. 26083/94, judgment of 18 February 1999, para 68 ('a material factor'); *Roland Klausecker* v. *Germany*, Appl. no. 415/07, decision of 6 January 2015 on the admissibility, para 69 ('the Court therefore considers it decisive . . .').

147 OHCHR, Communication by the Special Rapporteur on adequate housing et al., Reference: JAL, HTI 3/2014, 25 Sep 2014, 3, 4–5; ILA, Berlin Conference (2004), Accountability of international organizations, Final report, 41.

148 Convention on the Privileges and Immunities of the UN (n 135), Article VIII(29)

149 *Infra*, Section 8.2.1.1.

administrator of the territory, it might assume certain human rights obligations, whereas as an unrecognised entity the community of States is reluctant to confer on it rights and obligations under IHRL. In line with the human rights obligations of peace operations, those of *de facto* regimes may be set out in extrinsic sources (Section 4.2.1), not subject to the will of the *de facto* regime, and in intrinsic sources (Section 4.2.2), adopted by the entity itself. As in the case of peace operations controlling an area, *de facto* regimes are bound by a core group of positive obligations to ensure public order and safety (Section 4.2.3). This section argues that *de facto* regimes are addressees of most positive obligations under IHRL as guarantors of human rights, but these duties are limited by their effectiveness and unrecognised status, with due respect to the rights of the territorial State.

4.2.1 Extrinsic Sources

Three types of extrinsic sources provide for human rights obligations of *de facto* regimes: customary international law and general principles of law (Section 4.2.1.1), human rights treaties (Section 4.2.1.2) and acts of IOs (Section 4.2.1.3).

4.2.1.1 Customary International Law and General Principles of Law

Contrary to peace operations, it is contested whether customary international human rights law and general principles of law bind *de facto* regimes. The classical scholarship on *de facto* regimes held that general international law applies *mutatis mutandis* to these subjects, except for norms addressed exclusively to States.[150] There is consensus that an armed opposition group (AOG) has rights and obligations in IHL governing non-international armed conflicts: several judgments of international criminal tribunals have recognised that AOGs are bound by customary international law.[151] Without identifying all such norms, it suffices to note that at least Common Article 3 of the Geneva

[150] Jochen A. Frowein, *Das De facto-Regime im Völkerrecht: eine Untersuchung zur Rechtsstellung nichtanerkannter Staaten und ähnlicher Gebilde* (C Heymann 1968) 34.

[151] SCSL, *Prosecutor* v. *Sam Hinga Norman*, SCSL-2004-14-AR72(E), Decision on preliminary motion based on lack of jurisdiction (child recruitment), 31 May 2004, para 22; *Prosecutor* v. *Morris Kallon and Brima Bazzy Kamara*, SCSL-2004-15-AR72(E) and SCSL-2004-16-AR72(E), Decision on challenge to jurisdiction: Lomé Accord amnesty, Appeals Chamber, 13 March 2004, para 47; ICTY, *Prosecutor* v. *Stanislav Galić*, IT-98-29-A, judgment, Appeals Chamber, 30 November 2006, paras 86, 119.

Conventions[152] and the heart of Additional Protocol II (AP II), such as fundamental guarantees (Article 4)[153] and the respect for and protection of the civilian population (Article 13)[154] are considered customary rules. AP II is regarded as a development of Common Article 3 and as equally 'binding upon both government forces and armed opposition groups'.[155]

Beyond customary IHL, there are good reasons to consider customary human rights norms binding on *de facto* regimes. The first reason is a regulatory need: with the normalisation of the situation in the 'grey zone', the relevance of humanitarian norms decreases, as IHL does not protect a number of human rights, such as the right to education, freedom of expression and the right to respect private and family life.[156] In such a situation, the life of the local population requires a body of laws to protect it against the authority exercised by the *de facto* authorities.[157] Customary IHRL might fill this vacuum and provide for adequate protection.

A second reason to consider customary human rights norms binding on *de facto* regimes is the evolving idea in international documents that *de facto* regimes are addressees of IHRL due to their exercise of territorial control and government-like authority over the population, in analogy with the relationship governor/governed in IHRL. A high number of

152 *Military and Paramilitary Activities in and against Nicaragua (Nicaragua* v. *United States of America)*, Merits, judgment, *I.C.J. Reports* 1986, 113–114, para 218; *Corfu Channel case*, judgment of April 9th, 1949, *I.C.J. Reports* 1949, 22.

153 ICTR, *Prosecutor* v. *Jean-Paul Akayesu*, ICTR-96-4-T, judgment, Chamber I, 2 September 1998, paras 609–610; Report of the Secretary-General on the establishment of a Special Court for Sierra Leone, UN Doc. S/2000/915 (4 October 2000), para 14; ICTY, *The Prosecutor* v. *Milan Martić*, IT-95-11-x R61, Decision, Trial Chamber, 8 March 1996, para 14.

154 ICTY, *The Prosecutor* v. *Pavle Strugar, Miodrag Jokić et al.*, IT-01-42-PT, Decision on Defence Preliminary Motion Challenging Jurisdiction, Trial Chamber, 7 June 2002, paras 17–21; *The Prosecutor* v. *Milan Martić*, Case n° IT-95-11-T, judgment, Trial Chamber I, 12 June 2007, para 45; Yves Sandoz, Christophe Swinarski and Bruno Zimmermann (eds), *Commentary on the Additional Protocols of 8 June 1977 to the Geneva Conventions of 12 August 1949* (Martinus Nijhoff Publishers 1987) 1448, para 4761.

155 Jean-Marie Henckaerts and Louise Doswald-Beck, *Customary International Humanitarian Law*, vol. 1 (Rules) (Comité international de la Croix-Rouge ed, Cambridge University Press 2005) 437 (Commentary of Rule 137); Sandoz, Swinarski and Zimmermann (n 154) 1345, para 4442 (Commentary of Part I).

156 Aristotle Constantinides, 'Human Rights Obligations and Accountability of Armed Opposition Groups: The Practice of the UN Security Council' (2010) 4 *Human Rights & International Legal Discourse* 89, 94; Cedric Ryngaert, 'Human Rights Obligations of Armed Groups' (2008) 41 *Revue belge de droit international* 355, 378.

157 Sandesh Sivakumaran, 'Re-Envisaging the International Law of Internal Armed Conflict' (2011) 22 *European Journal of International Law* 219, 244.

reports issued by UN expert bodies such as fact-finding missions,[158] UN Special Rapporteurs,[159] independent experts,[160] and the UN High Commissioner for Human Rights,[161] accept that non-state AOGs are bound by certain rules of IHRL if they exercise government-like functions and *de facto* control over a territory.[162] A major difficulty with these reports is to first assess their content, that is, under what conditions and which rules of IHRL address *de facto* regimes and, second, their normative value.

Those reports of UN expert bodies have over time crystallised the content of their conclusion. While early reports provided for 'legitimate expectations of the international community',[163] using the verb 'should' instead of 'shall'[164] in the sense of a recommendation, reports adopted after 2011 mention a direct 'obligation' of *de facto* regimes to respect international human rights norms,[165] using the wording 'shall'. Beyond the problem that the reports hardly ever analyse whether the AOG in question fulfils the criteria mentioned in the formula, they also rarely specify the scope of their legal obligations.[166] At least some more recent

[158] E.g. Human Rights in Palestine and in other occupied Arab territories, Report of the United Nations Fact-Finding Mission on the Gaza Conflict, UN Doc. A/HRC/12/48 (25 September 2009), paras 305, 1370; Report of the International Commission of Inquiry to investigate all alleged violations of international human rights law in the Libyan Arab Jamahiriya, UN Doc. A/HRC/17/44 (12 January 2012), para 62.

[159] E.g. Human Rights situation in Palestine and other occupied Arab territories, UN Doc. A/HRC/10/22 (29 May 2009), para 22; Report of four Special Rapporteurs, Mission to Lebanon and Israel (7–14 September 2006), UN Doc. A/HRC/2/7 (2 October 2006), para 19.

[160] Report on Human Rights in the Transnistrian Region of the Republic of Moldova, by Thomas Hammarberg, Senior Expert, 14 February 2013, at www.undp.org/content/dam/unct/moldova/docs/pub/Senior_Expert_Hammarberg_Report_TN_Human_Rights.pdf (15 March 2020), 4.

[161] E.g. UNOHCHR (n 15) 25.

[162] Until 31 December 2019, the author could find 69 UN reports confirming the same formula.

[163] Extrajudicial, summary or arbitrary executions, Report of the Special Rapporteur, Philip Alston, Mission to Sri Lanka, UN Doc. E/CN.4/2006/53/Add.5 (27 March 2006), para 25; Report of the Special Rapporteur on extrajudicial, summary or arbitrary executions, UN Doc. A/62/265 (16 August 2007), para 43; UN Doc. A/HRC/2/7 (n 159), para 19.

[164] Report of the Special Rapporteur on freedom of religion or belief, Heiner Bielefeldt, Addendum, Summary of cases transmitted to Governments and replies received, UN Doc. A/HRC/16/53/Add.1 (14 February 2011), para 24.

[165] E.g. UN Doc. A/HRC/17/44 (n 158), para 72; UN Doc. A/HRC/10/22 (n 159), para 22; UN Doc. A/HRC/12/48 (n 158), paras 305, 1370.

[166] Katharine Fortin, *The Accountability of Armed Groups under Human Rights Law* (Oxford University Press 2017) 343–345.

reports specified that the relevant rules of IHRL are limited to customary human rights norms.[167]

As for the normative value of the conclusion, reports of UN expert bodies are not among the traditional sources of international law under Article 38 of the ICJ Statute but might be considered acts of IOs that bypass the classical consent of States, or even soft law.[168] Such reports usually contain both factual and legal conclusions, and their normative influence depends on the body that created them, the expertise of their members, their mandate and the care with which they formulate their normative conclusions.[169] While they have only the force of recommendation and do not themselves create obligations, they might reflect existing customary international law.[170] Furthermore, acts adopted within IOs can lead States to perform conducts that form State practice and develop custom.[171] Therefore, it is important to verify how far the standard formula used by the above-mentioned reports has generated State practice.

Considering the impact of the formula, there is a weak but evolving State practice confirming the bindingness of IHRL on *de facto* regimes. While UN member States rarely commented on the reports' above-mentioned conclusion, IOs have adopted some resolutions that might confirm it, thereby possibly contributing to a general practice accepted as law (accompanied by *opinio juris*).[172] Especially, resolutions adopted by the United Nations General Assembly (UNGA) or the Human Rights

[167] Report on Human Rights in the Transnistrian Region (n 160), 4; UN Doc. A/HRC/25/21 (n 4), para 11; Report of the detailed findings of the Independent International Fact-Finding Mission on Myanmar, UN Doc. A/HRC/39/CRP.2 (17 September 2018), para 49.

[168] On those sources: Malgosia Fitzmaurice, 'The History of Article 38 of the Statute of the International Court of Jusice. The Journey from the Past to the Present' in Jean d'Aspremont, Samantha Besson and Sévrine Knuchel (eds), *The Oxford Handbook of the Sources of International Law* (Oxford University Press 2017) 194–195, 197–198; *a contrario*: Rodenhäuser considers them 'akin to "judicial decisions", or "the teachings of the most highly qualified publicists"', and as such 'subsidiary means for the determination of rules of law' under Article 38(d) of the ICJ Statute. Tilman Rodenhäuser, *Organizing Rebellion: Non-State Armed Groups under International Humanitarian Law, Human Rights Law, and International Criminal Law* (Oxford University Press 2018) 150.

[169] Steven R. Ratner, 'Sources of International Humanitarian Law and International Criminal Law' in Jean d'Aspremont, Samantha Besson and Sévrine Knuchel (eds), *The Oxford Handbook of the Sources of International Law* (Oxford University Press 2017) 918.

[170] Allehone Mulugeta Abebe, 'Special Rapporteurs as Law Makers: The Developments and Evolution of the Normative Framework for Protecting and Assisting Internally Displaced Persons' (2011) 15 *The International Journal of Human Rights* 286, 292.

[171] ILC, Draft conclusions on identification of customary international law, with commentaries 2018, UN Doc. A/73/10 (2018), 134, para 5.

[172] Ibid., 146, Draft Conclusion 12(2).

Council referred to the reports that included the formula. According to their weight in confirming a possible customary rule, one can distinguish between three types of resolutions:

(a) Some resolutions only take note of or welcome the entire report, without mentioning its conclusions.[173] As the member States adopting those acts did not necessarily agree with the specific formula on the bindingness of IHRL on *de facto* regimes, the weight of such resolutions in contributing to a custom is low.

(b) Other resolutions take note of or welcome the report, and even reiterate the obligations of the given *de facto* regime expressly, but the voting record reflects the view of a restricted number of States. For instance, a resolution of the Human Rights Council on the cooperation with Georgia stressed that

> the findings of the High Commissioner in the reports, in which the High Commissioner underscored the responsibility of the authorities in control in Abkhazia, Georgia and the Tskhinvali region/South Ossetia, Georgia to uphold the fundamental freedoms and human rights of all people living therein.[174]

As the resolution was adopted by a vote of nineteen to three, with twenty-five abstentions, a relatively small number of member States supported the conclusion. Therefore, the weight of such resolutions in general practice is relatively low.[175]

(c) Finally, a third group of resolutions takes note of or welcomes the report, reiterates the obligations of the given *de facto* regime and was adopted either by a high majority[176] or without vote,[177] enshrining a

[173] E.g. UN Doc. A/RES/70/142 (9 February 2016), para 1; UN Doc. A/RES/70/179 (16 February 2016), preambular para 31; Human Rights Council, Res. S-12/1, UN Doc. A/HRC/RES/S-12/1 (21 October 2009), para 1; Res. 28/18, UN Doc. A/HRC/RES/28/18 (7 April 2015), para 13.

[174] Human Rights Council, Res. 40/28, UN Doc. A/HRC/RES/40/28 (4 April 2019), preambular para 12.

[175] Similar resolutions: Human Rights Council, Res. 35/26, UN Doc. A/HRC/RES/35/26 (14 July 2017), paras 2, 8–10, 12 (vote of 27-8, with 12 abstentions); Res. 36/20, UN Doc. A/HRC/RES/36/20 (9 October 2017), paras 2, 8, 11–12 (vote of 27-7, with 13 abstentions); Res. 40/17, UN Doc. A/HRC/RES/40/17 (12 April 2019), preambular para 17 and paras 11, 16, 22, 30 (vote of 28-5, with 14 abstentions); Res. 42/2, UN Doc. A/HRC/RES/42/2 (2 October 2019), preambular para 1 and dispositive para 2 (vote of 22-12, with 11 abstentions).

[176] Human Rights Council, Res. 21/26, UN Doc. A/HRC/RES/21/26 (17 October 2012), paras 1, 7 (vote of 41-3, with 3 abstentions).

[177] E.g. Human Rights Council, Res. 17/17, UN Doc. A/HRC/RES/17/17 (14 July 2011), paras 4, 6; Res. 30/18, UN Doc. A/HRC/RES/30/18 (12 October 2015), paras 1, 3; Res. 33/16, UN Doc. A/HRC/RES/33/16 (5 October 2016), paras 1, 3; Res. 36/31, UN Doc. A/HRC/RES/36/31 (3 October 2017), preambular para 12 and dispositive part, para 2.

consensus within the political body. Yet, consensus in UN votes of political bodies does not mean unanimity,[178] and the agreement of States should still be searched, for example by considering the number of States initiating the draft resolution. The more States supported it, the more the resolution reflects State practice.

Even beyond the UN, the overwhelming majority of OSCE member States[179] called on '*de facto* authorities and other groups in and around Ukraine ... to respect and protect human rights, and to conduct prompt and effective investigations into all allegations of human rights violations'.[180] While it is contestable whether 'human rights' are to be understood as the body of IHRL or the fundamental rights as enshrined in domestic law, the above-mentioned UN documents often expressly referred to IHRL.[181]

Some States excluded the bindingness of IHRL on non-state actors but they did so in general terms,[182] not mentioning the exceptional case where AOGs exercise territorial control. Few States, however, expressed their support for the bindingness of IHRL on *de facto* regimes.[183] The domestic law of the US also recognises that *de facto* authorities are bound by customary international human rights norms.[184] Beyond State practice, the ICRC[185] and a considerable group of authors also confirm the

[178] ILC, Draft conclusions on subsequent agreements and subsequent practice in relation to the interpretation of treaties, with commentaries, 2018, UN Doc. A/73/10 (2018), 90-91, para 30.

[179] Adopted by a vote of 96-7, with 32 abstentions. Report. OSCE Parliamentary Assembly's 24th Annual Session, Helsinki, 5–9 July 2015, 18.

[180] Resolution on the continuation of clear, gross and uncorrected violations of OSCE commitments and international norms by the Russian Federation, para 32, in: OSCE, 24th Annual Session, Helsinki, 2015, Helsinki Declaration and resolutions adopted by the OSCE Parliamentary Assembly, AS (15) DE.

[181] E.g. UN Doc. A/HRC/RES/17/17 (n 177), para 4; UN Doc. A/HRC/RES/33/16 (n 177), para 3; UN Doc. A/HRC/RES/36/31 (n 177), para 2; UN Doc. A/HRC/RES/40/17 (n 175), para 11.

[182] E.g. UNGA, UN Doc. A/C.3/65/SR.25 (7 December 2010), paras 14 (EU), 21 (UK) and 24 (Pakistan).

[183] UNGA, UN Doc. A/C.3/56/SR.40 (9 December 2002), para 25 (Japan); UN Doc. A/C.3/68/SR.32 (19 November 2013), para 82 (Norway); UNSC, UN Doc. S/PV.8619 (16 September 2019), 12 (Belgium, South Africa); UN Doc. S/PV.8642 (17 October 2019), 13 (Belgium), 15 (Equatorial Guinea).

[184] *S. Kadić* v. *Radovan Karadzic*, 13 October 1995, 70 F.3d 232, 245 ('The customary international law of human rights, such as the proscription of official torture, applies to states without distinction between recognized and unrecognized states').

[185] 'International Humanitarian Law and the challenges of contemporary armed conflicts', 31st International Conference of the Red Cross and Red Crescent, October 2011, 14–15.

formula,[186] whereas others contest it because human rights obligations, even customary norms, have been created in order to impose obligations on States.[187] The idea of the bindingness of IHRL on *de facto* regimes is supported by evolving State practice and, understandably, never opposed by States, as this would produce a vacuum of human rights protection in areas under their control. Whereas it would be premature to speak about an existing customary obligation of *de facto* regimes to respect human rights,[188] the more States accept the *de facto* control theory, the more the 'legitimate expectations of the international community' are stabilised as a customary norm.[189]

Consequently, *de facto* regimes have customary obligations under IHRL. Their content may be defined by reference to the core of IHRL binding on States and international law subjects controlling territory. As explained in Section 4.1.1.1 regarding peace operations, it covers at least non-derogable human rights, peremptory human rights norms and, in the case of an armed conflict, customary IHL.[190]

4.2.1.2 International Human Rights Treaties

As in the case of IOs, *de facto* regimes and *a fortiori* AOGs without territorial control cannot have access to treaties under IHRL. Nevertheless, akin to customary international law, treaty practice has evolved over time and nowadays provides on AOGs. International human rights monitoring bodies often addressed to AOGs obligations under IHL but also under IHRL. As *de facto* regimes, emerging from armed conflicts, are addressees of humanitarian obligations, it is not surprising that

[186] Liesbeth Zegveld, *Accountability of Armed Opposition Groups in International Law* (Cambridge University Press 2002) 54, 148–151, 230; Sivakumaran (n 157) 252–253; Clapham (n 52) 280; Daragh Murray, *Human Rights Obligations of Non-State Armed Groups* (Hart Publishing 2016) 120–271; Fortin (n 166) 240–284; Rodenhäuser (n 168) 181–193.

[187] Lindsay Moir, *The Law of Internal Armed Conflict* (Cambridge University Press 2002) 194; Jean D'Aspremont and Jérôme De Hemptinne, *Droit international humanitaire: thèmes choisis* (A Pedone 2012) 101, 104.

[188] Yaël Ronen, 'Human Rights Obligations of Territorial Non-State Actors' (2013) 46 *Cornell International Law Journal* 21, 46–50; *a contrario*, this is the opinion of Constantinides: Constantinides (n 156) 102–103.

[189] Ryngaert (n 156) 356.

[190] Report of the independent international commission of inquiry on the Syrian Arab Republic, UN Doc. A/HRC/19/69 (22 February 2012), para 106; Report of the Special Rapporteur on extrajudicial, summary or arbitrary executions on armed non-State actors: the protection of the right to life, UN Doc. A/HRC/38/44 (5 June 2019), paras 19, 56.

there is a high level of complementarity and overlap between their obligations under IHL and IHRL.

One may argue that provisions of IHL conventions that bind AOGs, mainly under AP II, also partially provide for human rights obligations. For example, the protection of life and the integrity of the person has a minimum threshold that both IHRL and AP II protect.[191] Another aspect of the interconnections between IHL and IHRL is the inclusion of some humanitarian rules in human rights treaties. The Convention on the Rights of the Child provides for some obligations related to the protection of children in armed conflicts (Article 38), which is further detailed by its Optional Protocol on the Involvement of Children in Armed Conflict (OPAC-CRC).[192] Article 4(1) of the OPAC-CRC is the only universal human rights treaty provision expressly addressed to AOGs 'that are distinct from the armed forces of a State', providing that they 'should not, under any circumstances, recruit or use in hostilities persons under the age of 18 years'.[193] The *travaux préparatoires* of the OPAC-CRC show that while the CRC in its preliminary draft only provided for the obligations of States,[194] most States insisted on dedicating a distinct clause to the prohibition of recruitment and participation of children in hostilities related to non-state AOGs, beyond the obligations of States.[195] While some delegates expressed doubts concerning the possibility of imposing obligations on non-state actors,[196] others emphasised that the provision should be drafted with care to avoid that AOGs would be equated with State parties.[197] A minority of delegates proposed a wording similar to the obligation of States, using the word 'shall' to the required conduct of AOGs.[198] Between those two extremities, most States supported a

191 ICC, *The Prosecutor* v. *Bosco Ntaganda*, Trial Chamber VI, ICC-01/04-02/06, judgment, 8 July 2019, para 991 (with other examples).

192 Optional Protocol to the Convention on the Rights of the Child on the involvement of children in armed conflict, New York, 25 May 2000.

193 The term 'armed groups' is considered to overlap with the definition of AP II, Article 1 (1). Tiny Vandewiele, *Optional Protocol: The Involvement of Children in Armed Conflicts* (Martinus Nijhoff Publishers 2006) 40.

194 Preliminary draft optional protocol on involvement of children in armed conflicts, in: UN Doc. CRC/C/16 (5 March 1993), 59–61, Article 2.

195 Report of the working group on a draft optional protocol to the Convention on the Rights of the Child on involvement of children in armed conflicts, UN Doc. E/CN.4/1995/96 (10 February 1995), para 24; Report of the working group on its second session, UN Doc. E/CN.4/1996/102 (21 March 1996), para 31; Report of the working group on its fourth session, UN Doc. E/CN.4/1998/102 (23 March 1998), para 32.

196 UN Doc. E/CN.4/1995/96 (n 195), para 25; UN Doc. E/CN.4/1998/102 (n 195), para 33.

197 UN Doc. E/CN.4/1995/96 (n 195), para 26; UN Doc. E/CN.4/1996/102 (n 195), para 31.

198 UN Doc. E/CN.4/1995/96 (n 195), paras 169 (Poland), 173 (India), 174 (China).

compromise solution that addressed the required conduct of AOGs by the wording 'should',[199] distinct from the States' obligation 'shall'. This solution has been finally adopted as Article 4(1).[200] States that insisted on addressing the required conduct of AOGs justified this provision by applicable IHL[201] or the persuasive force of the future treaty.[202]

Nevertheless, some authors point out that the provision binds the State parties and not directly the AOGs:[203] they note that the term 'should' in the English version is generally used to express recommendations, contrary to the term 'shall', used by Article 4(2), addressed to State parties. Others highlight that the phrasing 'under any circumstances' grants the provision a binding, non-derogable character.[204] The Committee on the Rights of the Child in its Concluding Observations confirm the first interpretation, as it recommends the territorial State to protect against non-state AOGs,[205] while usually expressing its 'concern' about the violations of Article 4(1) by AOGs.[206] While it exceptionally addressed recommendations to AOGs on their negative obligations to respect children's rights,[207] it invoked 'applicable international standards'[208] or IHL[209] and never Article 4(1) of the OPAC-CRC. Therefore, the Optional Protocol imposes treaty obligations on State parties, while Article 4(1) expresses customary obligations of AOGs.

[199] UN Doc. E/CN.4/1998/102 (n 195), 26–29, Annex II: Chairman's perception, Article 3 and paras 41(d) (Switzerland), 43 (Denmark), 49 (Netherlands), 59 (Venezuela), 63 (Belgium); Report of the working group on its sixth session, UN Doc. E/CN.4/2000/74 (27 March 2000), paras 36, 130 (USA), 145 (India).

[200] UN Doc. E/CN.4/2000/74 (n 199), 30–35, Article 4.

[201] Report of the working group on its third session, UN Doc. E/CN.4/1997/96 (13 March 1997), para 36.

[202] Ibid., para 35.

[203] Vandewiele (n 193) 42 (considering AOGs under a moral obligation); Sivakumaran (n 157) 249.

[204] Clapham (n 52) 75.

[205] E.g. CRC, Concluding observations: Iraq, UN Doc. CRC/C/OPAC/IRQ/CO/1 (4 February 2015), para 26.

[206] E.g. CRC, Concluding observations: Yemen, UN Doc. CRC/C/OPAC/YEM/CO/1 (26 February 2014), paras 24, 26–27; CRC, Concluding observations: Rwanda, UN Doc. CRC/C/OPAC/RWA/CO/1 (8 July 2013), para 15.

[207] CRC, Concluding observations: Sudan, UN Doc. CRC/C/15/Add.190 (9 October 2002), para 60; Concluding observations: Israel, UN Doc. CRC/C/15/Add.195 (9 October 2002), para 59; Concluding observations: Nepal, UN Doc. CRC/C/15/Add.261 (21 September 2005), para 12; Concluding observations: Democratic Republic of the Congo, UN Doc. CRC/C/15/Add.153 (9 July 2001), para 6 ('emphasizes the responsibilities of [. . .] certain other actors for the negative impact of the armed conflict upon children and for violations of some provisions of the Convention').

[208] UN Doc. CRC/C/15/Add.190 (n 207), para 60(a).

[209] UN Doc. CRC/C/15/Add.153 (n 207), para 6; UN Doc. CRC/C/15/Add.195 (n 207), para 59(a).

At the regional level, it is the African Union Convention for the Protection and Assistance of Internally Displaced Persons in Africa (Kampala Convention) which in a separate article addresses the role of 'armed groups', understood as 'dissident armed forces or other organised armed groups that are distinct from the armed forces of the state'.[210] In its Article 7, the Convention imposes negative obligations on members of AOGs, namely, prohibitions on violating the rights of displaced persons. The Kampala Convention, in its Preamble, refers to one of its precedents,[211] the UN Guiding Principles on Internal Displacement, which is an early human rights instrument to provide on expectations addressed to 'all authorities, groups and persons irrespective of their legal status and applied without any adverse distinction'.[212] The *travaux préparatoires* of the Kampala Convention show that the initial draft prepared by a group of experts went beyond the recommendatory wording of both the UN Guiding Principles and the OPAC-CRC as it provided for both positive and negative obligations of AOGs to respect and protect the rights of internally-displaced persons.[213] Non-governmental organisations (NGOs) criticised the draft convention for the equal treatment of the responsibilities of States and non-state actors,[214] with introductory references to 'states, armed groups and other relevant actors shall',[215] and States also preferred inserting treaty provisions on the criminal responsibility of individual members of AOGs to obligations of AOGs as such. More intensively than in the OPAC-CRC, obligations under the Kampala Convention bind mainly the State parties which 'shall take measures aimed at ensuring that armed groups act in conformity with their obligations under Article 7'.[216] Furthermore, both

210 African Union Convention for the protection and assistance of internally displaced persons in Africa, 22 October 2009 (Kampala Convention), Article 1(e).

211 Ibid., preambular para 10.

212 Guiding Principles on Internal Displacement (n 4), Principle 2(1).

213 Draft article 6, cited in Flavia Zorzi Giustiniani, 'New Hopes and Challenges for the Protection of IDPs in Africa: The Kampala Convention for the Protection and Assistance of Internally Displaced Persons in Africa' (2010) 39 *Denver Journal of International Law and Policy* 347, 360, n 73.

214 Amnesty International et al., The African Union Convention for the Prevention of Internal Displacement and the Protection of and Assistance to Internally Displaced Persons in Africa. NGO commentary, 6 June 2008, at www.fidh.org/IMG/pdf/IDPconventionAUngoComments.pdf (2 September 2019), 8.

215 Draft article 6.1.3, cited ibid.

216 Ibid., Article 5(11); Won Kidane, 'Managing Displacement by Law in Africa: The Role of the New African Union IDPS Convention' (2011) 44 *Vanderbilt Journal of Transnational Law* 1, 72.

the OPAC-CRC and the Kampala Convention express their State-centric focus by stressing that the above-mentioned provisions shall not affect the legal status of any AOG.[217]

These treaty provisions on AOGs may be explained by customary law, reiterated by the above-mentioned conventions which set out obligations of humanitarian origin, binding non-state actors. On the one hand, these obligations enshrined in human rights treaties do not explain how *de facto* regimes would be bound by other non-humanitarian obligations under IHRL. On the other hand, beyond the obligations of humanitarian origin, States are reluctant to consider rebel authorities bound by other conventions addressed to States, thereby legitimising them.[218]

The practice of human rights treaty bodies confirmed the role of customary IHRL and IHL in human rights treaties. Human rights monitoring bodies traditionally do not consider human rights treaties as binding upon non-state actors such as AOGs or *de facto* regimes – as the IACHR[219] and the ACommHPR[220] expressly confirmed. More categorically, the Human Rights Committee holds that '[t]he article 2, paragraph 1, obligations are binding on States [Parties] and do not, as such, have direct horizontal effect as a matter of international law'.[221]

Some resolutions of the ACommHPR, however, expressly addressed obligations to AOGs: in certain armed conflicts, the Commission 'urged' the rebels to put an immediate end to their attacks,[222] or to respect their obligations under the ACHPR and other international human rights instruments.[223] If one accepts the above-mentioned conclusion that human rights treaties do not directly impose obligations on non-state

[217] OPAC-CRC (n 192), Article 4(3); Kampala Convention (n 210), Articles 7(1) and 15(2).

[218] Nigel S. Rodley, 'Can Armed Opposition Groups Violate Human Rights?' in Kathleen E. Mahoney and Paul Mahoney (eds), *Human Rights in the Twenty-First Century: A Global Challenge* (Martinus Nijhoff Publishers 1993) 314–318; Ryngaert (n 156) 377.

[219] IACHR, Third report on the human rights situation in Colombia, OEA/Ser.L/V/II.102, Doc. 9 rev.1 (26 February 1999), Chapter IV, paras 13–14; Report No. 55/97, Case 11.137, *Juan Carlos Abella* v. *Argentina*, 18 November 1997, para 174.

[220] ACommHPR, *Amnesty International, et al.* v. *Sudan*, Communications nos. 48/90–50/91–52/91–89/93, 15 November 1999, para 186.

[221] HRC, General Comment No. 31 [80], Nature of the General Legal Obligation on States Parties to the Covenant (29 March 2004), UN Doc. CCPR/C/21/Rev.1/Add.13 (26 May 2004), para 8.

[222] ACommHPR, Resolution 209: Resolution on the Human Rights Situation in the North of Mali, 24 February 2012, para 3; Resolution 210: Resolution on Refugees and Internally Displaced Persons fleeing the conflict in the North of Mali, 29 February 2012, para 1; in the same sense: Resolution 68: Resolution on Darfur, 21 May–4 June 2004, para 2.

[223] Resolution 109: Resolution on the Situation in Somalia, 16–30 May 2007, para 4; in the same sense: Statement by the African Commission on the Present Human Rights

actors, the resolutions of the ACommHPR must be interpreted as reiterating the customary human rights obligations of AOGs, as enshrined in the cited human rights instruments.

The Committee on the Rights of the Child, '[w]hile noting the *de facto* control by non-State actors of areas of the State party's territory', urged 'the Communist Party of Nepal (the Maoists) to respect child rights within the areas in which they operate'.[224] The Committee addressed similar Concluding observations to certain *de facto* regimes.[225] Similarly, the Committee against Torture recommended that Hamas authorities in the Gaza Strip 'should take immediate steps to end' human rights violations, 'and to punish those responsible'.[226] The Committee on the Elimination of Discrimination Against Women goes beyond even the obligations of humanitarian origin: it confirmed in its General Recommendation 30 that

> [u]nder international human rights law, although non-State actors cannot become parties to the Convention, the Committee notes that, under certain circumstances, in particular where an armed group with an identifiable political structure exercises significant control over territory and population, non-State actors are obliged to respect international human rights.[227]

Thus, the Committee is the first human rights treaty-monitoring body to expressly confirm that a *de facto* regime is bound by IHRL. Even if this opinion is interpreted in a minimalist way, restricted to customary IHRL, without the binding effect of the CEDAW on *de facto* regimes, it is remarkable that a treaty supervisory body adopted the *de facto* control theory. Moreover, the Committee went further when it urged 'non-State actors such as armed groups' to 'respect women's rights in conflict and post-conflict situations, in line with the Convention' and to 'commit themselves to abiding by codes of conduct on human rights and the prohibition of all forms of gender-based violence'.[228] In line with the CEDAW practice, the Committee on the Protection of the Rights of All

Situation in Mali, 18 January 2013, at www.achpr.org/press/2013/01/d140/ (24 January 2013).

224 CRC, Concluding observations: Nepal, UN Doc. CRC/C/15/Add.261 (21 September 2005), para 12.

225 UN Doc. CRC/C/15/Add.195 (n 207), para 59(a); UN Doc. CRC/C/15/Add.153 (n 207), para 6.

226 CAT, Concluding observations: Israel, UN Doc. CAT/C/ISR/CO/4 (23 June 2009), para 34.

227 CEDAW, General recommendation No. 30 on women in conflict prevention, conflict and post-conflict situations, UN Doc. CEDAW/C/GC/30 (1 November 2013), para 16.

228 Ibid., para 18; CEDAW, Concluding observations: Syria, UN Doc. CEDAW/C/SYR/CO/2 (18 July 2014), para 23.

Migrant Workers urged 'other actors that exercise territorial control to immediately take the necessary measures to protect migrants' in Lybia.[229]

Consequently, human rights treaties and the practice of certain treaty-monitoring bodies demonstrate a tendency to recognise the 'legitimate expectations of the international community', especially customary IHRL and IHL, as binding *de facto* regimes.

4.2.1.3 Acts of International Organisations

The practice of political organs of IOs, such as the UNGA, the UNSC or the European Parliament,[230] set out the obligations under IHRL not only of AOGs exercising territorial control but also of 'all parties to the conflict', including AOGs without territorial control.

The UNSC has addressed provisions to AOGs not only in non-binding resolutions under chapter VI of the UN Charter but increasingly in binding resolutions adopted under chapter VII requiring all parties to the conflict, including rebel militia, to put an immediate end to the violation of human rights[231] or comply with their obligations under IHL and IHRL.[232] It is accepted that the UNSC decisions can deploy an international binding effect on international legal subjects other than States independently of their consent, thanks to the special quality of the UN Charter.[233] The ICJ establishes 'on a case-by-case basis, considering all relevant circumstances, for whom the Security Council intended to create binding legal obligations', including non-state actors.[234]

The UNSC has been criticised for using vague wording,[235] not specifying which human rights obligations it imposes on which actors. However, one may observe a development in the wording: on the one

[229] Committee on the Protection of the Rights of All Migrant Workers and Members of Their Families, Concluding observations: Libya, UN Doc. CMW/C/LBY/CO/1 (12 April 2019), para 11.

[230] E.g. European Parliament, Resolution on the situation in the Central African Republic (17 January 2013) (2013/2514(RSP)), para 9.

[231] E.g. UN Doc. S/RES/2071 (12 October 2012), para 5; UN Doc. S/RES/2098 (28 March 2013), paras 7–8.

[232] UN Doc. S/RES/2140 (26 February 2014), para 9; UN Doc. S/RES/2216 (14 April 2015), para 8.

[233] Anne Peters, 'Article 25' in Bruno Simma, Daniel-Erasmus Khan, Georg Nolte and Andreas Paulus (eds), *The Charter of the United Nations: A Commentary* (Third Edition, Oxford University Press 2012) 803–804, para 44.

[234] *Accordance with International Law of the Unilateral Declaration of Independence in Respect of Kosovo*, Advisory Opinion, *I.C.J. Reports* 2010, 450–451, para 117.

[235] Ryngaert (n 156) 367.

hand, the resolutions define with increasing precision the obligations of AOGs, while referring not only to treaties of IHL but sometimes also to instruments of IHRL such as the CRC and the OPAC-CRC,[236] the CEDAW and its Optional Protocol[237] or Convention 182 of the International Labour Organization on the Worst Forms of Child Labour.[238] On the other hand, beyond the mere negative obligations to respect, UNSC resolutions increasingly stipulate well-defined positive obligations: to prevent[239] and expressly prohibit human rights violations,[240] to protect human rights,[241] 'to issue clear orders prohibiting all violations and abuses committed against children, in violation of applicable international law',[242] to guarantee the instruction in minority language,[243] and so forth.

The fact of the exercise of territorial control by an AOG seems to slightly influence the wording of the resolutions. First, the UNSC and the Human Rights Council are more willing to use the wording 'violation' – reserved for States – when it comes to AOGs controlling territory than the term 'abuse' – reserved for AOGs.[244] Second, there were few instances where the UNSC noted the *de facto* control exercised by the given AOG. For instance, in respect of the *Rassemblement Congolais pour la Democratie-Goma*, it reiterated that 'as the *de facto* authority' it was 'responsible to bring to an end all extrajudicial executions, human rights violations and arbitrary harassment of civilians'[245] and called on 'the *de facto* authorities in the regions affected to ensure the protection of civilians and the rule of law'.[246] Likewise, the UNGA adopted the Declaration on the Protection of All Persons from Being Subjected to Torture and Other Cruel, Inhuman or Degrading Treatment or Punishment of 1975 'as a guideline for all States and other entities exercising effective power'.[247]

236 E.g. UN Doc. S/RES/1314 (10 August 2000), para 3; UN Doc. S/RES/1998 (12 July 2011), Preamble, para 3.
237 UN Doc. S/RES/1325 (31 October 2000), para 9.
238 UN Doc. S/RES/1379 (20 November 2001), para 8(a).
239 UN Doc. S/RES/1464 (4 February 2003), para 7 (adopted under Chapter VII); UN Doc. S/RES/1479 (13 May 2003), para 8.
240 UN Doc. S/RES/2127 (5 December 2013), paras 22–23 (adopted under Chapter VII).
241 UN Doc. S/RES/1291 (24 February 2000), para 10.
242 UN Doc. S/RES/2134 (28 January 2014), para 22 (adopted under Chapter VII).
243 UN Doc. S/RES/1427 (29 July 2002), para 13; UN Doc. S/RES/1554 (29 July 2004), para 20.
244 Fortin (n 166) 340–341.
245 UN Doc. S/RES/1417 (14 June 2002), para 4.
246 Ibid., para 5.
247 UNGA Res. 3452 (XXX), UN Doc. A/RES/3452 (9 December 1975), preambular para 5.

One may ask whether the political organs of IOs, and especially the UNSC, in this way impose new obligations on non-state actors or, according to a less progressive interpretation, it reminds AOGs of their pre-existing obligations under IHRL.[248] This latter conclusion is more accurate concerning customary obligations such as the prohibition on the recruitment of child soldiers or the participation of child soldiers in hostilities,[249] while it is difficult to maintain that all provisions of human rights conventions such as the CRC or the CEDAW bind AOGs. One should interpret UNSC resolutions referring to these treaties, adopted until now without exception under chapter VI, as invoking treaty provisions on AOGs such as Article 4(1) of the OPAC-CRC, and excluding the other provisions binding State parties. Nevertheless, one cannot exclude the possibility of the UNSC inventing new obligations of AOGs in the future under chapter VII, without any customary basis.

4.2.2 *Intrinsic Sources*

The conduct of *de facto* regimes, despite the fact that it is neither creative nor expressive of customary international law,[250] can be analysed as an indicator of the engagements undertaken by non-state actors. Once a *de facto* regime has expressed its will to assume obligations under IHRL, the principle of estoppel applies to it.[251] While these intrinsic sources may constitute a means of propaganda, without any legal force, if the *de facto* regime respects them, they must be taken seriously.[252] One can distinguish between agreements concluded by the *de facto* regimes (Section 4.2.2.1) and their unilateral commitments (Section 4.2.2.2).

4.2.2.1 Agreements Concluded by *De Facto* Regimes

De facto regimes might conclude agreements, in particular ceasefire agreements, peace agreements, arrangements on normalisation or the protection of human rights, with the territorial State, IOs or even with

[248] Christian Tomuschat, 'The Applicability of Human Rights Law to Insurgent Movements', *Krisensicherung und humanitärer Schutz: Festschrift für Dieter Fleck* (BWV Berliner Wissenschatfs-Verlag 2004) 586; Tshibangu Kalala, *Les résolutions de l'ONU et les destinataires non étatiques* (Larcier 2009) 97; Peters (n 233) 803, para 39.

[249] Henckaerts and Doswald-Beck (n 155) 482–488 (Rules 136–137).

[250] ILC, Draft conclusions on identification of customary international law (n 171), 130, Draft Conclusion 4(3).

[251] Ronen (n 188) 37.

[252] Sandesh Sivakumaran, *The Law of Non-International Armed Conflict* (Oxford University Press 2012) 108.

other AOGs.[253] It is accepted that *de facto* regimes have the capacity to undertake obligations in such agreements,[254] for instance, under Common Article 3 of the Geneva Conventions.[255]

The legal status of these agreements is more contested. While the International Criminal Tribunal for the Former Yugoslavia (ICTY) and the International Commission of Inquiry on Darfur held that they constitute binding international agreements,[256] other tribunals concluded that such agreements are not governed by international law.[257] The law governing the agreement concluded by a *de facto* regime in fact is not necessarily international law but may be the law of the territorial State or another domestic law – everything depends on the wording of the agreement which must be interpreted on a case-by-case basis.[258]

In any event, such agreements set out obligations of the *de facto* regime: the respect for IHL[259] or that of human rights in general[260] or, though rarely, some international instruments and/or the internal law on human rights of the territorial State. A rule under human rights law and IHL may be identical, 'such that it is immaterial whether the Parties to the agreement have referred to the rule as stemming from one or the other body of law'.[261] Some agreements refer to the laws and inter-

[253] Ibid., 124–133; All agreements cited below are available at http://peacemaker.un.org (22 July 2014).

[254] Frowein (n 150) 94–166; Stefan Talmon, *Kollektive Nichtanerkennung illegaler Staaten: Grundlagen und Rechtsfolgen einer international koordinierten Sanktion dargestellt am Beispiel der Türkischen Republik Nord-Zypern* (Mohr Siebeck 2006) 370–458.

[255] CG IV, Article 3(2).

[256] ICTY, *Prosecutor* v. *Dusko Tadić*, decision on the Defence Motion for Interlocutory Appeal on Jurisdiction, decision of 2 October 1995, paras 89, 143; Report of the International Commission of Inquiry on Darfur to the Secretary-General, UN Doc. S/2005/60 (1 February 2005), para 174.

[257] Colombian Constitutional Court, C-225/95, *Derecho internacional humanitario-Naturaleza imperativa/Ius cogens*, 18 May 1995, para 17; SCSL, *The Prosecutor* v. *Sesay, Kallon and Gbao*, Decision on constitutionality and lack of jurisdiction, SCSL-2004-15-AR72(E), Appeals Chamber, 13 March 2004, paras 45–50.

[258] Frowein (n 150) 114; Olivier Corten and Pierre Klein, 'Are Agreements between States and Non-State Entities Rooted in the International Legal Order?' in Enzo Cannizzaro (ed), *The Law of Treaties beyond the Vienna Convention* (Oxford University Press 2011) 10.

[259] GC IV, Common Article 3(3); AP I, Article 96(2); Hague Convention for the Protection of Cultural Property (1954), Article 19(2).

[260] E.g. 12-point understanding reached between the Seven Political Parties and Nepal Communist Party (Maoists), 22 November 2005, points 4, 8; Framework Agreement on the Bangsamoro between the Philippine Government and the Moro Islamic Liberation Front, 15 October 2012, Article VI.

[261] GC I, Commentary of 2016, para 851.

national conventions in force in the territorial State,[262] whereas others include substantial provisions protecting human rights.[263] Yet other agreements refer expressly to IHRL instruments such as the UDHR, CAT, CRC or the ACHPR.[264] In the latter cases the obligations of *de facto* regimes are undoubtedly subject to the international legal order.[265]

Once concluded, such an agreement produces rights and obligations, if not under international law, at least under the general principle of the law of *pacta sunt servanda*. It causes the referenced international instruments to be binding on the *de facto* regime.[266] The UNSC[267] and human rights monitoring bodies[268] refer to such agreements to reiterate the obligations of the parties to the conflict. This practice illustrates that at least some States and IOs, parties to the agreement, accept that a *de facto* regime could be the addressee of obligations under IHRL when it attains a certain level of effectiveness by reason of its permanence and/or the intensity of the conflict.[269]

4.2.2.2 Unilateral Commitments

More often than concluding agreements, *de facto* regimes declare their commitment to respect IHL, human rights in general or IHRL. The notion 'unilateral commitments' is understood as all types of unilateral acts adopted by a *de facto* regime: mere declarations, codes of conduct, instructions, regulations, laws and other sources that express the non-

262 E.g. Comprehensive Agreement on Respect for Human Rights and International Humanitarian Law between the Government of the Republic of the Philippines and the National Democratic Front of the Philippines, The Hague, 16 March 1998, Part II, Article 4.

263 E.g. Agreement on Human Rights between the Government of El Salvador and the Frente Farabundo Martí para La Liberación Nacional, San José, 26 July 1990, UN Doc. A/44/971-S/21541 (16 August 1990), Annex; Comprehensive Agreement on Respect for Human Rights GRP-NDFP (n 262).

264 E.g. Peace Agreement between the Government of Sierra Leone and the RUF (Lomé Peace Agreement), 7 July 1999, in: UN Doc. S/1999/777 (12 July 1999), Annex, Article XIV, para 1; Comprehensive Peace Agreement GN-CPN-M (n 263), Article 7; Comprehensive Agreement on Respect for Human Rights GRP-NDFP (n 262), Article 5.

265 Corten and Klein (n 258) 12–13.

266 ICTY, *Prosecutor* v. *Tihomir Blaskić*, IT-95-14-T, Decision, Trial Chamber, 3 March 2000, para 172; *Prosecutor* v. *Stanislav Galić*, IT-98-29-T, judgment, Trial Chamber, 5 December 2003, para 25; *Galić* appeals judgment (n 151), para 119.

267 E.g. UN Doc. S/RES/1261 (30 August 1999), para 9; UN Doc. S/RES/1706 (31 August 2006), para 14 (Chapter VII); UN Doc. S/RES/2088 (24 January 2013), paras 4–5 (Chapter VII).

268 E.g. ACommHPR, Resolution 68 (n 222), Preamble, para 7; Resolution 238: Resolution on the Political Situation in the Republic of Mali, 20–24 July 2013, dispositive part, para 6.

269 Sivakumaran (n 252) 97.

state entity's policy related to human rights.[270] Various *de facto* regimes declared their commitment to international law, human rights and/or international human rights instruments in a declaration of independence. Eurasian *de facto* regimes referred to the UN Charter,[271] the UDHR, the ICCPR, the ICESCR and other international human rights instruments,[272] whereas other *de facto* regimes have issued declarations with a more general wording such as the commitment to respect human rights.[273]

The legal force of these declarations is questionable, as *de facto* regimes might use them as mere rhetoric tools to strengthen their legitimacy. Unilateral commitments must be analysed on a case-by-case basis, under their own terms and taking into account their practice.[274] In practice, many *de facto* authorities ignore IHRL instruments, especially because of their lacking human resources and appropriate training in IHRL.[275] Some *de facto* judges nonetheless are ready to apply international human rights instruments especially where the legal system of the territorial State that they oppose had a legal tradition to apply them.[276] The practice also shows that *de facto* authorities are more willing to respect these engagements if the latter are set out in written codes.[277]

[270] Ibid., 140–143.

[271] E.g. 'MRT', Declaration of independence, 25 August 1991, at http://mfa-pmr.org/ru/DTp (16 March 2020); 'TRNC', Declaration of independence, 15 November 1983, at www.cm.gov.nc.tr/Bilgi/bildirge.pdf (15 November 2014), paras 11, 23(a); 'Donetsk People's Republic', Memorandum on the foundation of State building, political and historical continuity, 2014, at https://dnrsovet.su/zakonodatelnaya-deyatelnost/memorandumy/ (15 September 2019).

[272] South Ossetia, Declaration of independence, 20 September 1990, at www.parliament.ge/files/613_8104_291446_5a.pdf (15 March 2020); Abkhazia, Act on the Declaration of independence, 12 October 1999, at http://abkhazia-apsny.ru/suverinitet.html (15 March 2020); 'TRNC', Declaration of independence (n 271), para 18.

[273] E.g. the declaration of the National Transitional Council of Libya in March 2011, in: A/HRC/17/44 (n 158), para 72; FMLN, La Legitimidad de nuestros métodos de lucha, El Salvador, 10 October 1988, 89, in: ICTY, *Tadić*, decision on the defence motion for interlocutory appeal on jurisdiction (n 256), para 107.

[274] Sivakumaran (n 252) 122.

[275] For a socio-legal analysis of the rule of law in *de facto* regimes: Christopher Waters, 'Law in Places That Don't Exist' (2006) 34 *Denver Journal of International Law and Policy* 401, 407–418.

[276] E.g. 'TRNC', judgment in Case No. D.4/2003, 26 June 2003 (holding that the ECHR is part of domestic law of the 'TRNC'); 'Donetsk People's Republic', judgment in Case No. 6/023/135/2016, 29 November 2016 (applying the ECHR and its Protocol No. 4); other examples available at https://sites.manchester.ac.uk/armjust/courts-of-aogs/ (15 March 2020).

[277] International Council on Human Rights Policy, *Ends & Means: Human Rights Approaches to Armed Groups*, 2000, 52; Sivakumaran (n 252) 563.

State practice considers these unilateral engagements as binding on the *de facto* regime: the UNSC called on AOGs 'to make and implement specific time-bound commitments to combat sexual violence',[278] while the Human Rights Council called on AOGs to honour their commitments to prevent the recruitment and use of children.[279] Human rights treaty-monitoring bodies recommended that AOGs commit themselves to abiding by codes of conduct on human rights.[280]

In conclusion, norms of IHRL that *de facto* regimes voluntarily accept are binding on them. Territorial control is a relevant factor in taking those commitments seriously as the effectiveness that the *de facto* regime exercises ensures the ability necessary to implement its human rights obligations. This is the reason why some commentators exclude the fact that IHRL could bind AOGs without stable effective control.[281]

4.2.3 *The Maintenance of Public Order and Safety*

As explained in Sections 4.2.1–4.2.2, *de facto* regimes are bound by certain human rights obligations under extrinsic and intrinsic sources. State practice increasingly tends to assimilate the obligations of *de facto* regimes to those of States, codified by the works of the Secretary-General under the title 'Fundamental standards of humanity'.[282] Similarly to the State in a territory under its control, the *de facto* regime is considered the guarantor of human rights in its area.[283] By analogy, it may be required to maintain public order and safety similarly to an occupying State. Even though *de facto* regimes lack legitimacy, they are the main subject able to fulfil this obligation and to protect human rights on the ground. As this section explains, *de facto* regimes are addressees of this obligation, which has two crucial aspects: positive obligations towards the local population

[278] UN Doc. S/RES/2106 (24 June 2013), para 10.

[279] Human Rights Council, Res. 39/19, UN Doc. A/HRC/RES/39/19 (3 October 2018), para 12.

[280] CEDAW, General recommendation No. 30 (n 227), para 18(b); UN Doc. CEDAW/C/SYR/CO/2 (n 228), paras 11, 28; UN Doc. CRC/C/15/Add.195 (n 207), para 59(a).

[281] Sivakumaran (n 252) 97; Ryngaert (n 156) 376, 379.

[282] E.g. Fundamental standards of humanity, Report of the Secretary-General submitted pursuant to Commission resolution 1998/29, UN Doc. E/CN.4/1999/92 (18 December 1998); UN Doc. E/CN.4/2001/91 (12 January 2001); UN Doc. A/HRC/8/14 (3 June 2008) etc.

[283] Human Rights Council, Res. 22/18, UN Doc. A/HRC/RES/22/18 (10 April 2013), para 5 ('Calls upon all forces and all armed groups present within the territory to ensure that international human rights law' is 'strictly respected') (Adopted without a vote); UN Doc. A/HRC/12/48 (n 158), paras 498, 1682, 1954; CoE Parliamentary Assembly, Resolution 1648, The humanitarian consequences of the war between Georgia and Russia (28 January 2009), paras 24.1, 24.13; Resolution 1633 (2008), The consequences of war between Georgia and Russia, para 23.1.1.

(Section 4.2.3.1) and the maintenance of laws in force in the country (Section 4.2.3.2).

4.2.3.1 Positive Obligations

De facto regimes are subject to the entire range of obligations to respect in IHRL. The reason for this is that they can comply with negative obligations not to violate human rights. The scope of their positive obligations to protect and fulfil, however, depends on their effectiveness and, therefore, the functional approach is recommended to determine their content (a). This section applies the functional approach to two examples of positive obligations, the obligation to guarantee economic and social rights (b) and access to justice (c).

a. Functional Approach

The entire spectrum of IHRL is applicable to *de facto* regimes, as in the case of States, but the scope of their obligations might be different. Their effectiveness, that is, their exercised authority, available resources or capacity to fulfil the obligations in IHRL might be more limited than those of States. It is clear that the obligation to conduct effective investigations requires a series of procedures and institutions such as the hearing of witnesses, gathering evidence, trajectory analysis and ballistic and forensic analyses, autopsy and so forth – which some *de facto* regimes cannot implement.[284] Because of their lack of resources, some *de facto* regimes might not be able to fulfil certain socio-economic rights to the same extent as States, such as the right to social security, the right to join trade unions and the right of the child to education. Likewise, because of their limited participation in international life, *de facto* regimes might not be able to satisfy the obligation of international assistance and cooperation in matters of socio-economic rights or in cross-border trafficking of human beings. Some AOGs are unable to establish stable institutions such as civil or administrative tribunals, whereas others set up sophisticated institutions: for instance, Eurasian *de facto* regimes dispose of an institutional structure comparable to that of a State. Consequently, the huge variety of *de facto* regimes require a flexible standard of their positive obligations, depending on their effectiveness. As in the case of outside States controlling an area outside their borders, the functional approach of the scope of obligations imposes positive obligations commensurate to the local authorities' effectiveness in the

[284] Sivakumaran (n 157) 255–256.

given case at hand (Section 3.2.2). As this approach imposes the maximum human rights protection realistically, in light of the specific circumstances, it is equally applicable to non-state *de facto* regimes.[285]

Nonetheless, as in the case of States, *de facto* regimes are also required to satisfy a certain minimum threshold of humanity, independently of their capabilities. First, customary IHL norms applicable in non-international armed conflicts impose certain minimum thresholds, for instance the obligation to respect the fundamental guarantees of civilians and persons *hors de combat*,[286] the obligation to search for, respect and protect the wounded, sick and shipwrecked,[287] the obligation to protect persons deprived of their liberty[288] or the specific protection afforded to women and children.[289]

Second, minimum core obligations in IHRL equally apply to *de facto* regimes, irrespective of their resources and capabilities.[290] For instance, all detained persons have the right to an adequate standard of living, including the rights to food and water, as well as the right to health,[291] irrespective of the legal status of the detaining authority.[292] Likewise, the Guiding Principles on Internal Displacement, recognised by States as 'the key international framework for the protection of internally displaced persons',[293] require *de facto* authorities to provide internally-displaced persons with certain minimum services such as essential food and potable water, basic shelter and housing, appropriate clothing and essential medical services and sanitation.[294]

Beyond those minimum thresholds, the scope of positive obligations in IHRL depends on the effectiveness of the given *de facto* regime. IHL has recognised this: for example in respect of detained persons, AP II

[285] Clapham (n 52) 68–69; Constantinides (n 156) 110; Murray (n 186) 177–180.

[286] Henckaerts and Doswald-Beck (n 155) 299–383 (Rules 87–105).

[287] Ibid., 396–405 (Rules 109–111).

[288] Ibid., 428–433, 435–437, 445–447 (Rules 118–119, 121 and 125).

[289] Ibid., 474–488 (Rules 134–137).

[290] *Supra*, Section 3.2.3.4.

[291] Standard Minimum Rules for the Treatment of Prisoners, approved by the Economic and Social Council by its resolutions 663 C (XXIV) of 31 July 1957 and 2076 (LXII) of 13 May 1977, paras 20, 22–26.

[292] Report of the Independent International Commission of Inquiry on the Syrian Arab Republic, UN Doc. A/HRC/40/70 (31 January 2019), para 92 (violation of the right to an adequate standard of living by the Syrian Democratic Forces); CPT, Report to the Government of the Republic of Moldova on the visit to Prison Establishment No. 8 in Bender, CPT/Inf (2008) 37 (4 December 2008), paras 18, 20 (recommendations to the 'MRT' to allow access to running water and electricity supplies for a Moldovan prison).

[293] UNGA Res. 73/298, UN Doc. A/RES/73/298 (7 June 2019), preambular para 3.

[294] Guiding Principles on Internal Displacement (n 4), Principle 18(2).

provides that AOGs 'shall also, within the limits of their capabilities, respect the following provisions'.[295] Several provisions refer to the capacity of the parties to the armed conflict ('all appropriate steps shall be taken', 'to the fullest extent practicable', 'all possible measures shall be taken') which set the limit of positive obligations.[296] In IHRL, international monitoring bodies have also applied the functional approach to *de facto* regimes. For instance, the UN report on the Gaza conflict concluded that 'the Gaza authorities have an obligation to respect and enforce the protection of the human rights of the people of Gaza, *inasmuch as* they exercise effective control over the territory, including law enforcement and the administration of justice' [emphasis added].[297] Likewise, Special Rapporteurs have held that *de facto* regimes have obligations under IHRL in accordance with 'the extent and nature of their capacities to exercise territorial control and governance functions'.[298] Consequently, *de facto* regimes have an obligation to guarantee human rights in the area under their control in accordance with their effectiveness.

b. Economic and Social Rights

The functional approach is particularly important for economic, social and cultural rights, as they expect from authorities their progressive realisation by all appropriate means to the maximum of the available resources.[299] Due to the replacement of State authority by the *de facto* regime, the latter has the authority to adopt long-term measures and the effectiveness to implement them.[300]

The rule on progressive realisation of socio-economic rights entails a strong presumption that retrogressive measures taken in relation to those rights are not permissible.[301] In other words, *de facto* authorities are expected to preserve the threshold of protection of socio-economic rights guaranteed in the area. Any deliberately retrogressive measures 'would require the most careful consideration and would need to be fully

[295] AP II, Article 5(1)–5(2). [296] Ibid., Articles 4 (3)(b), 7(2), 8, 17(1).

[297] UN Doc. A/HRC/12/48 (n 158), para 1369.

[298] Report of the Special Rapporteur on extrajudicial, summary or arbitrary executions on her mission to Iraq, UN Doc. A/HRC/38/44/Add.1 (20 June 2018), para 17; UN Doc. A/HRC/38/44 (n 190), paras 52, 75.

[299] ICESCR, Article 2(1). [300] Murray (n 186) 191.

[301] CESCR, General Comment No. 14 (2000): The right to the highest attainable standard of health (article 12 of the ICESCR), UN Doc. E/C.12/2000/4 (11 August 2000), para 32.

justified by reference to the totality of the rights provided for in the Covenant and in the context of the full use of the maximum available resources'.[302]

Taking the example of the right to education, not every *de facto* regime can set up schools, especially during an ongoing armed conflict. They nonetheless have the capacity to maintain and the duty to protect the existing schools in armed conflict as civilian objects[303] and to ensure education to children under IHL.[304] IHRL complements and specifies these duties. Authorities are expected to guarantee the right to education within their existing capacities: depending on their resources, *de facto* authorities are expected to make available buildings or other protection from the elements, sanitation facilities for both sexes, safe drinking water, trained teachers who receive domestically-competitive salaries and teaching materials for educational institutions and programmes.[305] They are also required to ensure the right to education of children from vulnerable groups such as children with disabilities or ethnic minorities, especially in times of severe resource constraints, by the adoption of relatively low-cost targeted programmes.[306] A language policy applied to schools that intends to enforce a separatist ideology and change the language and culture of a given community living in the area, however, constitutes an impermissible retrogressive measure.[307]

Another example is the right to an adequate standard of living, including the right to housing. The takeover of control by *de facto* authorities often has a negative impact on housing, especially on property rights of vulnerable people, internally-displaced persons or a conflict-affected population whose property the military has damaged, destroyed or used. Local authorities are required to take measures to defend the interests of people who have lost housing or land rights and initiate housing and livelihood programmes that allow them to normalise their living

[302] CESCR, General comment No. 3: The nature of States parties' obligations (art. 2, para 1, of the Covenant), in: UN Doc. HRI/GEN/1/Rev.9 (Vol. I) (27 May 2008), 7–10, para 9.

[303] Henckaerts and Doswald-Beck (n 155) 32–36 (Rules 9–10). [304] AP II, Article 4(3)(a).

[305] ICESCR, Article 13(2); CESCR, General comment No. 13 (1999): The right to education (article 13 of the Covenant), UN Doc. E/C.12/1999/10 (8 December 1999), para 6(a).

[306] CESCR, General comment No. 3 (n 302), para 12; CESCR, General comment No. 5: Persons with disabilities, in: Ibid., 17–27, para 10; Report on Human Rights in the Transnistrian Region (n 160), 44–48, Recommendations nos. 25, 28; Follow-up Report on Human Rights in the Transnistrian Region by Thomas Hammarberg Senior UN Human Rights Expert, 2018, at www.undp.org/content/dam/unct/moldova/docs/Follow-up_Report_TH_2018.pdf (23 August 2019), 38–39.

[307] ECtHR, *Catan and Others* v. *Moldova and Russia* [GC], Appl. Nos. 43370/04, 8252/05 and 18454/06, judgment of 19 October 2012, paras 144, 138.

situation.[308] The degree to which they are expected to fulfil the right to housing depends on their resources such as annual budget, the availability of safe and uninhabitated buildings, material assistance received from the civil society and humanitarian organisations and so forth.

Similarly to States, any *de facto* regime is expected to seek international assistance and cooperation on mutually-agreed terms if it is unable, despite its best efforts, to guarantee economic, social and cultural rights within the territory under its control.[309] In this case it is required to seek assistance from and cooperation with the territorial State or relief organisations, including NGOs and IOs so as to satisfy the obligation to protect and fulfil. It follows from AP II and customary IHL that AOGs are also obliged to allow and facilitate the provision of humanitarian assistance.[310] However, assistance provided by IOs and especially other States is subject to the consent of the territorial State,[311] as this might otherwise constitute a violation of its sovereignty.

c. *Access to Justice*

State practice has recognised the obligation of AOGs to 'take all the measures necessary to ensure effective, impartial and independent investigations into all alleged violations and abuses of human rights'.[312] This applies *a fortiori* to *de facto* regimes, as they have effective control over territory and persons, necessary for providing remedies, and they have been called on to and repress violations of IHL and IHRL, and bring perpetrators to justice.[313]

IHL obliges all parties to a non-international armed conflict to guarantee the right to a fair trial.[314] AOGs are authorised to hold trials only for

[308] Report of the Representative of the Secretary-General on the human rights of internally displaced persons, Walter Kälin, Follow-up to the report on the mission to Georgia, UN Doc. A/HRC/13/21/Add.3 (14 January 2009), 2 (summary) and paras 40, 54; UNOHCHR, Report on the human rights situation in Ukraine, 16 February to 15 May 2019, at www.ohchr.org/Documents/Countries/UA/ReportUkraine16Feb-15May2019_EN.pdf (13 August 2019), para 118(d).

[309] *Supra*, Section 3.1.5.1.

[310] AP II, Article 18(1); Henckaerts and Doswald-Beck (n 155) 193–202 (Rules 55–56).

[311] UNGA Res. 46/182, UN Doc. A/RES/46/182 (19 December 1991), Annex, para 3.

[312] UN Doc. A/HRC/RES/36/31 (n 177), para 11; Res. 39/16, UN Doc. A/HRC/RES/39/16 (5 October 2018), para 11.

[313] E.g. UNGA Res. 54/189, UN Doc. A/RES/54/189A-B (14 February 2000), para 25; UN Doc. S/RES/1509 (2003), para 10 (adopted under Chapter VII); UN Doc. CAT/C/ISR/CO/4 (n 226), para 34 (with regard to Hamas).

[314] GC IV, Article 3(1)(d); AP II, Article 6; Rome Statute of the International Criminal Court, Rome, 17 July 1998, Article 8(2)(c)(iv); Henckaerts and Doswald-Beck (n 155) 352–375 (Rules 100–103).

'a regularly constituted court, affording all the judicial guarantees which are recognized as indispensable by civilized peoples',[315] understood as a court either constituted in accordance with the 'laws' of the AOG or a pre-existing court continuing its operation under the control of the AOG.[316] Such a court must offer the essential guarantees of independence and impartiality.[317] In IHRL, these fundamental principles guaranteeing fair trial (such as the presumption of innocence, the principle of legality) are considered non-derogable even in states of emergency.[318] On the one hand, these customary obligations of fair trial bind AOGs only if they choose to have recourse to convictions,[319] but they are not required *a priori* to create a justice system. On the other hand, IHL, namely, the rule of responsible command, supposes a mechanism of investigation and sanction within the AOGs.[320] One can at least affirm that there is an interest to require *de facto* regimes to set up a functioning judicial system in order to prevent impunity and anarchy.[321]

This interest is recognised by numerous resolutions of IOs such as the UNSC[322] and the CoE Parliamentary Assembly,[323] which called on AOGs to prohibit serious breaches of human rights and open investigations so that the perpetrators will be brought to justice and held accountable. International monitoring bodies such as the UNSC Working Group on Children and Armed Conflict,[324] Special Rapporteurs[325] and fact-finding

[315] GC IV, Article 3(1)(d). [316] GC I, Commentary of 2016, para 692.

[317] Ibid., paras 693–694; ICC, Elements of Crimes, 2011, 34.

[318] HRC, General comment no. 29, States of emergency (Article 4), UN Doc. CCPR/C/21/Rev.1/Add.11 (31 August 2001), para 11; IACtHR, *Habeas corpus in Emergency Situations (Arts. 27(2), 25(1) and 7(6) American Convention on Human Rights)*, Advisory Opinion OC-8/87 of 30 January 1987, Series A No. 8, para 32; *Judicial Guarantees in States of Emergency (Arts. 27(2), 25 and (8) American Convention on Human Rights)*, Advisory Opinion OC-9/87 of 6 October 1987, Series A No. 9, paras 23–25.

[319] Report of the Special Rapporteur on Extrajudicial, Summary or Arbitrary Executions, Philip Alston, Mission to Philippines, UN Doc. A/HRC/8/3/Add.2 (16 April 2008), para 32.

[320] Sivakumaran (n 252) 557. [321] Ibid., 550.

[322] E.g. UN Doc. S/RES/1291 (24 February 2000), para 15; UN Doc. S/RES/1509 (19 September 2003), para 10; UN Doc. S/RES/1960 (16 December 2010), para 5.

[323] CoE Parliamentary Assembly, Resolution 1647, The implementation of Resolution 1633 (2008) on the consequences of the war between Georgia and Russia (28 January 2009), para 7; Resolution 1648 (n 283), para 25.3.

[324] Working Group on Children and Armed Conflict, Conclusions on children and armed conflict in Afghanistan, UN Doc. S/AC.51/2009/1 (13 July 2009), para d)(vi); Conclusions on children and armed conflict in the Central African Republic, UN Doc. S/AC.51/2009/2 (13 July 2009), para g)(iv).

[325] Situation of human rights in the Sudan, Report of the Special Rapporteur, Gáspár Bíró, UN Doc. E/CN.4/1996/62 (20 February 1996), para 87; Special process on missing persons

missions[326] often recommended AOGs to take the necessary measures to investigate the cases that came to their attention and hold the perpetrators accountable. The IACHR also urged AOGs to respect, implement and enforce, 'through their command and control structures', the rules of IHL, with particular emphasis on those norms providing for the protection of civilians.[327] The UN Secretary-General went even further, urging AOGs to 'restore' the justice system in Côte d'Ivoire.[328]

An obligation of *de facto* regimes to maintain a justice system presupposes that such a system might comply with IHRL irrespective of the entity's unrecognised status.[329] For instance, the International Criminal Court (ICC) recognised that there was a functioning judicial system set up by the *Mouvement pour la Libération du Congo*, which permitted the commanders to punish the crimes committed and to prevent their future repetition.[330] Thereby, the ICC rejected the argument that a tribunal set up by an AOG cannot be considered 'a regularly constituted court' under Article 8(2)(c)(iv) of the Rome Statute as it was not established by 'a parliamentary statute or equivalent unwritten norm of common law'.[331] Human rights monitoring bodies are also ready to recognise procedures instituted by *de facto* regimes as 'tribunal' or 'effective investigation' if they comply with fair trial guarantees under IHRL. The ECtHR used this pragmatic approach and concluded that

> [i]n certain circumstances, a court belonging to the judicial system of an entity not recognised under international law may be regarded as a tribunal 'established by law' provided that it forms part of a judicial system operating on a 'constitutional and legal basis' reflecting a judicial tradition compatible with

in the territory of the former Yugoslavia, Report submitted by Mr. Manfred Nowak, UN Doc. E/CN.4/1995/37 (12 January 1995), paras 55–56.

326 UN Doc. A/HRC/12/48 (n 158), paras 1682, 1963.

327 Third report on the human rights situation in Colombia, OEA/Ser.L/V/II.102, Doc. 9 rev. 1 (26 February 1999), Chapter IV, Recommendation 1.

328 Report of the Secretary-General on children and armed conflict in Côte d'Ivoire, UN Doc. S/2006/835 (25 October 2006), para 51.

329 Report on Human Rights in the Transnistrian Region (n 160), 13 (recognising that several provisions of the 'MRT' laws are consistent with IHRL).

330 ICC, *Prosecutor* v. *Jean-Pierre Bemba Gombo*, ICC-01/05-01/08, Decision pursuant to article 61 (7) (a) and (b) of the Rome Statute on the charges of the Prosecutor, Pre-Trial Chamber, 15 June 2009, para 501.

331 ICC, *Prosecutor* v. *Jean-Pierre Bemba Gombo*, Amicus curiae observations on superior responsibility submitted pursuant to rule 103 of the rules of procedure and evidence, ICC-01/05-01/08-406, Pre-trial Chamber, 20 April 2009, paras 22–23.

the Convention, in order to enable individuals to enjoy the Convention guarantees.[332]

While examining these criteria and the quality of the *de facto* regime's law,[333] the ECtHR recognised that the 'TRNC' has an operational justice system where local tribunals could be regarded as 'established by law'.[334] Similarly, the Court concluded that the remedies existing in the 'TRNC', especially the procedure of the Immovable Property Commission, could be considered 'domestic remedies' from the point of view of Article 35(1) of the ECHR.[335] While one might criticise this case law as legitimising unrecognised *de facto* entities, the interest to maintain public order and safety prevails over the interest of non-recognition of the *de facto* institutions.[336]

Because of the great variety of their effectiveness, one cannot expect all *de facto* regimes to establish a sophisticated justice system. However, they may reasonably be required to maintain the pre-existing mechanisms: it is in that sense that the UN High Commissioner for Human Rights called upon the *Fuerzas armadas revolucionarias de Colombia* (FARC), at the time controlling the demilitarised region, to respect 'the people's legitimate exercise of human rights and their access to the mechanisms and resources that guarantee these, especially in the demilitarized zone'.[337] Similarly, as Eurasian *de facto* regimes, which emerged mainly from the former USSR 'inherited' a well-established judicial system from the territorial State, it is legitimate to require them to at least maintain it operationally to guarantee the normality of individuals' lives. Depending on their effectiveness, they can be expected to set up, alternatively, new remedies to comply with IHRL. For instance, Eurasian *de facto* regimes were required to establish dispute settlement mechanisms involving international expertise to decide on individuals' property

[332] *Ilaşcu and Others* v. *Moldova and Russia* [GC], Appl. no. 48787/99, judgment of 8 July 2004, para 460.

[333] On the indirect justiciability of non-state conduct: *Infra*, Section 7.2.5.

[334] *Cyprus* v. *Turkey* [GC], Appl. no. 25781/94, judgment of 10 May 2001, paras 231–240, esp. para 237; *Ahmet Djavit AN* v. *Turkey*, Appl. no. 20652/92, judgment of 20 February 2003, paras 30–31; *Protopapa* v. *Turkey*, Appl. no. 16084/90, judgment of 24 February 2009, para 87.

[335] *Demopoulos and Others* v. *Turkey* [GC], Appl. nos. 46113/99 et al., decision of 1 March 2010 on the admissibility, para 103.

[336] Sivakumaran (n 252) 559.

[337] Report of the United Nations High Commissioner for Human Rights on the human rights situation in Colombia, UN Doc. E/CN.4/2002/17 (28 February 2002), para 382.

claims[338] or a juvenile justice system where it was lacking.[339] Finally, a *de facto* regime is expected to use the available formal or informal, indirect channels of cooperation with IOs and States including the territorial State to ensure investigation and prosecution of crimes.[340]

4.2.3.2 The Maintenance of Laws in Force in the Area

Limited State practice and scholarship expect from *de facto* regimes the protection of persons on the model of the occupying power.[341] Given the lack of sovereignty of *de facto* regimes recognised by the community States over the territory, their authority is temporary, while international law protects the rights of the displaced sovereign, similarly to military occupation. Therefore, it is reasonable to require *de facto* regimes, in line with Article 43 of The Hague Regulations, to maintain the laws in force in the territory under their control, 'unless absolutely prevented'.[342] As an exception from the main rule to maintain local laws of the ousted sovereign, as in the case of occupying powers and peace operations controlling territory, it is appropriate to enable *de facto* authorities to modify local laws incompatible with IHRL or adopt new legislation in order to harmonise them with IHRL (Section 4.1.3.2).

In practice, the United Nations Observer Mission in El Salvador (ONUSAL) examined the conformity of the criminal law of the AOG

[338] UN Doc. A/HRC/13/21/Add.3 (n 308), 2 and paras 44, 49; ECtHR, *Xenides-Arestis* v. *Turkey*, Appl. no. 46347/99, judgment of 22 December 2005, para 40 (obligation addressed directly to Turkey, indirectly to the 'TRNC').

[339] Report on Human Rights in the Transnistrian Region (n 160), 18–19; On this obligation: CRC, Articles 37, 40; CRC, General Comment No. 10 (2007): Children's rights in juvenile justice, UN Doc. CRC/C/GC/10 (25 April 2007).

[340] E.g. CoE Commissioner for Human Rights, Monitoring of Investigations into cases of missing persons during and after the August 2008 armed conflict in Georgia, CommDH (2010)35 (29 September 2010), 21, para 67; Report of the Representative of the Secretary-General on the human rights of internally displaced persons, Walter Kälin, Mission to Georgia, UN Doc. E/CN.4/2006/71/Add.7 (24 March 2006), para 49(b); UN Doc. S/RES/2166 (21 July 2014), paras 6, 9; UN Doc. A/RES/54/189A-B (n 313), para 25; UN GA Res. 67/183, UN Doc. A/RES/67/183 (12 February 2013), para 7; see the analogous and parallel obligation of the territorial State: *Supra*, Section 3.1.5.4.

[341] CoE Parliamentary Assembly, Resolution 1648 (n 283), paras 24.1, 24.13; Resolution 1633 (n 283), para 23.1.1; Sivakumaran (n 157) 245–246; Marco Sassòli, 'Taking Armed Groups Seriously: Ways to Improve Their Compliance with International Humanitarian Law' (2010) 1(1) *International Humanitarian Legal Studies* 5, 35; Dieter Fleck, 'The Law of Non-International Armed Conflicts' in Dieter Fleck (ed), *The Handbook of International Humanitarian Law* (Oxford University Press 2008) 628.

[342] Zegveld (n 186) 71; Sivakumaran (n 252) 560; Murray (n 186) 230.

FMLN both with the territorial State's law and international norms.[343] According to this logic, whenever the *de facto* regime is unable to adapt its laws and institutions to international law, it must have recourse to those of the territorial State.[344] This approach favours the law and institutions of the territorial State and is preferable to a legal vacuum, especially in a transitional period, while with stabilisation *de facto* authorities might adapt their law to IHRL. For instance, Eurasian *de facto* regimes typically continued to apply the former laws in force in the territorial State – the laws of the former USSR in the ex-soviet States, the law of Ukraine in Eastern Ukraine and the laws of common law origin in Northern Cyprus.[345] However, at the time of taking territorial control by the *de facto* regime, the territorial State often was not yet party to human rights conventions and its legislation was not in harmony with the latter. In this scenario, obsolete local laws require reform in conformity with IHRL.

Human rights monitoring bodies have adopted a pragmatic approach: they recommended the *de facto* authorities to revise their 'law' in compliance with instruments of IHRL.[346] For example, they recommended *de facto* authorities to strengthen rules and procedures for implementing the principle of equal treatment and adopt rules for alternative service for conscientious objectors instead of military service;[347] to revise the existing rules concerning accessibility of places of worship in conformity with IHRL;[348] to adopt a new criminal code in conformity with the ECHR and CoE recommendations concerning the death penalty and custody pending trial;[349] and to elaborate a code of conduct for police interviews.[350] Similarly, international human rights monitoring bodies urged the Abkhazian *de facto* authorities to abolish the death penalty and to adopt

[343] Third report of ONUSAL, UN Doc. A/46/876-S/23580 (19 February 1992), paras 111–113, 125–126.

[344] Zegveld (n 186) 73–74.

[345] *Supra*, n 276.

[346] See a series of recommendations on the law of the 'MRT': Report on Human Rights in the Transnistrian Region (n 160), 14.

[347] Report of the Special Rapporteur on freedom of religion or belief, Heiner Bielefeldt, Mission to the Republic of Moldova, UN Doc. A/HRC/19/60/Add.2 (27 January 2012), para 87(b)–(c).

[348] Report of the Special Rapporteur on freedom of religion or belief, Heiner Bielefeldt, Mission to Cyprus, UN Doc. A/HRC/22/51/Add.1 (24 December 2012), paras 51, 82.

[349] CPT, Report on the visit to the Transnistrian region of the Republic of Moldova, CPT/Inf (2002) 35, 12 December 2002, paras 7, 11–12.

[350] Ibid., para 29.

schemes for the classification and differentiation of sentenced prisoners in accordance with CoE norms.[351]

Both approaches, maintaining the law in force and reforming it in accordance with IHRL, have a certain legitimacy: it is reasonable to require *de facto* authorities to maintain the laws in force of the territorial State to the extent that they are unable to adopt new rules and able to enforce old rules. The obligation to maintain the laws in force serves the normalisation of the lives of the civilian population and the protection of the sovereignty of the territorial State. However, if *de facto* authorities are able to adopt and implement new laws, the international community has a legitimate interest to expect 'legislation' in harmony with universal and regional human rights standards. This typically is the case in a phase of stabilisation of the *de facto* administration.

In conclusion, the obligations of *de facto* regimes have certain limits, understood as objective restrictions of human rights obligations, due to their effectiveness, which generally is lower than that of a State, and their non-recognition as legitimate subjects of international law. As the international community has a preoccupation not to legitimise unrecognised *de facto* regimes, it carefully avoids imposing on them positive obligations that conflict with the sovereign interests of the territorial State. This is the reason why human rights monitoring bodies used to refuse to engage in any assistance of the institutions of unrecognised entities fulfilling governmental functions in parallel with or against the territorial State.[352] Nevertheless, the balance between the rights of the State and the pragmatic protection of human rights is changing: monitoring bodies are ready to address positive obligations, especially the maintenance of law and public order, to *de facto* regimes. Even if *de facto* regimes are obliged to maintain the pre-existing law and remedies, IHRL leaves room for the creation and operation of *de facto* laws and institutions to comply with IHRL, especially those responsible for the maintenance of public order and justice. Instead of rejecting the validity of such parallel structures with the institutions of the territorial State

351 CPT, Report on the visit to the region of Abkhazia, Georgia, CPT/Inf (2009) 38, 23 December 2009, paras 23, 50; Report of the Special Rapporteur on torture and other cruel, inhuman or degrading treatment or punishment, Manfred Nowak, Mission to Georgia, UN Doc. E/CN.4/2006/6/Add.3 (23 September 2005), paras 54, 61.

352 Sivakumaran (n 252) 558; International Council on Human Rights Policy, *Ends & Means* (n 277), 50; this is the reason why ONUSAL refused to formulate recommendations on the justice system of the FMLN: First report of the United Nations Observer Mission in El Salvador, UN Doc. A/45/1055-S/23037 (16 September 1991), para 38.

under the rule of non-recognition, they must be considered functionally as an alternative to ensure compliance with IHRL.

4.3 Concluding Remarks

The international community has a tendency to increasingly recognise obligations of peace operations and *de facto* regimes under IHRL, mostly originating from IHL, whether it is in the form of general international law, treaty obligations, acts of IOs or obligations voluntarily assumed by those non-state actors. On account of their exercise of control over territory and authority over individuals, these non-state actors have positive obligations arising from the standard of due diligence, especially the duty to maintain public order and safety in the area. The specificity of the limits of their positive obligations result from the immunities of peace operations, on the one hand, and from the non-recognised status of *de facto* regimes, on the other.

The binding effect of IHRL towards peace operations and *de facto* regimes is in harmony with Article 28 of the UDHR which enshrines the right of everyone 'to a social and international order in which the rights and freedoms set forth in this Declaration can be fully realized'.[353] Nevertheless, the risk to promote a 'horizontal direct effect' of obligations under IHRL is the weakening of the international system of the protection of human rights. A perverse effect of the obligations of non-state actors in IHRL is to provide States with an excuse for the violations of human rights (the argument *tu quoque*).[354] It must be stressed, as human rights monitoring bodies did, that the obligations imposed on non-state actors are parallel to the primary responsibility of the States in IHRL,[355] especially that of the territorial State and the outside State.

[353] Forteau (n 41) 13–14. [354] Ryngaert (n 156) 376. [355] UNOHCHR (n 15) 27, 28–29.

5 The Responsibility of States

The Articles on the Responsibility of States for Internationally Wrongful Acts (ARSIWA) of the ILC provides that every internationally wrongful act of a State entails the international responsibility of that State.[1] It is generally recognised that two conditions are required for establishing the existence of an internationally wrongful act of a State: first, the concerned conduct must be attributable to the State under international law; second, the conduct must constitute a breach of an international legal obligation in force for that State.[2] Whereas the previous chapters examined the States' substantive obligations, this chapter focuses on the other constitutive element of the internationally wrongful act, namely, the attributability of the conduct. Since States can act only through individuals,[3] attribution determines the persons who are considered as acting on behalf of the State, and whose conduct thus constitutes an 'act of the State' for the purposes of the responsibility of States. Attribution (the French *imputation*)[4] is a normative operation that determines more precisely whether 'a given event is sufficiently connected to conduct (whether an act or omission) which is attributable to the State under one or other of the rules set out' by the rules of attribution.[5]

Human rights violations in 'grey zones' are usually committed by subjects other than the territorial State. The wrongful conduct can be performed either by agents or organs of another State, or by non-state

1 Article 1 ARSIWA. 2 Ibid., Article 2.

3 PCIJ, *Certain questions relating to settlers of German origin in the territory ceded by Germany to Poland*, advisory opinion, 10 September 1923, Series B, no. 6, 22.

4 Considered as synonyms: ARSIWA Commentary, 36, para 12.

5 That is under Articles 4 to 11 ARSIWA. ARSIWA Commentary, 35, para 6; Dionisio Anzilotti, 'La Responsabilité Internationale Des États à Raison Des Dommages Soufferts Par Des Étrangers' (1906) 13 *Revue générale de droit international public* 5, 291.

actors. The first situation raises fewer difficulties for the law of State responsibility than the second: when an area of the State's territory is controlled by the organs (typically the army) of another State, their unlawful conduct is attributable to that State. The responsibility of the State for the conduct of its own *de jure* organs is a customary norm codified in Article 4 ARSIWA.[6]

However, it is much more common that an outside State acts on foreign soil under the cover of a non-state actor and refuses the attribution of the latter's conduct. Because of the frequency of this situation, especially the conduct of *de facto* regimes in 'grey zones', this chapter focuses on the responsibility of States for the internationally wrongful conduct of non-state actors rather than for human rights violations committed by the State's *de jure* organs.[7] The situation is often complex as non-state actors and organs of the outside State simultaneously operate in the same area: in this case, the judge must separately examine the State's responsibility for the wrongful act committed by its own organs, on the one hand, and by the non-state actor, on the other. From the two main types of non-state actors analysed in the book, peace operations and *de facto* regimes, the present chapter only examines the latter, whereas the responsibility of States for the conduct of peace operations necessarily raises the complex question of the responsibility of the IO conducting the operation and that of the State sending agents to the operation. This will be analysed in a separate chapter (Chapter 6).[8]

When an area of the State's territory is controlled by subjects other than the territorial State, the committed human rights violations may engage the responsibility of States in two different ways: States (especially the territorial State or the outside State) can be held responsible for the conduct of the non-state actor, through attribution, or for the violation of their own obligation of due diligence, independently of the attributability of the non-state conduct. Accordingly, Section 5.1 focuses on the attributability of the conduct of non-state actors. Even if the conduct cannot be attributed to any of the States concerned, the latter

[6] *Difference Relating to Immunity from Legal Process of a Special Rapporteur of the Commission on Human Rights*, Advisory Opinion, *I.C.J. Reports* 1999, 87, para 62; *Application of the Convention on the Prevention and Punishment of the Crime of Genocide (Bosnia and Herzegovina* v. *Serbia and Montenegro)*, judgment, *I.C.J. Reports* 2007, 202, para 385.

[7] Furthermore, the chapter does not analyse the rare case codified by Articles 17–18 of the ILC's ARSIWA either, where an organ of the State acts under the direction or control or under the coercion of another State.

[8] For the same reason, the ILC excluded from the scope of the ARSIWA issues of the responsibility of a State for the acts of an IO. ARSIWA Commentary, 142, para 4.

can be responsible for the non-compliance with their own obligation of due diligence to prevent and repress human rights violations by others (Section 5.2).

5.1 Attribution of the Conduct of Non-state Actors

Whereas a minority view proposed to attribute to the State all wrongful acts of private persons performed in its territory,[9] State practice rejected this theory.[10] Thus, as a main rule, the State is not responsible for the conduct of non-state actors, unless their conduct satisfies any of the hypotheses of attribution foreseen in the international law of State responsibility. The codification works of the general international law of responsibility[11] and arbitral awards[12] have firmly established this principle that the ARSIWA commentary equally enshrines.[13] General international law recognises that the territorial State is not responsible for unlawful acts which occurred in an area outside of its effective control which were impossible to prevent.[14] The main reason of the principle of non-responsibility for the conducts of third parties undoubtedly is *force majeure*, defined as the 'the occurrence of an irresistible force or of an unforeseen event, beyond the control of the State, making it materially impossible in the circumstances to perform' an obligation.[15] As the arbitral case law recognised:

[9] Agostino Soldati, *La responsabilité des États dans le droit international* (Libr de Jurisprudence ancienne et moderne E Duchemin 1934) 84; Proposition of Mongolia: State responsibility, Comments and observations received from Governments, UN Doc. A/CN.4/488 (25 March 1998), 107.

[10] E.g. *Corfu Channel case*, judgment of 9 April 1949, *I.C.J. Reports* 1949, 18; First report on State responsibility, by Mr. James Crawford, Special Rapporteur, UN Doc. A/53/10, in: *YbILC*, 1998, vol. II(1), 33, para 154(a) and 49, para 250.

[11] E.g. Basis of discussion n° 22, Bases of dicussion drawn up in 1929 by the Preparatory Committee of the Conference for the codification of international law, The Hague, 1930, in: UN Doc. A/CN.4/96, in: *YbILC*, 1956, vol. II, 224; Draft convention on the international responsibility of States for injuries to aliens, prepared by the Harvard Law School, 1961, Article 18(2), in: *YbILC*, 1969, vol. II, 146; Text of the draft articles provisionally adopted by the Commission on first reading, in: Eighth report on State responsibility, by Mr. Gaetano Arangio-Ruiz, Special Rapporteur, UN Doc. A/51/10, in: *YbILC*, 1996, vol. II(2), 58–64 [Draft articles adopted on first reading], draft article 14(1).

[12] E.g. *Affaire des biens britanniques au Maroc espagnol (Espagne contre Royaume Uni)*, 1 May 1925, *UNRIAA*, vol. II, 642 ; precedents cited by Ago in: Fourth report on State responsibility, by Mr. Roberto Ago, Special Rapporteur, UN Doc. A/CN.4/264 and Add. 1, in: *YbILC*, 1972, vol. II, 132–133, para 161; *Asian Agricultural Products Ltd. (AAPL)* v. *Republic of Sri Lanka*, ICSID, ARB/87/3, 21 June 1990, *ILM*, 1991, vol. 30, 577–655, para 72.

[13] ARSIWA Commentary, 50, paras 2–4.

[14] *Affaire des biens britanniques au Maroc espagnol* (n 12), 722.

[15] Article 23(1) ARSIWA.

> The principle of non-responsibility for acts of rebel enemies in time of civil war rests upon the ground that the latter have withdrawn themselves by force of arms from the control and jurisdiction of the sovereign, putting it out of his power, so long as they make their resistance effectual, to extend his protection within the hostile territory to either strangers or his own subjects [. . .].[16]

Most codification works consider revolutions, wars or, more generally, the loss of control over a portion of the State territory as cases of *force majeure*.[17]

The exceptions from the main rule are the codified situations of attribution of non-state actors' conducts to the State.[18] State practice has foreseen the attribution of the conduct of *de facto* regimes to a State as a *de facto* organ of the latter, codified in Article 4 ARSIWA (Section 5.1.1), or as a *de facto* agent, governed by Article 8 ARSIWA (Section 5.1.2). The difference between the two results from the scope of application of the attributability: whereas all conducts of a *de facto* organ are attributable to the State, including *ultra vires* acts ('attribution *ratione personae*'/organic attribution), only specific acts and omissions of the *de facto* agent are attributable to the State that were performed on the instructions of, or under the direction or control of that State ('attribution *ratione materiae*'/functional attribution).[19] Another possible basis for attributing the conduct of *de facto* authorities to a State is the case of the so-called agent of necessity, that is, a person exercising governmental authority in circumstances such as to call for the exercise of those elements of authority, codified in Article 9 ARSIWA (Section 5.1.3). Finally, two other scenarios of attribution seem worth mentioning, both based on facts occurring after the wrongful act or the omission in question. This fact can be the victory of the insurrectional movement (Section 5.1.4), codified in Article 10 ARSIWA, or the acknowledgement or the adoption of

[16] *Prats case (Mexico/United States of America)*, 1974, cited in: '*Force majeure*' and 'fortuitous event' as circumstances precluding wrongfulness: survey of State practice, international judicial decisions and doctrine-Study prepared by the Secretariat, UN Doc. A/CN.4/315, in: *YbILC*, 1978, vol. II(1), 153, para 341.

[17] E.g. Eighth report on State responsibility, by Mr. Roberto Ago, Special Rapporteur, UN Doc. A/CN.4/318 and Add.l to 4, in: *YbILC*, 1979, vol. II(1), 49–50, para 107; ARSIWA Commentary, 76–77, para 3.

[18] Draft articles adopted on first reading (n 11), draft article 14(2); First report of Crawford (n 10), 57, draft article 15(1)–15(2) and its commentary: Ibid., 54, para 277.

[19] Patrick Jacob, 'L'imputation d'un fait à l'Etat en droit international de la responsabilité' (Thèse de doctorat, Université de Rennes 2010) 170 ('*attribution ratione personae / ratione materiae*'); Pierre D'Argent, *Les réparations de guerre en droit international public: la responsabilité internationale des États à l'épreuve de la guerre* (Bruylant 2002) 525 ('*rattachement organique/fonctionnel*').

the wrongful conduct by the State as its own (Section 5.1.5), codified in Article 11 ARSIWA. As the analysis of those attribution scenarios will illustrate, human rights treaty bodies flexibly interpret the ARSIWA provisions with a view to avoiding the risk of a 'vacuum' of responsibility and to normalise 'grey zones'.

5.1.1 De Facto *Organs (Article 4 ARSIWA)*

A *de facto* organ is understood as a person or entity acting in such close links with the State that all its conducts are attributable to the latter without having such a status under the domestic law of that State.[20] The idea of attribution of the conduct of *de facto* regimes to a State as its *de facto* organ is recognised both in general international law (Section 5.1.1.1) and in IHRL (Section 5.1.1.2). However, the adopted solutions are different as regards the threshold of the required links between the State and the non-state actor.

5.1.1.1 General International Law

It is widely recognised that the *de facto* authority created by the occupying power in the occupied territory is considered a *de facto* organ, whose conducts are all attributable to the occupying State. For the attribution of the conduct of 'puppet States' to the occupying power, one finds examples in the case law of domestic courts[21] and international arbitrations.[22]

In its early codification works on State responsibility, the ILC considered the attribution of the conduct of 'puppet States', defined as 'States or Governments, normally set up in a given territory on the initiative or an occupying State, which, while purporting to be free, are in fact dependent, often to a very high degree, on the State which brought them into existence'.[23] According to Roberto Ago's report, when

20 Jacob (n 19) 169–170; Stefan Talmon, 'The Responsibility of Outside Powers for Acts of Secessionist Entities' (2009) 58 *International & Comparative Law Quarterly* 493, 498–499.

21 E.g. *Socony Vacuum Oil Co. Claim*, United States International Claims Commission, *ILR*, 1954, vol. 21, 55–63, esp. 62; *Carl Zeiss Stiftung Appellants* v. *Rayner & Keeler Ltd. and Others Respondents (Original Appeal)*, [1967] 1 A.C. 853, esp. 860–861; *Autocephalous Greek-Orthodox Church of Cyprus and The Republic of Cyprus* v. *Goldberg & Feldman Fine Arts, Inc., and Peg Goldberg*, 3 August 1989, 717 F.Supp. 1374, 1378.

22 E.g. *Case of Holland*, Arbitration United States–France, 1820, in: John Bassett Moore, *History and Digest of the International Arbitrations to Which the United States Has Been a Party: Together with Appendices Containing the Treaties Relating to Such Arbitrations, and Historical Legal Notes ...*, vol. 5 (GPO 1898) 4473–4476; *Portugal* v. *Germany*, 30 June 1930, *UNRIAA*, vol. II, 1040.

23 Eighth report of Ago (n 17), 22, para 36.

such an entity cannot be considered as a State and it is 'in fact, wholly subject in its actions to the State which created it', '[t]he actions of the organs of the entity in question are then directly attributable to the latter State'.[24] The last Rapporteur on the topic, James Crawford, has excluded relationships of dependence between a State and a territory from the scope of application of Article 17 (Direction and control exercised over the commission of an internationally wrongful act). He concluded that the normal principles specified in Articles 4–9 ARSIWA apply to other relationships of dependence, 'such as dependent territories'.[25] However, the commentary to Article 4 on the conduct of organs of a State seems to permit the assimilation of a non-state entity to an organ of fact of the State. The Rapporteur expressly emphasised that the internal law of the State is not decisive to determine whether a person or a body is an 'organ' of that State, because its internal law may be silent on the question, whereas in some States even the practice can define it.[26] The commentary of Article 4 ARSIWA recognises *de facto* organs when it highlights that 'a State cannot avoid responsibility for the conduct of a body which does in truth act as one of its organs merely by denying it that status under its own law'.[27] The case law of the ICJ specified such a *de facto* relationship.

The ICJ has elaborated a very high threshold of attribution that allows assimilating persons, groups of persons or non-state entities to an organ of the State based on close factual links with the State. In the *Nicaragua* case the Court for the first time recognised the possibility of such assimilation when it examined whether the *contras*, an AOG conducting military and paramilitary operations against the Nicaraguan government, could be considered a *de facto* organ of the US. It emphasised that for such as assimilation,

> [w]hat the Court has to determine at this point is whether or not the relationship of the *contras* to the United States Government was so much one of dependence on the one side and control on the other that it would be right to equate the *contras*, for legal purposes, with an organ of the United States Government, or as acting on behalf of that Government.[28]

[24] Seventh report on State responsibility, by Mr. Roberto Ago, Special Rapporteur, UN Doc. A/CN.4/307 and Add.1 and 2, in: *YbILC*, 1978, vol. II(1), 56, note 105.

[25] ARSIWA Commentary, 68, para 4.

[26] First report of Crawford (n 10), 35, para 163; ARSIWA Commentary, 42, para 11.

[27] Ibid.

[28] *Military and Paramilitary Activities in and against Nicaragua (Nicaragua* v. *United States of America)*, Merits, judgment, *I.C.J. Reports* 1986, 62, para 109.

In the *Nicaragua* case the only element of control that the US could exercise was a cessation of foreign aid, which did not prevent the *contras* from continuing their activities and, consequently, it was not clearly established whether the US had 'actually exercised such a degree of control in all fields as to justify treating the *contras* as acting on its behalf'.[29] In other terms, the required threshold was an authority exercised over all activities of the armed group, that is, a 'complete dependence on United States aid' and not only various forms of assistance provided to the *contras* which have been crucial to the pursuit of their activities.[30]

In the *DRC* v. *Uganda* case the Court concluded that Uganda gave training and military support for the *Mouvement de libération du Congo* (MLC), a rebel group acting in the territory of the Democratic Republic of the Congo (DRC), but held that there was no 'probative evidence that Uganda controlled, or could control, the manner' in which the armed group used this assistance.[31] Consequently, the Court concluded that 'the conduct of the MLC was not that of "an organ" of Uganda (article 4 [ARSIWA]), nor that of an entity exercising elements of governmental authority on its behalf (Art. 5)'.[32] The *DRC* v. *Uganda* judgment confirms that a certain degree of control is essential for the attribution as a *de facto* organ, but the threshold of this control was only elaborated in the *Genocide* case.

In the *Genocide case (Bosnia and Herzegovina* v. *Serbia and Montenegro)* Bosnia and Herzegovina argued that the 'Republika Srpska' and its army could be equated with *de facto* organs of the Federal Republic of Yugoslavia (FRY) by reason of their 'total dependence'.[33] As for the Court, it confirmed first that

> persons, groups of persons or entities may, for purposes of international responsibility, be equated with State organs even if that status does not follow from

[29] Ibid. [30] Ibid., 62–63, para 110.

[31] *Armed Activities on the Territory of the Congo (Democratic Republic of the Congo* v. *Uganda)*, judgment, *I.C.J. Reports* 2005, 226, para 160.

[32] Ibid.; The reference to Article 5 of the ILC's ARSIWA is surprising: it is difficult to qualify a rebel group as an entity exercising elements of governmental authority since the latter shall be 'empowered by the law of that State to exercise elements of the governmental authority'. Article 5 ARSIWA; criterion also examined, but non fulfilled in *Genocide case (Bosnia and Herzegovina* v. *Serbia and Montenegro)* (n 6), 215, para 414.

[33] ICJ, *Application of the Convention on the Prevention and Punishment of the Crime of Genocide (Bosnia and Herzegovina* v. *Serbia and Montenegro)*, CR 2006/10, Public sitting, 6 March 2006, 12, para 6 and p. 21, para 27 (Mr. Condorelli).

internal law, provided that in fact the persons, groups or entities act in 'complete dependence' on the State, of which they are ultimately merely the instrument.[34]

As a consequence of such assimilation, all acts accomplished of the non-state entity in this quality are attributable to the State for the purposes of international responsibility.[35] The Court added that such attribution can only be exceptional since it requires 'proof of a particularly great degree of State control over them, a relationship which the Court's judgment described as "complete dependence"'.[36] In the specific case 'neither the Republika Srpska nor its *de facto* army, the VRS could be regarded as mere instruments through which the FRY was acting, and as lacking any real autonomy', despite the close political, military and logistical relations between the federal authorities in Belgrade and the authorities in Pale, between the Yugoslav army and the VRS.[37] The 'Republika Srpska' 'has however enjoyed some *de facto* independence' rather than a total dependence.[38] Consequently, the judgment of the ICJ only foresees attribution where a 'total dependence' exists between the State and the *de facto* regime, amounting to a 'subordination',[39] without any real margin of autonomy of the latter. This threshold of control seems firmly confirmed in the case law of the ICJ[40] and certain fact-finding commissions.[41]

The test of 'total dependence', considered the threshold for the assimilation of a non-state actor to a *de facto* organ of the State, nevertheless is questionable, as the ICJ has not specified the factors that would satisfy the test. Such factors can only be discerned from the three above-mentioned judgments (*Nicaragua*, *DRC* v. *Uganda*, *Genocide* case) where the ICJ did not find that 'total dependence' had been satisfied. In those judgments the Court took into consideration the following

[34] *Genocide case (Bosnia and Herzegovina* v. *Serbia and Montenegro)* (n 6), 205, para 392.

[35] Ibid., 207, para 397.

[36] Ibid., 205, para 393.

[37] Ibid., 205–206, para 394; neither could the 'Scorpions' be regarded as acting in fact under the tota dependence of Serbia, see ibid., 206, para 395.

[38] Ibid., 138, para 233.

[39] Jacob (n 19) 212.

[40] In the *Croatia* v. *Serbia* case, the parties also accepted this threshold and disputed only its applicability to the facts, e.g. *Application of the Convention on the Prevention and Punishment of the Crime of Genocide (Croatia* v. *Serbia)*, Counter-memorial submitted by the Republic of Serbia, vol. I, December 2009, paras 313, 511, 1013–1014; Reply of the Republic of Croatia, vol. I, 20 December 2010, paras 9.59–9.60; Rejoinder submitted by the Republic of Serbia, vol. I, November 2011, paras 546–547, 556.

[41] Although for purposes other than State responsibility, to determine an armed attack. Report of the Independent International Fact-Finding Mission on the Conflict in Georgia, September 2009, at www.ceiig.ch (visited on 15 February 2013) [IIFFMG-CEIIG report], vol. II, 259–260.

elements: the creation of the entity by the State;[42] heavy subsidies, training, military support and other forms of assistance provided by the State to the non-state actor;[43] political, military and logistic links between the State and the non-state actor;[44] a particularly high degree of control exercised in all fields;[45] the lack of real autonomy of the *de facto* regime and of differences of opinions between the State authorities and the leaders of the non-state actor over strategic options (as a proof of a real autonomy).[46] It is difficult to establish *in abstracto* the weight that the Court attributes to each of these elements: for example, the heavy subsidies and the other forms of assistance to the *de facto* regime and the payment of the salaries and other benefits to officials did not automatically render these officials organs of the State.[47] Moreover, the list is open: one could foresee other pieces of evidence such as the administrative and territorial annexation of the *de facto* regime by the outside State.[48]

Despite the uncertainty about the positive criteria of a 'total dependence', the Court established a very strict, even exceptional threshold of control, requiring a total subordination of the non-state entity to the State. However, at a certain degree of effectiveness that some *de facto* regimes have reached, especially those situated in Eurasia, some autonomy of the non-state entity undoubtedly exists *vis-à-vis* the outside State that it created, supports and controls in various ways. It suffices to think of the presidential elections in some of those *de facto* regimes that led to the electoral victory of a candidate not supported by the outside State.[49] Under these conditions, it is unlikely that the test of 'total dependence' would be satisfied. Until now the ICJ has never found that the evidence brought to its knowledge was sufficient to fulfil the test of 'total

[42] *Nicaragua* (n 28), 61–62, para 108; *DRC* v. *Uganda* (n 31), 225–226, paras 158–160.

[43] *Nicaragua* (n 28), 61, paras 106–107 and 62, para 109; *DRC* v. *Uganda* (n 31), 226, para 160; *Genocide case (Bosnia and Herzegovina* v. *Serbia and Montenegro)* (n 6), 203, para 388.

[44] *Genocide case (Bosnia and Herzegovina* v. *Serbia and Montenegro)* (n 6), 205–206, para 394.

[45] *Nicaragua* (n 28), 62, para 109; *Genocide case (Bosnia and Herzegovina* v. *Serbia and Montenegro)* (n 6), 205, para 393.

[46] *Genocide case (Bosnia and Herzegovina* v. *Serbia and Montenegro)* (n 6), 205–206, para 394.

[47] *Nicaragua* (n 28), 62, paras 109–110; *Genocide case (Bosnia and Herzegovina* v. *Serbia and Montenegro)* (n 6), 203, para 388.

[48] Talmon (n 20) 500.

[49] E.g. in Abkhazia (2004), Transnistria (2011) and South Ossetia (2011). Donnacha Ó Beacháin, Giorgio Comai and Ann Tsurtsumia-Zurabashvili, 'The Secret Lives of Unrecognised States: Internal Dynamics, External Relations, and Counter-Recognition Strategies' (2016) 27 *Small Wars & Insurgencies* 440, 447.

dependence'[50] and it is not sure whether 'total dependence' is the only possible test of attribution under Article 4 ARSIWA. The major examples for alternative thresholds of control are the less demanding test that human rights treaty bodies have applied, on the one hand, and the 'overall control' test in international criminal law (Section 5.1.2.2), on the other.

5.1.1.2 International Human Rights Law

Both universal and regional human rights monitoring bodies assimilated *de facto* regimes to *de facto* organs of a State by using thresholds of control that were less stringent than that of 'total dependence' in general international law.

a. *Universal Monitoring Bodies*

Among universal bodies, the Human Rights Committee used a summary test in the *Serna and Others* v. *Colombia* case on the enforced disappearance of two persons in an area that was under the control of paramilitary forces. The Human Rights Committee noted that 'the State party encouraged the establishment of "self-defence" groups – according them legal recognition – to assist law enforcement bodies in fighting insurgents and provided them subsequently with training, weapons, logistical support and, in some instances, active involvement by the military in their operations'.[51] The Committee also took into account that enforced disappearance was a widespread practice used by paramilitary groups, with the complicity of the Colombian armed forces. In the specific case the Committee added that

> the group Autodefensas Campesinas del Magdalena Medio controlled parts of the Middle Magdalena region, including the Medellín-Bogotá motorway where Mr Anzola and Mr Molina were disappeared, and that the group operated with the

[50] Eventually an exception could be admitted: in the *Nicaragua* case, the conduct of the UCLAs, defined as 'persons of the nationality of unidentified Latin American countries, paid by, and acting on the direct instructions of, United States military or intelligence personnel' (45, para 75). Without detailing the type of attribution and referring to the 'total dependence', the Court attributed the operations of the UCLAs to the US, because 'agents of the United States participated in the planning, direction, support and execution of the operations'. See *Nicaragua* (n 28), 50–51, para 86; *a contrario*: Ibid., Separate opinion of Judge Ago, 187–188, para 15 (considering the UCLAs as 'public entities empowered within its domestic legal order to exercise certain elements of the government authority').

[51] HRC, *Rosa María Serna* v. *Colombia*, Communication No. 2134/2012, Views of 9 July 2015, UN Doc. CCPR/C/114/D/2134/2012 (22 September 2015), para 9.3.

acquiescence of the Colombian army, which had provided training, weapons and cover for the group's actions.[52]

Because of the link of these groups with the military, the Human Rights Committee concluded 'that the forced disappearances of Mr Anzola and Mr Molina are attributable to the Colombian State'.[53] While this conclusion does not necessarily relate to all conducts of the paramilitary group but might concern only the specific operation of the enforced disappearance, the above-mentioned factors related to the general conduct of the armed group rather than to specific acts. As noted in Section 2.2.2.4, the Committee members disagreed only about the role of the paramilitary group in the challenged enforced disappearance, but not about the State's control over the group.[54] The summary analysis of the facts does not confirm whether the Committee regarded the group as a mere instrument through which the State was acting, and lacking any real autonomy as required by the 'total dependence' test. Support and the acquiescence of the State to the operation of the paramilitary group prove some dependence and influence, but not necessarily a lack of autonomy.

Another universal human rights body, the Working Group on Arbitrary Detention, also used a flexible threshold. It had to examine whether the conduct of the South Lebanon Army (SLA), a non-state entity administrating the detention centre of Al-Khiam, situated in South Lebanon under Israeli occupation, could be attributed to Israel or Lebanon.[55] Contrary to the test of 'total dependence' elaborated by the ICJ, the Working Group limited its analysis to general factual links between the SLA and the Israeli army, especially to financial aid, logistical assistance and other forms of assistance and support, cooperation and coordination. While recognising that the Israeli Defence Forces (IDF) have 'influence over SLA', the Working Group added that the latter 'also has its own judgment concerning its military activities'.[56] Since the Working Group concluded that 'it has been sufficiently demonstrated that the SLA is acting on behalf of the IDF',[57] it assimilated it to a *de facto* organ without researching Israel's implication in the detentions

[52] Ibid. [53] Ibid.

[54] Ibid., Individual opinion by Committee member Yuval Shany (partly concurring and partly dissenting), para 3; Individual opinion by Committee members Víctor Rodríguez-Rescia and Fabián Omar Salvioli (concurring), para 4.

[55] Report of the Working Group on Arbitrary Detention, UN Doc. E/CN.4/2000/4 (28 December 1999), para 11.

[56] Ibid., para 17. [57] Ibid., para 18.

specified in the communication. The applied test of attribution, focusing on a dependence/influence, is far more general and less stringent than that of 'total dependence'.

b. Inter-American Treaty Bodies

The Inter-American treaty bodies attribute all conducts of an armed group to the territorial State as its *de facto* organ with respect to some Latin-American countries where, during a first period, the State actively contributed to the creation of self-defence groups whereas, during a second period, it dissociated itself from their paramilitary activity that it considered unlawful.[58] The case law shows that the assimilation of the paramilitary group to a *de facto* organ is only possible during the first stage when the group acts as a self-defence group with the approval of the State, whereas at the second stage the paramilitary group acts outside the State's control, with a partial legal personality, separate from that of the State.

The IACtHR attributed the conduct of militia groups to the State when they acted at the first stage, in close links with the territorial State. In the *Blake* v. *Guatemala* case concerning the killing of two US citizens by a self-defence patrol group, the Court took into account that the paramilitary civilian patrols enjoyed an institutional link with the national army, acting with the support and under the supervision of the latter, and received from it resources, arms, training and direct orders.[59] Consequently, the IACtHR concluded that 'the acquiescence of the State of Guatemala in the perpetration of such activities by the civil patrols indicates that those patrols should be deemed to be agents of the State and that the actions they perpetrated should therefore be imputable to the State'.[60] Likewise, the IACHR considered the paramilitary groups as organs of the State when they committed human rights violations in close collaboration and with the direct participation of the Colombian military forces and under cover of State authorities.[61]

58 E.g. IACtHR, *19 Merchants* v. *Colombia*, judgment of 5 July 2004 (Merits, Reparations and Costs), paras 116–121.

59 *Case of Blake* v. *Guatemala*, judgment of 24 January 1998 (Merits), paras 75–77.

60 Ibid., para 78.

61 IACHR, Third report on the human rights situation in Colombia, OEA/Ser.L/V/II.102, Doc. 9 rev. 1 (26 February 1999), Chapter IV, paras 234, 249, 258, 262, 335, 337; Report No. 37/00, Case 11.481, *Monsignor Oscar Arnulfo Romero y Galdámez* v. *El Salvador*, 13 April 2000, paras 64, 71; Application to the IACtHR in the case of *Mariela Morales Caro y otros (Masacre de La Rochela) c. la República de Perú*, Case 11.995, 10 March 2006, para 106; Application to the IACtHR in the case of *Jesús María Valle Jaramillo et al.* v. *Colombia*, Merits,

Whereas the required threshold of the State's control is unclear in the Inter-American case law, it suffices to note that these close links with the State and the direct participation of the *de jure* authorities in the commission of the wrongful act suffice to assimilate the paramilitaries to *de facto* organs. Such close links arguably do not amount to a 'total dependence' required by the ICJ, as the IACHR and the IACtHR often recognised the relative autonomy of paramilitary groups from the central government.[62] Consequently, the Inter-American treaty bodies apply a less demanding threshold than the ICJ, similar to the test of dependence/influence of UN monitoring bodies.

c. *European Court of Human Rights*

The ECtHR developed a more detailed threshold than universal and Inter-American bodies, but one that is similarly more flexible than the 'total dependence' test of the ICJ. Formally, the Court analyses the attribution of the conduct of a *de facto* regime to the respondent State to decide on a preliminary question, namely, on the respondent State's jurisdiction. Consequently, it is a question of primary norms which, according to the Court, 'does not in any way prejudge the questions to be determined at the merits stage of the proceedings', such as attribution, belonging to secondary norms.[63] Whereas the Court aims to distinguish the two different subjects in its recent case law,[64] there has been much confusion in this regard: for instance, the Court sometimes referred in the phase of the preliminary objections to State responsibility[65] or 'imputability' of

Case 12.415, 13 February 2007, para 66; Report No. 64/11, Case 12.573, *Marino López et al. (Operation Génesis)* v. *Colombia*, Merits, 31 March 2011, para 227.

[62] E.g. IACHR, Third report on the human rights situation in Colombia (n 61), para 238; IACtHR, *Case of the Pueblo Bello Massacre* v. *Colombia*, judgment of 31 January 2006 (Merits, Reparations and Costs), para 96(a); *Operation Génesis* (n 61), para 226.

[63] *Cyprus* v. *Turkey*, Appl. no. 25781/94, decision of the Commission of 28 June 1996 on the admissibility, 131; *Loizidou* v. *Turkey (Preliminary objections)* [GC], Appl. no. 15318/89, decision of 23 March 1995 on the admissibility, paras 61, 64.

[64] *Al-Skeini and Others* v. *United Kingdom* [GC], Appl. no. 55721/07, judgment of 7 July 2011, para 130; *Catan and Others* v. *Moldova and Russia* [GC], Appl. nos. 43370/04, 8252/05 et 18454/06, judgment of 19 October 2012, para 115; *Jaloud* v. *the Netherlands* [GC], Appl. no. 47708/08, judgment of 20 November 2014, para 154; *Ukraine* v. *Russia (re Crimea)* [GC], Appl. nos. 20958/14 and 38334/18, decision of 14 January 2021 on the admissibility, paras 266, 311, 313; *Georgia* v. *Russia (II) (Merits)* [GC], Appl. no. 38263/08, judgment of 21 January 2021, para 162.

[65] E.g. *Ilaşcu and Others* v. *Moldova and Russia* [GC], Appl. no. 48787/99, judgment of 8 July 2004, para 315; *Ivanţoc and Others* v. *Moldova and Russia*, Appl. no. 23687/05, judgment of 15 November 2011, para 120; *Catan* (n 64), para 106.

the challenged conduct.[66] Moreover, in the phase on the merits, the Court has systematically referred to the same test, namely, to the examination of the 'effective control' applied in the phase of preliminary objections. Despite the confusion of the two questions, jurisdiction and attribution, it will be shown that the test used by the Court to decide on jurisdiction in cases involving occupation through proxies (Section 2.1.1.2) is also appropriate to decide on attribution.

Some authors argued that the ECtHR used the 'overall control' test not as control over persons, a question of attribution, but as control over territory, a question of jurisdiction and thus primary rules.[67] In fact, the two are inherently related where a subject other than the respondent State exercises effective control over the territory: to establish the State's jurisdiction – preliminary condition of the State's responsibility – the acts and omissions leading to the alleged violation must at least *prima facie* be attributable to the State.[68] Therefore, the Court's reason for engaging the outside State's responsibility must be read according to the following logic: 'it is because Turkey controls the territory of Northern Cyprus (question of jurisdiction) and because it controls the authorities of this region (question of attribution) that this State's responsibility can be engaged' for the violations of the ECHR.[69] The same logic applies to other *de facto* regimes, where the Court applied the same 'effective control' test both to jurisdiction and attribution.[70]

[66] E.g. *Loizidou* v. *Turkey (Merits)* [GC], Appl. no. 15318/89, judgment of 18 December 1996, paras 49–57 ('imputability issue'), esp. paras 52, 56 and dispositive para 2; *Loizidou* v. *Turkey (Article 50)* [GC], Appl. no. 40/1993/435/514, judgment of 28 July 1998, paras 2, 25; *Cyprus* v. *Turkey* [GC], Appl. no. 25781/94, judgment of 10 May 2001, paras 75, 77, 101.

[67] Marko Milanovic, 'State Responsibility for Genocide' (2006) 17 *European Journal of International Law* 553, 586–587; Gábor Kajtár, *A Nem Állami Szereplők Elleni Önvédelem a Nemzetközi Jogban [Self-Defence against Non-State Actors in International Law]* (ELTE Eötvös Kiadó 2015) 236–237; *a contrario*: Antonio Cassese, 'The Nicaragua and Tadić Tests Revisited in Light of the ICJ Judgment on Genocide in Bosnia' (2007) 18 *European Journal of International Law* 649, 658, notes 17–18.

[68] *Ilaşcu* (n 65), para 311; *Al-Skeini* (n 64), para 130; *Issa and Others* v. *Turkey*, Appl. no. 31821/96, judgment of 16 November 2004, para 66; HRC, 26 October 1998 (Initial report of Armenia), UN Doc. CCPR/C/SR.1710 (17 December 1998), para 30 (Mr. Klein).

[69] Translated by the author. Jérôme Reymond, *L'attribution de comportements d'organes de facto et d'agents de l'Etat en droit international: étude sur la responsabilité internationale des Etats* (Schulthess 2013) 214.

[70] E.g. *Catan* (n 64), paras 122 (jurisdiction), 150 (State responsibility); *Mozer* v. *the Republic of Moldova and Russia* [GC], Appl. no. 11138/10, judgment of 23 February 2013, paras 110 (jurisdiction), 157 and 217 (State responsibility); *Chiragov and Others* v. *Armenia (Merits)* [GC], Appl. no. 13216/05, judgment of 16 June 2015, paras 186 (jurisdiction), 192 (State responsibility).

As explained in Sections 2.1.1.1 and 2.1.1.2, in its decisions on Northern Cyprus the Court used the test of 'effective control' to decide on jurisdiction, which is a test (i) based on a spatial rather than a personal jurisdictional link and (ii) defined mainly on account of the military control exercised over foreign soil.[71] The Court referred to the occupation of Northern Cyprus by Turkish troops, to the creation of the 'TRNC'[72] and to the 'overall control' exercised over the territory. In addition, in the *Cyprus* v. *Turkey* case the Grand Chamber talked about 'military and other support' that Turkey allocates to the *de facto* authorities of the 'TRNC'.[73] The Court has never detailed what it understands as 'other support'.[74] Be that as it may, the 'effective/overall control' over the territory entailed not only Turkey's jurisdiction (control over territory), but also 'her responsibility for the policies and actions of the "TRNC"' (control over person).[75] In the *Cyprus* v. *Turkey* case the Court confirmed this 'broad statement of principle as regards Turkey's general responsibility under the Convention for the policies and actions of the "TRNC" authorities'.[76] The legal consequence of this test is the same as that foreseen by general international law under Article 4 ARSIWA: all unlawful conducts of the *de facto* organ, including *ultra vires* acts, are attributable to the State. Since *Loizidou*, the Court has consistently attributed all conduct of the 'TRNC' to Turkey.[77]

The test of 'effective/overall control' in the Northern Cyprus cases is undoubtedly summary, as the Court did not examine the factual links between the *de facto* regime and the outside State in detail, especially whether 'Turkey actually exercises detailed control over the policies and actions of the authorities of the "TRNC"',[78] but satisfied itself that there is a relationship of dependence/influence. Some dissenting judges criticised the *Loizidou* judgment precisely for the absence of a detailed examination of the facts.[79] Two judges held that the mere presence of Turkish troops and the support provided by Turkey to the 'TRNC' are not

[71] *Supra*, Chapter 2.
[72] *Loizidou (Preliminary objections)* (n 63), para 63; *Loizidou (Merits)* (n 66), para 54.
[73] *Cyprus* v. *Turkey* [GC] (n 66), para 77.
[74] E.g. *Chriso Kakoulli and Others* v. *Turkey*, Appl. no. 38595/97, Decision of 4 September 2001 on the admissibility, 8; *Ahmet Djavit AN* v. *Turkey*, Appl. no. 20652/92, judgment of 20 February 2003, para 12; *Ilaşcu* (n 65), para 316.
[75] *Loizidou (Merits)* (n 66), para 56.
[76] *Cyprus* v. *Turkey* [GC] (n 66), para 77.
[77] *Loizidou (Merits)* (n 66), para 56; *Foka* v. *Turkey*, Appl. no. 28940/95, judgment of 24 June 2008, para 83; *Demopoulos and Others* v. *Turkey* [GC], Appl. nos. 46113/99, etc., decision of 1 March 2010 on the admissibility, para 95.
[78] *Loizidou (Merits)* (n 66), para 56.
[79] Ibid., Dissenting opinion of Judge Pettiti, 36.

sufficient to conclude that the unlawful facts are attributable to Turkey and 'that Turkey is therefore responsible for more or less everything that happens in Northern Cyprus'.[80]

One may criticise the summary character of the Court's attribution analysis as it does not sufficiently examine the factual links required by general international law, namely, the 'total dependence' between the State and the *de facto* regime and the latter's lack of real margin of autonomy. In fact, it is defensible that the 'TRNC' has certain autonomy *vis-à-vis* Turkey. Turkey invoked the lack of its direct or indirect control over the conduct of the 'TRNC' and the latter's autonomy, confirmed implicitly by the Foundation Agreement – The Comprehensive Settlement of the Cyprus Problem ('Annan Plan') of 31 March 2004. The latter agreement provided for the settlement of the conflict by two separate referenda in the northern and southern parts of the island, which effectively was approved by the electors of Northern Cyprus.[81] The Court nevertheless rejected this argument, holding that no change concerning the exercise of overall control by Turkey has been proved.[82] Thus, the Court avoided engaging in a detailed examination of the leeway left for the subordinate local administration.

In its subsequent case law on Transnistria and Nagorno-Karabakh, the Court engaged in a more detailed analysis of the outside State's control over the *de facto* regime, going beyond the military relations to various factual links substantiating dependence/influence. In its Transnistrian judgments (*Ilaşcu*, *Catan*) the Court engaged in a detailed analysis of factual links between the 'MRT' and Russia in the part on Russia's jurisdiction. It insisted on the role played by Russia in the creation and the maintenance of the 'MRT'; it took into account the stationing of the forces of the 14th Army in Transnistria, their participation in the combats with and on behalf of the Transnistrian separatist forces, the transfer of large quantities of weapons from the stores of the 14th Army (which later became the ROG) to the separatists and the political support of the separatist authorities by the leaders of the Russian Federation.[83] At first sight these numerous factual links could lead to an assimilation

[80] Ibid., Dissenting opinion of Mr Bernhardt, joined by Mr Lopes Rocha, 26, para 3.

[81] *Myra Xenides-Arestis* v. *Turkey*, Appl. no. 46347/99, decision on admissibility of 14 March 2005, 11; citing: The Comprehensive Settlement of the Cyprus Problem, 31 March 2004.

[82] *Myra Xenides-Arestis* v. *Turkey*, Appl. no. 46347/99, decision on admissibility of 14 March 2005, 17.

[83] *Ilaşcu* (n 65), paras 379–382.

of the 'MRT' to a *de facto* organ of Russia,[84] because the Court, in *Ilaşcu*, seemed to talk about attribution when it concluded that 'the Russian Federation's responsibility is engaged in respect of the unlawful acts committed by the Transdniestrian separatists'[85] and, in *Catan*, the Court even referred to Article 4 ARSIWA and its subsequent case law.[86] Most importantly, as in the case of the Northern Cyprus cases, the Court attributed all conducts of the 'MRT' to Russia (without the need 'to determine whether or not Russia exercised detailed control over the policies and actions of the subordinate local administration') and not only certain specific operations over which the latter had influence.[87] The qualification of the 'MRT', like the 'TRNC', as 'local subordinate administration' and the recognition of Russia's 'effective control *and* decisive influence' over the 'MRT'[88] in *Catan* also brought the control tests used in the Northern Cyprus and Transnistrian cases under the same umbrella.

Since the assimilation of the non-state entity to a *de facto* organ of the State leads to the attribution of all wrongful acts and omissions of the entity to the State, it is not by accident that applicants from other 'grey zones' are interested in arguing in this sense. For example, in the *Georgia* v. *Russia (II)* case, Georgia argued that the Abkhazian and South Ossetian military formations 'had acted as agents or *de facto* organs of the Russian Federation and as such constituted a simple continuation of the Russian armed forces'.[89] Similarly, less expressly, the applicants in *Chiragov* submitted that, by reason of several factual links, the 'NKR' is under the authority of Armenian agents operating in Nagorno-Karabakh,[90]

[84] In this sense: the applicants in the *Ilaşcu* case, see *Ilaşcu* (n 65), para 367; ICJ, *Application of the International Convention on the Elimination of All Forms of Racial Discrimination (Georgia* v. *Russian Federation)*, Memorial of Georgia, vol. I, 2 September 2009 [*Georgia* v. *Russian Federation*, Memorial of Georgia], paras 9.36–9.41; Paolo Palchetti, *L'organo di fatto dello Stato nell'illecito internazionale* (Giuffrè Editore 2007) 92–93; Reymond (n 69) 219; *a contrario*, see the authors proposing Article 8 ARSIWA as legal basis, *infra*, Section 5.1.2.3.

[85] *Ilaşcu* (n 65), para 382.

[86] *Alexei Catan and Others* v. *Moldova and Russia*, Appl. nos. 43370/04, 8252/05 and 18454/06, decision of 15 June 2010 on the admissibility [*Catan* (admissibility)], para 73 (citation of Article 4 of the ILC's ARSIWA); *Catan* (n 64), para 76 (citation of the paragraphs of the *Genocide* judgment of the ICJ on the assimilation to a *de facto* organ).

[87] *Catan* (n 64), paras 106, 150; *Mozer* (n 70), paras 157, 217; *Ilaşcu* (n 65), para 315 (as a general principle).

[88] *Catan* (n 64), para 122; *Mozer* (n 70), para 110.

[89] *Georgia* v. *Russia (II)*, Appl. no. 38263/08, decision of 13 December 2011 on the admissibility, para 25.

[90] *Elkhan Chiragov and Others* v. *Armenia* [GC], Appl. no. 13216/05, Decision of 14 December 2011 on the admissibility, paras 69–76.

whereas the Azerbaijani government claimed that it is a subordinate local administration of Armenia.[91] Unlike in Northern Cyprus and as in Transnistria, in Nagorno-Karabakh it was contested whether the outside State had the status of occupying power, and consequently the Court could have followed the Transnistrian test on the military, economic, financial and political support provided to the *de facto* regime rather than the Cypriot test on the military control over foreign soil. In the *Chiragov* case the Court analysed in detail both the military and other types of support between Armenia and the 'NKR': the military support provided by Armenia to the 'NKR' in the conflict of Nagorno-Karabakh, which continues to be 'decisive' and proves that 'the armed forces of Armenia and the "NKR" are highly integrated';[92] other types of support such as the various political links, legislative, enforcement and judicial integration of the two entities, Armenia's financial support and further assistance given to the 'NKR'.[93] On the basis of the evidence, the Court expressly recognised that Armenia 'exercises effective control over Nagorno-Karabakh and the surrounding territories' with 'a significant and decisive influence over the "NKR"', thus control over both the territory and the *de facto* regime.[94] Moreover, it affirmed that the control test used for the spatial model of jurisdictional link equally determines the question of attribution: 'the issue to be determined on the facts of the case is whether the Republic of Armenia exercised and continues to exercise effective control over the mentioned territories and as a result may be held responsible for the alleged violations'.[95] As in the Northern Cyprus and Transnistrian cases, the Court satisfied itself that there was a relationship of dependence/influence between the State and the *de facto* regime. While integrating the conclusions on the control over territory and person in one single test, the Court brought closer the control tests applied in its former case law. The Court has consistently applied the same legal consequence of the test, the automatic attribution of all conducts of the *de facto* regime to the outside State.[96]

[91] Ibid., paras 77–78; *Chiragov (Merits)* (n 70), para 165.

[92] *Chiragov (Merits)* (n 70), paras 172–180. [93] Ibid., paras 181–185. [94] Ibid., para 186.

[95] Ibid., para 169.

[96] Confirmed in: *Muradyan* v. *Armenia*, Appl. no. 11275/07, judgment of 24 November 2016, paras 126–127; *Zalyan and Others* v. *Armenia*, Appl. nos. 36894/04 and 3521/07, judgment of 17 March 2016, paras 214–215; The Court applied the same test of attribution to the conduct of the *de facto* authorities in South Ossetia and Abkhazia: *Georgia* v. *Russia (II) (Merits)* (n 64), paras 214, 248, 276 ('the "strict control" that' Russia 'exercised over the South Ossetian forces'), 298.

Even if one accepts that the Court's analysis on both jurisdiction and attribution has become more detailed, covering all factual links between the outside State and the *de facto* regime, it remains questionable as to how far it is compatible with the threshold of 'total dependence' required in general international law. After the Court concluded that the 'MRT' remained 'under the effective authority, or at the very least under the decisive influence' of Russia, the latter raised the argument of the non-conformity of this test with that of 'total dependence' required by the ICJ.[97] However, the Court rejected this argument, noting that the ICJ had decided on the attribution of conduct, whereas the Court is 'concerned with a different question, namely whether facts complained of by an applicant fell within the jurisdiction of a respondent State within the meaning of Article 1 of the Convention'.[98] Consequently, the Court concluded that the more demanding threshold was not applicable. Despite the commendable distinction between jurisdiction and attribution, the explanation is problematic because, while engaging the responsibility of the respondent State, the Court uses the same control test as it used to establish the jurisdiction.

This case law may be regarded as the maintenance of a less demanding threshold of control than that of 'total dependence'. The autonomy of the subordinate entity is much clearer in the *Catan* case than in the case of the 'TRNC': the violations against the rights of the pupils and their family members in the Moldovan schools were committed by the Transnistrian *de facto* authorities without Russia's active participation. The Court expressly recognised the positive effect of the Russian/international mediation in the schools' crisis,[99] the lack of evidence of any direct participation by Russia in the measures taken against the applicants or of its 'involvement in or approbation for the "MRT"'s language policy in general'.[100] Despite Russia's non-involvement in the unlawful conduct and mediation attempts, which demonstrate the leeway of the 'MRT', the Court engaged Russia's responsibility '[b]y virtue of its continued military, economic and political support for the "MRT", which could not otherwise survive'.[101] Because of the leeway left for the 'MRT', this attribution test does not fulfil the criterion of 'total dependence' in general international law.

[97] *Catan* (n 64), para 96; Armenia also raised the same argument in the *Chiragov* case, but the Court did not take it into account. *Chiragov (Merits)* (n 70), para 158.

[98] *Catan* (n 64), para 115. [99] Ibid., paras 49, 56, 66, 149. [100] Ibid., para 149.

[101] Ibid., para 150.

A possible explanation to reconcile the tension between 'total dependence', on the one hand, and dependence/influence/'effective/overall control', on the other, is to consider the less stringent thresholds of human rights treaty bodies as a 'human rights' type interpretation of the same Article 4 ARSIWA.[102] It is submitted that a flexible interpretation in IHRL is justified: human rights treaty bodies have to settle, as a main rule, State–individual disputes and it would be exaggerated to expect the same threshold of evidence on control as in an interstate dispute before the ICJ.[103] Furthermore, massive, systematic and often continuing human rights violations in 'grey zones' require answers adapted to the context of human rights. The application of a flexible control test (based on dependence/influence/'effective/overall control') as a special interpretation of Article 4 ARSIWA facilitates the procedure of human rights treaty bodies, especially in cases of repetitive or massive applications concerning the same region.

5.1.2 De Facto *Agents (Article 8 ARSIWA)*

The notion of *de facto* agents is understood as persons or groups of persons whose specific conduct is attributable to the State on account of the State's instructions, direction or control over the conduct, as codified under Article 8 ARSIWA. Contrary to a *de facto* organ, deprived of real autonomy from the State, a *de facto* agent is defined as a private person or a group of persons outside the State's administrative structure, with a real autonomy. It follows that the criteria of the factual links between the non-state actor and the State are less demanding than in the case of *de facto* organs. International courts and fact-finding missions only examined the attribution of non-state conduct as a *de facto* agent to the State if the assimilation of the entity to a *de facto* organ of the State failed.[104] This analysis of attribution in two steps seems firmly entrenched in international case law. However, the required degree of factual links between the State and the *de facto* agent is contested: whereas general international law defines the required degree narrowly (Section 5.1.2.1), special branches of international law, namely, international criminal law (Section 5.1.2.2) and IHRL (Section 5.1.2.3) satisfy with a less demanding threshold of control.

[102] For another possible explanation, using *lex specialis*: *Infra*, Section 5.1.2.3.

[103] In this sense: *Chiragov (Merits)* (n 70), Concurring opinion of Judge Motoc, 84.

[104] *Nicaragua* (n 28), 62–65, paras 110–115; *Genocide case (Bosnia and Herzegovina* v. *Serbia and Montenegro)* (n 6), 207, para 397; IIFFMG-CEIIG report (n 41), 259–261.

5.1.2.1 General International Law

Both the ICJ and the ILC define the *de facto* agent narrowly, requiring that the conduct is committed on the instructions of, or under the direction or control of, the State. They have developed this secondary norm in a reciprocal exchange that has led to Article 8 ARSIWA.

In the *Nicaragua* case, after the ICJ rejected the equation of the *contras* with a *de facto* organ, it examined whether the US could be held responsible for the assistance of the *contras*, which the Court found crucial to the pursuit of their activities,[105] considering this assistance a partial dependence. The conclusion of the Court requires the State's effective control over the challenged operation: for this conduct to give rise to legal responsibility of the State, 'it would in principle have to be proved that that State had effective control of the military or paramilitary operations in the course of which the alleged violations were committed'.[106] In other terms, the factual links must be proved between the outside State and the specific operation, and not between the State and the non-state entity. Consequently, the Court took the following view:

> United States participation, even if preponderant or decisive, in the financing, organizing, training, supplying and equipping of the *contras*, the selection of its military or paramilitary targets, and the planning of the whole of its operation, is still insufficient in itself, on the basis of the evidence in the possession of the Court, for the purpose of attributing to the United States the acts committed by the *contras* in the course of their military or paramilitary operations in Nicaragua. All the forms of United States participation mentioned above, and even the general control by the respondent State over a force with a high degree of dependency on it, would not in themselves mean, without further evidence, that the United States directed or enforced the perpetration of the acts contrary to human rights and humanitarian law alleged by the applicant State.[107]

Thus, for effective control over the challenged operation, it should be demonstrated by evidence that the State 'directed or enforced the perpetration' of the wrongful act. Since in the instant case the Court found that the acts of the *contras* could have been committed without the control of the US, the criterion of 'effective control' was not fulfilled.[108] Unlike Judge Ago who, in his separate opinion, required a detailed analysis of effective control over all specific acts forming part of the entire operation,[109] the majority only required an effective control over the operation in which the given violations occurred.

[105] *Nicaragua* (n 28), 62–63, para 110. [106] Ibid., 64–65, para 115. [107] Ibid.
[108] Ibid. [109] Ibid., Separate opinion of Judge Ago, 188–189, para 16.

The other case where the Court reaffirmed the so-called effective control attribution test is the *Genocide case (Bosnia and Herzegovina* v. *Serbia and Montenegro)*, where the Court relied on Article 8 ARSIWA that the ILC had finalised some years earlier. In the specific case, the Court examined whether the persons having committed acts of genocide in Srebrenica, although not having the quality of organs of the respondent State, were acting on the instructions of or under the direction or control of the latter. The Court first confirmed that the test of effective control under Article 8 ARSIWA is less demanding than that of 'total dependence': a relationship of 'complete dependence' between the respondent State and the non-state actor does not need to be demonstrated, but only that the persons acted on the instructions or under the 'effective control' of the State. In other words, factual links between the State and the operation need to be substantiated:

> It must however be shown that this 'effective control' was exercised, or that the State's instructions were given, in respect of each operation in which the alleged violations occurred, not generally in respect of the overall actions taken by the persons or groups of persons having committed the violations.[110]

As the evidence did not confirm the involvement of the FRY authorities in the preparation and commission of the massacres,[111] the Court could not attribute the genocide of Srebrenica and the killings committed by the 'Scorpions' to the FRY.[112]

In a reciprocal exchange with the above-mentioned case law of the ICJ, the ILC codified the norm governing the attribution of the conduct of a *de facto* agent in Article 8 ARSIWA. Very early in the ILC's work on State responsibility the Special Rapporteur Ago accepted the hypothesis of attribution of the conduct of persons who 'in fact act on behalf of the State', without having acquired the status of organs of that State.[113] The ILC adopted this wording at the first reading.[114] Following the *Nicaragua* judgment and a great deal of criticism under which the criterion of acting in fact 'on behalf of' opens the way too broadly to attribution even without any control of the State over the person acting

[110] Ibid., 208, para 400. [111] Ibid., pp 213–214, paras 411–412.

[112] Ibid., pp 214–215, para 413.

[113] Third report on State responsibility, by Mr. Roberto Ago, Special Rapporteur, UN Doc. A/CN.4/246 and Add.1–3, in: *YbILC*, 1971, vol. II(1), 182, para 197, draft Article 8.

[114] Report of the ILC on the work of its twenty-sixth session (6 May–26 July 1974), UN Doc. A/96101/Rev.1, in: *YbILC*, 1974, vol. II(1), 283, draft article 8.

spontaneously,[115] the ILC adopted a new wording for Article 8 at the second reading:

> The conduct of a person or group of persons shall be considered an act of a State under international law if the person or group of persons is in fact acting on the instructions of, or under the direction or control of, that State in carrying out the conduct.[116]

Unlike the former wording, Article 8 ARSIWA requires that the State has 'a direct and real influence on the entire operation' in question.[117] The two different types of State contribution to the unlawful conduct, that is, instructions, on the one hand, and directives or control, on the other, do not seem well distinguished, but rather they are synonyms of the State's active participation in the wrongful act. These elements are disjunctive and it suffices to establish the existence of any of these.[118] They all express the ILC's intention to require, in contrast to the criterion of acting in fact 'on behalf of' the State, the State's active participation in the internationally wrongful conduct.

This secondary norm that the ICJ considered customary[119] foresees two sorts of attributable conducts: the conduct performed on the instructions of the State, on the one hand, and the conduct accomplished under the direction or control of the State, on the other. The first case refers to individuals or private groups who, 'though not specifically commissioned by the State and not forming part of its police or armed forces, are employed as auxiliaries or are sent as "volunteers" to neighbouring countries, or who are instructed to carry out particular missions abroad'.[120] Without explaining expressly, the Rapporteur seemed to understand under the notion of instruction an authorisation or a mandate to commit the unlawful act.[121]

115 First report of Crawford (n 10), 40, para 197; Reymond (n 69) 122; Luigi Condorelli, 'L'imputation à l'Etat d'un Fait Internationalement Illicite: Solutions Classiques et Nouvelles Tendences' (1984) 189 *Recueil des Cours* 9, 101–102.

116 Article 8 ARSIWA.

117 Translated by the author, see: Jérôme Reymond, *L'attribution de comportements d'organes De facto et d'agents de l'Etat en droit international: étude sur la responsabilité internationale des Etats* (Schulthess 2013) 208.

118 ARSIWA Commentary, 48, para 7; *Tulip Real Estate and Development Netherlands B.V.* v. *Republic of Turkey*, ICSID, ARB/11/28, Award, 10 March 2014, para 303.

119 *Genocide case (Bosnia and Herzegovina* v. *Serbia and Montenegro)* (n 6), 207, para 398 and 208–209, para 401 and 210–211, paras 406–407.

120 ARSIWA Commentary, 47, para 2.

121 First report of Crawford (n 10), 40, para 197 and 43, para 212.

Contrary to instruction that relates to a specific conduct, in the second hypothesis direction or control by the State relates to an entire operation.[122] This condition is interpreted as the State's decisive influence on the implementation or the continuation of the operation.[123] Article 8 does not define the required degree of factual links: the commentary highlights that '[t]he principle does not extend to conduct which was only incidentally or peripherally associated with an operation and which escaped from the State's direction or control'.[124] The ILC quotes the *Nicaragua* judgment to stress the criterion of effective control over the operation where the violation concerned occurred, adding that a general situation of dependence and support would be insufficient to justify attribution of the conduct to the State.[125] Contrary to the Drafting Committee which limited the direction or the control to the specific conduct,[126] the *Nicaragua* judgment and the ILC's commentary only require direction or control over the entire operation of which the conduct forms an integral part.[127]

Contrasting the *Nicaragua* judgment to the *Tadić* judgment of the Appeals Chamber of the International Criminal Tribunal for the Former Yugoslavia (ICTY) which satisfied itself with a less demanding overall control test, the ILC concluded that 'it is a matter for appreciation in each case whether particular conduct was or was not carried out under the control of a State, to such an extent that the conduct controlled should be attributed to it'.[128] Consequently, the wording of the article leaves a certain flexibility as to the interpretation of the required links and, as a State observed, '[t]his inbuilt ambiguity is a positive element and offers scope for progressive development of the legal rules on State responsibility'.[129]

The legal effect if this secondary norm is the above-mentioned limitation of the attribution to the specific conduct, contrary to the

122 Ibid., 43, para 212.

123 Jörn Griebel, *Die Zurechnungskategorie der De-facto-Organe im Recht der Staatenverantwortlichkeit* (Lit 2004) 96.

124 ARSIWA Commentary, 47, para 3.

125 Ibid., 47–48, para 4.

126 Declaration of the chairman of the Drafting Committee: 2562nd meeting, 13 August 1998, *YbILC*, 1998, vol. I, 282–292, para 79; Griebel (n 123) 74–75.

127 ARSIWA Commentary, 49, para 3; ibid., 77.

128 Ibid., 48, para 5; ILC members stressed the varying degree of sufficient control required in different legal contexts: Report of the ILC on the work of its fiftieth session, UN Doc. A/53/10 (1998), in: *YbILC*, 1998, vol. II(2), 83, para 395.

129 Comments and observations received from Governments, UN Doc. A/CN.4/515 and Add.1–3 (2001), in: *YbILC*, 2001, vol. II(1), 49 (Netherlands).

assimilation of a *de facto* organ of which the acts and omissions are automatically attributed to the State.[130] The narrow definition of Article 8 rarely led to an attribution of the conduct of a *de facto* regime to an outside State and other branches of international law, international criminal law and IHRL have used broader definitions.

5.1.2.2 International Criminal Law

International criminal law uses another test for attribution, that of 'overall control', satisfying with a less demanding degree of State control than that of 'effective control' required by the ICJ under Article 8 ARSIWA. This attribution test, for the first time elaborated by the ICTY Appeals Chamber in the *Tadić* case, has provoked a great deal of criticism, but has henceforth been consistently applied in international criminal law.

In the *Tadić* case the ICTY had to decide on the question of the applicability of Article 2 of its Statute which only applies to acts committed against 'protected persons' in the sense of the Geneva Conventions (GC). As a precondition of its applicability, the central question was whether the victims found themselves 'in the hands of a Party to the conflict or Occupying Power of which they are not nationals' under Article 4 of Convention (IV) Relative to the Protection of Civilian Persons in Time of War (GC IV), or in other terms whether the armed conflict was international. To decide on the international or non-international character of the armed conflict, both the Trial Chamber and the Appeals Chamber chose to follow an analysis of attribution, namely, to determine whether the armed forces of the 'Republika Srpska' could be considered '*de facto* organs or agents' of the FRY (Serbia and Montenegro),[131] but they followed completely different attribution tests.

The Trial Chamber, for its part, turned to the analysis of attribution of the *Nicaragua* judgment, without distinguishing the two tests of 'total dependence' and 'effective control'.[132] It interpreted the judgment of the ICJ as requiring for the attribution a threshold of evidence which goes

130 See the wording of the article which emphasizes that the attribution is limited to the specific conduct ('in fact acting [...] in carrying out the conduct'); First report of Crawford (n 10), 42–43, para 211.

131 *The Prosecutor* v. *Duško Tadić a.k.a. 'Dule'*, IT-94-1-T, judgment, Trial Chamber, 7 May 1997, para 584; ICTY, *The Prosecutor* v. *Duško Tadić*, IT-94-1-A, judgemnt, Appeals Chamber, 15 July 1999, para 98 and para 105.

132 *Tadić*, Trial Chamber (n 131), para 585.

beyond dependence, even complete dependence, between the person or group of persons and the State, and furthermore demonstrates that the FRY (Serbia and Montenegro) 'exercised the potential for control inherent in that relationship of dependency or that the VRS had otherwise placed itself under the control' of the FRY.[133] The majority found that in the instant case there were 'various forms of assistance provided' to the armed forces of the 'Republika Srpska' by the government of the FRY and that there was a form of coordination, alliance and high dependence between them,[134] but no evidence allowed the Court to conclude that the FRY 'made use of the potential for control inherent in that dependence', or that it exercised effective control over the forces of the 'Republika Srpska'.[135] Consequently, the majority did not consider the 'Republika Srpska' as a *de facto* agent of the FRY. The Trial Chamber ruled so not in terms of State responsibility, but strictly in terms of the qualification of the armed conflict.[136]

The Appeals Chamber completely reversed the judgment of the Trial Chamber. While insisting on the analysis of general international law, it rejected the argument of the Prosecutor and of Judge McDonald who claimed that the ICJ only applied the criterion of 'effective control' as a second test after having concluded that the *contras* did not have the quality of organs of the US.[137] Instead, the majority considered *Nicaragua* as applying one single 'effective control' test.[138] The Appeals Chamber strongly criticised the Trial Chamber for relying on the *Nicaragua* judgment that it considered not 'consonant with the logic of the law of State responsibility'[139] and at variance with judicial and State practice.[140] Instead of only one test of effective control, the Appeals Chamber, according to the degree of State control over persons,[141] distinguished three situations to which two different attribution tests are applicable. In the case of a private individual who is engaged by a State to perform some specific illegal acts in the territory of another State and when an unorganised group of individuals commits internationally wrongful acts, the Appeals Chamber requires that the State 'issued specific instructions to them concerning the performance of the acts at issue, or that it *ex post facto* publicly endorsed those'.[142] Consequently, in these cases the ICTY applies the 'effective control' test of the *Nicaragua* judgment.[143] The third situation is constituted by 'individuals making

[133] Ibid., para 588. [134] Ibid., paras 604–606. [135] Ibid., para 605.
[136] Ibid., 229–230, paras 584 and 606. [137] *Tadić*, Appeals Chamber (n 131), para 111.
[138] Ibid., para 112. [139] Ibid., paras 116–123. [140] Ibid., paras 124–145.
[141] Ibid., para 117. [142] Ibid., para 118. [143] Ibid., para 124.

up an organised and hierarchically structured group, such as a military unit or, in case of war or civil strife, armed bands of irregulars or rebels'.[144] As opposed to the first two cases, an organised group has a structure and a chain of command, where the members of the group do not act on their own but conform to the standards prevailing in the group.[145] In this case, to attribute the group's conduct to the State, it suffices 'to require that the group as a whole be under the overall control of the State'.[146]

This 'overall control' is established when the State exercises a control over the group 'not only by equipping and financing the group, but also by coordinating or helping in the general planning of its military activity'.[147] In other words, the degree of overall control can be considered established 'when a State ... has a role in organising, coordinating or planning the military actions of the military group, in addition to financing, training and equipping or providing operational support to that group'.[148] On the basis of these elements of fact, it is not necessary to require that the State gave instructions or directives to commit certain specific acts[149] or certain operations.[150] The State thus is responsible for the unlawful acts of the organised group, whether or not it gave specific instructions to the group.[151] The legal consequence of this type of attribution, for the Appeals Chamber, is the equation of the organised group 'with State organs proper': the latter is responsible for all the conduct, including *ultra vires* acts of the group acting under its overall control.[152] The ICTY thereby transformed the test of 'total dependence' of the ICJ into a test of 'overall control'.[153]

The *Tadić* judgment of the Appeals Chamber has provoked an intense scholarly and judicial debate in matters of attribution. The major criticism, rightly, is that the Appeals Chamber founded all its analysis on an erroneous reading of the *Nicaragua* judgment of the ICJ. Instead of examining first of all whether the entity can be assimilated to a *de facto* organ under the test of total dependence (*Nicaragua*, para 109) and, in the negative, whether the specific conducts were performed on the instructions or under the effective control of the State (*Nicaragua*, para 115),[154]

[144] Ibid., para 120. [145] Ibid. [146] Ibid. [147] Ibid., para 131. [148] Ibid., para 137.
[149] Ibid., para 131. [150] Ibid., para 137. [151] Ibid., para 123.
[152] Ibid., paras 121–122 and 137.
[153] James Crawford, *State Responsibility: The General Part* (Cambridge University Press 2013) 152.
[154] See this reading as proposed by the Prosecutor: *Tadić*, Appeals Chamber (n 131), paras 73, 106; Separate and dissenting opinion of Judge McDonald, *Tadić*, Trial Chamber (n

the Appeals Chamber interpreted the *Nicaragua* judgment as requiring one single criterion for attribution, that of 'dependence and control', as specified by 'the evidently stringent application of the "effective control" test'.[155] It follows that the Appeals Chamber mixed the thresholds of attribution under Articles 4 and 8 ARSIWA and created the 'overall control' test which results in the assimilation of the group not only to a *de facto* agent, but to a *de facto* organ of the State.[156]

In the *Genocide* case *(Bosnia and Herzegovina* v. *Serbia and Montenegro)* the ICJ firmly rejected the 'overall control' test of the *Tadić* appeal judgment. It noted that the ICTY ruled on a question beyond the exercise of its jurisdiction,[157] namely, State responsibility – a question that falls within the jurisdiction of the ICJ.[158] The Court observed first that logic does not require the same test to be adopted in resolving the two above-mentioned issues, namely, State responsibility and the question of the international character of the armed conflict, which are different in nature: the degree and nature of a State's involvement can very well, without logical inconsistency, be different in the two cases.[159] Contrary to the Court's insistence to maintain the distinction between primary and secondary rules, it is not uncommon that attribution rules are used to determine the scope of application of substantive (primary) rules. This is typically necessary to determine whether, when acting through non-state actors, a State has breached its obligations[160] – as the analysis of jurisdiction in IHRL also showed. After the *Tadić* case international criminal courts have widely applied the 'overall control' test to qualify the armed conflict as international or non-international, satisfying with a less demanding degree of State control than that of 'effective control' in general international law.[161]

131), paras 22, 25; *Nicaragua* (n 28), Separate opinion of Judge Ago, 188–189, para 16.

155 *Tadić*, Appeals Chamber (n 131), para 112.

156 Ibid., paras 121–123, esp. 122.

157 *Genocide case (Bosnia and Herzegovina* v. *Serbia and Montenegro)* (n 6), 209, para 403.

158 Ibid., 210, para 404.

159 Ibid., 210, para 405.

160 Remy Jorritsma, 'Where General International Law Meets International Humanitarian Law: Attribution of Conduct and the Classification of Armed Conflicts' (2018) 23 *Journal of Conflict and Security Law* 405, 416.

161 E.g. ICTY: *The Prosecutor* v. *Tihomir Blaškic*, IT-95-14-T, judgment, Trial Chamber, 3 March 2000, 28–44, paras 75–123; *The Prosecutor* v. *Jadranko Prlić et al.*, IT-04-74, Trial Chamber, judgment, 29 May 2013, Vol. 3/6, paras 545–568; SCSL, *Prosecutor* v. *Issa Hassan Sesay et al.*, SCSL-04-15-T, Trial Chamber, judgment, 2 March 2009, 306, paras 975–976; ICC: *The Prosecutor* v. *Thomas Lubanga Dyilo*, ICC-01/04-01/06-2842, judgment pursuant to Article 74 of the Statute, 14 March 2012, 246–248, para 541; *The Prosecutor* v. *Germain*

Second, the ICJ rejected the ICTY's criterion of 'overall control' as it goes well beyond the threshold of acting 'on the instructions of, or under the direction or control of' the State and thus it 'is unsuitable, for it stretches too far, almost to breaking point, the connection which must exist between the conduct of a State's organs and its international responsibility'.[162] As opposed to the Court's insistence to ensure the uniformity of the attribution test under Article 8 ARSIWA, it was explained above that the latter provision leaves some leeway for international courts as to the required threshold of control.

Alternatively, the threshold of 'overall control' of *Tadić* could perfectly constitute an attribution test under Article 4 ARSIWA. The Appeals Chamber itself pointed out that its test would attribute all conduct of the non-state entity to the State exercising the 'overall control'.[163] This reading confirms the case law of the regional human rights courts according to which, to attribute all acts and omissions of the entity to the State controlling it under Article 4 ARSIWA, the 'total dependence' of the ICJ is not the only threshold.

5.1.2.3 International Human Rights Law

Some (a) universal and (b) regional human rights monitoring bodies apply a less stringent threshold of attribution of conduct committed on the instructions or the directives or under the control of the State than general international law.

a. Universal Monitoring Bodies

Among UN treaty-monitoring bodies, the Convention on the Elimination of All Forms of Discrimination against Women (CEDAW) Committee and the Committee on Economic, Social and Cultural Rights (CESCR) expressly accepted the 'effective control' test under Article 8 ARSIWA.[164] Various universal monitoring bodies, deprived of (quasi-) judicial competence, have invoked Article 8 ARSIWA with regard to the

Katanga, ICC-01/04-01/07, Trial Chamber, judgment, 7 March 2014, 446–447, para 1178.

162 *Genocide case (Bosnia and Herzegovina* v. *Serbia and Montenegro)* (n 6), 210, para 406.

163 *Tadić*, Appeals Chamber (n 131), 50, para 122; Reymond (n 69) 227.

164 CEDAW, General recommendation No. 35 on gender-based violence against women, UN Doc. CEDAW/C/GC/35 (26 July 2017), para 24(a); CESCR, General comment No. 24 (2017) on State obligations under the ICESCR in the context of business activities, UN Doc. E/C.12/GC/24 (10 August 2017), para 11.

conduct of paramilitary or self-defence groups,[165] without applying it to a specific case. An exception is the Special Rapporteur on Extrajudicial, Summary or Arbitrary Executions who foresaw, in conformity with Article 8, an example 'where State officials fund the formation of a vigilante group and instructs it to kill certain named individuals or to patrol a certain area and kill suspected criminals'.[166]

Other monitoring bodies apply broader tests of attribution. The Committee against Torture attributes to the State the conduct of non-state actors 'acting on behalf of the State, in conjunction with the State, under its direction or control'.[167] As mentioned in Section 5.1.2.1, the formulation 'on behalf of the State' not necessarily requires the active participation of the State in the internationally wrongful conduct. Furthermore, a report established by three Special Rapporteurs on the situation of human rights in East Timor attributed the atrocities committed by pro-integration militia to Indonesia on account of the support, planning, assistance and organisation of these acts by the Indonesian National Army.[168] In the instant case, the analysis of attribution was limited to summarising the major factual links between the militias and the outside State, without examining the instructions or directives or the control exercised over the specific conducts/operation, thus resembling the *Tadić* test.[169] These examples show that some universal monitoring bodies have required a less stringent threshold of attribution of conduct than general international law. Regional human rights monitoring bodies also follow a broad concept of attribution of conduct committed

[165] E.g. Report of the Special Rapporteur on the situation of human rights defenders, UN Doc. A/65/223 (4 August 2010), para 41; Report of the Special Rapporteur on extrajudicial, summary or arbitrary executions, UN Doc. A/64/187 (29 July 2009), para 56; Report of the Special Rapporteur on extrajudicial, summary or arbitrary executions on the right to life and the use of force by private security providers in law enforcement contexts, UN Doc. A/HRC/32/39 (6 May 2016), para 63.

[166] UN Doc. A/64/187 (n 165), para 56.

[167] CAT, General comment No. 2: Implementation of article 2 by States parties, UN Doc. CAT/C/GC/2 (24 January 2008), para 15; *Ms. M.C.M.V.F.* v. *Sweden*, Communication No. 237/2003, UN Doc. CAT/C/35/D/237/2003 (12 December 2005), para 6.4 (no evidence that 'those incidents be attributable to state agents or to groups acting on behalf of or under the effective control of state agents').

[168] Situation of Human Rights in East Timor, UN Doc. A/54/660 (10 December 1999), paras 59–65, 72.

[169] The rapporteurs themselves admit that in this regard, '[w]hat still remains to be determined is how much of TNI and to what level in the hierarchy there was either active involvement or, at least, culpable toleration of the activities'. Ibid., para 72; In favor of an analogy with the *Tadić* test: Cassese (n 67) 659, note 19.

on the instructions or under the directives or the control of the State, but as opposed to universal bodies, they apply it in judicial procedures.

b. Regional Monitoring Bodies

The IACtHR has attributed the conduct of non-state actors to the (territorial) State in the situations described in Section 5.1.1.2/b even at the second stage of the development of paramilitary groups, where the State dissociated itself from their activity that it considered unlawful. This was the case in areas controlled by a paramilitary group when the authorities of the State actively supported the group in the commission of a violation of the ACHR. The Court often established the attribution of private parties' conduct on the 'support' and tolerance of the conduct by State authorities.[170]

Chronologically the first case in which the Court attributed the conduct of paramilitaries to the territorial State is the *19 Merchants* v. *Colombia* case (2004). In the instant case a paramilitary group controlling the municipality of Boyacá abducted and killed 19 tradesmen who refused to pay the 'taxes' for transiting the region. The Court noted that the paramilitaries acted in the region with the support, collaboration and the tolerance of the Colombian armed forces and that they adopted their plan to abduct and kill the tradesmen with the acquiescence of some members of the Colombian armed forces.[171] While finding the Colombian State responsible for the committed violations of the ACHR, the Court also referred to its case law according to which for the attribution of private persons' conduct, it suffices to demonstrate that the State authorities supported or tolerated the unlawful conduct.[172] The Court did not further clarify the norm of attribution that it mixed with elements of violation of the State's obligations of due diligence (see Section 5.2), although some commentators hold that the *Nicaragua* test of 'effective control' was satisfied in that case.[173]

The second case in which the Court attributed the violation of the ACHR committed by a paramilitary group to the State was the *Mapiripán Massacre* v. *Colombia* (2005) case on the massacre committed by the

170 *'White Van' (Paniagua-Morales et al.)* v. *Guatemala*, judgment of 8 March 1998 (Merits), para 91; *19 Merchants* (n 58), para 141; *Mapiripán Massacre* v. *Colombia*, judgment of 15 September 2005 (Merits, Reparations and Costs), para 110; *Rochela Massacre* v. *Colombia*, judgment of 11 May 2007 (Merits, Reparations, and Costs), para 68.

171 *19 Merchants* (n 58), paras 86, 134–137.

172 Ibid., paras 141, 156, 205, 217,

173 Frédéric Vanneste, *General International Law before Human Rights Courts: Assessing the Speciality Claims of International Human Rights Law* (Intersentia 2010) 178.

paramilitary group *Autodefensas Unidas de Colombia* (AUC). In the instant case the AUC occupied the village of Mapiripán and detained, tortured and killed at least 49 civilians with the collaboration and acquiescence of Colombia's armed forces. As the Court recognised, the paramilitaries carried out their incursion to the town with the knowledge, logistic preparations and collaboration of the Colombian armed forces, who left the territory under their control for the paramilitary, leaving the civilian population defenceless.[174] However, the IACtHR admitted that the State authorities did not directly participate in the operation and that no relation of dependence existed between them and the paramilitary group.[175]

The IACHR proposed to establish Colombia's responsibility on attribution, in conformity with its earlier case law, on account of the support or tolerance of the unlawful conduct by State authorities, adding interestingly that this norm equally conforms to international law.[176] However, as the respondent State rightly argued, the criteria of Article 8 ARSIWA had not been fulfilled since the paramilitary group did not act on the instructions or under the control of the State, neither under the *Nicaragua* test, nor under the *Tadić* test.[177] The Court avoided to rule on the conformity of its case law with Article 8 ARSIWA, but confined itself to emphasising the special nature of the ACHR and the *effet utile* to be given to its provisions.[178] While confirming that the support or tolerance of the wrongful conduct by the State suffices for attribution, the Court confirmed that the test of support and collaboration had been fulfilled in the instant case and consequently engaged Colombia's responsibility.[179]

Collaboration with paramilitary groups also served as a basis of attribution in the *Afro-descendant communities displaced from the Cacarica River Basin (Operation Genesis)* v. *Colombia* (2013) case. In the instant case the military incursion of a paramilitary group, conducted at the same time as the operation of the Colombian armed forces in other areas of the same region, provoked a series of massive human rights violations such as the killing or forced displacement of civilians. The evidence has established that there was a collaboration of paramilitaries and the Colombian armed forces.[180] Consequently, the Court concluded that the torture and the killing of a civilian person, committed by the

174 *Mapiripán Massacre* (n 170), paras 120–121. 175 Ibid., para 120.
176 Ibid., para 98(a). 177 Ibid., para 97(d)–(e). 178 Ibid., paras 103–105.
179 Ibid., para 123.
180 *Afro-descendant communities displaced from the Cacarica River Basin (Operation Genesis)* v. *Colombia*, judgment of 20 November 2013 (Preliminary objections, Merits, Reparations and Costs), paras 255–280, 386, 389.

paramilitary group, 'can be attributed to the State owing to the acquiescence or collaboration that agents of the Armed Forces provided to the operations of those groups'.[181]

It is clear that the test of 'support or tolerance', collaboration and acquiescence of State authorities falls short of fulfilling the threshold of general international law, that is, the State's active participation in, direct and real influence on the entire operation in which the wrongful act occurred. It also does not satisfy the *Tadić* 'overall control' test,[182] as the ICTY Appeals Chamber also required general direction, coordination and supervision of the operation beyond the mere support. In other words, in all the tests analysed under Article 8 ARSIWA – those of the ICJ and the ICTY – there was a varying degree of dependence between the non-state actor and the State. Often the non-reference to attribution in the IACtHR's final conclusion on the State's responsibility and its frequent references to the State's positive obligations suggest that there could be a violation of the State's own obligations of due diligence rather than an attribution of conduct (see Section 5.2).[183] This is typically the case where there is evidence on the mere tolerance of the unlawful conduct, without any form of the State's active collaboration with the paramilitary group.

As far as the ECtHR is concerned, it was explained in Section 5.1.1.2/c that the Court's case law on *de facto* regimes may be considered an example of the application of Article 4 ARSIWA. Nevertheless, some commentators, including the ILC, classify the Court's attribution analysis in its Northern Cyprus[184] and Transnistrian cases[185] in terms of Article 8 ARSIWA. However, the legal consequence of the attribution test applied by the ECtHR, that is, the automatic attribution of all conduct of the *de facto* regime to the outside State (organic attribution),

[181] Ibid., para 281. [182] *A contrario*, in this sense: Vanneste (n 173) 178–179.

[183] This is confirmed by the reference in subsequent cases to the above cited paragraphs of the *19 Merchants* and *Mapiripán Massacre* cases as precedents of due diligence violations. *Rochela Massacre* (n 170), para 68, note 34.

[184] E.g. ARSIWA Commentary, 50, para 5, note 160; First report of Crawford (n 10), 41–42, paras 207–208; Vassilis P. Tzevelekos, 'The Use of Article 31(3)(C) of the VCLT in the Case Law of the ECtHR: An Effective Anti-Fragmentation Tool or a Selective Loophole for the Reinforcement of Human Rights Teleology – Between Evolution and Systemic Integration' (2009) 31 *Michigan Journal of International Law* 621, 672.

[185] E.g. Gérard Cohen-Jonathan and Jean-François Flauss, 'Cour Européenne Des Droits de l'homme et Droit International Général' (2004) 50 *Annuaire français de droit international* 778, 785; Jan Arno Hessbruegge, 'Introductory Note to the European Court of Human Rights: Catan and Others v. Moldova and Russia' (2013) 52 *International Legal Materials* 217–218.

including *ultra vires* acts, excludes the application of Article 8 ARSIWA, which relates only to specific conducts (functional attribution). Moreover, the Court never examines instructions, directives or the control over the specific conducts challenged in the disputes but satisfies itself with the 'effective/overall control' exercised over the *de facto* regime. These elements make the hypothesis of an attribution under Article 8 ARSIWA unlikely.

As has been shown, neither the ECtHR's case law on *de facto* organs, nor the IACtHR's case law on *de facto* agents corresponds to the general international law threshold under Articles 4 and 8 ARSIWA. As mentioned in Section 5.1.1.2/c, the regional monitoring bodies have applied a *sui generis* interpretation of general international law secondary norms in IHRL. Another possible explanation is that regional human rights courts apply a *lex specialis* in matters of attribution under Article 55 of the ILC's Articles.[186] As the ICJ noted, '[t]he rules for attributing alleged internationally wrongful conduct to a State do not vary with the nature of the wrongful act in question in the absence of a clearly expressed *lex specialis*'.[187] It is possible that a human rights treaty specifies only some aspects of the general law of State responsibility, whereas other aspects remain applicable – this is the case of Article 41 of the ECHR on just satisfaction.[188]

However, international human rights treaties foresee no derogation to the attribution rules of general international law. Quite to the contrary, the ECtHR several times observed that 'the Convention cannot be interpreted in a vacuum and should so far as possible be interpreted in harmony with other rules of international law of which it forms part'.[189] Specifically in matters of State responsibility, the Court often refers to

[186] E.g. as a *sui generis* test of attribution applied by the ECtHR: Andrea Bianchi, 'The Act of the State: The State of the Act Judicial Interpretation and Human Rights Enforcement' in Marcelo G. Kohen (ed.), *Promoting Justice, Human Rights and Conflict Resolution through International Law: Liber Amicorum Lucius Caflisch* (M Nijhoff Publishers 2007) 136; Ioana Petculescu, 'La Contribution Du Droit International de La Responsabilité à La Protection Des Droits de l'homme. L'arrêt de La Cour Européenne Des Droits de l'homme Du 8 Juillet 2004 Dans l'affaire Ilascu et Autres c. La République de Moldova et La Fédération de Russie' (2005) 109 *Revue Générale de Droit International Public* 581, 587–588.

[187] *Genocide case (Bosnia and Herzegovina* v. *Serbia and Montenegro)* (n 6), 208–209, para 401.

[188] ARSIWA Commentary, 140, para 3; ECtHR, *Cyprus* v. *Turkey* [GC], Appl. no. 25781/94, judgment (just satisfaction) of 12 May 2014, para 42.

[189] E.g. *Loizidou (Merits)* (n 66), para 43; *Hassan* v. *United Kingdom* [GC], Appl. no. 29750/09, judgment of 16 September 2014, paras 77, 102.

'the relevant principles of international law governing State responsibility'[190] or the ILC's ARSIWA as 'relevant international law',[191] including Article 8 ARSIWA.[192] While the Court does not apply the ARSIWA directly in the part on the merits, it confirmed its intent to conform to the ILC's interpretation of Article 8 ARSIWA.[193] It follows that it establishes international responsibility on the provisions of the ECHR, as interpreted in light of the purposes of the Convention and general international law.[194]

As in the case of the ECtHR, the IACtHR often refers to the international law on State responsibility in general,[195] and on attribution in particular.[196] In the *Mapiripán Massacre* v. *Colombia* case, however, the IACtHR noted that the ACHR

> constitutes *lex specialis* regarding State responsibility, in view of its special nature as an international human rights treaty *vis-à-vis* general International Law. Therefore, attribution of international responsibility to the State ... must take place in light of the Convention itself.[197]

In this sense, some authors submitted that the particularism of IHRL could lead to rules of attribution different from those codified by the ILC,[198] while others maintain that the IACtHR applies general

[190] E.g. *Loizidou (Merits)* (n 66), para 52; *Cyprus* v. *Turkey* [GC] (n 66), para 76 (citing *Loizidou*).

[191] E.g. *Jaloud* (n 64), para 98; *Catan* (admissibility) (n 86), para 73.

[192] *Mikhail Vitalevich Samsonov* v. *Russia*, Appl. no. 2880/10, decision of 16 September 2014 on the admissibility, para 45–46; *Liseytseva and Maslov* v. *Russia*, Appl. nos. 39483/05 and 40527/10, judgment of 9 October 2014, paras 128–129.

[193] *Samsonov* (n 192), para 73; *Liseytseva* (n 192), para 205.

[194] E.g. *Stichting mothers of Srebrenica and Others* v. *the Netherlands*, Appl. no. 65542/12, decision of 11 June 2013 on the admissibility, para 144; *Avşar* v. *Turkey*, Appl. no. 25657/94, judgment of 10 July 2001, para 284; Fragmentation of International Law: difficulties arising from the Diversification and Expansion of International Law, Report of the Study Group of the ILC, UN Doc. A/CN.4/L.682 (13 April 2006), para 469.

[195] *Velásquez-Rodríguez* v. *Honduras*, judgment of 29 July 1988 (Merits), para 164; in matter of reparation: *Almonacid-Arellano et al* v. *Chile*, judgment of 26 September 2006 (Preliminary objections, Merits, Reparations and Costs), para 135; *19 Merchants* (n 58), para 220.

[196] On *ultra vires* acts: *Velásquez-Rodríguez* (n 195), para 170; *Kawas-Fernández* v. *Honduras*, judgment of 3 April 2009 (Merits, Reparations and Costs), para 72; on attribution: *'The Last Temptation of Christ' (Olmedo-Bustos et al.)* v. *Chile*, judgment of 5 February 2001 (Merits, Reparations and Costs), para 72; *19 Merchants* (n 58), para 140; *Afro-descendant communities* ... (n 180), para 224.

[197] *Mapiripán Massacre* (n 170), para 107; confirmed in: *Santo Domingo Massacre* v. *Colombia*, judgment of 30 November 2012 (Preliminary objections, Merits and Reparations), para 23 (reiterating the reference to *lex specialis*).

[198] Gérard Cohen-Jonathan, 'Responsabilité pour atteinte aux droits de l'homme' in Société française pour le droit international (ed.), *La responsabilité dans le système international*.

international law codified by the ILC in matters of attribution.[199] In fact, the European and Inter-American case law does not differ significantly: both courts interpret the relevant instrument in conformity with the general rules of State responsibility. In turn, regional human rights courts interpret the general rules in a flexible manner to make human rights effective and to fill the gap of the lacking special rules on attribution in human rights treaties. The IACtHR emphasised that legal norms of attribution as codified by the ILC's ARSIWA do not constitute a *numerus clausus* and may be applied flexibly, in light of the factual circumstances of each case.[200] Thus, the links between general international law and IHRL in matters of attribution confirm the general tendency of mutual enrichment in which, contrary to a hypothesis of exclusivity between the two regimes ('unity *or* fragmentation'), IHRL is inspired by and develops general international law through its own case law ('signs of unity *and* fragmentation').[201] With a flexible threshold of attribution, IHRL ultimately contributes to the normalisation of the human rights situation in 'grey zones': it facilitates the engagement of the State's responsibility, and sanctions its influence on the wrongful conduct of the non-state actor directly controlling the territory, even if such influence is less intensive than the thresholds required in general international law.

5.1.3 *Agents of Necessity (Article 9 ARSIWA)*

On the so-called agent of necessity case,[202] Article 9 ARSIWA provides:

> The conduct of a person or group of persons shall be considered an act of a State under international law if the person or group of persons is in fact exercising elements of the governmental authority in the absence or default of the official authorities and in circumstances such as to call for the exercise of those elements of authority.

Société française pour le droit international, colloque du Mans, [31 mai–2 juin 1990] (A Pedone 1991) 115.

199 Vanneste (n 173) 178–180; Jo M. Pasqualucci, *The Practice and Procedure of the Inter-American Court of Human Rights* (Cambridge University Press 2003) 228–229.

200 *Pueblo Bello Massacre* (n 62), para 116.

201 Christina Binder and Konrad Lachmayer, 'Introduction. The Reception of Public International Law in the Jurisprudence of the European Court of Human Rights: Sign of Fragmentation or Unity?' in Christina Binder and Konrad Lachmayer (eds.), *The European Court of Human Rights and Public International Law: Fragmentation or Unity?* (Nomos-Verl-Ges 2014) 10.

202 Griebel (n 123) 78.

The Representative of the Secretary-General on the human rights of internally-displaced persons suggested that this article could constitute a legal basis for the attribution of the conduct of *de facto* regimes to the territorial State.[203] Furthermore, some authors and codification works defended the idea under which the principle of non-attribution of the insurgents' conduct to the territorial State has an exception, namely, the conduct performed in the interests of society such as acts of administrative routine, which should be attributed to the State.[204]

The commentaries of Article 9 partially confirm this view. As the ILC's commentary notes, '[s]uch cases occur only rarely, such as during revolution, armed conflict or foreign occupation, where the regular authorities dissolve, are disintegrating, have been suppressed or are for the time being inoperative'.[205] Furthermore, the commentary specifies that '[t]he cases envisaged by article 9 presuppose the existence of a Government in office and of State machinery whose place is taken by irregulars or whose action is supplemented in certain cases', for example 'on part of the territory of a State which is for the time being out of control, or in other specific circumstances'.[206] One of the conditions, the expression 'in the absence or default of' the official authorities 'is intended to cover both the situation of a total collapse of the State apparatus as well as cases where the official authorities are not exercising their functions in some specific respect, for instance, in the case of a partial collapse of the State or its loss of control over a certain locality'.[207] These references confirm the hypothesis of the Representative of the Secretary-General.

Nevertheless, the spontaneous character of the conduct of individuals distinguishes Article 9 from the conduct of a *de facto* regime. As the codification works of this rule stressed, the private persons act 'spontaneously', on their own initiative,[208] and the circumstances are such as to

[203] Report of the Representative of the Secretary-General on the human rights of internally displaced persons, Walter Kälin, Mission to Georgia, UN Doc. E/CN.4/2006/71/Add.7 (24 March 2006), para 5; Follow-up mission to Georgia, UN Doc. A/HRC/10/13/Add.2 (13 February 2009), para 8.

[204] Paul Reuter, 'La responsabilité internationale. Problèmes choisis (1955–1956)', in *Le développement de l'ordre juridique international: écrits de droit international* (Économica 1995) 465; Haig Silvanie, 'Responsibility of States for Acts of Insurgent Governments' (1939) 33 *American Journal of International Law* 78, 93–103; ILC, 1259th meeting, 17 May 1974 (A/CN.4/SR.1259), *YbILC*, 1974, vol. I, 36–43, para 8 (Mr. Ramangasoavina); Restatement (Third) of The Foreign Relations Law of the United States Part, para 207(b).

[205] ARSIWA Commentary, 49, para 1. [206] Ibid., 49, para 4. [207] Ibid., 49, para 5.

[208] Ibid., 49, para 4; Third report of Ago (n 113), 263, para 189; UN Doc. A/96101/Rev.1 (n 114), 285, paras 9–11.

'call' for the exercise of those elements of authority such as police or other functions in the absence of any constituted authority.[209] The ILC foresaw a situation in which, on the one hand, private persons act 'on behalf of the State, as a subject of international law, without having received any formal appointment as organs under the internal law of that State', while there is 'no formal or real link with the machinery of the State or of one of the entities entrusted by the internal law of the State with the exercise of elements of the governmental authority'.[210] On the other hand, acting 'on behalf of the State' seems to exclude cases where persons act on behalf of other subjects of international law, namely, as members of an insurrectional movement which refuses the authority of the territorial State and which itself contributed to the situation of the absence or default of the official authorities. Contrary to the above-mentioned suggestions to attribute routine administrative acts of *de facto* regimes to the territorial State, the majority of the ILC firmly refused this idea which seems to confuse the recognition of some acts of insurgents under domestic law – which has some State practice – and the attribution of their conduct.[211] Indeed, it would be unjust to attribute the wrongful conducts of a *de facto* regime opposing the central government to the territorial State,[212] even if the acts concerned belong to governmental functions, 'in the absence or default of the official authorities'.

Beyond the works of the ILC, the rare case law cited for Article 9 consists of cases where irregular and self-defence groups acted spontaneously on behalf of the territorial State's (*de facto* or *de jure*) government, and not on behalf of other subjects of international law such as a *de facto* regime.[213] Likewise, one of the sources inspiring Article 9, the old

[209] ARSIWA Commentary, 49, para 6.

[210] UN Doc. A/96101/Rev.1 (n 114), 285, para 10, 286, para 13.

[211] Fourth report of Ago (n 12), 142, para 186; Text of articles 1–15 adopted by the Commission at its twenty-fifth, twenty-sixth and twenty-seventh sessions and commentaries, UN Doc. A/10010/Rev.1, in: *YbILC*, 1975, vol. II, 98, para 26; First report of Crawford (n 10), 51, para 263.

[212] Draft article 12(2), Fourth report of Ago (n 12), 143; Draft articles adopted on first reading (n 11), draft article 14(1); Gérard Cahin, 'L'État défaillant en droit international : quel régime pour quelle notion ?', in *Droit du pouvoir, pouvoir du droit: mélanges offerts à Jean Salmon* (Bruylant 2007) 204.

[213] *Kenneth P. Yeager* v. *The Islamic Republic of Iran*, Case No. 10199, Iran – United States Claims Tribunal, Chamber One, Award No. 324-10199-1, 2 November 1987, *Iran – United States Claims Tribunal Reports*, 1987, vol. 17, 1987-IV, 104, paras 43–44; *Charles S. Stephens and Bowman Stephens (U.S.A.)* v. *United Mexican States*, 15 July 1927, *UNRIAA*, vol. IV, 267; France, Conseil d'Etat, *Sieur Marion and Others et Commune de Saint Valéry-sur-Somme*,

idea of the *levée en masse*, that is, the self-defence of the inhabitants in the absence of regular forces, aims to apply to 'inhabitants of a territory which has not been occupied'.[214] Therefore, the scenario of Article 9 is applicable during a transition period, in a vacuum of governmental authority but not in an area under the effective control of a *de facto* regime or another State.[215] As this situation is extremely rare in the case law, Article 9 forms part of the progressive development of international law rather than the existing practice.[216]

For the above-mentioned reasons – the spontaneous character of the conduct, the exercise of governmental authority on behalf of the territorial State, the lack of formal appointment by State authorities and vacuum of governmental authority – it is not surprising that very few if no precedents have attributed the conduct of agents of necessity in 'grey zones'. Cases of the IACtHR discussed under the precedent point, where the territorial State collaborated with paramilitary groups, do not seem to satisfy the criteria of Article 9: where the paramilitary group acted in its second phase of development, unlawfully, conducting criminal activities, it is difficult to submit that it exercised in fact prerogatives of governmental authority.[217] The *Rochela Massacre* v. *Colombia* case seems much closer to the hypothesis of Article 9: contrary to precedents, at the time of the facts, the paramilitary group acted under the cover of the law on the creation of self-defence groups still in force, exercising certain functions of public power of the State (patrol, counter guerrilla activities), whereas such paramilitary groups were only criminalised with some delay.[218] In the instant case the armed group thus acted in a phase of transition, as entity habilitated to exercise governmental functions and the judgment of the Court referred to that element, which allows interpreting the attribution under Article 9.[219] Nonetheless, the fact that Colombia adopted legal regulations in force which expressly

Section, Cases No. 86.937 and 77.688, 5 March 1948, *Recueil des arrêts du Conseil d'Etat*, 1948, 113–114.

214 Regulations respecting the laws and customs of war on land (annexed to the Conventions respecting the Laws and Customs of War on Land of 1899 and 1907), Article 2; GC III, Article 4(A)(6).

215 The notion 'agency of necessity' used by Crawford seems to express this situation of vacuum and need of authorities exercising governmental functions. Crawford (n 153) 169.

216 Jacob (n 19) 378; *a contrario*: UNCITRAL, *Sergei Paushok et al.* v. *The Government of Mongolia*, Award on jurisdiction and liability, 28 April 2011, para 576 (considering Article 9 as custom).

217 *A contrario*: Vanneste (n 173) 179–180.

218 Ibid., paras 84–85, 101(b)–(c).

219 In this sense, arguing for the applicability of Article 9 ARSIWA: Vanneste (n 173) 180.

authorised the exercise of those governmental functions by the paramilitary group[220] and the latter's close link to the Colombian armed forces suggest that the conduct was performed under some sort of State control (as a *de facto* agent) rather than spontaneously.

A clearer example that arguably satisfied all conditions is the *African Commission on Human and Peoples' Rights* v. *Libya* case, where the ACtHPR had to decide on the attribution of conduct of a so-called revolutionary brigade that illegally detained the applicant, Saïf Al-Islam Kadhafi, Muammar Gaddafi's unspoken successor. The applicant's arrest and detention occurred in November 2011, when the National Transitional Council was already the recognised government of Libya, without controlling the entire national territory.[221] The revolutionary armed groups, one of them keeping the applicant in secret detention, were later placed under the nominal authority of the government, while they have continued to operate with significant autonomy, and have consolidated effective control over large territorial areas.[222] Therefore, the ACtHPR rightly took note of the 'volatile political and security situation in Libya', that is, the transitional vacuum of authority, cited Article 9 ARSIWA and concluded that 'the Respondent is responsible for the latter's action as well as its acts of omission'.[223]

5.1.4 *Conduct of a Victorious Insurrectional Movement (Article 10 ARSIWA)*

Article 10 ARSIWA governs the responsibility of the territorial State for the conduct of an insurrectional or other movement as follows:

> 1. The conduct of an insurrectional movement which becomes the new Government of a State shall be considered an act of that State under international law.
> 2. The conduct of a movement, insurrectional or other, which succeeds in establishing a new State in part of the territory of a pre-existing State or in a territory under its administration shall be considered an act of the new State under international law.
> 3. This article is without prejudice to the attribution to a State of any conduct, however related to that of the movement concerned, which is to be considered an act of that State by virtue of Articles 4 to 9.

[220] *Rochela Massacre* (n 170), paras 88–89.

[221] ACtHPR, *The African Commission on Human and Peoples' Rights* v. *Libya*, App. No. 002/2013, judgment of 3 June 2016, para 6.

[222] Investigation by the Office of the United Nations High Commissioner for Human Rights on Libya, UN Doc. A/HRC/31/47 (15 February 2016), para 12.

[223] *The African Commission on Human and Peoples' Rights* v. *Libya* (n 221), paras 49–50.

The attribution of the conduct of an insurrectional or other movement to the State thus depends on whether the movement becomes the new government of the State or succeeds in establishing a new State. Despite the actuality and the controversy that this norm generates, the hypothesis provided for in Article 10 exceeds the limits of the present book, which focuses on areas controlled by ongoing insurrections in a pending state.[224]

5.1.5 *Conduct Acknowledged and Adopted by a State As Its Own (Article 11 ARSIWA)*

Article 11 ARSIWA provides:

> Conduct which is not attributable to a State under the preceding articles shall nevertheless be considered an act of that State under international law if and to the extent that the State acknowledges and adopts the conduct in question as its own.

This provision, arguably enshrining a customary norm,[225] enables the attribution of wrongful conduct that at the time of its commission was not attributable to the State, but which the State later acknowledged and adopted as its own. As in the case of victorious insurrectional movements, this attribution rule helps to avoid 'gaps in the extent of responsibility for what is, in effect, the same continuing act'.[226] It may serve as a basis of responsibility of both the territorial State and the outside State: in some cases the policy of acquiescence of the authorities of the territorial State *vis-à-vis* paramilitary groups could amount to an acknowledgement and adoption of the conduct by the State as its own, whereas outside States are often accused of expressly acknowledging and adopting the unlawful conducts of voluntary groups acting on foreign soil.

The most remarkable precedent is the *United States Diplomatic and Consular Staff in Tehran* case. In the instant case the ICJ concluded that since Ayatollah Khomeini and other organs of the Iranian State approved the occupation of the US embassy and the detention of the hostages by

[224] In details: Jacob (n 19) 236–245; Patrick Dumberry, 'New State Responsibility for Internationally Wrongful Acts by an Insurrectional Movement' (2006) 17 *European Journal of International Law* 605.

[225] *Responsibilities and obligations of States with respect to activities in the Area*, Advisory Opinion, 1 February 2011, *ITLOS Reports* 2011, 59–60, para 182.

[226] ARSIWA Commentary, 52–53, para 4.

the militants, the unlawful acts had become acts by the State itself.[227] Whereas in the specific case it was unclear whether the Iranian State approved and acknowledged the conduct as its own only prospectively or with regard to the occupation of the embassy and the detention of the personnel *ab initio*,[228] the ILC confirmed that '[w]here the acknowledgement and adoption is unequivocal and unqualified there is good reason to give it retroactive effect'.[229] Later cases have not clarified this question, and scholarship is equally divided in this respect.[230] However, it is accepted that the State may acknowledge and adopt a conduct as its own only to a certain extent, that is, partially.[231] It follows that a State can acknowledge and adopt in part or entirely the conduct of a non-state actor controlling an area as its own, which makes the conduct attributable to the State. While so doing, it might even go as far as to consider and treat the entity as one of its organs under its 'total dependence', which would assimilate it to a *de facto* organ.

The specificity of the acknowledgement and the adoption of the conduct nonetheless raises several controversies. Taking the example invoked by Ago, it is doubtful whether the amnesty granted for a crime could constitute an approval and acknowledgement of the unlawful act by the State as its own and that it would have the effect of making the conduct in question a public act of the State.[232] Similarly, in the *Genocide* case *(Croatia* v. *Serbia)* Croatia argued that the FRY, predecessor State of Serbia, 'validated' the genocidal acts committed by the JNA (Yugoslav People's Army), and also the occupation and the administration of certain Croatian territories during the Balkan war, in particular by the

[227] *United States Diplomatic and Consular Staff in Tehran*, judgment, *I.C.J. Reports* 1980, 35, para 74.

[228] Crawford (n 153) 185.

[229] ARSIWA Commentary, 53–54, para 4.

[230] For the retroactive effect: Crawford (n 153) 185–186; Against: Condorelli (n 115) 102; Luigi Condorelli and Claus Kress, 'The Rules of Attribution: General Considerations' in James Crawford, Alain Pellet and Simon Olleson (eds), *The Law of International Responsibility* (Oxford University Press 2010) 231–232; Griebel (n 123) 88, 174, 222 (accepting Article 11 only for continuing violations); Frédéric Dopagne, 'La Responsabilité de l'Etat Du Fait Des Particuliers: Les Causes d'imputation Revisitées Par Les Articles Sur La Responsabilité de l'Etat Pour Fait Internationalement Illicite' (2001) 34 *Revue Belge de Droit International* 492, 514, 518–519.

[231] ARSIWA Commentary, 56, para 8.

[232] Fourth report of Ago (n 12), 101, para 77; *YbILC*, 1975, vol. II (n 211), 98, para 26; however, in favor of this hypothesis: *Case of Cotesworth & Powell*, Arbiration Great Britain–Colombia, August 1875, in: John Bassett Moore, *History and Digest of the International Arbitrations to Which the United States Has Been a Party: Together with Appendices Containing the Treaties Relating to Such Arbitrations, and Historical Legal Notes ...*, vol. 2 (GPO 1898) 2082–2085; Reuter (n 204) 464–465.

honours and decorations bestowed by the Serbian leadership and the JNA on persons involved in the genocidal campaign, amounting to the subsequent adoption and ratification of the conduct by Serbia as its own.[233] In turn, Serbia submitted that the general recognition of a factual situation, namely, that of the existence of the 'Republika Srpska Krajina' by the FRY cannot be considered an acknowledgement and adoption of the conduct as its own.[234] While the ICJ has not ruled on the question, the ARSIWA commentary is instructive in this regard. The latter notes that 'conduct will not be attributable to a State under article 11 where a State merely acknowledges the factual existence of conduct or expresses its verbal approval of it' and that more than a general acknowledgement of a factual situation, it is necessary 'that the State identifies the conduct in question and makes it its own'.[235] In other terms, the acknowledgment and adoption of the conduct by the State as its own must refer to specific unlawful conduct and 'must be clear and unequivocal', whether it takes the form of words or conduct.[236]

Some commentators proposed that the responsibility of the outside State with regard to the conduct of the *de facto* regime that it controls, as established by the ECtHR in the Transnistrian and Cypriot cases, could be interpreted as an application of Article 11 ARSIWA.[237] Indeed, the Grand Chamber invoked a similar argument in the *Cyprus* v. *Turkey* and *Ilaşcu* cases:

> [T]he acquiescence or connivance of the authorities of a Contracting State in the acts of private individuals which violate the Convention rights of other individuals within its jurisdiction may engage the State's responsibility under the Convention … That is particularly true in the case of recognition by the State in question of the acts of self-proclaimed authorities which are not recognised by the international community.[238]

[233] ICJ, *Application of the Convention on the Prevention and Punishment of the Crime of Genocide (Croatia* v. *Serbia)*, Memorial of the Republic of Croatia, vol. I, 1 March 2001, paras 8.53–8.55.

[234] ICJ, *Application of the Convention on the Prevention and Punishment of the Crime of Genocide (Croatia v. Serbia)*, Counter-memorial submitted by the Republic of Serbia, vol. I, December 2009, paras 1034–1043.

[235] ARSIWA Commentary, 53, para 6. [236] Ibid., 53, para 8.

[237] Petculescu (n 186) 590.

[238] *Ilaşcu* (n 65), para 318; *Cyprus* v. *Turkey* [GC] (n 66), para 81; confirmed in: *Solomou and Others* v. *Turkey*, Appl. no. 36832/97, judgment of 24 June 2008, para 46; *Minas Sargsyan* v. *Azerbaijan* [GC], Appl. no. 40167/06, decision of 14 December 2011 on the admissibility, para 73 (citing *Ilaşcu*); *Chiragov (admissibility)* (n 90), para 82.

However, the Court did not expressly apply Article 11 ARSIWA and Russia itself had not approved the acts of the Transnistrian *de facto* authorities, not even implicitly. As it was noted, such conduct 'must be clear and unequivocal': for example, the ICTY confirmed that the fact of passively accepting the advantages of the unlawful conduct cannot amount to an 'adoption' or 'acknowledgement' of the illegal conduct by the State as its own.[239] No such 'clear and unequivocal' State conduct referred to the unlawful acts challenged in the Cypriot and Transnistrian cases.

While the case law of the ECtHR uses the notions 'acquiescence' and 'connivance' of the State, these cannot be equated with an acknowledgement and adoption of the wrongful conduct. The Court held the territorial State responsible for its 'acquiescence' and for its 'connivance' in an activity of other subjects acting in its territory such as CIA prisons operated by the US in European States, despite the fact that the State authorities were not exactly aware of the nature of the operation.[240] In those cases, the Court held the State responsible for having permitted the operation of other subjects which presented a predictable and serious risk of human rights violations and not for having acknowledged and adopted the unlawful conduct as its own. Rather than attributing the unlawful conduct, the Court thus follows an approach based on the State's responsibility for the violation of its own due diligence (see Section 5.2). The ACommHPR established State responsibility on similar conducts as it held that '[a] State can be held responsible for killings by non-State actors if it approves, supports or acquiesces in those acts'.[241] The generality of this conclusion makes it uncertain whether those conducts could be equated with an acknowledgement and adoption of the wrongful conduct under Article 11 ARSIWA. As it has been explained, the two hypotheses of attribution by reason of subsequent links after the commission of the violation, Articles 10 and 11 ARSIWA, have little relevance in 'grey zones', especially where a *de facto* regime opposes the territorial State's government.

[239] ICTY, *Prosecutor* v. *Dragan Nikolić ('Sušica Camp')*, Case No. IT-94-2-PT, Decision on defence motion challenging the exercise of jurisdiction by the Tribunal, 9 October 2002, Trial Chamber II, paras 66–67.

[240] *El-Masri* v. *The Former Yugoslav Republic of Macedonia* [GC], Appl. no. 39630/09, judgment of 13 December 2012, para 206; *Al-Nashiri* v. *Poland*, Appl. no. 28761/11, judgment of 24 July 2014, paras 452, 517.

[241] ACommHPR, General comment No. 3 on the African Charter on Human and Peoples' Rights: The Right to Life (Article 4), 4–18 November 2015, para 9.

As the above cases of attribution demonstrated, human rights treaty bodies interpret the general rules of attribution in a flexible manner to make human rights effective in the 'grey zone'. Furthermore, attribution rules do not depend on the place where the unlawful act occurs: the same secondary rules apply to the State acting in its own territory as to the outside State acting beyond its borders.[242] However, certain types of attribution typically are applicable to the territorial State (agents of necessity, conduct of a victorious insurrectional movement), whereas others are applicable to both States.

5.2 Responsibility for Non-compliance with Due Diligence

Where the human rights violations committed in the 'grey zone' by non-state actors cannot be attributed to any State, the territorial State and outside State can be held responsible not only for the conduct of non-state actors, but also for their own omissions, namely, for the violation of their obligations of due diligence (Chapter 3). In general international law, the ICJ and arbitral tribunals consistently apply this gradual approach to violations committed by non-state entities: as a first step, they examine whether the conduct of the non-state actor is attributable to the respondent State and, if not, as a second step, they scrutinise the State's responsibility for the breach of its obligation of due diligence.[243]

Rather than trying to extend the threshold of control required by secondary norms such as Articles 4 and 8 ARSIWA, this solution bases the responsibility on a primary norm of IHRL[244] and, therefore, is more harmonious to general international law. A second advantage of this solution is that it is likely to eliminate the risk of a vacuum of a responsible State in the 'grey zone' by engaging the State's responsibility for its positive obligations. Finally, a third advantage is a question of proof:

[242] *Legal consequences for States of the continued presence of South Africa in Namibia (South West Africa) notwithstanding Security Council resolution 276 (1970)*, Advisory Opinion, *I.C.J. Reports* 1971, 54, para 118; Fourth report of Ago (n 12), 127, para 148; First report of Crawford (n 10), 33, para 154(a) and 49, paras 150–151.

[243] *DRC* v. *Uganda* (n 31), 230-231, para 177 and 231, paras 178–180; *Genocide case (Bosnia and Herzegovina* v. *Serbia and Montenegro)* (n 6), 202–215, paras 385–415 and 219–229, paras 425–450, esp. 200–201, para 382; *Affaire des biens britanniques au Maroc espagnol* (n 12); Eritrea-Ethiopia Claims Commission, *Partial Award: Central Front – Eritrea's Claims 2, 4, 6, 7, 8 & 22*, 28 April 2004, *UNRIAA*, vol. XXVI, 138–139, para 67; *Partial Award: Western Front, Aerial Bombardment and Related Claims – Eritrea's Claims 1, 3, 5, 9–13, 14, 21, 25 & 26*, 19 December 2005, *UNRIAA*, vol. XXVI, 313–314, paras 46–47.

[244] Crawford (n 153) 157–161; Reymond (n 69) 186–193.

whereas it often is difficult to establish for attribution the factual links between the non-state conduct and the State that the applicant has to prove, it is the State that shall prove that it respected its positive obligations of due diligence.[245] Provided that the applicant established that the risk was predictable, that is, that the State knew or should have known about the wrongful act, the burden of proof is incumbent on the State to demonstrate that it took sufficient measures to prevent or repress the violation. In this sense, it is not exaggerating to talk about a 'presumption' of the responsibility of the State for the violation of its obligations of diligence.[246]

Both general international law (Section 5.2.1) and IHRL (Section 5.2.2) recognise the State's responsibility for non-compliance with due diligence, regarding both the territorial State and the outside State. While their effectiveness and thus the degree of the required diligence might be different, their responsibility for non-compliance with due diligence operates under the same rules.

5.2.1 *General International Law*

Even before the codification works of the ILC's ARSIWA, abundant arbitral case law[247] and codification drafts[248] established the same rule: the responsibility of the State is engaged in cases of damage caused to foreigners by an insurrection or riot, or mob violence, if the State failed to use such diligence as was due in the circumstances to prevent the damage and punish its authors. This rule constitutes the limit of the above-mentioned non-responsibility of the State for the conduct of non-state actors, in general, and failed insurrections, in particular.[249]

Article 10(3) ARSIWA leaves the door open to this sort of responsibility. As its commentary specifies, the State incurs responsibility where 'the State was in a position to adopt measures of vigilance, prevention or punishment in respect of the movement's conduct but improperly failed

[245] *Supra*, Section 3.1.3.

[246] *DRC* v. *Uganda* (n 31), Declaration of Judge Tomka, 352, para 4; Condorelli (n 115) 154–155. (talking about 'automatic' responsibility).

[247] E.g. *Don Jacinto Gadino case*, 30 September 1901, *UNRIAA*, vol. XV, 415; *Affaire des biens britanniques au Maroc espagnol* (n 12), 644–645.

[248] Basis of discussion n° 22(d) (n 11), 224; Draft prepared by the Institute of International Law, 1927 (n 11), 228, Article III; Draft of the Harvard Law School, 1929 (n 11), 229, Article XI; International responsibility: Second report by F. V. Garcia Amador, Special Rapporteur, UN Doc. A/CN.4/106 (1957), in: *YbILC*, 1957, vol. II, 121, Article 11 and 121, paras 1–2.

[249] *Affaire des biens britanniques au Maroc espagnol* (n 12), 642.

to do so'.[250] For example, this is the case of 'the failure by a State to take available steps to protect the premises of diplomatic missions, threatened from attack by an insurrectional movement'.[251]

Certain circumstances precluding the wrongfulness of conduct confirm that a State failing to comply with its due diligence shall incur responsibility. While it was explained in Section 5.1 that the character *force majeure* of the loss of territorial control excludes the responsibility of the territorial State for the conduct of third parties, this secondary norm is not unqualified. Article 23(2)(a) ARSIWA provides that *force majeure* as a circumstance precluding wrongfulness does not apply if 'the situation of *force majeure* is due, either alone or in combination with other factors, to the conduct of the State invoking it'. In other words, if the territorial State's omission contributed to the loss of territorial control, its responsibility for human rights violations cannot be excluded. Another provision confirming the same rule is necessity, understood as an exceptional case where 'a factual situation of grave and imminent peril for the essential interests of a State would legally justify a breach of an international obligation by such State as the only means to safeguard such essential interests'.[252] Under Article 25(2)(b) ARSIWA the State cannot invoke necessity as a ground for precluding wrongfulness if 'the State has contributed to the situation of necessity'.[253] These provisions suggest that wrongfulness, and thus the territorial State's responsibility, is not precluded if it contributed, through its action or omission, to the situation of the loss of territorial control in general or to the unlawful acts in particular.

The case law of the ICJ also confirmed the State's responsibility for the non-compliance with due diligence. In the *United States Diplomatic and Consular Staff in Tehran* case, after the Court had concluded that the attacks against the consulate of the US (before the acknowledgement and adoption of the unlawful act by Iran as its own) could not be attributed to the Iranian State, it reviewed whether Iran respected its international obligations under various rules of international law on consular relations.[254] The Court examined both classical preconditions of due diligence, knowledge and capacity. First, the Court held that the Iranian authorities were aware of the risk since they received urgent and

[250] ARSIWA Commentary, 52, para 15. [251] Ibid.

[252] Attila Tanzi, 'Necessity, State Of', *MPEPIL* (Oxford University Press 2013) para 1.

[253] Article 25(2)(b) ARSIWA.

[254] *Diplomatic and Consular Staff in Tehran* (n 227), 30, para 61.

repeated appeals for help.[255] Second, concerning the capacity to adopt reasonable measures, the Court concluded that the government of Iran had completely failed to take any 'appropriate steps' to protect the premises and the staff of the US' mission against attack by the militants, either to prevent this attack or to stop it, while this failure was due to more than mere negligence or lack of appropriate means.[256] In IHRL, treaty bodies have followed the approach of the ICJ and examined State responsibility for non-compliance with due diligence in cases of non-attributability of the non-state conduct.

5.2.2 *International Human Rights Law*

If attribution of the wrongful conduct to the State is not possible, universal and regional, namely the Inter-American, African and European treaty bodies, establish the State's responsibility on its obligations of due diligence, in line with general international law.

5.2.2.1 Universal Monitoring Bodies

The Committee against Torture engages the responsibility of the territorial State in each case where the applicants substantiate that the authorities failed to take appropriate measures to protect while they were aware of the immediate risk of torture or ill-treatment by non-state actors and had the power to react to it. This failure allows the Committee to conclude that the State had a 'tacit consent' in the sense of Article 16 of the Convention,[257] or 'a form of encouragement and/or *de facto* permission', or even complicity.[258] Other treaty bodies, such as the Committee on the Elimination of Discrimination against Women[259] and the Human Rights Committee,[260] confirmed this responsibility in their quasi-judicial practice. For instance, from the fact that the territorial State did not provide any pertinent explanations on a kidnapping and murder committed by non-state actors, the Human Rights Committee

[255] Ibid., 31, para 64 and 32–33, para 68. [256] Ibid., 31, para 63 and 32–33, para 68.

[257] CAT, *Hajrizi Dzemajl et al.* v. *Yugoslavia*, Complaint No. 161/2000, UN Doc. CAT/C/29/D/161/2000 (2 December 2002), para 9.2.

[258] CAT, General comment No. 2 (n 167), para 18.

[259] *The Vienna Intervention Centre against Domestic Violence et al.* v. *Austria*, Communication No. 6/2005, UN Doc. CEDAW/C/39/D/6/2005 (1 October 2007), paras 12.1.1–12.1.4; *The Vienna Intervention Centre against Domestic Violence et al.* v. *Austria*, Communication No. 5/2005, UN Doc. CEDAW/C/39/D/5/2005 (1 October 2007), paras 12.1.1–12.1.4.

[260] HRC, *Willian Eduardo Delgado Paez* v. *Colombia*, Communication no. 195/85, UN Doc. A/45/40(VOL.II)(SUPP) (4 October 1990), 43–49, para 5.6.

concluded that the absence of investigations amounted to a denial of justice.[261]

Universal bodies prefer resorting to State responsibility for non-compliance with due diligence to attribution when the latter is contested.[262] It is easier to establish in a quasi-judicial procedure that the State did not take all measures of prevention within its power than to research the factual links between the State and the non-state actor. For example, in the *Evangeline Hernandez* v. *Philippines* case, four members of a human rights organisation who were in an enquiry mission in the separatist region of Mindanao were killed by a paramilitary group. Whereas the author of the communication affirmed that the killing had been committed by State security forces or groups acting under their control, inducement, acquiescence or tolerance, the State party denied that the murder was attributable to its armed forces. The Human Rights Committee avoided to rule on attribution and concluded that the State was responsible for the victims' death because it submitted no convincing information on the compliance with 'its obligation to protect the right to life under article 6, paragraph 1, to prevent and refrain from arbitrary deprivation of life'.[263] This practice confirms that assessing compliance with due diligence allows treaty bodies to enforce the State's positive obligations where attribution of non-state conduct is not possible. Regional monitoring bodies have followed this approach.

5.2.2.2 Inter-American Treaty Bodies

The IACtHR also prefers the responsibility for non-compliance with due diligence to that of attribution of non-state conduct, especially if there are no direct links between the territorial State and the armed groups controlling the area, but where the State can be held responsible for its omissions.[264] The IACtHR, however, blurs the distinction between the two approaches and refers to the violation of the State's obligation of due diligence while equally mentioning the 'attribution' of the conduct of non-state entities:

[261] E.g. HRC, *Orly Marcellana and Daniel Gumanoy* v. *The Philippines*, Communication No. 1560/2007, UN Doc. CCPR/C/94/D/1560/2007 (17 November 2008), para 7.4.

[262] E.g. Report of the United Nations High Commissioner for Human Rights on the human rights situation in Colombia, UN Doc. E/CN.4/2002/17 (28 February 2002), para 357.

[263] HRC, *Evangeline Hernandez* v. *The Philippines*, Communication No. 1559/2007, UN Doc. CCPR/C/99/D/1559/2007 (20 August 2010), para 7.3.

[264] *Pueblo Bello Massacre* (n 62), para 140.

> The State's international responsibility can also be generated by the attribution to it of acts that violate human rights committed by third parties or private individuals when the State fails to comply ... with its obligation to take the necessary measures to ensure the effective protection of human rights.[265]

The IACtHR often considered the territorial State as having created the situation of risk, especially if it promoted the creation of self-defence groups[266] or left its region for the free action of paramilitary groups.[267] As the Court combines the State's action and omission, support or tolerance of,[268] acquiescence to or the collaboration with the non-state conduct,[269] it interprets notions of attribution and State responsibility for non-compliance with due diligence in a flexible manner. Despite the confusing wording, references to the State's omission to respect its positive obligations suggest State responsibility for a failure to exercise due diligence rather than attribution.

In other cases, Inter-American bodies more clearly refer to due diligence. For instance, the IACtHR could have attributed the conduct of paramilitaries, in their first phase of operation, to the territorial State on account of the delegation of the exercise of certain elements of governmental authority (such as patrol or other armed activities) to the militias under Article 5 ARSIWA. However, the Court preferred to stress the non-compliance with the State's due diligence obligations,[270] which some authors classify as 'complicity' in the wrongful conduct of private parties.[271] Even the IACtHR referred to the complicity of the Colombian authorities in the conduct of paramilitaries in the *Mapiripán Massacre* judgment where it established the State's responsibility on the

[265] *Afro-descendant communities* ... (n 180), paras 224, 281; *Pueblo Bello Massacre* (n 62), paras 113, 140; *Mapiripán Massacre* (n 170), para 111 (Spanish: '*La atribución de responsabilidad al Estado por actos de particulares puede darse en casos* ...'; the English version does not use the notion of attribution: 'The State may be found responsible for acts by private individuals in cases in which ...').

[266] *Pueblo Bello Massacre* (n 62), para 151; *Ituango Massacres* v. *Colombia*, judgment of 1 July 2006 (Merits, Reparations and Costs), para 134.

[267] *Mapiripán Massacre* (n 170), para 120; *Pueblo Bello Massacre* (n 62), para 151.

[268] *19 Merchants* (n 58), para 141; *Mapiripán Massacre* (n 170), para 110; *Pueblo Bello Massacre* (n 62), para 96(c) (opinion of the IACHR); *Rochela Massacre* (n 170), para 68.

[269] *Afro-descendant communities*... (n 180), para 281; Idem regarding the IACHR: Third report on the human rights situation in Colombia (n 61), chapter IV, para 236; *Monsignor Oscar Arnulfo Romero* (n 61), para 71.

[270] *Rochela Massacre* (n 170), para 102.

[271] Felipe Medina Ardila, 'La Responsabilidad Interacional Del Estado Por Actos de Particulares : Análisis Jurisprudencial Interamericano' in Comite Editorial Ministerios de Relaciones Exteriores (ed.), *Debate Interamericano* (Ministerio de Relaciones Exteriores 2009) 104–105.

violation of its obligations of due diligence.[272] The IACtHR, as do the CAT, the ACommHPR,[273] the African Committee of Experts on the Rights and Welfare of the Child[274] and the ECtHR,[275] expressly considers the State's failure to comply with its obligations of due diligence as complicity in the commission of wrongful acts by private persons. This use of the term 'complicity' does not correspond to Article 16 ARSIWA which only applies to the wrongful assistance given by one State to another State,[276] but covers non-compliance with due diligence as the State's contribution to the wrongful act by non-state actors. Shortly, while the Inter-American case law combines elements of attribution and non-compliance with due diligence, the latter clearly is a common basis of State responsibility.

5.2.2.3 African and European Treaty Bodies

Contrary to the Inter-American treaty bodies, the African and European treaty bodies distinguish between attribution and responsibility for the non-compliance with due diligence. The ACommHPR follows the ICJ's gradual approach under which, in the absence of attribution of the non-state conduct to the State, it examines the State's responsibility for the non-respect of its due diligence.[277] The Commission engaged the State's responsibility for the failure to prevent[278] and investigate[279] violations committed by non-state actors. In line with the African Commission's case law, the ACtHPR and the African Committee of Experts on the Rights and Welfare of the Child engaged the State's responsibility for

[272] *Mapiripán Massacre* (n 170), para 119.

[273] ACommHPR, *Zimbabwe Human Rights NGO Forum* v. *Zimbabwe*, Communication no. 245/02, 15 May 2006, para 160; *Noah Kazingachire, et al.* v. *Zimbabwe*, Communication no. 295/04, 2 May 2012, para 132.

[274] ACERWC, *Minority Rights Group International and SOS-Esclaves* v. *The Government of The Republic of Mauritania*, Communication No. 008/Com/002/2016, May 2017, para 54.

[275] *Al-Nashiri* (n 240), para 517; *El-Masri* (n 240), paras 206, 211.

[276] ARSIWA Commentary, 67, para 11.

[277] E.g. ACommHPR, Communication no. 74/92, *Commission nationale des droits de l'Homme et des libertés* v. *Chad* [English], 11 October 1995, para 22; *Zimbabwe Human Rights NGO Forum* v. *Zimbabwe* (n 273), paras 139, 141; *Noah Kazingachire et al.* (n 273), para 134; regarding the occupying power' obligations of due diligence: *Democratic Republic of Congo* v. *Burundi, Rwanda and Uganda*, Communication no. 227/99, 15–29 May 2003, paras 79, 86.

[278] E.g. *Commission nationale des droits de l'Homme et des libertés* v. *Chad* (n 277), para 22.

[279] Communication no. 323/2006, *Egyptian Initiative for Personal Rights* v. *Egypt*, 12–16 December 2011, para 156.

its failure to prosecute violations committed by non-state actors, together with the violation of Article 1 of the ACHPR.[280]

The *Sudan Human Rights Organisation & Centre on Housing Rights and Evictions (COHRE)* v. *Sudan* case is exemplary: in 2003, in the region of Darfur the applicants alleged that paramilitary groups and militias committed a series of human rights violations, supported by the authorities of the Sudanese State.[281] In conformity with the international case law, the ACommHPR recognised that it is the State that has to demonstrate that it took appropriate measures to protect the victims,[282] which Sudan failed to do in the instant case. Without deciding on the question of attribution of the conduct of militia troops to the State, the Commission found Sudan responsible for the violations of the right to property by not protecting the victims from the attacks by militias.[283]

The ECtHR is equally ready to establish the State's responsibility on non-compliance with due diligence if the wrongful non-state conduct is not attributable to the State. The analysis followed by the Court in the *Kiliç* v. *Turkey* case is enlightening in this regard. In the instant case a journalist of the Turkish Kurdish community was killed by unknown persons, after the victim had requested protection, referring to attacks on others associated with the newspaper. The Court, as 'it has not been established beyond reasonable doubt that any State agent or person acting on behalf of the State authorities was involved in the killing' of the victim, examined the question of 'whether the authorities failed to comply with their positive obligation to protect him from a known risk to his life'.[284] The Court first concluded that the authorities were aware of the real and immediate risk[285] and, second, it reviewed whether the authorities had taken all measures that could reasonably be expected to prevent the materialisation of the risk, which was not proven in the case.[286] The same type of analysis should be followed in all cases where

[280] ACtHPR, *Beneficiaries of Late Norbert Zongo et al.* v. *Burkina Faso*, Appl. no. 013/2011, judgment of 28 March 2014, paras 156, 199; ACERWC, *Minority Rights Group International and SOS-Esclaves* (n 274), paras 58, 63–64, 69–70, 73, 75, 78, 84, 88, 92.

[281] *Sudan Human Rights Organisation & Centre on Housing Rights and Evictions (COHRE)* v. *Sudan*, Communication no. 279/03-296/05, 27 May 2009, paras 2, 5, 11–12.

[282] Ibid., para 179.

[283] Ibid., para 205; Nevertheless, the Commission also talks about the non-prevention of violations by the State's own armed forces, which contradicts the logic of the limitation of due diligence to third parties (*supra*, Chapter 3): Ibid., para 216.

[284] *Kiliç* v. *Turkey*, Appl. no. 22492/93, judgment of 28 March 2000, para 64.

[285] Ibid., paras 67–68. [286] Ibid., paras 69–77.

the conduct of the non-state actor controlling the territory is not attributable to the territorial State.

Several authors interpret the Cypriot and the Transnistrian case law of the ECtHR as the outside State's responsibility for non-compliance with its due diligence rather than attribution.[287] Since the attribution of the conduct of the 'TRNC' or that of the 'MRT' to the outside State (Turkey and Russia, respectively) does not fully correspond to the control thresholds of general international law, responsibility for non-compliance with due diligence provides for a solution more harmonious to international law. The consequence of this interpretation is that, unlike assimilation of the non-state actor to a *de facto* organ of the outside State, non-compliance with due diligence entails the State's responsibility only as far as it had the knowledge about the risk and the capacity to effectively influence the non-state conduct.[288] If the Court had consistently followed the approach of diligence, it should have taken into account Russia's mediation attempts between the 'MRT' and the applicants, the pupils of the Moldovan schools and their families in the *Catan* case.[289] However, the fact that the Court did not examine Russia's positive obligations in the part on responsibility[290] but held the State responsible for all conducts of the *de facto* regime (Section 5.1.1.2c) reflects the logic of attribution rather than responsibility for non-compliance with due diligence. This normative choice may be explained by the Court's intention to eliminate a 'vacuum' of responsibility in a foreseeable manner.

As this summary illustrated, regional monitoring bodies establish the State's responsibility on its non-compliance with due diligence under the jurisdictional clause (Article 1 of the ACHR) or the general obligations clause of the given convention (Article 1 of the ACHPR; Article 1 of the African Charter on the Rights and Welfare of the Child [ACRWC]). This approach, based on knowledge and capacity, that is, effectiveness of the State, insists on the State's positive obligations and is likely to contribute to the normalisation of 'grey zones'. An empirical sign of normalisation is the impact of regional monitoring bodies on the domestic case law of

[287] Hessbruegge (n 185) 218; Anthony Cullen and Steven Wheatley, 'The Human Rights of Individuals in De Facto Regimes under the European Convention on Human Rights' (2013) 13 *Human Rights Law Review* 691, 705–706; Jacob (n 19) 206.

[288] *Supra*, Section 3.1.3.

[289] Marko Milanovic, 'Grand Chamber Judgment in Catan and Others' (*EJIL: Talk!*, 21 October 2012) <www.ejiltalk.org/grand-chamber-judgment-in-catan-and-others/> accessed 7 June 2013.

[290] *Catan* (n 64), para 150.

certain States. For example, in accordance with the case law of the ECtHR, domestic courts of the Republic of Cyprus engaged the responsibility of the Cypriot State for its failure to comply with the procedural limb of the right to life and awarded damages to the claimants, relatives of missing persons who disappeared during the Turkish invasion.[291] Likewise, in line with the Inter-American case law, the Colombian Council of State applies the same approach: in the absence of evidence on the active participation (support, authorisation) of State authorities in the human rights violations committed by *de facto* regimes, it examines whether the violation is due to an omission of the authorities. If the latter were unable to foresee the risk of the violation, the State does not incur responsibility.[292] However, if both the activity and the military objectives of the guerrillas in a given region were of public knowledge – this was the case in the 'demilitarised enclave'[293] – the Council of State engaged the State's responsibility for its own omission.[294] As in the case of the IACtHR, the Council of State stresses that through the non-respect for the obligations of due diligence, the territorial State itself created the situation of risk.[295]

5.3 Concluding Remarks

Human rights monitoring bodies can establish the responsibility of the State on numerous legal bases of attribution, both in respect of the outside State and the territorial State. While secondary norms of general international law inspire the case law of IHRL, it is difficult to classify the decisions adopted by international human rights monitoring bodies under the ILC's ARSIWA. Whereas regional human rights courts insist that their case law in matters of attribution is in conformity with general

[291] *Vasos Vasiliou and others* v. *Cyprus*, Nicosia Court, Appeal Chamber, 13863/2002, 5 November 2010; *Palma* v. *Attorney General*, Nicosia Court, Appeal Chamber, 6661/2001, 28 November 2012.

[292] Consejo de Estado, *Luis Miguel Fernández Vega c. Nación/Ministerio de Defensa/Ejercito Nacional/Policía nacional*, no. 11837, 8 May 1998, 18.

[293] *Supra*, Section 1.3.

[294] E.g. Consejo de Estado, *Martha Morales y Otros c. Nación/Ministerio de Defensa nacional/Policía nacional*, 5001-23-31-000-1994-4398-01(13553), 20 September 2001, 27–28; *Blanca Rosalba Prieto Rubio y otros c. Nación/Ministerio de Defensa y Otro*, 20001-23-31-000-1997-03529-01 (18274), 18 February 2010, 30.

[295] E.g. *José Ignacio Ibañez Diaz y Otros c. Nación/Ministerio de Defensa nacional/Ejercito nacional*, 52001-23-31-000-1997-08789-01, 25 May 2011, 91, para 60; *Petrona Casarrubia Berrocal c. Nación/Ministerio de Defensa/Policía nacional*, 23001-23-31-000-1999-00967-01(25087), 30 January 2013, 41.

international law, they are *sui generis* compared to the interpretation of Articles 4 or 8 ARSIWA given by the ICJ. Because of the lack of special attribution rules enshrined in the respective conventions, human rights treaty-monitoring bodies interpret the general rules flexibly in order to make human rights effective, in conformity with the principle of *effet utile*.[296] A reason why they apply less demanding attribution thresholds than the ICJ is the treaty-monitoring bodies' expressed policy not to leave 'vacuums' in the responsibility for the violations of human rights of individuals in territories covered by the given convention.[297] In so doing, human rights monitoring bodies respect and develop the norms of general international law in matters of attribution.

Whereas the attribution of non-state conduct is often not feasible, engaging the responsibility of the outside State and the territorial State is less problematic when human rights monitoring bodies resort to the violation of the obligation of due diligence rather than to attribution. When international monitoring bodies establish the State's responsibility for non-compliance with its obligations of due diligence in respect of violations committed by non-state actors, their case law is in full harmony with general international law.

The idea of concurrently examining the responsibility of both the territorial State and the outside State follows from their concurrent jurisdiction and obligations under IHRL: the more they exert effectiveness on the human rights situation, the more they incur responsibility for wrongful conduct. The concurrent and independent responsibility of both States, the engagement of their responsibility both for attributable non-state conducts and the non-compliance with their obligations of due diligence all contribute to the normalisation of the 'grey zone'.

296 *Mapiripán Massacre* (n 170), para 105; *Cyprus* v. *Turkey* [GC] (n 66), para 78; *Catan* (n 64), para 136.

297 *Supra*, Chapter 2.

6 The Responsibility of Non-state Actors

This chapter explains that non-state actors controlling the area outside the effective control of the State can incur responsibility under international law for the violations of their obligations under IHRL. The responsibility of a non-state actor only arises if its wrongful act cannot be attributed to a State.[1] Contrary to the responsibility of States for internationally wrongful acts, international law has developed much less legal basis for the responsibility of non-state actors. As for peace operations, one can find a positive law basis, albeit not a solid one, in the codification of the ILC of the responsibility of international organisations (IOs), whose rules are inspired by the law of State responsibility. While much uncertainty exists as to their application, IHRL could slightly contribute to their development. The responsibility of *de facto* regimes, however, has even less legal basis and most of the secondary norms may be identified based on analogies with the rules of the ARSIWA. As the present chapter will demonstrate, the norms of the responsibility of peace operations (Section 6.1) and *de facto* regimes (Section 6.2) provide an existing but rarely applied legal framework. Peace operations and *de facto* regimes incur responsibility not only for wrongful acts committed by persons or groups of persons whose conduct is attributable to them, but also for the failure to comply with their own due diligence obligations, as detailed in Sections 4.1.3 and 4.2.3.

6.1 The Responsibility of Peace Operations

As opposed to State responsibility, the responsibility of peace operations is more complex because of the multiple forms of such peace missions,

[1] *Military and Paramilitary Activities in and against Nicaragua (Nicaragua* v. *United States of America)*, Merits, judgment, *I.C.J. Reports* 1986, 65, para 116.

the derived nature of their legal personality and the parallel participation of States and IOs. Given this complexity, it is reasonable to distinguish between two possible responsibilities for human rights violations in peace operations: the responsibility of the IO conducting the peace operation (Section 6.1.1) and that of the States participating in the operation through their military or civilian agents (Section 6.1.2). The focus of the responsibility for the violation of IHRL, as in Chapter 5, is the attributability of the conduct. As this section will explain, the two types of attribution, attribution to the IO and that to States, do not exclude each other: joint or parallel attribution can be envisaged for the same conduct.

6.1.1 *Attribution to the International Organisation*

As explained in Section 1.4, IOs often assume a leadership in the conduct of peace operations. The peacekeeping mission in Cyprus and the two territorial administrations in Eastern Timor and Kosovo were all conducted under the auspices of an IO: the United Nations Peacekeeping Force in Cyprus (UNFICYP), the United Nations Interim Administration Mission in Kosovo (UNMIK) and the United Nations Transitional Administration in East Timor (UNTAET) under the leadership of the United Nations (UN), whereas the security component of the Kosovo international administration, the Kosovo Force (KFOR), was an operation led by the North Atlantic Treaty Organization (NATO). Their responsibility thus is governed by the law of the responsibility of IOs, recognised by the ICJ as a principle[2] and consisting of norms elaborated through the transposition of analogue rules of State responsibility. Although in 2011 the ILC concluded its almost decade-long codification work on the responsibility of IOs and adopted the draft articles (DARIO)[3] and its detailed commentary (DARIO Commentary),[4] the State practice and case law on the matter remain scarce. Nevertheless, the DARIO serve as authoritative guidance for any attribution of conduct to IOs.

[2] *Difference Relating to Immunity from Legal Process of a Special Rapporteur of the Commission on Human Rights*, Advisory Opinion, *I.C.J. Reports* 1999, 88–89, para 66.

[3] Draft articles on the responsibility of international organizations, with commentaries, *YbILC*, 2011, vol. II (Part Two), 40–46, para 87 [DARIO], of which the General Assembly took note [Resolution 66/100. Responsibility of international organizations, UN Doc. A/RES/66/100 (9 December 2011)].

[4] Ibid., 46–105, para 88 [DARIO Commentary].

As in the case of States, every internationally wrongful act of an IO entails the international responsibility of that IO,[5] and there is an internationally wrongful act of an IO when the conduct '(a) is attributable to that organization under international law; and (b) constitutes a breach of an international obligation of that organization'.[6] The attribution norms DARIO were all inspired by the attribution norms of the ILC's ARSIWA. As a basic distinction, a human rights violation may be committed by entities forming part of the IO's institutional structure, that is, organs or agents of the IO (Section 6.1.1.1) and entities not forming part of its institutional structure but of which the conduct nevertheless under certain circumstances could be attributed to the IO (Section 6.1.1.2).

6.1.1.1 Organs or Agents of the International Organisation

Similar to States, IOs are legal personalities that can carry out their activities only through natural persons. Codifying the existing practice, Article 6(1) of DARIO provides:

> The conduct of an organ or agent of an international organization in the performance of functions of that organ or agent shall be considered an act of that organization under international law, whatever position the organ or agent holds in respect of the organization.

The most important element of this norm is the attributability of the conduct of any organ or agent through whom the IO performs its acts. This corresponds to the ICJ's advisory opinion that defined an agent of IOs as 'any person who, whether a paid official or not, and whether permanently employed or not, has been charged by an organ of the Organization with carrying out, or helping to carry out, one of its functions – in short, any person through whom it acts'.[7] Similar to States, an organ or agent may have formal organic ties to the IO or its conduct may be *de facto* assimilated to a *de jure* organ of the IO.[8]

The second case, *de facto* organs of an IO, has only little practice so far, but analogies seem to support this hypothesis. As the law of State responsibility, the law of the responsibility of IOs is based on effectiveness, thus it is necessary to look beyond situations of formal links and

[5] DARIO, Article 3. [6] DARIO, Article 4.

[7] *Reparation for injuries suffered in the service of the United Nations*, Advisory Opinion, *I.C.J. Reports* 1949, 177.

[8] Pierre Klein, 'The Attribution of Acts to International Organizations' in James Crawford, Alain Pellet and Simon Olleson (eds), *The Law of International Responsibility* (Oxford University Press 2010) 298.

analyse the actual relations between individuals and an IO.[9] Whenever the factual links reveal dependence between the IO and the individual or group of individuals amounting to 'effective control', it is reasonable to apply Article 6 of DARIO. The commentary foresees such an attribution[10] and the ICJ also observed that in practice 'the United Nations has had occasion to entrust missions – increasingly varied in nature – to persons not having the status of United Nations officials'.[11] In peace operations, the IO could entrust certain functions to persons in their individual capacity such as Special Rapporteurs or experts responsible for fact finding[12] or NGOs charged with the assistance of refugees.[13] Furthermore, the definition of 'agent' in the DARIO seems to rely on factual links rather than institutional links between the individual and the IO: the draft articles understand under agent of an IO 'an official or other person or entity, other than an organ, who is charged by the organization with carrying out, or helping to carry out, one of its functions, and thus through whom the organization acts'.[14]

As for the first case, *de jure* organs of IOs, defined by the ILC as 'any person or entity which has that status in accordance with the rules of the organization',[15] the norm is less problematic since the practice provides a strong basis for this norm. Attribution of conduct of *de jure* organs or agents neither depends on the type of power exercised in the peace operation nor on the hierarchical status of the organ or agent in the organisational structure of the IO. However, what is crucial is the requirement that the organ or agent acts 'in the performance of functions of that organ or agent' – thus, the conduct is attributable to the IO only if the organ or agent exercises functions that have been given to that organ or agent, and not attributable if the organ or agent acts in a private capacity.[16] As the United Nations Security Council (UNSC) or the United Nations General Assembly (UNGA) create UN peacekeeping operations as its subsidiary organs, they are *de jure* organs of the IO. On the question of the attribution of the conduct of peacekeeping forces to the UN or to contributing States, the UN Secretariat submitted the following comment:

> As a subsidiary organ of the United Nations, an act of a peacekeeping force is, in principle, imputable to the Organization, and, if committed in violation of an

[9] Ibid., 299. [10] DARIO Commentary, 55, paras 2–3.

[11] *Applicability of Article VI, Section 22, of the Convention on the Privileges and Immunities of the United Nations*, Advisory Opinion, *I.C.J. Reports* 1989, 194, para 48.

[12] Ibid. [13] Klein (n 8) 301. [14] DARIO, Article 2(d). [15] DARIO, Article 2(c).

[16] DARIO Commentary, 55–56, para 7.

international obligation, entails the international responsibility of the Organization and its liability in compensation. The fact that any such act may have been performed by members of a national military contingent forming part of the peacekeeping operation does not affect the international responsibility of the United Nations *vis-à-vis* third States or individuals.[17]

This view is slightly nuanced by the fact that a troop-contributing State may be held responsible for unlawful conduct related to its exclusive disciplinary and criminal jurisdiction over its national contingent (see Section 6.1.2.2). At any rate, the conduct of components of peace operations that form part of the institutional structure of an IO are attributable to that IO as long as they were performed within the functions of the peace mission.

International human rights monitoring bodies haved confirmed this rule. The ECtHR usually recognised the attributability of conduct committed by *de jure* organs of the IO within the framework of peace operations. For example, in the *Kyriakoula Stephens* v. *Cyprus, Turkey and the United Nations* case the ECtHR noted that UNFICYP is under the exclusive control and command of the UN and that as a subsidiary organ of the UN 'its actions and inactions are in principle attributable to the UN'.[18] Likewise, in the *Behrami/Saramati* decision the Court concluded that the conduct of UNMIK, a subsidiary organ of the UN, in principle is attributable to the UN.[19] These precedents are in conformity with general international law.

Consultative monitoring bodies, especially the Human Rights Advisory Panel (Kosovo) (HRAP) and the Human Rights Review Panel (Kosovo) (HRRP) that review complaints against UNMIK and EULEX Kosovo, respectively, consistently attributed the conduct of organs forming part of the IO concerned to that IO. For example, the HRAP without difficulty attributed the conduct of the Director of the UNMIK Department of Justice to UNMIK, and thus to the UN.[20] Likewise, the HRRP attributed the conduct of the Financial Intelligence Centre, established pursuant to a UNMIK regulation and integrated in 2008 in the EULEX Police

[17] Comments and observations received from international organizations, UN Doc. A/CN.4/545 (2004), in: *YbILC*, 2004, vol. II(1), 28.

[18] *Kyriakoula Stephens* v. *Cyprus, Turkey and the United Nations* , Appl. no. 45267/06, decision of 11 December 2008 on the admissibility. See its analysis, *supra*, Section 2.1.1.4.

[19] *Agim Behrami and Bekir Behrami* v. *France and Ruzhdi Saramati* v. *France, Germany and Norway* [GC], Appl. nos. 71412/01 and 78166/01, decision of 2 May 2007 on the admissibility, para 143.

[20] HRAP, *Milogorić et al.* v. *UNMIK*, 24 March 2010, para 46.

Component's Executive Department,[21] or the conduct of EULEX investigators and prosecutors to EULEX.[22]

Beyond UNMIK bodies, the HRAP in several cases faced the problem of human rights violations committed by the Provisional Institutions of Self-Government (of Kosovo) (PISG) whose status was contested. They were instituted under the Constitutional Framework for Provisional Self-Government, a UNMIK resolution which provided that 'the exercise of the responsibilities of the Provisional Institutions of Self-Government in Kosovo shall not in any way affect or diminish the ultimate authority of the SRSG for the implementation of UNSCR 1244 (1999)'.[23] As the ICJ confirmed, 'the Provisional Institutions of Self-Government were to function in conjunction with and subject to the direction of the Special Representative of the Secretary-General in the implementation of Security Council resolution 1244 (1999)' and in a legal order whose supervision the Special Representative of the Secretary-General (Kosovo) (SRSG) was charged with.[24] As the PISG were created by the SRSG, an organ of UNMIK, subsidiary body of the UN, one could argue that the PISG were also formed as part of the UNMIK structure at least until the unilateral declaration of independence of Kosovo.[25]

Whereas the attribution of organs and agents within the institutional structure of the IO to that IO has been rather unproblematic, peace operations composed of entities outside the institutional structure of the IO leading the mission have raised more controversies.

6.1.1.2 Entities outside the Institutional Structure of the International Organisation

Organs or agents of the IO participating in a peace mission may be defined on the basis of two articles of DARIO: Article 6, providing for the conduct of an organ or agent of an IO in the strict sense, and Article

[21] HRRP, *Blerim Rudi* v. *EULEX* , Case No. 2010-07, decision of 8 June 2011, paras 75–76.

[22] E.g. HRRP, *W.* v. *EULEX*, decision of 10 April 2013, Case No. 2011-07, para 38 (attribution of the conduct of EULEX prosecutors and investigators); *Goran Becić* v. *EULEX*, Case No. 2013-03, decision of 12 November 2014, paras 56, 58–63 (attribution of the conduct of the EULEX and the EULEX Property Rights Co-ordinator).

[23] UNMIK/REG/2001/9 (15 May 2001) on a Constitutional Framework For Provisional Self-Government in Kosovo, Preamble, para 9.

[24] *Accordance with International Law of the Unilateral Declaration of Independence in Respect of Kosovo*, Advisory Opinion, *I.C.J. Reports* 2010, 440–441, para 90.

[25] Paolo Palchetti, 'Les Autorités Provisoires de Gouvernement (PISG) Du Kosovo, EULEX et ONU: Les Principes d'attribution à l'épreuve' (2013) 47 *Revue belge de droit international* 45, 48–49 (arguing for such attribution irrespectively of whether the PISG have international legal personality).

7, providing for the conduct of organs of a State or organs or agents of an IO placed at the disposal of another IO. The latter are outside the institutional structure of the IO conducting the peace operation, but in fact act under the operational control of that IO. Since most military and civilian agents participating in peace missions are placed under the disposal of the IO by a contributing State, this scenario is especially important in peace operations. Article 7 of DARIO provides that

> [t]he conduct of an organ of a State or an organ or agent of an international organization that is placed at the disposal of another international organization shall be considered under international law an act of the latter organization if the organization exercises effective control over that conduct.

Under this rule, the conduct of the organ seconded to an IO, in which the seconded organ or agent still to a certain extent acts as an organ of the seconding State or as an organ or agent of the seconding organisation, would be attributable to the receiving organisation only if that organisation exercises effective control over the unlawful conduct.[26] This is the question when a State places military contingents at the disposal of the UN for a peacekeeping operation, as the State retains disciplinary powers and criminal jurisdiction over the members of the national contingent.[27]

The central criterion of attribution, 'effective control', directs us to the law of State responsibility. However, as the DARIO Commentary notes, 'effective control' over the conduct in the case of IOs 'does not concern the issue whether a certain conduct is attributable at all to a State or an international organization, but rather to which entity – the contributing State or organization or the receiving organization – conduct has to be attributed'.[28] In other words, to decide whether the agents provided by contributor States or an IO to another IO that exercises the operational control over the peace mission is attributable to the receiving IO or the seconding State or IO, the degree of effective control over the conduct needs to be analysed on a case-by-case basis.

The practice of peace missions provides a strong basis for the attribution norm under Article 7. Insofar as the UN exercised the operational control over the wrongful conduct of a peacekeeping mission, it has usually accepted its responsibility for the wrongful acts.[29] Under this

[26] DARIO Commentary, 56, para 1. [27] Ibid. [28] DARIO Commentary, 57, para 5.

[29] Exchange of letters constituting an agreement relating to the settlement of claims filed against the United Nations in the Congo by Belgian nationals, 199, cited by Second report on responsibility of international organizations, by Mr. Giorgio Gaja, Special Rapporteur, UN Doc. A/CN.4/541 (2 April 2004), 17, para 35; Memorandum of the United Nations

practice, whereas the contributing States retain disciplinary power and criminal jurisdiction over the members of their national contingents, it is the IO that is responsible for the conduct of peacekeepers performed in their official capacity as far as the IO was in effective control over the conduct.[30] For the same reason, the Secretary-General held that, in joint operations, those composed of a UN peacekeeping operation and an operation conducted under national or regional command and control, 'international responsibility lies where effective command and control is vested and practically exercised'.[31]

The central criterion of effective control distinguishes peace operations conducted under the operational control of an IO, especially the UN, on the one hand, and UN-mandated multinational operations conducted by States, on the other. In the latter case the UNSC authorises the given peace operation without creating factual links amounting to effective control of the UN over the operation in the command structure. As some authors observe, in this case the UNSC exercises only a more general, political, or even merely nominal control over the operation.[32] In such a mandated multinational operation, the States exercise effective control over the troops on the ground, whereas the UN retains only a political control without much influence on the operational control. Consequently, the DARIO Commentary,[33] most authors,[34]

Legal Counsel, Mr. Hans Corell, of 3 February 2004 to the Director of the Codification Division, cited in ibid., 17–18, para 36.

30 Second report of Gaja (n 29), 19–20, para 40.

31 Comments and observations received from international organizations, UN Doc. A/CN.4/545 (2004), in: *YbILC*, 2004, vol. II(1), 28; Administrative and budgetary aspects of the financing of the United Nations peacekeeping operations: financing of the United Nations peacekeeping operations, Report of the Secretary-General, UN Doc. A/51/389 (20 September 1996), paras 17–18.

32 Linos-Alexandre Sicilianos, 'L'(ir)responsabilité des forces multinationales?' in Laurence Boisson de Chazournes and Marcelo G Kohen (eds), *International Law and the Quest for Its Implementation: Liber Amicorum Vera Gowlland-Debbas* (Brill 2010) 98.

33 DARIO Commentary, 54, para 5.

34 Sicilianos (n 32) 98; Klein (n 8) 302–303; Sadia R. Sorathia, '*Behrami* v. *France*: An Unfortunate Step Backwards in the Protection of Human Rights' (2011) 26 *Maryland Journal of International Law* 271, 285–287; *A contrario*: Danesh Sarooshi, *The United Nations and the Development of Collective Security: the Delegation by the UN Security Council of its Chapter VII Powers* (Clarendon Press 1999) 165.

State practice,[35] and the UN's consistent policy[36] confirm that wrongful acts committed in multinational operations authorised by the UNSC cannot be attributed to the UN, but to the State(s) exercising the operational control over the given contingent. However, this general trend has been challenged by the practice of human rights treaty bodies, especially that of the ECtHR.

Contrary to the attribution of the conduct of UNFICYP or UNMIK to the UN by the ECtHR, the attribution of the conduct of KFOR, a multinational operation authorised by the UNSC, to the UN in the *Behrami/Saramati* decision is contestable case law. In the instant case the Court concluded that the UNSC retained ultimate authority and control over the challenged conduct, detention by KFOR during more than one year, and that NATO retained effective command of the relevant operational matters. Consequently, it held that the detention power delegated by the UNSC under chapter VII of the UN Charter, in principle, was 'attributable' to the UN.[37] If the Court seriously scrutinised effective control on the ground, it would have drawn a different conclusion.

First of all, the UNSC resolution on the establishment of the international territorial administration of Kosovo, Resolution 1244 (1999), adopted under chapter VII, envisaged the 'authorisation'[38] of a security force rather than a deployment of KFOR under UN command. The enforcement of the resolution confirmed this view: the structure of KFOR resembled a multinational operation authorised by the UNSC rather than a peace operation under the operational control of the UN. The applicants in the *Behrami/Saramati* cases provided several elements proving that neither the acts nor omissions of KFOR soldiers were attributable to the UN or NATO. Among other arguments, they emphasised that KFOR was not established as a UN force or organ, there was no operational command link between the UNSC and NATO, while the

[35] E.g. Second report of Gaja (n 29), 15–16, para 32 (US practice in the Korean war); Letter dated 50/09/26 from the Deputy Representative of the United States of America addressed to the Secretary-General concerning the bombing by Air Forces of the territory of China, UN Doc. S/1813 (26 September 1950) (US practice in the Korean war); Letter of the Prime Minister of Rwanda addressed to the UN Secretary-General about the non-attributability of the wrongful conduct committed by the "Opération Turquoise" to the UN, 11 November 1996, cited in: *Report of the ILC*, UN Doc. A/60/10 (2005), 104, para 12.

[36] Letter of the Director of the Field Administration and Logistics Division of the Department of Peacekeeping Operations of the United Nations to the Permanent Representative of Belgium to the United Nations, 25 June 1998, cited in Second report of Gaja (n 29), 16, para 33.

[37] *Behrami/Saramati* (n 19), paras 134–141.

[38] UN Doc. S/RES/1244 (10 June 1999), paras 5, 7.

Troop Contributing Nations (TCNs) retained such significant power that there was no unified chain of command from the UNSC; the link between KFOR and the UNSC was described as one of 'consultation/ interaction'.[39] The respondent States, however, argued that the UN was the controlling umbrella over the civilian and security presence, which 'was consistent with UNMIK and KFOR having independent command and control structures and applied regardless of whether KFOR was a traditionally established UN security presence under direct UN operational command'.[40] The fact that the UN did not exercise direct operational command was left in the background and the third party interveners also supported the respondent States' view.[41]

Before deciding, the Court cited some provisions of the ILC's DARIO, among others the draft article on the 'conduct of organs or agents placed at the disposal of an international organisation by a State or another international organisation' (later Article 7), including its commentary.[42] However, it failed to consider the ILC's commentary about the non-attributability of wrongful conducts committed in multinational operations authorised by the UNSC to the UN[43] which hypothesis seemed to apply to KFOR. Furthermore, circumventing the text of Article 7 and especially the criterion of 'effective control', the Grand Chamber considered that 'the key question is whether the UNSC retained ultimate authority and control so that operational command only was delegated'.[44] The 'ultimate authority and control' test, however, bears no resemblance to the 'effective control' test,[45] supported by the State practice and scholarship, and the Court cited no support for this choice except for some scholarly views. Moreover, even some of the scholarship cited does not support the Court's final conclusion.[46] While the Court departed from the right observation that the UNSC lawfully delegated

39 *Behrami/Saramati* (n 19), para 77. 40 Ibid., para 91.

41 Ibid., paras 97–98 (Denmark), 104 (Germany), 109 (Greece), 110 (Poland), 113 (United Kingdom).

42 Ibid., paras 30–31. 43 DARIO Commentary, 54, para 5.

44 *Behrami/Saramati* (n 19), para 133.

45 E.g. Kjetil Mujezinovic Larsen, 'Attribution of Conduct in Peace Operations: The "Ultimate Authority and Control" Test' (2008) 19 *European Journal of International Law* 509, 522.

46 E.g. the article of Gowlland-Debbas. Andrew Clapham, 'The Subject of Subject and the Attribution of Attribution' in Laurence Boisson de Chazournes and Marcelo G. Kohen (eds), *International Law and the Quest for Its Implementation: Liber Amicorum Vera Gowlland-Debbas* (Brill 2010) 55; Vera Gowlland-Debbas, 'Is the UN Security Council Bound by Human Rights Law? Remarks' (2009) 103 *American Society of International Law Proceedings* 199, 201 (the author herself disapproving of *Behrami*).

some of its powers to 'Member States and relevant international organisations', its conclusion, the UNSC's ultimate authority and control over the security presence and the attributability of KFOR's conduct to the UN, is erroneous.

The Court suggested that the legality of the delegation of the 'effective command' by the UNSC makes the UN automatically responsible for the conduct performed in the given multinational operation.[47] However, a cautious analysis of the UNSC's role in the conduct of KFOR contingents reveals that the UN's involvement was rather nominal or symbolic. The supervision it exercised over the security forces was limited to formal reports submitted by national contingents, without a regular basis and any formal evaluation on their substance by the UNSC. The latter monitored the discharge of the security mandate through the reports presented by KFOR to the Secretary-General who forwarded them to the UNSC. Whereas the Court invoked this mechanism as an argument in favour of the 'ultimate authority and control' of the UNSC,[48] it was by definition *a posteriori* and rather superficial control, constituting a 'self-control' by KFOR rather than a supervisory mechanism.[49] As opposed to the UN-UNMIK command structure, where the chain of command is continuous from the UNSC to the UNMIK organs without the interference of contributing States, in the case of KFOR the chain of command stopped at the level of the commanders of national contingents. In fact, troop-contributing States had only military objectives to reach, as defined by the UNSC Resolution 1244 (1999), whereas they had a wide margin for manœuvre as to the choice of the means of execution, without the interference of the UNSC.[50] After the decision, in his report of June 2008 on UNMIK, the UN Secretary-General not surprisingly distanced himself from the criterion of 'ultimate authority and control' and stated that '[i]t is understood that the international responsibility of

[47] *Behrami/Saramati* (n 19), para 140. [48] Ibid., para 134.

[49] See Serbia's view: ICESCR, Second periodic report: Serbia, UN Doc. E/C.12/SRB/2 (12 February 2013), Annex 1, para 94; Pierre Klein, 'Responsabilité Pour Les Faits Commis Dans Le Cadre d'opérations de Paix et Étendue Du Pouvoir de Contrôle de La Cour Européenne Des Droits de l'homme: Quelques Considérations Critiques Sur l'arrêt Behrami et Saramati' (2007) 53 *Annuaire français de droit international* 43, 54; Philippe Lagrange, 'Responsabilité Des Etats Pour Actes Accomplis En Application Du Chapitre VII de La Charte Des Nations Unies – Observations à Propos de La Décision de La Cour Européenne Des Droits de l'homme (Grande Chambre) Sur La Recevabilité Des Requêtes Behrami et Behrami c. France et Saramati c. Allemagne, France et Norvège, 31 Mai 2007' (2008) 112 *Revue générale de droit international public* 85, 97–98; Sicilianos (n 32) 104.

[50] Klein (n 49) 51; Lagrange (n 49) 99–100.

the United Nations will be limited in the extent of its effective operational control'.[51]

Shortly, the command structure and the effectiveness of the UN's role in the operation or, in other words, the 'effective control' test reveals that the security presence acted under the operational command of the TCNs. Consequently, had the Court applied the 'effective control' test instead of the 'ultimate authority and control' test, it would have concluded that the conducts challenged in the *Saramati* case were not attributable to the UN, but to the individual States whose troops were involved and/or, alone or jointly with the TCNs, to NATO.[52] The latter's responsibility again depends on the consistent application of the 'effective control' test on a case-by-case basis.[53] On the one hand, KFOR acted under the unified command and control of NATO but, on the other hand, it included both NATO and non-NATO member TCNs whose contingents usually operated on the commands of their national commanders. Not all conduct performed by KFOR troops in the course of an operation 'under the unified command and control' in fact were under the operational control of the COMKFOR.[54] For instance, the conduct of the Russian contingent participating in KFOR could not have been attributed to NATO since, under a separate agreement, the Russian contingent in Kosovo was 'under the political and military control of the Russian Command'.[55]

However, other monitoring bodies have not followed the ECtHR's approach. The two consultative bodies active in Kosovo, the HRAP and the HRRP, both applied the 'effective control' test rather than the 'ultimate authority and control' test. For example, after UNMIK transferred its

[51] Report of the Secretary-General on the United Nations Interim Administration Mission in Kosovo, UN Doc. S/2008/354 (12 June 2008), para 16.

[52] Seventh report on responsibility of international organizations, by Giorgio Gaja, Special Rapporteur, UN Doc. A/CN.4/610 (27 March 2009), para 26 and the authors cited therein; DARIO Commentary, 58, para 10; European Commission for Democracy through Law (Venice Commission), Opinion on human rights in Kosovo, Possible establishment of review mechanisms, Opinion no. 280/2004, Venice, 8–9 October 2004, CDL-AD(2004)033, para 79; CoE, Parliamentary Assembly, Protection of human rights in Kosovo, Report, Doc. 10393 (6 January 2005), para 33(ii).

[53] In this sene, accepting the attributability of the unlawful conducts committed by KFOR both to NATO and to TCNs, depending on the circumstances: Alain Pellet, 'L'imputabilité d'éventuels actes illicites – Responsabilité de l'OTAN ou des Etats membres?' in Christian Tomuschat (ed), *Kosovo and the International Community: a Legal Assessment* (2002) 199–201.

[54] Ibid.

[55] Agreed Points on Russian Participation in KFOR, concluded between the Secretary of Defense of the United States and the Minister of Defense of the Russian Federation, Helsinki, 18 June 1999, at www.nato.int/kosovo/docu/a990618a.htm (4 April 2015).

responsibility with regard to police and justice in Kosovo on 9 December 2008 to EULEX ,which assumed full operational control in the area of the rule of law, the HRAP concluded that UNMIK bears no more responsibility for any violation of human rights allegedly committed by the judiciary and law enforcement authorities of Kosovo after that date.[56]

Beyond attribution, it is worth noting that human rights bodies recognise the responsibility of the IO for the violation of its own due diligence obligations, as it is in the case of States. In other terms, an IO is responsible not only for the unlawful attributable conduct in the framework of a peace operation, but also for the violation of its own positive obligations to prevent, investigate and punish, as detailed above.[57] The example of the PISG is also pertinent here: even if it is not accepted that the PISG constituted *de jure* organs of the UNMIK, the human rights violations committed by the PISG could engage the responsibility of the UN if UNMIK failed to comply with its due diligence obligations. In this sense, the HRAP held that the SRSG retained a power of oversight of the PISG, their officials and their agencies under the Constitutional Framework.[58] The HRAP concluded that it is within the power of the SRSG to take action when human rights are violated and that '[t]his in itself leads to the conclusion that UNMIK remains responsible, from a human rights perspective, for any action or omission imputable to a Provisional Institution of Self-Government'.[59] Likewise, there is no institutional relationship between the PISG and EULEX Kosovo, but the latter has positive obligations to protect human rights wherever it knows or ought to have known of a real and immediate risk of a human rights violation.[60] For example, EULEX incurred responsibility for the violation of the complainants' right to private life, freedom of assembly and freedom of religion as a result of inadequate training, insufficient operational guidelines and resources allocated to the planning and controlling of EULEX operations at the annual ethnic Serbian celebration of Vidovdan.[61]

[56] E.g. *HRAP, N.G.* v. *UNMIK*, Case No. 45/10, 13 April 2011, para 13; *Snežana Zdravković* v. *UNMIK*, Case No. 46/08, 25 February 2013, para 68.

[57] *Supra*, Section 4.1.3.1. [58] Constitutional Framework (n 23), sections 3.2 and 12.

[59] HRAP, *Nexhmedin Spahiu* v. *UNMIK*, Case No. 02/08, Partial opinion, 20 March 2009, para 29; *Tomë Krasniqi* v. *UNMIK*, 6 June 2013, Case No. 08/10, para 36; *Milogorić et al.* v. *UNMIK* (n 20), para 18.

[60] HRRP, *H & G* v. *EULEX*, decision of 30 September 2013, Case No. 2012-19 & 2012-20, para 42 and other sources cited in Section 4.1.3.1, n 76.

[61] HRRP, *H & G* v. *EULEX* (n 60), para 53; in a similar sense: *A, B, C and D* v. *EULEX*, decision of 20 June 2013, Case No. 2012-09, 2012-10, 2012-11 and 2012-12, paras 65, 67.

After *Behrami/Saramati*, the Court consistently found all applications challenging conduct of troop-contributing States performed within the activities of KFOR inadmissible.[62] The 'ultimate authority and control' test as applied by the ECtHR opened the way to a contestable State practice, hiding the State's responsibility behind that of the IO that authorised the multinational operation. The practice of consultative bodies, however, corresponds to general international law and provides for the attribution of conduct to the IO exercising the 'effective control' over the challenged conduct or bases the IO's responsibility on the failure to comply with its due diligence obligations.

6.1.2 *Attribution to States Participating in the Operation*

The responsibility of IOs for conduct performed in a peace operation does not exclude the joint or parallel responsibility of States participating in the operation for the same conduct.[63] From the point of view of individuals, such a dual responsibility is desirable as it takes into account the effectiveness of various subjects implicated in the operation. One must again emphasise the difference between multinational operations conducted by States whose responsibility shall be assessed under the 'effective control' test (Section 6.1.2.1) and contributing States to peace operations where the dual or parallel responsibility of the IO should be also assessed (Section 6.1.2.2).

6.1.2.1 Contributing States of Multinational Operations

As a logical consequence of Article 7 of DARIO, contributing States of multinational operations are responsible for the unlawful conduct of the contingents they effectively control. The case law in IHRL provides support to the 'effective control' test, notwithstanding the continued application of the *Behrami/Saramati* 'ultimate authority and control' test by certain domestic courts such as in the UK.[64]

[62] *Ilaz Kasumaj* v. *Greece*, Appl. no. 6974/05, decision of 5 July 2007 on the admissibility, 2–3; *Slavisa Gajic* v. *Germany*, Appl. no. 31446/02, decision of 28 August 2007 on the admissibility, 5–6.

[63] Second report of Gaja (n 29), 4-5, para 7; DARIO Commentary, 54, para 4; *Al-Jedda* v. *the United Kingdom* [GC], Appl. no. 27021/08, judgment of 7 July 2011, para 80; James Crawford, *State Responsibility: The General Part* (Cambridge University Press 2013) 204.

[64] *R. (on the application of Al-Jedda)* v. *Secretary of State for Defence*, House of Lords, 12 December 2007, [2007] UKHL 58; *Serdar Mohammed* v. *Ministry of Defence*, High Court of Justice, 2 May 2014, [2014] EWHC 1369 (QB), para 178; *Serdar Mohammed & Others* v. *Secretary of State for Defence*, Court of Appeal, 30 July 2015, [2015] EWCA Civ 843, para 65.

The *Al-Jedda* case challenged the lawfulness of the detention of an Iraqi national by British armed forces in Iraq. The majority of the British House of Lords found that the situations of Kosovo and that of Iraq were different,[65] while the minority view considered the case analogous to that of the *Behrami/Saramati* cases and entirely admitted the 'ultimate authority and control' test.[66] The case was subsequently filed with the ECtHR which had to review its *Behrami/Saramati* decision in the context of Iraq occupied by the Multi-national Force.

Before the ECtHR the UK argued that similarly to UNSC Resolution 1244 (1999) which authorised the operation by KFOR in Kosovo, UNSC Resolutions 1511 and 1546 authorised the Multi-National Force (MNF) in Iraq under chapter VII of the UN Charter.[67] It added that the five factors underlining the UN's 'ultimate authority and control' over KFOR all applied in Iraq and that the UNSC retained greater control over the MNF than over KFOR under Resolution 1244.[68] By contrast, the ECtHR confirmed the applicant's position under which the UNSC's position towards the UK forces in Iraq was clearly distinguishable from that in *Behrami/Saramati*.[69] Analysing the facts of the UN's involvement in the operation of the MNF in Iraq, the Court did not consider that, as a result of the authorisation contained in Resolution 1511, the acts of soldiers within the MNF became attributable to the UN or – more importantly in the instant case – ceased to be attributable to the TCNs.[70] Both the US and the UK, through the Coalition Provisional Authority that they had established at the start of the occupation, continued to exercise governmental powers in Iraq. Although the US was requested to report periodically to the UNSC about the activities of the MNF, 'the United Nations did not, thereby, assume any degree of control over either the force or any other of the executive functions of the Coalition Provisional Authority'.[71] In Resolution 1546 the UNSC reaffirmed the authorisation for the Multi-National Force, without indicating any intention to assume any greater degree of control or command over the MNF than it had exercised previously.[72]

[65] *R. (on the application of Al-Jedda)* v. *Secretary of State for Defence* (n 64), paras 22–25 (Lord Bingham of Cornhill), 124 (Baroness Hale), 131 (Lord Carswell), 145–148 (Lord Brown of Eaton-under-Heywood).

[66] Ibid., paras 59, 61, 87–88 (Lord Rodger of Earlsferry).

[67] *Al-Jedda* (n 63), para 65.

[68] Ibid., para 66.

[69] Ibid., esp. paras 70–72.

[70] Ibid., para 80.

[71] Ibid.

[72] Ibid., para 81.

The Court recognised that the test to be applied in order to establish attribution was that set out in Article 7 of DARIO and its commentary.[73] In the instant case the ECtHR considered that the UNSC 'had neither effective control nor ultimate authority and control over the acts and omissions of troops within the Multi-National Force and that the applicant's detention was not, therefore, attributable to the United Nations'.[74] While this conclusion is correct, the reference to the 'ultimate authority and control' indicates that the Grand Chamber still insists on the continued applicability of its erroneous case law. At any rate, the Court recognised that the impugned internment took place within a detention facility controlled exclusively by British forces, and the applicant was therefore within the authority and control of the UK. Consequently, the internment of the applicant was attributable to the UK and not to the UN.[75] As the ECtHR focused on the operational control held by the UK over the challenged conduct, it correctly relied on the 'effective control' test to engage the responsibility of a troop-contributing State.

6.1.2.2 Contributing States of Peace Operations

The 'effective control' test under Article 7 of DARIO has the consequence that in all cases where the troop-contributing State exercises effective control over the unlawful conduct, its responsibility is engaged. The contributing States' responsibility is reasonable as they retain disciplinary power, criminal jurisdiction and sometimes operational control over their agents operating abroad in peace operations. Both general international law and IHRL confirms this type of attribution.

In general international law, various domestic court decisions engaging the responsibility of troop-contributing States to peace missions provided support for the 'effective control' test under Article 7 of DARIO[76] and the concept of dual attribution.[77] An example is a Belgian decision in the *Mukeshimana-Ngulinzira and Others* v. *Belgium* case, relating to the United Nations Assistance Mission for Rwanda (UNAMIR), to which Belgium also contributed a contingent that operated in the Kigali sector

[73] (former draft Article 5) Ibid., para 84. [74] Ibid. [75] Ibid., para 86.

[76] DARIO Commentary, 59–60, para 14.

[77] E.g. *Mehida Mustafic-Mujic, Damir Mustafic, Alma Mustafic* v. *the State of the Netherlands*, Supreme Court of the Netherlands, 12/03329 LZ/TT, 6 September 2013, para 3.9.4; *Hasan Nuhanovic* v. *the State of the Netherlands*, Supreme Court of the Netherlands, 12/03324 LZ/TT, 6 September 2013, para 3.9.4; *Mothers of Srebrenica* v. *the State of the Netherlands*, Court of Appeal of The Hague (Gerechtshof Den Haag), 200.158.313/01 and 200.160.317/01, 27 June 2017, para 12.1; *State of The Netherlands* v. *Stichting Mothers of Srebrenica et al.*, Supreme Court of the Netherlands, 17/04567(Eng), 19 July 2019, para 3.3.5.

under the command of a Belgian officer. While a unit of the Belgian contingent was based at a compound built around a school where some 2 000 Tutsi and moderate Hutu sought refuge, in April 2004 the Belgian soldiers evacuated the compound. This leave had the consequence that shortly afterwards Interahamwe militias massacred the majority of the refugees inside the compound. Nine applicants (survivors or relatives of the killed) brought civil lawsuits against the Belgian State. The court of Brussels distinguished between the situation in Rwanda and that of Kosovo and rejected the respondent State's argument that the challenged conduct would be attributable to the UN and other States.[78] To decide whether the decision to evacuate was attributable to Belgium or to UNAMIR, the Court took into account the fact that the commandant of UNAMIR expressly complained about his lack of control over the Belgian contingent and that there was absolutely no consultation between UNAMIR and the commander of the Belgian army. Consequently, the Court concluded that the decision to evacuate the compound was made by the Belgian army and not by UNAMIR.[79]

The numerous civil procedures initiated before the Dutch courts against The Netherlands concerning the alleged unlawful conduct of the Dutch Battalion (Dutchbat) also confirm the 'effective control' test. Dutchbat was tasked with protecting the 'safe areas' assigned by the UNSC near to Srebrenica during the Bosnian war. In July 1995 some 5 000 Muslim Bosnian refugees fleeing Bosnian Serb attacks on Srebrenica sought refuge in the 'safe area' under Dutchbat protection. After the takeover of Srebrenica by the Bosnian Serbs, Dutchbat was instructed to withdraw and evacuate the 'safe area'. Although the commander of Bosnian Serbian forces assured the Dutchbat commander that his troops would not attack the civilian population, shortly after the evacuation and Dutchbat's withdrawal Bosnian Serbs took away refugees who were inside the compound, during which operation they almost immediately separated and massacred the able-bodied men. The families of several victims brought civilian actions against The Netherlands under Dutch tort law. The court of first instance concluded that the challenged Dutchbat actions were attributable exclusively to the UN, as the 'operational command and control' over the Dutch troops had been

[78] *Mukeshimana-Ngulinzira et Autres c. Etat belge*, Brussels First Instance Court, R.G.no. 04/4807/A and 07/15547/A, 8 December 2010, para 26.

[79] Ibid., para 38.

transferred to the UN.[80] However, based on the 'effective control' test, the Court of Appeal reversed the decisions and found that the impugned conduct could be attributed to The Netherlands.[81] The Supreme Court confirmed the Court of Appeal's ruling, holding that the judgment was in conformity with both Article 7 of DARIO and Article 8 ARSIWA.[82] All instances interpreted 'effective control' in the same sense, researching in the facts whether the Dutch government was closely involved in the evacuation and its preparations to prevent the unlawful conduct.[83] This corresponds to the academic reading of the 'effective control' test under which the command and control powers – either of the contributing State or the IO – best positioned in legal terms to a given conduct are those most likely to be useful in preventing that conduct from occurring.[84] The importance of the Dutch case law is the possibility of dual attribution: even after the command and control over the peacekeeping troops had been transferred to the IO, and the IO exercised effective control over troops in principle, there might be exceptional instances where the troop-contributing State also exercised effective control over certain aspects of acts performed by the contingent.[85]

The practice in IHRL has confirmed the importance of factual control over conduct in peace operations. Some international cases implied the attributability of human rights violations committed within a peace mission under UN command to the troop-contributing State. In the *Kurbogaj* and the *Atallah and Others* cases before the Human Rights Committee and the ECtHR, respectively, the applicants complained of harassment by the Spanish police unit of UNMIK and a fatal shooting by the French contingent of the United Nations Interim Force in Lebanon

[80] *H.N.* v. *the State of the Netherlands*, District Court in The Hague, 265615 / HA ZA 06-1671, 10 September 2008, esp. paras 4.8–4.9, 4.14.5; *M.M.-M, D.M., A.M.* v. *the State of the Netherlands*, District Court in The Hague, 265618 / HA ZA 06-1672, 10 September 2008, esp. paras 4.10–4.11, 4.16.5.

[81] *Mehida Mustafic-Mujic, Damir Mustafic, Alma Mustafic* v. *the State of the Netherlands*, Appeal Court in The Hague, 265618/ HA ZA 06-1672, 5 July 2011, esp. paras 5.8–5.20; *Hasan Nuhanovic* v. *the State of the Netherlands*, Appeal Court in The Hague, Civil Law Section, 265618/ HA ZA 06-1672, 5 July 2011, esp. paras 5.8–5.20.

[82] Supreme Court decisions (*Mustafic-Mujic et al.*; *Nuhanovic*) (n 77), paras 3.11.3, 3.13.

[83] First instance decisions (n 80), para 4.14.1; Second instance decisions (n 81), para 5.18; Supreme Court decisions (n 77), para 3.12.3.

[84] Crawford (n 63) 206, 209; Tom Dannenbaum, 'Translating the Standard of Effective Control into a System of Effective Accountability: How Liability Should Be Apportioned for Violations of Human Rights by Member State Troop Contingents Serving as United Nations Peacekeepers' (2010) 51 *Harvard International Law Journal* 113, 157.

[85] *Supra*, n 77.

(UNIFIL), respectively. Without pronouncing on the questions of jurisdiction and attributability, the monitoring bodies found the applications inadmissible for procedural grounds (for non-exhaustion of available Spanish domestic remedies and the non-respect of the sixth-month rule, respectively).[86] This implies that, despite the UN command over the peacekeeping operation, the troop-contributing States might have exercised effective control over the challenged conduct. Moreover, unlike Spain in the *Kurbogaj* case, France in the *Atallah* case did not even challenge the attributability of the alleged human rights violation.

Likewise, the same implied attributability characterises the Concluding Observations of universal monitoring bodies on the (personal model of) jurisdiction exercised by the troop-contributing State in peacekeeping operations.[87] In other words, when a monitoring body asserts the applicability *ratione personae* of the convention to a national contingent, it presumes that human rights violations committed by the contingent may be attributable to the sending State, irrespective of their parallel attribution to an IO.

In conclusion, international law has started to elaborate the law of responsibility of IOs to which IHRL largely contributes. Factual control over the given conduct rather than the general command and control over the operation is the key test that human rights monitoring bodies should apply. Effective control over the conduct also means that monitoring bodies should examine dual or even multiple attribution of conduct: the attribution of the wrongful act to an IO does not exclude the fact that the same conduct may be attributed to a State and *vice versa*. Alternatively, the IO controlling the territory can incur responsibility for the failure to comply with due diligence.

6.2 The Responsibility of *De Facto* Regimes

While positive international law has not codified any rules on the international responsibility of armed opposition groups (AOGs), including *de facto* regimes, States and IOs have increasingly recognised and developed its concept (Section 6.2.1). Based on certain similarities between States and *de facto* regimes, the law of State responsibility is a useful tool to

[86] HRC, *Azem Kurbogaj and Ghevdet Kurbogaj* v. *Spain*, Communication No. 1374/2005, decision of 14 July 2006, UN Doc. CCPR/C/87/D/1374/2005 (11 August 2006), para 6.3; ECtHR, *Arlette Atallah and Others* v. *France*, Appl. No. 51987/07, decision of 30 August 2011 on the admissibility.

[87] *Supra*, Section 2.1.2.1.

govern the responsibility of the latter (Section 6.2.2). The analogous application of the law of State responsibility helps to identify certain rules on attribution (Section 6.2.3) regarding *de facto* regimes.

6.2.1 *The International Recognition of the Concept*

Under draft Article 14(3) ARSIWA, as provisionally adopted on first reading, the fact that the conduct of an organ of an insurrectional movement is not to be considered an act of State 'is without prejudice to the attribution of the conduct of the organ of the insurrectional movement to that movement in any case in which such attribution may be made under international law'.[88] Although this article was subsequently deleted, the Special Rapporteur noted that 'the responsibility of such movements, for example for breaches of international humanitarian law, can certainly be envisaged'.[89] The ARSIWA Commentary and the study by the International Committee of the Red Cross (ICRC) on customary international humanitarian law (IHL) also recognise the possibility to hold unsuccessful insurrectional or other movements internationally responsible.[90]

Since *de facto* regimes, at least under certain special regimes such as IHL, have partial legal personality,[91] limited to certain rights and obligations, it is logical to accept their responsibility for the violation of their obligations.[92] While in IHRL numerous States reject both AOGs' obligations and responsibility,[93] several organs of IOs, especially the ICJ,[94] the

[88] Eighth report on State responsibility, by Mr. Gaetano Arangio-Ruiz, Special Rapporteur, UN Doc. A/51/10, in: *YbILC*, 1996, vol. II(2), 57–73.

[89] First report on State responsibility, by Mr. James Crawford, Special Rapporteur, UN Doc. A/53/10, in: *YbILC*, 1998, vol. II(1), 53, para 272 and 51, para 263.

[90] ARSIWA Commentary, 52, para 16; Jean-Marie Henckaerts and Louise Doswald-Beck, *Customary International Humanitarian Law*, vol. 1 (Rules) (Comité international de la Croix-Rouge, ed., Cambridge University Press 2005) 536.

[91] *Supra*, Section 1.4.

[92] Fourth report on State responsibility, by Mr. Roberto Ago, Special Rapporteur, UN Doc. A/CN.4/264 et Add. 1, in: *YbILC*, 1972, vol. II, 139, para 180.

[93] Minimum humanitarian standards. Analytical report of the Secretary-General submitted pursuant to Commission on Human Rights resolution 1997/21, UN Doc. E/CN.4/1998/87 (5 January 1998), para 60; The right to a remedy and reparation for victims of violations of international human rights and humanitarian law, Note by the High Commissioner for Human Rights, UN Doc. E/CN.4/2003/63 (27 December 2002), para 18.

[94] *Military and Paramilitary Activities in and against Nicaragua (Nicaragua* v. *United States of America)*, Merits, judgment, *I.C.J. Reports* 1986, 65, para 116; in the *Croatia* v. *Serbia* case, the Court did not exclude this possibility: *Application of the Convention on the Prevention and Punishment of the Crime of Genocide (Croatia* v. *Serbia)*, judgment, *I.C.J. Reports* 2015, 53, para 105.

Special Court for Sierra Leone (SCSL),[95] the International Criminal Court (ICC),[96] fact-finding commissions[97] and even human rights treaty-monitoring bodies[98] confirmed the responsibility of AOGs, without the *stricto sensu* power to engage it. Finally, there were few precedents where States have presented claims to an insurrectional movement for injuries caused to them or their nationals by organs of that movement[99] and where *de facto* regimes paid reparations.[100]

6.2.2 *The Analogous Application of State Responsibility*

Unlike the responsibility of States and IOs, the ILC has not examined the topic of the international responsibility of AOGs. However, several arguments militate in favour of and against the idea of developing a legal framework of responsibility of AOGs. One of the counterarguments is the States' reluctance to adopt any regulation that is likely to contribute to the legitimisation or formal status of AOGs, and unduly limit the State's freedom to suppress a rebellion by all the means and prosecute its members.[101] An argument for such a legal regime is the substantive obligations of AOGs, including *de facto* regimes, recognised under IHL, IHRL and international criminal law.[102] Furthermore, States and IOs

[95] SCSL, *Prosecutor* v. *Sam Hinga Norman*, Decision on preliminary motion based on lack of jurisdiction (child recrutement), Appeals Chamber, SCSL-2004-14-AR72(E), 31 May 2004, para 22.

[96] ICC, *The Prosecutor* v. *Bosco Ntaganda*, ICC-01/04-02/06, Trial Chamber, 8 July 2019, para 993.

[97] E.g. Report of the Independent International Commission of Inquiry on the Syrian Arab Republic, UN Doc. A/HRC/23/58 (4 June 2013), para 156; Report of the United Nations Fact-Finding Mission on the Gaza Conflict, UN Doc. A/HRC/12/48 (25 September 2009), para 1836.

[98] E.g. ACommHPR, *Zimbabwe Human Rights NGO Forum* v. *Zimbabwe*, Communication no. 245/02, 15 May 2006, para 183; *Amnesty International et al.* v. *Sudan*, Communications nos. 48/90-50/91-52/91-89/93, 15 November 1999, para 186; CRC, Concluding observations: Democratic Republic of the Congo, UN Doc. CRC/C/15/Add.153 (9 July 2001), para 6; CERD, Concluding observations: Colombia, UN Doc. CERD/C/304/Add.76 (12 April 2001), para 12.

[99] Fourth report of Ago (n 92), 139, paras 180–181.

[100] Ibid.; Jochen A. Frowein, *Das De facto-Regime im Völkerrecht: eine Untersuchung zur Rechtsstellung nichtanerkannter Staaten und ähnlicher Gebilde* (C Heymann 1968) 72–80.

[101] Jean Pictet, Frédéric Siordet and International Committee of the Red Cross, *Geneva Convention for the Amelioration of the Condition of the Wounded and Sick in Armed Forces in the Field: Commentary* (International Committee of the Red Cross 1952) 44.

[102] Jann K. Kleffner, 'The Collective Accountability of Organised Armed Groups for System Crimes' in André Nollkaemper and Harmen van der Wilt (eds), *System Criminality in International Law* (Cambridge University Press 2009) 258.

have increasingly made conclusions about the responsibility of AOGs, indicating the need to set international secondary norms on the issue.

In the absence of codified norms on the responsibility of AOGs/*de facto* regimes, the ARSIWA may be invoked by analogy. The basis of this analogy is a certain similarity between States and *de facto* regimes, both being collective entities with a certain degree of organisation, exercising effective control over territory and quasi-governmental powers.[103] However, the limits of this analogy must be kept in mind, as the responsibility of AOGs has some specialities with regard to the ARSIWA. First, as opposed to States, *de facto* regimes do not have a right to exist. Therefore, 'the underlying rationales of a legal responsibility of organized armed groups for system crimes may not only include the termination, prevention of recurrence, but also the more far-reaching aim to dismantle organized armed groups'.[104] Second, AOGs dispose of rights and obligations under certain special regimes, and thus they have partial legal personality, as opposed to the State's full legal personality, not limited to certain rights and obligations. While bearing in mind these differences between the responsibility of States and that of *de facto* regimes, some rules of the ARSIWA can be applied by analogy to *de facto* regimes, especially the rules of attribution.

6.2.3 *Attribution Norms*

A *de facto* regime, as in the case of a State, can act only through individuals. However, it may be difficult to determine whether an internationally wrongful act was actually performed by an 'organ', 'agency', 'official' or 'employee' of the *de facto* regime or by unorganised supporters of the entity without official status.[105] In the absence of an international instrument defining the rules of attribution regarding AOGs/*de facto* regimes, the practice of States and IOs provides some support for the presumed application of the ARSIWA rules on attribution (Articles 4–11) by analogy.[106]

[103] Ibid., 260; Liesbeth Zegveld, *Accountability of Armed Opposition Groups in International Law* (Cambridge University Press 2002) 154.

[104] Kleffner (n 102) 261.

[105] Convention on the international responsibility of States for injuries to aliens, Final draft with explanatory notes by Louis B. Sohn and R. R. Baxter, in: F. V. García Amador y Rodríguez, Louis B. Sohn and Richard Reeve Baxter, *Recent Codification of the Law of State Responsibility for Injuries to Aliens* (Oceana Publications 1974) 258–259.

[106] ICJ, *Croatia* v. *Serbia*, Public sitting, 21 March 2014, CR 2014/21, 24–25, para 50 (Mr. Crawford, on behalf of Croatia).

There is consensus that the conduct of organs of the *de facto* regime is attributable to that entity.[107] To define an organ of an insurrectional movement, the normative order of the *de facto* regime is decisive. Ago referred to 'individuals and groups belonging to the organization of an insurrectional movement and acting in its name and on its behalf'.[108] In a similar sense the ARSIWA commentary mentions the 'apparatus' of the movement.[109] Likewise, the International Commission of Inquiry on Darfur by analogy applied Article 4 ARSIWA when it held that international crimes are attributable to 'the international non-state entity to which those authors belong as officials (or for which they acted as *de facto* organs)'.[110] The US considered 'agencies and instrumentalities' of the Taliban as part of the non-state entity.[111] Civilian or military agents from the ranks of the *de facto* regime, even if not acting on orders from the senior leadership,[112] may be considered 'organs' of the entity analogously to Article 4 ARSIWA. The conduct of those persons is attributable to the *de facto* regime even if they act *ultra vires*, under the the logic of Article 7 ARSIWA.

While the normative order of the *de facto* regime may designate its *de jure* organs, it is contested whether it may have *de facto* organs, that is organs not expressly designated as its bodies but in fact acting under its dependence and, in the affirmative, which threshold applies to them. Some truth commissions held AOGs responsible for wrongful acts committed by individuals belonging to the group,[113] while others based attribution on the fact that the internationally wrongful acts either derived from the AOG's political-military strategy or were committed

[107] Fourth report of Ago (n 92), 129, para 153 and 142, para 188; Report of the ILC on the work of its twenty-seventh session, 5 May–25 July 1975, in: *YbILC*, 1975, vol. II, 91–92, para 3 (commentary to draft article 14); Eighth report on State responsibility, by Mr. Gaetano Arangio-Ruiz (n 88), 59, draft Article 14(3); In 1998, this draft paragraph was supported by ILC members, see *YbILC*, 1998, vol. II(2), 86, para 437.

[108] Fourth report of Ago (n 92), 129, para 153.

[109] ARSIWA Commentary, 50, para 5.

[110] Report of the International Commission of Inquiry on Darfur to the United Nations Secretary-General, UN Doc. S/2005/60 (1 February 2005), para 175.

[111] The White House Executive Order blocking property and prohibiting transactions with the Taliban, Executive Order 13129 of 4 July 1999, *Federal Register*, vol. 64, no. 129, section 4(c).

[112] Interim report on the situation of human rights in the Sudan prepared by Mr. Gáspár Bíró, Special Rapporteur of the Commission on Human Rights, UN Doc. A/50/569 (16 October 1995), para 73.

[113] From Madness to Hope: the 12-year war in El Salvador, Report of the Commission on the Truth for El Salvador, UN Doc. S/25500 (1 April 1993), 152–153, 157 (attacks planned by individuals belonging to AOG 'as part of the FMLN policy').

in compliance with decisions taken at the highest level of the AOG.[114] Those reports suggest that official and unofficial organs of AOGs might be hardly distinguishable, while they do not specify an applicable attribution test. If ignoring the existence of *de facto* organs in State responsibility would have the effect of States escaping their responsibility, then the same rationale must apply to *de facto* regimes. Therefore, the conduct of their *de facto* organs should be attributable to those entities to eliminate a vacuum of responsibility.

As to the applicable threshold, one might invoke the tests used by the case law in State responsibility focusing on control by the State over the person/group of persons[115] or that proposed by the ICRC to determine individual membership in AOGs. The latter depends on 'whether a person assumes a continuous function for the group involving his or her direct participation in hostilities'.[116] This might lead to the responsibility of AOGs for the conduct of individuals whom they do not control – a consideration that also led the ILC to exclude the criterion 'on behalf' of the State from its attribution articles.[117] As special Rapporteur Crawford opined, attribution to insurrectional movements should not apply to 'the more or less uncoordinated conduct of the supporters of such a movement'.[118] Therefore, attribution based on control by the entity over the individual seems preferable. Nonetheless, there are good arguments to allow a more flexible approach than the 'complete dependence' test applied by the ICJ: *de facto* regimes more often act through units having some degree of automony than State organs as their institutional and normative system may be less sophisticated than those of a State. A less demanding test, such as the 'overall control' of international criminal law or the 'effective control' test of the ECtHR allows more autonomy for such *de facto* organs and therefore should be applied to *de facto* regimes.[119] However, it should be limited to *de facto* regimes capable

[114] Commission for Historical Clarification, *Guatemala: Memory of Silence*, Conclusions and Recommendations, UN Doc. A/53/928 (27 April 1999), Annex, 31, para 142.

[115] Zegveld (n 103) 154–155.

[116] Nils Melzer and International Committee of the Red Cross, *Interpretive Guidance on the Notion of Direct Participation in Hostilities under International Humanitarian Law* (International Committee of the Red Cross 2009) 33.

[117] *Supra*, Section 5.1.2.1.

[118] First report on State responsibility (n 89), 57, para 3.

[119] Sten I. Verhoeven, 'International Responsibility of Armed Opposition Groups: Lessons from State Responsibility for Actions of Armed Opposition Groups' in Noemi Gal-Or, Math Noortmann and Cedric Ryngaert (eds), *Responsibilities of the Non-State Actor in Armed Conflict and the Market Place* (Brill 2015) 300–301.

of controlling individuals, leaving aside AOGs with heterogeneous membership and a loose structure.

Furthermore, nothing prevents the attribution of specific conduct to a *de facto* regime, when a person or group of persons in fact is acting on the instructions of or under the direction or control of the entity, analogously to Article 8 ARSIWA. The ICTY Trial Chamber in the *Prosecutor v Hadžihasanović* case found that an AOG could exercise 'effective control' over a group of persons, extending the superior–subordinate relationship to relations between groups. The Trial Chamber held that a superior–subordinate relationship existed between the 3rd Corps Command and the *El Mujahedin* detachment,[120] whereas the Appeals Chamber found no relationship of subordination and reversed the conclusion about effective control of the commander over the said group.[121] Beyond the evaluation of the concrete facts, there was also disagreement on the relevant evidence proving effective control: from the elements that the Trial Chamber considered to determine the existence of a commander's effective control over his forces (the power to give orders and have them executed; the conduct of combat operations involving the forces in question; the absence of any other authority over the forces in question),[122] the Appeals Chamber accepted only the power to give orders and have them executed as relevant evidence on effective control.[123] Although the Trial Chamber limited its findings to superior responsibility, excluding any conclusion on attribution, the decision indicates that persons or a group of persons, not dependent from the AOG, may execute orders from an AOG in the framework of a given operation, similarly to the hypothesis of Article 8 ARSIWA.[124]

As a further example of the analogous application of Article 8 ARSIWA, the Independent Fact-Finding Committee on Gaza proposed to apply the 'effective control' test to the attribution of the conduct of certain factions to an AOG: it held 'that Hamas ultimately had effective control over the actions of these factions and could be held responsible

[120] ICTY, *Prosecutor* v. *Enver Hadžihasanović and Amir Kubura ("Central Bosnia")*, Case n° IT-01-47-T, Trial Chamber, judgment of 15 March 2006 [*Hadžihasanović*, Trial Chamber], paras 844–853, 1036 (superior–subordinate relationship within the meanings of Article 7(3) of the Statute of the ICTY).

[121] ICTY, *Prosecutor* v. *Enver Hadžihasanović and Amir Kubura ("Central Bosnia")*, Case n° IT-01-47-A, Appeals Chamber, judgment of 22 April 2008 [*Hadžihasanović*, Appeals Chamber], paras 194–232.

[122] See *Hadžihasanović*, Trial Chamber (n 120), paras 82–84 (in general) and 851 (in the concrete case).

[123] *Hadžihasanović*, Appeals Chamber (n 121), para 199.

[124] Kleffner (n 102) 264.

for them'.[125] Similarly, when it provided for the freezing of assets of persons or entities designated by the Sanctions Committee established pursuant to Resolution 1533 (2004) concerning the Democratic Republic of the Congo (DRC), the UNSC determined the concerned scope of the assets as those 'held by entities owned or controlled, directly or indirectly, by them or by any persons or entities acting on their behalf or at their direction'.[126]

In the *Application of the Convention on the Prevention and Punishment of the Crime of Genocide (Croatia* v. *Serbia)* case before the ICJ, Croatia claimed that the conduct of Serb and Serbian paramilitary groups, which were not formally integrated into the Yugoslav People's Army (JNA) as 'volunteers', but acted under the direction and control of the JNA, was attributable to the Federal Republic of Yugoslavia.[127] However, Serbia considered that claim as an attribution of paramilitary conduct to an insurgent movement, and stressed that 'in the exceptional case of movement responsibility, there can be no equivalent to article 8 of the ILC text'.[128] It seemed to accept attribution of the conduct of the 'apparatus' to an insurgent movement under Article 4 ARSIWA, but not of individuals under Article 8 ARSIWA.[129] Croatia objected and held that '[t]he usual principles of attribution apply' to a 'movement *qua* state in embryo'.[130] There is no reason to exclude that insurrectional movements including *de facto* regimes act through *de facto* agents in specific operations, without controlling them in all their performance. If the *de facto* regime has decisive influence only over the specific conduct through its instructions, direction or effective control, it should be responsible for the wrongful conduct by analogy with Article 8 ARSIWA. If it is accepted that the conduct of *de facto* organs could be attributed to the entity under a control test of Article 4 ARSIWA which is more flexible than the 'complete dependence' test of the ICJ, this might overlap with the 'effective control' test under Article 8 ARSIWA. The difference is that, in the former case, all conduct of the person or group of persons is

125 Report of the Independent Fact-Finding Committee on Gaza, UN Doc. S/2009/537 (14 October 2009), Annex, para 575.

126 UN Doc. S/RES/1807 (31 March 2008), para 11.

127 ICJ, *Croatia* v. *Serbia*, Memorial of the Republic of Croatia, vol. I, 1 March 2001, para 8.49.

128 ICJ, *Croatia* v. *Serbia*, Public sitting, 12 March 2014, CR 2014/15, 37, para 18 (Mr. Lukić); Public sitting, 27 March 2014, CR 2014/22, 36–37, para 29 (Mr. Tams).

129 ICJ, *Croatia* v. *Serbia*, Public sitting, 12 March 2014, CR 2014/16, 16, para 83 (Mr. Ignjatović).

130 ICJ, *Croatia* v. *Serbia*, Public sitting, 21 March 2014, CR 2014/21, 24–25, paras 49–50 (Mr. Crawford).

attributable to the *de facto* regime, whereas in the latter case only the specific conduct it controlled.

Article 5 ARSIWA could also apply by analogy, providing on the 'conduct of persons or entities exercising elements of governmental authority'. If a person or entity cannot be considered an organ of the *de facto* regime, but it 'is empowered by the law' – that is, the normative system of the *de facto* regime – 'to exercise elements of the governmental authority', its conduct may be considered an act of the *de facto* regime, 'provided the person or entity is acting in that capacity in the particular instance'.[131] Article 5 ARSIWA can be applied by analogy, for instance, where a *de facto* regime contracts private military companies, as several AOGs did in some armed conflicts.[132] Furthermore, similarly to the logic of Article 11 ARSIWA, truth and fact-finding commissions attributed internationally wrongful acts to AOGs when the latter 'approved and adopted' the acts as their own[133] or simply acknowledged their responsibility for their commission.[134]

Generally speaking, the more effective the *de facto* regime is, the easier is the analogous application of the attribution rules of State responsibility. A *de facto* regime with a permanent and sophisticated structure is more likely to perform its conduct in a visible manner than one with an unstable organisation. For lawyers, this facilitates the process of attribution, while for the *de facto* regime, attribution paves the way to its responsibility and arguably for greater legitimacy.

Finally, the responsibility of *de facto* regimes complements that of States. For instance, the International Commission of Inquiry on Darfur held that not only is the State obliged to pay compensation for all crimes perpetrated by its organs, but '[a] similar obligation is incumbent upon rebels for all crimes they may have committed, whether or not the perpetrators are identified and punished'.[135] Limited State practice confirms that *de facto* regimes are obliged to participate in the redress of victims, at least as far as their effectiveness allows. Colombian courts have engaged the collective civil liability of all members of AOGs,[136] while the Lord's Resistance Army recognised its

131 Article 5 ARSIWA; Zegveld (n 103) 154. 132 Kleffner (n 102) 263.

133 From Madness to Hope: the 12-year war in El Salvador, Report of the Commission on the Truth for El Salvador, UN Doc. S/25500 (1 April 1993), 152.

134 Ibid., 162, 163, 166; UN Doc. A/HRC/12/48 (n 97), para 1687.

135 Report of the International Commission of Inquiry on Darfur to the United Nations Secretary-General, UN Doc. S/2005/60 (1 February 2005), para 600.

136 Colombia, Corte Constitucional, Sentencia C-370/06, 18 May 2006, para 6.2.4.4.13.

obligation to redress victims in an agreement signed with Uganda.[137] Some AOGs offered symbolic reparations to their victims,[138] which shows that even low effectiveness might allow compliance with the obligation of reparation.

6.3 Concluding Remarks

International law has recognised and started to elaborate on the law of responsibility of IOs, to which IHRL largely contributes. Beyond the international responsibility of States and IOs, international law recognises the concept of responsibility of AOGs. In the case of both IOs and *de facto* regimes, their effectiveness over the conduct of individuals enhances the likelihood of attribution, while non-attribution does not necessarily mean that there is no other subject internationally responsible for the wrongful act. The responsibility of non-state actors for the violations of IHRL does not exclude but is independent from and complementary to the responsibility of the territorial and the outside State(s). For instance, while an IO might incur responsibility for the conduct of the peace operation under its effective control, the territorial State might be responsible for failing to comply with its due diligence to take all administrative or diplomatic measures to protect the individual from abuses by the peace operation. The dual or multiple responsibility for violations of concurrent obligations is beneficious for individuals, as the latter can enforce the obligations of all international legal subjects primarily involved in the territorial situation.

137 Agreement on accountability and reconciliation between the Government of the Republic of Uganda and the Lord's Resistance Army/Movement, Juba, Sudan, in: UN Doc. S/2007/435 (17 July 2007), Annex, preambular para 3 and Article 9.

138 Ron Dudai, 'Closing the Gap: Symbolic Reparations and Armed Groups' (2011) 93 *International Review of the Red Cross* 783.

7 Judicial Control Mechanisms

This chapter argues that judicial control mechanisms can provide effective remedies for individuals in 'grey zones' provided that the applicant can establish the responsibility of the respondent State and the (quasi-) judicial body is willing to exercise certain judicial activism to promote individuals' access to international justice.

Judicial control mechanisms are understood as procedures of international human rights courts and quasi-judicial treaty-monitoring bodies having a competence to give opinions on individual petitions. The latter category of monitoring bodies is quasi-judicial in the sense that the procedure 'involves the resolution of a dispute as to facts, or as to the existence of legal rights or duties, by means of finding facts, deciding what the law is, and applying the law to the facts'[1] but, as opposed to human rights courts, does not lead to a final and binding decision. Such human rights treaty bodies have the competence to hear individual complaints against those parties that have ratified the respective human rights treaty (and its optional protocol). Human rights courts are the three regional courts (ECtHR, IACtHR, ACtHPR), whereas quasi-judicial bodies include regional (for instance IACHR, ACommHPR, African Committee of Experts on the Rights and Welfare of the Child (ACERWC)) and UN treaty-monitoring bodies (Committee on Economic, Social and Cultural Rights (CESCR), Committee on the Elimination of Discrimination against Women (CEDAW), Committee against Torture (CAT), Committee on the Elimination of Racial Discrimination (CERD), Committee on the Rights of the Child (CRC), Committee on the Rights of

[1] Volker Röben, 'Conference (Meeting) of States Parties', *MPEPIL* (Oxford University Press 2010) para 35.

Persons with Disabilities (CRPD), Committee on Enforced Disappearances, Human Rights Committee).

Several characteristics of 'grey zones' hinder the effective recourse to judicial control mechanisms. First, domestic remedies may be lacking or dysfunctional in an ongoing armed or 'frozen conflict'. Second, the time-consuming procedure of international human rights bodies may not be appropriate to address massive human rights violations that require urgent answers. Third, the complicated factual situation; the likely coexistence of several international law subjects on the ground may require a labyrinthine legal analysis that would discourage individuals from filing an application. Such features raise the question of how judicial control mechanisms can guarantee effective remedies for individuals. The chapter highlights certain major deficiencies of judicial control mechanisms (Section 7.1), before recommending certain tools of judicial activism that may promote individual applications from 'grey zones' (Section 7.2).

7.1 Deficiencies of Judicial Control Mechanisms

The major limit of judicial human rights control mechanisms in cases arising from 'grey zones' is the politicised territorial dispute in their background. This entails various deficiencies in human rights mechanisms, especially time-consuming procedures (Section 7.1.1), and difficulties in enforcing their decisions (Section 7.1.2) which restrict the effectiveness of international remedies in 'grey zones'.

7.1.1 *Time-Consuming Procedure*

The average time for the receipt and finalisation of an application is 22.9 months before the IACtHR[2] and only twelve months before the ACtHPR.[3] Before the ECtHR the procedure is generally much longer: although the Court endeavours to deal with cases within three years after they are brought, the examination of some cases can take longer depending on the case, the formation to which it is assigned, the diligence of the parties in providing the Court with information and many other factors, such as the holding of a hearing or referral to the Grand Chamber.[4] The Grand Chamber during several years considered the leading cases related to 'grey zones' until its inadmissibility or merits decision: *Loizidou* (seven

2 Inter-American Court of Human Rights, Annual Report 2018, 60.

3 ACtHPR, Activity report of the African Court for the Year 2013, Executive Council, Twenty-Fourth Ordinary Session, EX.CL/825(XXIV) (21–28 January 2014), para 107.

4 ECtHR, The ECHR in 50 questions, 2014, 9.

years); *Varnava and Others* v. *Turkey* (nineteen years); *Demopoulos and Others* v. *Turkey* (decided in 2010, involving applications lodged between 1999 and 2004); *Ilaşcu* (five years); *Catan* (eight years); *Behrami/Saramati* (six years); *Chiragov* and *Sargsyan* cases (ten and eleven years, respectively). The time-consuming procedure is contrary to the urgent interests of applicants in cases of ongoing conflicts and continuing violations.

The more an inter-State (territorial) dispute lies in the background of the case, the less human rights courts are willing to promptly decide it. For instance, the IACHR only decided on the merits in the *Salas Galindo and Others* v. *United States* case concerning the US invasion of Panama of December 1989 in October 2018, after 28 years.[5] In inter-State applications that the ECHR, the ACHPR and the ACHR authorise under certain circumstances,[6] and the Inter-American Commission and Court in cases of acceptance of this competence by both the respondent and the applicant States,[7] the length of the procedure as a deficiency of the mechanism applies *a fortiori*. The ACommHPR needed four years to decide on the *DRC* v. *Burundi, Rwanda and Uganda* case, whereas the *Franklin Guillermo Aisalla Molina (Ecuador* v. *Colombia)* case, initiated in June 2009, was resolved four years later by friendly settlement.[8] As for the ECtHR, the Court settled the fourth *Cyprus* v. *Turkey* case more than six years after the case was submitted to the European Commission of Human Rights (ECommHR) and two years after it was referred to the Court, while the Court decided only 13 years later on the just satisfaction. The Court decided in the merits of the *Georgia* v. *Russia (II)* after twelve years, following an admissibility decision (2011) and three different hearings (on the admissibility; witness hearing; on the merits).[9] All other inter-State cases related to 'grey zones' are still pending in December 2020: the *Georgia* v. *Russia (IV)* application[10] was submitted in 2018, while the numerous *Ukraine* v. *Russia* inter-State applications related to various aspects of the armed conflicts in Crimea and Eastern Ukraine were

[5] IACHR, Report No. 121/18, Case 10.573, *Jose Isabel Salas Galindo and others* v. *United States* (Merits), 5 October 2018.

[6] ACHR, Article 45; ACHPR, Articles 47–54 (before the ACommHPR); ECHR, Article 33.

[7] ACHR, Article 45(1)–45(2).

[8] IACHR, Report No. 96/131, Decision to archive inter-State case 12.779, *Ecuador* v. *Colombia*, 4 November 2013, paras 14–16.

[9] *Georgia* v. *Russia (II) (Merits)* [GC], Appl. no. 38263/08, judgment of 21 January 2021.

[10] The application relates to the alleged deterioration of the human rights situation along the administrative boundary lines between Georgian-controlled territory and Abkhazia and South Ossetia. See *Georgia* v. *Russia* (IV), Appl. no. 39611/18, in: Press release, ECHR 287 (2018), 31 August 2018.

submitted between 2014 and 2018.[11] As at 2020 there were approximately 7 000 individual applications before the Court concerning events in Crimea, Eastern Ukraine and the Donbass region,[12] with various overlapping claims. To save as much time as possible, the Court has decided that any related individual applications that are not declared inadmissible or struck out at the outset will be adjourned, pending a judgment in the inter-State case, with a view to having the files complete and ready for decision or judgment as soon as possible thereafter.[13] This is a welcome policy that is likely to accelerate the procedures. The same policy seems adaptable to similar overlapping inter-State and individual applications that were filed with the Court relating to the shooting down of Malaysia Airlines Flight MH17 over Eastern Ukraine on 17 July 2014,[14] and the 2020 armed conflict in and around the region of Nagorno-Karabakh.[15]

The ECtHR has traditionally been reluctant to deal with highly-politicised inter-State cases. Human rights courts, mandated to protect individuals against State parties, are not the appropriate forum to deal with inter-State cases that fall within the competence of the ICJ or diplomatic dispute settlement mechanisms.[16] Nonetheless, as States

[11] Chronologically, as to their submission date: *Ukraine* v. *Russia (re Crimea)* (Appl. no. 20958/14), joined with *Ukraine* v. *Russia (VII)* (Appl. no. 38334/18) on the alleged politically motivated detention and prosecution of Ukrainian nationals on various criminal charges; *Ukraine* v. *Russia (V) (re Eastern Ukraine)* (Appl. no. 8019/16), joined with *Ukraine* v. *Russia (II)* (Appl. no. 43800/14) on the alleged abduction of three groups of children in Eastern Ukraine and their temporary transfer to Russia and *The Netherlands* v. *Russia* (Appl. no. 28525/20) concerning downing of Malaysia Airlines flight MH17 (together: *Ukraine and the Netherlands* v. *Russia* (Appl. nos. 8019/16, 43800/14 and 28525/20)); *Ukraine* v. *Russia (VIII)* (Appl. no. 55855/18) concerning events on the Kerch Strait in November 2018. In January 2021, the Grand Chamber declared the application *Ukraine* v. *Russia (re Crimea)* partly admissible. See *Ukraine* v. *Russia (re Crimea)* [GC], Appl. nos. 20958/14 and 38334/18, decision of 14 January 2021 on the admissibility.

[12] Press release, ECHR 213 (2020), 15 July 2020.

[13] Press release, ECHR 432 (2018), 17 December 2018.

[14] *Netherlands* v. *Russia*, Appl. no. 28525/20, in: Press release, ECHR 213 (2020), 15 July 2020; individual applications include *Ayley and Others* v. *Russia*, Appl. nos. 25714/16 and 56328/18, and *Elena Ioppa* v. *Ukraine and 3 Other applications*, Appl. no. 73776/14.

[15] *Armenia* v. *Azerbaijan*, Appl. no. 42521/20; *Armenia* v. *Turkey*, Appl. no. 43517/20; *Azerbaijan* v. *Armenia*, Appl. no. 47319/20; individual applications concern for instance individual captives. See Press release, ECHR 314 (2020), 4 November 2020.

[16] *A contrario*, claiming that States parties 'that wage war, invade or support foreign armed intervention in other member States … must be made judicially accountable for their actions, without prejudice to additional political consequences'. *Cyprus* v. *Turkey* [GC], Appl. no. 25781/94, judgment (just satisfaction) of 12 May 2014, Concurring opinion of Judge Pinto de Albuquerque, joined by Judge Vučinić, 24, para 1.

granted regional human rights courts the competence to hear inter-State claims, the latter should use their available means to proceed with those cases.

7.1.2 *Enforcement*

The enforcement of the conclusions of quasi-judicial bodies enjoys fewer guarantees than that of human rights courts: since their recommendations are non-binding, the monitoring bodies at the most can monitor compliance through a follow-up procedure. In this follow-up procedure the treaty body seeks information from the respondent State and monitors the measures taken by the State Party to give effect to its recommendations on each communication. This is the case of the ACommHPR,[17] although it could decide, if it considers that the State has not complied or is unwilling to comply with its recommendations or provisional measures, to submit the communication to the ACtHPR.[18] The referral to the Court, if the respondent State is party to the Protocol on the Establishment of the ACtHPR,[19] may function as a political threat to enforce the Commission's conclusions. A further possibility is the mere information of the political organs of the African Union (AU), although they have not instituted any enforcement mechanism: the ACommHPR 'shall bring all its recommendations to the attention of the Sub-Committee on the Implementation of the Decisions of the African Union of the Permanent Representatives Committee'.[20] The IACHR can similarly refer the case to the IACtHR in case of non-compliance, if the respondent State has accepted the jurisdiction of the Court,[21] or – as in the *Salas Galindo and Others* v. *United States* case – publish its final report and adopt the follow-up measures it deems appropriate.[22]

As for the enforcement mechanism of regional courts, the ACtHPR can only express its grave concern in case of non-compliance with its provisional measures and judgments.[23] Unlike in the case of the Council of Europe (CoE), there is no enforcement mechanism by the political organs

17 Rules of Procedure of the ACommHPR, Rule 112.

18 Ibid., Rule 118(1)–118(2).

19 Protocol to the African Charter on Human and Peoples' Rights on the Establishment of the African Court on Human and Peoples' Rights, 9 June 1998, OAU/LEG/EXP/AFCHPR/PROT(III) [ACtHPR-Protocol], Articles 3(1) and 5(1)(a).

20 Rules of Procedure of the ACommHPR, Rule 125(2).

21 Rules of Procedure of the IACHR, Article 45.

22 Ibid., Articles 47–48.

23 ACtHPR, Activity report of the African Court for the Year 2013, Executive Council, Twenty-Fourth Ordinary Session, EX.CL/825(XXIV) (21–28 January 2014), para 110 (non-compliance by Libya with provisional measures).

of the AU: the Court is limited to reporting once a year in one of the two annual summits of the Union.[24] The IACtHR's enforcement procedure is special and different from the other regional systems: the Court itself supervises compliance through the submission of reports by the State and observations to those reports by the victims or their representatives, with the observations of the IACHR.[25] However, the Court cannot itself sanction non-compliance and the eventual follow-up by political bodies is similar to the African Court's enforcement mechanism: the IACtHR shall submit to each regular session of the General Assembly of the Organization of American States, for the Assembly's consideration, a report on its work during the previous year and 'specify, in particular, the cases in which a State has not complied with its judgments, making any pertinent recommendations'.[26]

As for the ECtHR, the enforcement mechanism is based on political pressure: the Committee of Ministers, responsible for the supervision of the enforcement of the Court's judgments, might note and condemn the non-compliance with the Court's decision. This was the case in the Cypriot and the Transnistrian cases, both of them involving a frozen conflict and two opposing States. As of 2020 the Turkish and Russian authorities have not yet enforced the *Cyprus* v. *Turkey* (just satisfaction) and *Catan* judgments, respectively, and the Committee of Ministers confined itself to calling on the respondent States to make efforts to comply with the judgments.[27] Other political bodies such as the Parliamentary Assembly may also support the enforcement of the Court's case law. For example, the Assembly 'strongly condemn[ed] instances of outright violations ... of the interim measures in relation to Russia's military actions in Georgia (see *Georgia* v. *Russia II*)'.[28]

As the former president of the ECtHR, Judge Jean-Paul Costa, opined, political sanctions might be more effective in cases of massive human rights violations than the rulings of the Court and, likewise, the frozen conflicts could more effectively be settled through political settlement

[24] ACtHPR-Protocol, Article 31; ACtHPR, Activity report of the African Court for the Year 2013, para 111; however, the ACtHPR expressed its concern and recommended a non-compliance procedure by policy organs of the Union; ibid., paras 113, 127(iii).

[25] Rules of procedure of the IACtHR, Article 69(1).

[26] ACHR, Article 65; Statute of the IACtHR, Article 30.

[27] CM/Del/Dec(2020)1377bis/H46-37, 3 September 2020 (*Cyprus* v. *Turkey*) (just satisfaction not yet executed); CM/Del/Dec(2020)1377bis/H46-29, 3 September 2020 (*Catan*).

[28] CoE Parliamentary Assembly, Resolution 1991 (2014), Urgent need to deal with new failures to co-operate with the European Court of Human Rights, 10 April 2014, para 4.

than by the Court.[29] However, the above-mentioned deficiencies of judicial control mechanisms may be compensated by certain judicial tools promoting individuals' access to courts.

7.2 Promotion of Individuals' Application

7.2.1 *Lis pendens*

Several respondent States invoked the ongoing status talks on the 'grey zone' as a preliminary objection precluding the admissibility of the application. They argued that since the area's status was subject to diplomatic negotiations, there is a *lis pendens*. While *lis pendens* excludes the admissibility of the application before most judicial and quasi-judicial control mechanisms,[30] monitoring bodies have required for identical litigations the same complaint, by the same applicants, on the same legal ground. For instance, the Human Rights Committee held that non-treaty-based (that is, Charter-based) mechanisms instituted by the former Commission of Human Rights or the Human Rights Council, such as the proceedings of the Working Group on Enforced or Involuntary Disappearances or a country visit by a Special Rapporteur, do not constitute 'another procedure of international investigation or settlement'.[31] The ECtHR held that a criterion for the *lis pendens* rule is the submission of another petition lodged formally or substantively by the same applicants, which is not the case with the inter-State status talks conducted under the auspices of an IO such as the OSCE negotiations on Nagorno-Karabakh.[32] Furthermore, the Court limited the *lis pendens* rule to individual applications and seemed to admit parallel inter-State proceedings in inter-State applications.[33] Likewise, the IACHR shall not refrain from considering cases where the pending

[29] Jean-Paul Costa, *La Cour européenne des droits de l'homme: des juges pour la liberté* (Dalloz 2013) 80.

[30] ECHR, Article 35(2)(b); ACHR, Article 46(1)(c); OP-ICCPR, Article 5(2)(a); before the ACommHPR, the communication shall contain information about *lis pendens*: Rules of Procedure of the ACommHPR, Rules 87(2)(b)–(c), 93(2)(j).

[31] HRC, *Halima Louddi* v. *Algeria*, Communication No. 2117/2011, UN Doc. CCPR/C/112/D/2117/2011 (25 November 2014), para 6.2; *Evangeline Hernandez* v. *The Philippines*, Communication No. 1559/2007, UN Doc. CCPR/C/99/D/1559/2007 (20 August 2010), para 6.4.

[32] *Chiragov and Others* v. *Armenia*, Appl. no. 13216/05, decision of 14 December 2011 on the admissibility, para 61.

[33] ECtHR, *Georgia* v. *Russia II*, Appl. no. 38263/08, decision of 13 December 2011 on the admissibility, para 79.

settlement before an IO 'is limited to a general examination of the human rights situation' in the respondent State 'and there has been no decision on the specific facts that are the subject of the petition before the Commission, or it will not lead to an effective settlement'.[34] In the *DRC* v. *Burundi, Rwanda and Uganda* case the Commission examined the exhaustion of local remedies rule, but not the information about any *lis pendens*, although the DRC's inter-state applications against the same States were already pending before the ICJ.[35] These examples demonstrate that IHRL defines *lis pendens* narrowly. Ongoing status talks, non-judicial international human rights mechanisms or fact-finding do not constitute *lis pendens*, as far as they do not constitute submission of the same complaint, by the same applicants, on the same legal ground before judicial or quasi-judicial bodies.

7.2.2 *Exhaustion of Domestic Remedies*

Individuals can have recourse to regional human rights courts only after having exhausted the available domestic remedies, a preliminary condition to all applications.[36] However, in 'grey zones' domestic remedies of both the territorial State and the outside State controlling the area are likely to be unavailable or ineffective. In such cases, human rights courts have interpreted the criterion of the exhaustion of domestic remedies with flexibility, allowing certain exceptions.

Human rights courts generally recognise that the rule of exhaustion of domestic remedies 'must never lead to a halt or delay that would render international action in support of the defenceless victim ineffective'.[37] In other words, the exhaustion rule does not apply in cases of impossibility or unavailability of domestic remedies. For example, the ACHR sets out exceptions to the requirement precisely in situations in which such remedies, for a variety of reasons, are ineffective.[38] The ECtHR similarly recognises that the exhaustion rule 'is neither absolute nor capable of being applied automatically; in reviewing whether it has been observed

[34] Rules of Procedure of the IACHR, Article 33(2)(a).

[35] ACommHPR, *Democratic Republic of Congo* v. *Burundi, Rwanda, Uganda*, Communication no. 227/99, 29 May 2003, para 45 (Uganda's objection).

[36] ACHR, Article 46(1)(a); ECHR, Article 35(1); ACtHPR-Protocol, Article 6(2).

[37] IACtHR, *Case of Velásquez-Rodríguez* v. *Honduras*, judgment of 26 June 1987 (Preliminary Objections), para 93.

[38] E.g. ACHR, Articles 46(2), 56(5).

it is essential to have regard to the particular circumstances of each individual case'.[39]

Specifically in a case related to military invasion, in the *Issa* v. *Turkey* case the Turkish government invoked the exhaustion rule as a preliminary objection, while the Court took into account the fact that the judicial mechanism of the invading State, Turkey, physically and financially was inaccessible to the Iraqi applicants.[40] It noted that the Turkish military authorities remained in Northern Iraq at the time of the killing of the victims for less than three weeks and that they failed to conduct a meaningful investigation into the victims' detention.[41] In these circumstances the Court concluded that 'the applicants were not required under Article 35 §1 of the Convention to apply for an inquiry to the Turkish army authorities in Northern Iraq, this not having been shown to constitute a remedy the existence of which was sufficiently certain in practice'.[42] In a stable occupation, in Nagorno-Karabakh, the ECtHR likewise considered the realities of using domestic remedies, especially the intensity of the hostilities, the hostile rhetoric at the political level and ceasefire breaches. The Court found that, as the occupying power, Armenia denied involvement or jurisdiction, 'it would not be reasonable to expect the applicants to bring claims for restitution or compensation before the Armenian courts and authorities'.[43] Examining the realities on the ground also supposes that the effectiveness of a domestic remedy may change over time and must be reviewed in each case. For instance, the ECtHR held in *Demopoulos and Others* v. *Turkey* that the procedure before the Immovable Property Commission (IPC) set up by the 'TRNC' provided an adequate and effective remedy for Greek Cypriot property claims relating to properties located in Northern Cyprus.[44] In the *Joannou* case, however, it concluded that the non-exhaustion rule did not apply as the IPC did not act with coherence, diligence and appropriate expedition concerning the applicant's compensation claim.[45]

In the *Salas Galindo and Others* v. *US* case the US invoked the exhaustion rule as a ground for inadmissibility, whereas the claimants argued that

[39] ECtHR, *Issa and Others* v. *Turkey*, Appl. no. 31821/96, decision of 30 May 2000 on the admissibility, 7.

[40] Ibid., 6–7. [41] Ibid., 7–8. [42] Ibid., 8.

[43] ECtHR, *Chiragov and Others* v. *Armenia (Merits)* [GC], Appl. no. 13216/05, judgment of 16 June 2015, para 119.

[44] *Demopoulos and Others* v. *Turkey* [GC], Appl. nos. 46113/99 et al., Decision of 1 March 2010 on the admissibility, para 127.

[45] *Joannou* v. *Turkey*, Appl. no. 53240/14, judgment of 12 December 2017, paras 104–106.

domestic remedies were inoperative in the post-invasion conditions.[46] The IACHR found that the US claims programme established to handle claims arising from Panama's invasion was limited to the payment of non-combat-related claims, whereas the petitioners' claims were combat-related and that, therefore, the exhaustion rule did not apply.[47] Likewise, in the *Franklin Guillermo Aisalla Molina* case the State of Colombia argued that the inter-State communication of Ecuador should be declared inadmissible as domestic remedies had not been exhausted before the Colombian courts.[48] The IACHR accepted that the Colombian authorities had initiated a criminal investigation and trial but held that Colombia had failed to discharge the burden of proof upon it as to the effectiveness of those remedies and, thus, Ecuador was exempted from the exhaustion rule.[49]

Since in the *Franklin Guillermo Aisalla Molina* case the victim died and it was the territorial State that presented an inter-State communication, the Commission, as the ECtHR,[50] assumed that the exhaustion rule equally applied in inter-State cases.[51] The ECtHR specified that in inter-State cases the exhaustion rule is inapplicable 'where an administrative practice, namely a repetition of acts incompatible with the Convention and official tolerance by the State authorities, has been shown to exist and is of such a nature as to make proceedings futile or ineffective'.[52] Furthermore, the non-exhaustion rule does not apply where the applicant State does not adopt the cause of one or more of its nationals, but challenges an administrative practice of violations without asking the Court to give a decision on each of the cases put forward as proof or illustrations of that practice.[53] With a less clearer guideline, the ACommHPR likewise held in the *DRC* v. *Burundi, Rwanda and Uganda* case

46 IACHR, Report No. 31/93, Case 10.573, *Salas* v. *United States*, 14 October 1993, paras 13–16, 27–32.

47 Ibid., Analysis, para 14–17.

48 IACHR, Report No. 112/10, Inter-State petition IP-02, *Franklin Guillermo Aisalla Molina, Ecuador* v. *Colombia*, Admissibility, 21 October 2010, OEA/Ser.L/V/II.140, Doc. 10, para 141.

49 Ibid., paras 158, 160.

50 *Georgia* v. *Russia II* (n 33), paras 91–94.

51 *Franklin Guillermo* (n 48), paras 152–160; More expressly, see IACHR, *Nicaragua* v. *Costa Rica*, Report No. 11/07, Interstate case 01/06, 8 March 2007, para 231.

52 ECtHR, *Cyprus* v. *Turkey* [GC], Appl. no. 25781/94, judgment of 10 May 2001, para 99.

53 *Application of the International Convention for the Suppression of the Financing of Terrorism and of the International Convention on the Elimination of All Forms of Racial Discrimination (Ukraine* v. *Russian Federation)*, Preliminary Objections, Judgment, *I.C.J. Reports* 2019, 606, para 130; *Ukraine* v. *Russia (re Crimea)* (n 11), paras 363–365; the Court concluded that such an administrative practice existed in: *Georgia* v. *Russia (II) (Merits)* (n 9), paras 221, 251, 255, 280, 300.

that since 'the violations complained of are allegedly being perpetrated by the Respondent States in the territory of the Complainant State', in the circumstances, 'local remedies do not exist, and the question of their exhaustion does not, therefore, arise'.[54] More generally, the ACommHPR does not apply the exhaustion rule in cases of serious or massive violations, as 'the scale and nature of the alleged abuses, the number of persons involved *ipso facto* make local remedies unavailable, ineffective and insufficient'.[55] In sum, to promote access to international justice, monitoring bodies should consider the particular realities to decide whether effective domestic remedies of the respondent State are available to the petitioner without disproportionate burden.

7.2.3 Priority Policy

A solution for the time-consuming procedure is special treatment given to applications from 'grey zones'. Unlike the African and Inter-American monitoring bodies where the order of the treatment of cases is chronological, based on the petition's submission date, the ECtHR's rules of procedure foresee a priority policy: in determining the order in which cases are to be dealt with, 'the Court shall have regard to the importance and urgency of the issues raised on the basis of criteria fixed by it'.[56] Furthermore, '[t]he Chamber, or its President, may, however, derogate from these criteria so as to give priority to a particular application'.[57] To have regard to the importance and urgency of the issues raised in the cases filed with the Court, the Court has fixed certain criteria that will enable it to give some cases priority before others. Among seven main categories of cases, the two first categories are:

- I Urgent applications (in particular risk to life or health of the applicant, other circumstances linked to the personal or family situation of the applicant, particularly where the well-being of a child is at issue, application of Rule 39 of theRules of Court);
- II Applications raising questions capable of having an impact on the effectiveness of the Convention system (in particular a structural or endemic situation that the Court has not yet examined, pilot-judgment procedure) or applications raising an important question of general interest (in particular a serious question capable of having major

[54] *DRC* v. *Burundi, Rwanda, Uganda* (n 35), para 63.

[55] ACommHPR, *Sudan Human Rights Organisation & Centre on Housing Rights and Evictions (COHRE)* v. *Sudan*, Communication no. 279/03-296/05, 27 May 2009, para 100; *Zimbabwe Human Rights NGO Forum* v. *Zimbabwe*, Communication no. 245/02, 15 May 2006, para 71.

[56] ECtHR, Rules of Court, 1 July 2014, Rule 41. [57] Ibid.

implications for domestic legal systems or for the European system), inter-State cases.[58]

Especially the second category is likely to cover applications submitted from 'grey zones', representing a conflict situation having an impact on the effectiveness of the Convention system, an important question of general interest or an inter-State case. In practice, the Court has prioritised the cases submitted from 'grey zones' such as Transnistria, Nagorno-Karabakh, Crimea or the eastern separatist regions of Ukraine. Some of them, the *Catan*, *Chiragov* and *Sargsyan* cases, had two,[59] while the *Georgia* v. *Russia (II)* case had three hearings[60] – unique in the history of the Court. The prioritisation is further expressed by the referral of the highly-politicised cases concerning 'grey zones' before the Grand Chamber – which was the case in *Loizidou*, *Cyprus* v. *Turkey*, *Ilaşcu*, *Catan*, *Chiragov*, *Sargsyan*, *Mozer*, *Güzelyurtlu*, *Georgia* v. *Russia (II)* and the *Ukraine* v. *Russia* cases related to the events in Crimea or Eastern Ukraine.[61] Furthermore, since thousands of individual applications relate to the Georgian and Ukrainian inter-State cases, the Court has to creatively use its procedural tools (for example, pilot procedure, joined or simultaneous examination of applications) to link together the interconnected legal and factual backgrounds.

Although the massive backlog of cases pending before the ECtHR is not comparable to the number of cases pending before the IACtHR or the ACtHPR, the priority treatment of cases concerning 'grey zones' is exemplary. Should various cases be filed from the same 'grey zone' with any of the regional courts, the latter can order the joinder of the related cases provided that there is commonality of the subject matter[62] such as the same geographic region outside the State's control.

7.2.4 *Facilitation of the Burden of Proof*

Under the classical rules of the burden of proof, the applicant has to prove the violation of human rights and the attributability, whereas the State has to prove that it complied with its obligations. As individuals often do not have access to all the evidence, monitoring bodies have

[58] ECtHR, The Court's priority policy.

[59] The first hearing on 9 June 2009 before the Chamber on admissibility and the merits and the second hearing, on 25 January 2012, before the Grand Chamber.

[60] Press release, ECHR 183 (2018), 23 May 2018.

[61] Press release, ECHR 173 (2018), 9 May 2018.

[62] Rules of procedure of the IACtHR, Article 30; ACtHPR, Rules of the Court, Rule 54; ECtHR, Rules of Court, Rule 42.

recognised that the State's defence cannot be based on the plaintiff's inability to provide evidence when it is the State that controls the means to clarify events that occurred in its territory.[63] Although not a reversal, it is an 'alleviation' of the burden of proof.[64]

Another judicial method of facilitating the applicant's burden of proof is the collection of evidence *ex officio*. Because of the controversial, complicated factual background and the oft-lacking or ineffective domestic remedies in 'grey zones', human rights courts should follow a particularly cautious examination of the facts. An appropriate tool for this could be a fact-finding investigation which the ECHR allows: it provides that the ECtHR shall, 'if need be, undertake an investigation, for the effective conduct of which the High Contracting Parties concerned shall furnish all necessary facilities'.[65] Among the cases related to 'grey zones', the Court effectuated a fact-finding on-the-spot investigation mission in Northern Cyprus and Transnistria. In the fourth *Cyprus* v. *Turkey* inter-State case, the ECommHR appointed three delegates to hear evidence on the Convention issues relating to the general living conditions of the so-called enclaved Greek Cypriots and the situation of Turkish Cypriots living in Northern Cyprus,[66] whereas in the *Ilaşcu* case the Court conducted the on-the-spot investigation 'in order to be able to determine whether Moldova and the Russian Federation had jurisdiction, particularly over the situation in Transdniestria, relations between Transdniestria, Moldova and the Russian Federation, and the applicants' conditions of detention'.[67] Although the Court's use of fact-finding missions has since then decreased mainly because of its huge backlog of pending applications, fact-finding investigation is strongly recommended in 'grey zones' where the State parties 'are not able, or willing, to carry out the essential role of adjudicating on fundamental factual

[63] IACtHR, *Velásquez-Rodríguez* v. *Honduras*, judgment of 29 July 1988 (Merits), para 135; *Case of the Afro-descendant Communities displaced from the Cacarica River Basin (Operation Genesis)* v. *Colombia*, judgment of 20 November 2013 (Preliminary Objections, Merits, Reparations and Costs), para 270; ACtHPR, Application 003/2015, *Kennedy Owino Onyachi* v. *United Republic of Tanzania*, judgment of 28 September 2017, para 143; ECtHR, *Salman* v. *Turkey* [GC], Appl. no. 21986/93, judgment of 27 June 2000, para 100; *Ireziyevy* v. *Russia*, Appl. no. 21135/09, judgment of 2 April 2015, para 57; specifically regarding an area under the effective control of the respondent State: *Ukraine* v. *Russia (re Crimea)* (n 11), para 390.

[64] Costa (n 29) 74. [65] ECHR, Article 38.

[66] *Cyprus* v. *Turkey* (n 52), paras 107, 110, 339–340.

[67] *Ilaşcu and Others* v. *Moldova and Russia* [GC], Appl. no. 48787/99, judgment of 8 July 2004, para 12; Moreover, contrary to most investigation missions, the Transnistrian fact-finding mission was conducted not by three, but by four judges, presided by the section president. See Costa (n 29) 173.

disputes'.[68] The same recommendation applies to the ACtHPR, of which the procedural rules allow for such an enquiry,[69] on the model of the ACommHPR which carried out various fact-finding visits under Article 46 of the African Charter.[70] In the case of the IACtHR, no such investigation mission is possible, but it is the IACHR that can conduct an investigation 'in serious and urgent cases' with the prior consent of the State in whose territory a violation has allegedly been committed.[71]

Other means used to facilitate factual evidence on 'grey zones' may include the authorisation of third party interventions and/or public hearings. Third party intervention[72] enables States, NGOs or IOs to express their position on a given application, which is especially important in *de facto* inter-State cases, understood as individual cases related to a territorial dispute (the territorial State intervening in favour of its citizens against the outside State or, conversely, the outside State intervening against the territorial State). The complicated factual situation may justify the recourse to public hearings where the parties and experts are heard. Procedural rules enable the courts to hold such a hearing when the respective court deems it appropriate to do so,[73] whereas before the ACtHPR it is the rule since the procedure includes an oral phase.[74] Some of the monitoring bodies even allow third parties to participate in the hearing.[75]

7.2.5 *Indirect Justiciability of Non-state Conduct*

International judicial and quasi-judicial human rights bodies are charged to review State conduct and do not have competence *ratione personae* to hear cases against non-state actors such as *de facto* regimes or IOs. It

[68] Philip Leach, Costas Paraskeva and Gordana Uzelac, 'Human Rights Fact-Finding – The European Court of Human Rights at a Crossroads' (2010) 28 *Netherlands Quarterly of Human Rights* 41, 77.

[69] ACtHPR-Protocol, Article 26(1); ACtHPR, Rules of the Court, Rule 45(3).

[70] E.g. *Sudan Human Rights Organisation & Centre on Housing Rights and Evictions (COHRE)* v. *Sudan*, Communication no. 279/03–296/05, 27 May 2009, para 151; Rachel Murray, *The African Charter on Human and Peoples' Rights: A Commentary* (Oxford University Press 2019) 634–636.

[71] ACHR, Article 48(2).

[72] ACtHPR-Protocol, Article 5(2) (States parties); Rules of Procedure of the ACommHPR, Rule 85; ACtHPR, Rules of the Court, Rule 53; ECHR, Article 36; ECtHR, Rules of Court, Rule 44; Rules of Procedure of the IACtHR, Rules 44, 73(3).

[73] Rules of Procedure of the IACtHR, Articles 15, 51; ECtHR, Rules of Court, Rules 63–64.

[74] ACtHPR, Rules of the Court, Rules 27(1), (3) and 43–44.

[75] Rules of Procedure of the ACommHPR, Rule 99(16); ECtHR, Rules of Court, Rule 44(1)(a), (2), (3)(a).

follows that for individuals, the only way to make non-state actors accountable is to initiate judicial or quasi-judicial procedures against States and to establish that the non-State entities' conduct is either attributable to the respondent State, or that the State breached its due diligence duties. Through the analysis of attribution and the material breach committed, human rights courts might draw conclusions, at least *prima facie*, on the material breach of IHRL by non-state actors.

First, by attributing the conduct of the non-state actor to the respondent State, the ECtHR examines the ECHR-conformity of the conduct, law and institutions of the non-state actor from a functional point of view, leaving open the possibility of their lawfulness.[76] The Court may recognise the legitimacy of domestic acts and institutions of *de facto* regimes for the purpose of its procedure provided that they have 'a constitutional and legal basis reflecting a judicial tradition compatible with the Convention' and that their law enforcement is not arbitrary.[77] The Court found that this test had been satisfied and presumed the validity of domestic acts only in respect of the 'TRNC', but not in respect of the 'MRT'.[78] As the Court examines the ECHR compatibility of the conduct of *de facto* regimes only as far as they are attributable to the State, this review falls within its competence.

Second, even if the non-state conduct is not attributable to the State, monitoring bodies might draw conclusions on the material breach of IHRL by the non-state actor, while examining the State's compliance with its due diligence or finding the case inadmissible.[79] This was the case in the *Behrami/Saramati* cases, where the ECtHR considered all the challenged conducts attributable to the UN. Neither the State parties to the dispute nor third party interveners, including the UN itself,[80] challenged the fact that the applicants' human rights under the ECHR had

[76] E.g. *Cyprus* v. *Turkey* (n 52), paras 90–102 (domestic remedies rule); *Ahmet Djavit AN* v. *Turkey*, Appl. no. 20652/92, judgment of 20 February 2003, paras 66–69 (violation of Article 11).

[77] *Ilaşcu and Others* v. *Moldova and Russia* [GC], Appl. no. 48787/99, judgment of 8 July 2004, para 436.

[78] *Foka* v. *Turkey*, Appl. no. 28940/95, judgment of 24 June 2008, paras 82–84 (no violation of Article 5); *Ilaşcu* (n 77), para 436.

[79] E.g. ACERWC, *Michelo Hunsungule and others (on behalf of children in northern Uganda)* v. *Uganda*, Communication No. 001/Com/001/2005, 15–19 April 2013, para 35 (condemnation of the conduct of an AOG).

[80] The UN only contested the attributability of the omission of de-mining. *Behrami/Saramati* [GC], Appl. no. 78166/01, decision of 2 May 2007 on the admissibility, para 119.

been violated. This implied a conclusion on the human rights violations by the UN.

Another case where the ECtHR more clearly recognised the material breach by a peace mission is the *Stichting Mothers of Srebrenica* case. In this case the ECtHR was asked to decide whether The Netherlands violated the applicants' right to remedy by respecting the jurisdictional immunity of the UN in its own courts. While focusing on the State party's obligations with regard to the immunity of the UN, the Court recognised that the only international instrument on which individuals could base their right to remedy against the conduct of the United Nations Protection Force (UNPROFOR) is the Agreement on the status of UNPROFOR in Bosnia and Herzegovina which requires that a claims commission be set up for that purpose.[81] However, since this has not been done, the Court noted that the UN had not ensured any alternative means of remedy for the applicants.[82] The Court also raised the question, while refusing to answer it, of 'whether Article VIII, paragraph 29 of the Convention on the Privileges and Immunities of the United Nations can be construed so as to require a dispute settlement body to be set up in the present case'.[83] Furthermore, another indirect way of recognition of the wrong committed by the UN is the ECtHR's detailed analysis in which the Court recounted the multiple investigative commissions, inquiries and judicial decisions relating to the Srebrenica massacre.[84] This may indicate that the Court was sensitive of the applicants' efforts to bring their claim before the Dutch courts and, albeit only impliedly, it recognised the wrongs committed.[85]

In sum, through the analysis of attribution or the respondent State's due diligence obligations, human rights courts may indirectly examine the lawfulness of non-state actors' conduct. However, such decisions

[81] Ibid., para 162; Agreement on the status of the United Nations Protection Force in Bosnia and Herzegovina, 15 May 1993, Article 48.

[82] *Stichting mothers of Srebrenica and Others* v. *the Netherlands*, Appl. no. 65542/12, para 165.

[83] Ibid., para 165. [84] Ibid., paras 21–53.

[85] Jacob Katz Cogan, 'Stichting Mothers of Srebrenica v. Netherlands. Application No. 65542/12. Decision on Admissibility. At Http://Hudoc.Echr.Coe.Int. European Court of Human Rights, June 11, 2013' (2013) 107 *American Journal of International Law* 884, 890.

might reveal judicial activism beyond the competence of the monitoring body,[86] not to mention their non-enforcability.

7.3 Concluding Remarks

Judicial control mechanisms over State conduct with respect to 'grey zones' have systematic deficiencies that hinder their availability for individuals. However, certain solutions of judicial activism are likely to promote their effectiveness. While the conduct of non-state actors are not justiciable before international judicial control mechanisms, through the analysis of attribution and the material breach committed, monitoring bodies can draw some conclusions on the human rights conformity of the non-state conduct. If the attributability of the conduct to the respondent State is established, judicial control mechanisms are likely to have an impact on the human rights situation in the 'grey zone'.

[86] *Mutatis-mutandis*: HRC, *Mohammad Munaf* v. *Romania*, Communication No. 1539/2006, UN Doc. CPR/C/96/DR/1539/2006 (13 July 2009), Dissenting opinion of Mr. Ivan Shearer, Sir Nigel Rodley and Mr. Yuji Iwasawa (criticizing strategic litigation against a State party to draw attention to violations by a non-Party State).

8 Non-judicial Control Mechanisms

Non-judicial control mechanisms in IHRL are international monitoring proceedings not covered by Chapter 7, where the monitoring body has no competence to give opinions on individual petitions.[1] They include a wide range of human rights accountability mechanisms such as special or periodic reports, advisory opinions, general comments, recommendations, resolutions, fact-finding missions, human rights or humanitarian negotiations, written or oral dialogue and so forth. The chapter focuses on procedures of international human rights monitoring bodies created under multilateral treaties or acts of IOs.

Non-judicial control mechanisms are not characterised by the systemic deficiencies of judicial mechanisms that hinder their availability for individuals. Their procedure is more flexible and open *ratione personae* to address recommendations to States and non-state actors involved in the territorial situation. According to the addressee, non-judicial control mechanisms can monitor the conduct of States (Section 8.1), non-state actors (Section 8.2) and multiple actors (Section 8.3).

8.1 Monitoring States

Non-judicial mechanisms, created primarily to monitor States' compliance with IHRL, can examine the conduct of both the territorial and outside States in the 'grey zone' in two types of procedures: periodic reporting mechanisms (Section 8.1.1) and *ad hoc* mechanisms (Section 8.1.2). While the distinction is based on the regularity of the monitoring,

[1] An important exception is the two internal human rights mechanisms instituted within the international territorial administration of Kosovo, the HRAP and the HRRP, see *infra*, Section 8.2.1.1.

practice shows that both types of mechanisms can effectively influence States' conduct if they rely on an informed examination of local realities and a constructive dialogue.

8.1.1 Periodic Reporting Mechanisms

Most human rights conventions, especially universal treaties, provide for the State parties' obligation to report to the monitoring body on the implementation of the given treaty. Monitoring bodies hold such reporting sessions only twice or three times a year, and members of the committees usually meet for a period of up to three weeks during each session. Whereas the burden of work on the members varies from one committee to the other depending on the number of State parties, the volume of State reports, the reports of civil societies submitted, and other functions of the monitoring body (individual communication procedure, country visits, and so forth), monitoring bodies generally have considerable time constraints. The lack of time, information and resources of monitoring bodies considerably limit periodic reporting about 'grey zones'. Furthermore, the relevant territorial or outside State might be unwilling or unable to cooperate and provide information about highly-politicised questions.[2] Monitoring bodies have answered to these limitations by adopting a proactive approach.

First, periodic reporting has an epistemological problem: committee members are not always aware of the human rights situation in 'grey zones', not even of the member designated as country rapporteur, who by definition cannot be a national of the given State. This epistemological gap can be improved by NGO reports about 'grey zones' submitted to the reporting procedure.

Second, even if the human rights problems of the area are well-known, few rapporteurs make the effort to enquire about 'grey zones' and to address questions to the territorial State when the latter either does not report on the area or makes the usual territorial declaration on the lack of territorial control. Furthermore, the case law on the continuing jurisdiction of the territorial State has not yet been widely disseminated among human rights experts, who are not necessarily lawyers. While considering the report of an outside State, which rarely addresses the

[2] As a historic example, the UNGA had difficulties in exercising political or legal control over South Africa's continued presence in Namibia (South West Africa). *Legal Consequences for States of the Continued Presence of South Africa in Namibia (South West Africa) notwithstanding Security Council Resolution 276 (1970)*, Written statements, Written Statement of the Secretary-General of the United Nations, *I.C.J. Reports* 1970, 95, para 77.

human rights situation in a foreign territory *de facto* under the State's control, committee members may be reluctant to deal with highly-politicised questions and focus rather on the State party's metropolitan territory. Those deficiencies can be addressed by raising the monitoring bodies' awareness about the applicable law and the proactive trend in other reporting mechanisms. Human rights monitoring bodies have interpreted their mandate as covering all territories over which the State has jurisdiction, notwithstanding the status question. For instance, the CESCR decided at an early stage of its operation that it was not competent to receive any information on occupied territories as this might implicitly legitimise the occupation.[3] However, it later revised its decision and decided that Israel could and should 'report on the situation in the occupied territories provided that Israel referred to them as "occupied territories" or it was explicitly stated in the report that those territories were not within the internationally-recognized borders of Israel'.[4]

Third, through a proactive approach, monitoring bodies can influence State practice even if a State is unwilling or unable to cooperate. For instance, Western Sahara, occupied by Morocco, is subject to the periodic reporting mechanism of the ACommHPR. The Sahrawi Arab Democratic Republic, which does not control most of its territory (except for negligible liberated territories and Sahrawi refugee camps), is a State party to the ACHPR and submits reports on its occupied territory to the ACommHPR.[5] The latter, among other recommendations, invited the international community to establish an international human rights monitoring mechanism in the occupied territories.[6] While it is questionable whether it can influence the outside State, as Morocco has not ratified the African Charter, the reporting mechanism can raise awareness and influence third States.

Armed conflict and systemic problems in the administration of the State might hinder the preparation of State reports. In this case, monitoring bodies used to postpone the examination of the report until its

3 CERD, Concluding observations: Israel, UN Doc. A/42/18 (1987), 119–122, para 588.

4 Ibid.

5 ACommHPR, Arab Democratic Sahrawi Republic, Initial Report and Periodic Reports 1 to 6, 1988–2002, 1 December 2002, 33rd Ordinary Session, 15–29 May 2003. Niamey, Niger; ACommHPR, Periodic Report of the Sahrawi Arab Democratic Republic to the African Commission on Human and Peoples' Rights containing all the outstanding reports in accordance with Article 62 of the Charter, October 2011.

6 ACommHPR, Resolution 282: Resolution on the situation in the Sahrawi Arab Democratic Republic, 55th Ordinary Session, 28 April–12 May 2014.

future elaboration. This was the case with Somalia, a genuine failed State, until the end of the Transitional Federal Government in 2012. However, some monitoring bodies have changed this practice and adopted a proactive policy. For instance, the Committee against Torture prepared its Concluding observations on Syria on the basis of available reports after Syria had failed to prepare a special report as required by the Committee.[7] In other words, through an activist approach, monitoring bodies can effectively supervise the human rights situation, raise awareness among the international community and try to influence the State concerned even if the latter's cooperation is lacking.

8.1.2 Ad Hoc *Mechanisms*

Most conventions,[8] resolutions of IOs[9] or rules of procedure[10] of treaty-monitoring bodies provide for the competence to initiate fact-finding inquiries. Universal human rights treaty bodies can do so with regard to State parties having accepted that competence of the monitoring body. Where necessary, and with the consent of the State party, the fact-finding procedure may include a visit to its territory. Within the UN, because of financial and time constraints, growing insecurity in some areas,[11] and the low acceptance of such inquiry competence by States, most treaty-monitoring or Charter-based bodies have not used the inquiry procedure.[12] Furthermore, if the territorial State refuses to authorise an on-site investigation and unless it has a treaty obligation to authorise it,[13] the monitoring body cannot institute an on-site visit.

[7] CAT, Concluding observations: Syrian Arab Republic, UN Doc. CAT/C/SYR/CO/1/Add.2 (29 June 2012).

[8] ECPT, Articles 1–2; CAT, Article 20; OP-CEDAW, Article 8; OP-CRPD, Article 6; CPPED, Article 33; OP-ICESCR, Article 11; Optional Protocol to the Convention on the Rights of the Child on a communications procedure, Article 13.

[9] Resolution Res(2002)8 on the statute of the European Commission against Racism and Intolerance, Article 11(2).

[10] Rules of procedure of the Committee of Experts of the European Charter for Regional or Minority Languages, Article 19.

[11] E.g. Mission report of the Special Rapporteur on the situation of human rights in the Democratic Republic of the Congo et al., UN Doc. E/CN.4/2003/44 (31 December 2002), para 6.

[12] Among UN bodies, by January 2020, three treaty bodies – the CEDAW (five States visited), the CAT (ten States visited), and the CRPD (two States visited) have undertaken confidential inquiries.

[13] E.g. the FRY during the Bosnian war, see Tenth periodic report on the situation of human rights in the territory of the former Yugoslavia, Special Rapporteur of the Commission on Human Rights, UN Doc. E/CN.4/1995/57 (16 January 1995), para 11.

Fact-finding inquiries provide a valuable evidential and awareness-raising tool. First, their conclusions can help international courts to clarify factual complexities: for instance, in the two contentious proceedings related to separatist areas before the ICJ, the *Georgia* v. *Russia* and *Ukraine* v. *Russia* cases, all parties intensively relied on international fact-finding reports. Second, they raise awareness about the human rights situation and might lead to constructive recommendations addressed to the authorities concerned by the monitoring body.

A further advantage of *ad hoc* mechanisms is their informal procedure and flexibility: special procedures of the UN Human Rights Council, such as Special Rapporteurs and other mechanisms of the Office of the UN High Commissioner for Human Rights (UNHCHR), can adapt to the needs of 'grey zones'. As they communicate with all components of the local population, including individuals and NGOs, they can forward credible information to the relevant State through confidential diplomatic channels and draw attention to actual or anticipated human rights violations.[14]

8.2 Monitoring Non-state Actors

Unlike international treaty-monitoring mechanisms that are as a main rule limited to controlling State parties, non-judicial control mechanisms can hold non-state actors accountable. *Ratione personae*, non-judicial human rights mechanisms can monitor the conduct of peace operations (Section 8.2.1) and *de facto* regimes (Section 8.2.2).

8.2.1 Monitoring Peace Operations

Contrary to judicial mechanisms, non-judicial monitoring bodies can supervise the conduct of peace operations without the procedural obstacle of immunity of IOs. Peace operations have been controlled by both internal (Section 8.2.1.1) and external (Section 8.2.1.2) human rights mechanisms, according to the monitoring body's position regarding the peace operation. Whereas peace operations have themselves set up internal mechanisms, other bodies of IOs, especially the UN and the Council of Europe (CoE), have instituted external monitoring mechanisms. As this section will explain, innovative procedures were created as

[14] Human Rights Council, Manual of Operations of the Special Procedures of the Human Rights Council, August 2008, para 28.

a reaction to the enhanced powers of peace operations controlling territory.

8.2.1.1 Internal Monitoring Mechanisms

As all peacekeeping operations, the UNMIK has created a standing claims commission to settle disputes of a private law character arising between the UN mission or any member thereof and private parties. Such claims commissions settled, according to the relevant UNMIK regulation, '[t]-hird party claims for property loss or damage and for personal injury, illness or death arising from or directly attributed to KFOR, UNMIK or their respective personnel and which do not arise from "operational necessity" of either international presence'.[15] Thus, any claim could be rejected under the exception of 'operational necessity', not defined by the regulation.[16] As its scope remained vague and did not fulfil the criterion of legality of admitted limitations under the ECHR,[17] this internal mechanism did not constitute an effective remedy. Following the proposals of the Venice Commission to design mechanisms allowing for adequate remedies,[18] the Special Representative of the Secretary-General (SRSG) in 2006 set up the Human Rights Advisory Panel (HRAP). The Panel's jurisdiction was limited to the violation of the international human rights conventions applicable under the Constitutional Framework, except for the two CoE conventions (the Framework Convention for the Protection of National Minorities (FCPNM) and European Charter for Regional or Minority Languages (ECRML)).[19] The three members of the HRAP were proposed by the President of the ECtHR and nominated by the SRSG.[20]

However, numerous factors limited the HRAP's effectiveness. First, its conclusions had no binding effect, while the SRSG decided on their implementation.[21] Especially in the early years of the Panel's operation, the SRSG did not or only partially complied with the HRAP's

[15] UNMIK/REG/2000/47 (18 August 2000), art. 7

[16] OIK, Special Report no. 1 (18 August 2000), paras 41–43; OSCE Mission in Kosovo, Department of Human Rights and Rule of Law, Property Rights in Kosovo, 2002–2003, 45–46.

[17] OIK, Special Report no. 1 (n 16), para 43.

[18] Venice Commission, Opinion on Human Rights in Kosovo: possible establishment of review mechanisms, Opinion no. 280/2004, CDL-AD(2004)033-e (11 October 2004), paras 114–124.

[19] UNMIK/REG/2006/12 (23 March 2006) on the Establishment of the Human Rights Advisory Panel, Article 1.2.

[20] Ibid., Article 5.1.

[21] Ibid., Articles 1.3 and 17.3.

conclusions.[22] Second, the Panel only examined claims after the petitioner had exhausted available domestic remedies (typically the Standing Claims Commission), thereby obliging individuals to use ineffective procedures.[23] Third, the HRAP was competent *ratione temporis* only as to alleged violations committed after April 2005,[24] excluding a high number of already-pending complaints againts UNMIK.[25] Fourth, human rights treaty-monitoring bodies held that the HRAP lacked the necessary effectiveness, independence and authority.[26] While it was the first human rights mechanism within an international territorial administration, without binding conclusions, the HRAP did not guarantee an effective remedy.

In all cases where the Panel found a human rights violation, it recommended that UNMIK award adequate compensation for non-pecuniary damage. Despite the Panel's innovative mechanism and impressive case law of more than 500 decided complaints, UNMIK followed none of the Panel's recommendations.[27] Opposing the idea of payment of non-material damage, it claimed that '[c]urrent UN General Assembly resolutions do not allow the Organization or its Missions to pay compensation other than for material damage or physical harm'.[28] Beyond payment of financial compensation, UNMIK could have offered a whole range of restorative measures of satisfaction and rehabilitation to the victims.[29]

The Human Rights Review Panel (HRRP), controlling the executive activity of EULEX Kosovo, suffers from similar deficiencies. Its conclusions likewise are non-binding, and deprived of procedural safeguards as the Head of Mission does not have to motivate a decision of

[22] Report of the CoE Commissioner for Human Rights' Special Mission to Kosovo, CommDH (2009)23 (2 July 2009), para 74.

[23] HRAP, *Kadri Balaj et al.* v. *UNMIK*, Case No. 04/07, 31 March 2010, para 55.

[24] UNMIK/REG/2006/12 (23 March 2006), ocit. (n 19), Article 2 (except for continuing violations).

[25] E.g. among other cases, inadmissible *ratione temporis*, the famous Behrami case: *Agim Behrami* v. *UNMIK*, Case No. 24/08, decision of 17 October 2008, paras 13–14.

[26] HRC, Concluding observations: Kosovo (Serbia), UN Doc. CCPR/C/UNK/CO/1 (14 August 2006), para 10; CESCR, Concluding observations: UNMIK, UN Doc. E/C.12/UNK/CO/1 (1 December 2008), para 11.

[27] Marek Nowicki, Christine Chinkin and Françoise Tulkens, 'Final Report of the Human Rights Advisory Panel' (2017) 28 *Criminal Law Forum* 77, 93.

[28] Venice Commission, Opinion on the existing mechanisms to review the compatibility with Human Rights Standards of Acts by UNMIK and EULEX in Kosovo, CDL-AD(2010) 051-e, 21 December 2010, para 45.

[29] Ibid., para 47.

non-compliance.[30] As another important limit of its effectiveness, the HRRP cannot recommend that monetary compensation be paid to the victim.[31] In this regard, the Commission of Venice was of the view that *restitutio in integrum* is the most suitable manner of redress; where it is not possible, the most effective remedy in some cases is financial compensation which, however, the HRRP cannot recommend. The Panel in several cases found that the head of mission failed to provide any financial compensation and concluded with regret that 'where this form or reparation would be appropriate, it would be unavailable to the complainant before the Panel'.[32] In sum, whereas internal review mechanisms in international territorial administration constitute welcome developments, much could still be done to make them an effective remedy.

8.2.1.2 External Monitoring Mechanisms

As a UN subsidiary organ responsible for '[p]rotecting and promoting human rights', the civilian component of the international administration of Kosovo, UNMIK wished to set the example and submitted itself to various human rights treaty mechanisms. First, it accepted the applicability of two CoE conventions, the FCPNM and the European Convention for the Prevention of Torture and Inhuman or Degrading Treatment or Punishment (ECPT), under technical agreements concluded between UNMIK and the CoE in 2004.[33] Under the ECPT, the European Committee for the Prevention of Torture and Inhuman or Degrading Treatment or Punishment (CPT) effectuated three periodic visits to Kosovo, in 2007, 2010 and 2015,[34] examining the human rights situation in police custody, penitentiary establishments and psychiatric/social welfare establishments similarly to its visits to any State party. Under the FCPNM, since its first report of June 2005, UNMIK submitted three further reports, all of them followed by an opinion of the Advisory

[30] Ibid., para 64.

[31] E.g. ibid., para 66; HRRP, *Zahiti* v. *EULEX*, Case No. 2012–14, decision on the implementation of the Panel's recommendations, 11 November 2014, para 16.

[32] HRRP, *Valbone Zahiti* v. *EULEX*, Case No. 2012–14, decision of 4 February 2014, para 66.

[33] *Supra*, Section 4.1.1.2.

[34] Report to the UNMIK on the visit of the CPT from 21 to 29 March 2007, CPT/Inf (2009) 3, 20 January 2009; CPT/Inf (2011) 26, 6 October 2011; CPT/Inf (2016) 23, 8 September 2016.

Committee and a resolution of the Committee of Ministers.[35] While reiterating its usual reference to status neutrality ('[a]ll reference to Kosovo, whether to the territory, institutions or population, in this text shall be understood in full compliance with United Nations Security Council Resolution 1244 and without prejudice to the status of Kosovo') as a precondition of their procedure, both the CPT and the Advisory Committee conducted their periodic reporting procedure essentially in the same way as with any State party. Without further analysis as to the status question, they addressed their recommendations to 'the relevant authorities' or 'the competent authorities' of Kosovo.[36]

Second, universal human rights mechanisms monitored international territorial administration, which had some historic precedents: the United Nations Trusteeship Council mechanisms supervised the UN members administering trust territories. In the context of the unlawful South African presence in Namibia, the Committee on the Elimination of All Forms of Racial Discrimination (CERD) addressed certain recommendations to the UN,[37] based on the latter's responsibility to 'secure the performance of the sacred trust of civilisation'.[38] Between 2006 and 2010 UNMIK also consented, without signing a formal technical agreement, to participate in the reporting mechanism of UN treaty-monitoring bodies similarly to the CoE. Importantly, in 2004 the Serbian government raised the following idea: whereas in its initial report Serbia and Montenegro reported on the situation of human rights in Kosovo and Metohija since the arrival of the United Nations International Forces (1999–2002)[39] on the basis of external sources, it proposed to the Human Rights Committee to invite UNMIK to present a separate report on Kosovo.[40] The Human Rights Committee welcomed the proposal and referred to two similar 'precedents': the ECtHR's *Ilaşcu* judgment, namely, the territorial State's jurisdiction over violations occurring in a region outside its

35 Report submitted by UNMIK, ACFC(2005)003, 2 June 2005; Progress Report, ACFC(2008) 001, 10 December 2008; Progress Report, 3rd Report, 13 September 2012; Progress Report, ACFC(2016)001, 8 March 2016.

36 E.g. Resolution CM/ResCMN(2014)13, 26 November 2014.

37 CERD, UN Doc. A/36/18(SUPP) (1981), 136–137, para 2; UN Doc. A/39/18(SUPP) (1984), 128–129, para 7.

38 *Legal Consequences for States of the Continued Presence of South Africa in Namibia (South West Africa) notwithstanding Security Council Resolution 276 (1970)*, Written Statement of the Secretary-General of the United Nations, *I.C.J. Reports* 1970, 95, para 77.

39 Initial report: Serbia and Montenegro, UN Doc. CCPR/C/SEMO/2003/1 (24 July 2003), Annex.

40 UN Doc. CCPR/C/SR.2206 (6 September 2004), para 9; confirmed in: UN Doc. CCPR/C/SR.2207 (27 July 2004), para 27.

effective control, and the Human Rights Committee's own practice of reporting about a specially-administered region within the State party's reporting proceeding. This has been the case of Hong Kong where the latter's representatives prepare and present the report in the presence of a representative of the People's Republic of China.[41] While admitting that none of these precedents poses exactly the same problems as Kosovo with UNMIK, the Human Rights Committee rightly observed that without any monitoring mechanism over UNMIK, Kosovo remains a 'black hole' that the Human Rights Committee shall remedy as far as possible within its power.[42] Consequently, the Committee invited UNMIK to prepare a report on the situation of human rights in Kosovo for its next session.[43]

Following the first report submitted by UNMIK to the Human Rights Committee in 2006,[44] the Committee criticised several measures taken by UNMIK contrary to the Covenant[45] and addressed various recommendations to UNMIK.[46] Unlike the CoE periodic reporting on Kosovo, the UN dialogue has not continued. While UNMIK presented several follow-up reports,[47] the follow-up procedure ended in December 2013[48] with no new report by UNMIK, despite the request by the Committee.[49]

Other UN treaty bodies followed the practice of the Human Rights Committee: the CESCR,[50] the Committee on the Elimination of All Forms of Discrimination against Women (CEDAW)[51] and the Committee on the

[41] UN Doc. CCPR/C/SR.2206 (n 40), para 46 (Mr. Scheinin). [42] Ibid.

[43] Ibid., para 53; HRC, Concluding observations: Serbia and Montenegro, UN Doc. CCPR/CO/81/SEMO (12 August 2004), para 3.

[44] Report submitted by the UNMIK, UN Doc. CCPR/C/UNK/1 (13 March 2006).

[45] UN Doc. CCPR/C/UNK/CO/1 (n 26), para 10 (e.g. transfer of the Ombudsperson's competence to the HRAP or the unwillingness of UNMIK to comply with the provisional measures ordered by the Ombudsperson).

[46] Ibid., para 8 (e.g. the designation of a competent authority to determine which provisions of the old Yugoslav laws would continue to apply in Kosovo).

[47] Further information received from UNMIK, UN Doc. CCPR/C/UNK/CO/1/Add.1 (1 April 2008); UN Doc. CCPR/C/UNK/CO/1/Add.2 (10 February 2009); UN Doc. CCPR/C/UNK/CO/1/Add.3 (8 December 2009).

[48] Follow-up letter sent to UNMIK, Letter of 2 December 2013, available at http://tbinternet.ohchr.org/Treaties/CCPR/ (visited on 2 March 2015).

[49] HRC, Concluding observations: Serbia, UN Doc. CCPR/C/SRB/CO/2 (20 May 2011), para 3.

[50] CESCR, Concluding observations: Serbia and Montenegro, UN Doc. E/C.12/1/Add.108 (23 June 2005), para 9.

[51] CEDAW, Concluding comments: Serbia, UN Doc. CEDAW/C/SCG/CO/1 (11 June 2007), para 7; General recommendation No. 30 on women in conflict prevention, conflict and post-conflict situations, UN Doc. CEDAW/C/GC/30 (1 November 2013), para 85.

Rights of the Child (CRC)[52] all invited UNMIK to present a report. UNMIK submitted its report on the Committee on Economic, Social and Cultural Rights (CESCR) in 2007, and the CESCR conducted a full periodic reporting procedure, treating UNMIK like any State party.[53] Whereas the Committee made several recommendations and requested further information in the next report,[54] UNMIK has made neither any follow-up, nor any new report since 2008, neither has it prepared any report before the CEDAW or the CRC.

Overall, these limited precedents demonstrate that human rights treaty bodies treated a peace operation controlling territory in every aspect as a State party to the given treaty,[55] and their non-binding Concluding observations could have had a practical impact if duly implemented by the peace operation. However, after some years of fructuous dialogue, UNMIK has lost the political will to continue this mechanism, especially with the transfer of its competences to other actors such as the local Kosovar authorities.

8.2.2 Monitoring De Facto *Regimes*

Traditionally, international human rights supervisory mechanisms are not empowered to monitor the activities of armed opposition group (AOG)/*de facto* regimes, while some monitoring bodies interpreted their mandate broadly by extending it to *de facto* regimes. While doing so, any human rights monitoring body should carefully balance between two competing needs: the pragmatic view to protect human rights notwithstanding the status of the entity, on the one hand, and the risk of the legitimising effect of monitoring *de facto* authorities, on the other.[56] First, pragmatism means that State-centred international human rights instruments should be interpreted according to the everyday circumstances of the 'grey zone', requiring *de facto* authorities to comply with IHRL.[57] Engaging with *de facto* authorities sometimes is the only way to ensure the international protection of human rights in the area under their control. Second, to minimise the risk of legitimisation, international monitoring bodies should conduct their procedure in a

52 CRC, Concluding observations: Serbia, UN Doc. CRC/C/SRB/CO/1 (20 June 2008), para 6.

53 E.g. CESCR, Concluding observations: UNMIK, UN Doc. E/C.12/UNK/CO/1 (1 December 2008).

54 Ibid., e.g. paras 23, 24, 25, 33.

55 UN Doc. CCPR/C/UNK/CO/1 (n 26), para 24.

56 International Council on Human Rights Policy, *Ends & Means: Human Rights Approaches to Armed Groups*, 2000, 50.

57 Manual of Operations of the Special Procedures (n 14), para 81.

transparent and status-neutral way, that is, without expressing any opinion about the legal status of the region or the *de facto* authorities.[58] Dialogue with a *de facto* regime requires the (at least tacit) consent of the territorial State. The designation of the *de facto* authorities as terrorist organisations by the latter, therefore, might severely restrict the operation of human rights mechanisms.[59]

Based on pragmatism, the idea of monitoring *de facto* regimes in a periodic reporting mechanism was first raised during the Bosnian war in 1992 in respect of the Bosnian Serb authorities. A member of the Human Rights Committee proposed to include in the periodic report of Bosnia and Herzegovina information about the areas controlled by the Bosnian Serb *de facto* authorities and to call on them to explain how they apply the provisions of the International Covenant on Civil and Political Rights (ICCPR).[60] Although the majority of the Committee did not consider this proposal appropriate, the idea has reappeared in other monitoring mechanisms.

Because of its flexibility and general competence, not limited to States parties to particular conventions, the UN High Commissioner for Human Rights has monitored certain 'grey zones' with or without the presence in the field: it could monitor the human rights situation in areas where it set up field offices such as in Colombia and the non-government-controlled areas of Eastern Ukraine,[61] and in other areas where it relied on open access sources such as Abkhazia and South Ossetia.[62]

Some regional treaty bodies have also extended their monitoring mechanism to areas controlled by *de facto* regimes. Within the CoE, the CPT is the only treaty body having examined in substance the practice and the domestic law of a *de facto* regime, that of Transnistria. Whereas the CPT examines by means of visits the treatment of persons deprived of liberty, followed by the preparation of a report in consultation with the

58 E.g. ibid., para 82; Report of the Secretary-General to the Security Council on the protection of civilians in armed conflict, UN Doc. S/2001/331 (30 March 2001), para 49; Report on Human Rights in the Transnistrian Region of the Republic of Moldova, by Thomas Hammarberg, Senior Expert, 14 February 2013 [2013 Hammarberg Report], 1.

59 E.g. in Colombia: Report of the Secretary-General to the Security Council on the protection of civilians in armed conflict, UN Doc. S/2004/431 (28 May 2004), para 41.

60 HRC, UN Doc. CCPR/C/SR.1178/Add.1 (19 January 1993), para 12 (Mr. Müllerson).

61 E.g. Report on the human rights situation in Ukraine 16 May to 15 August 2018, UN Doc. A/HRC/39/CRP.5 (21 September 2018), para 18, n 9.

62 Report of the United Nations High Commissioner for Human Rights on cooperation with Georgia, UN Doc. A/HRC/36/65 (17 August 2017); UN Doc. A/HRC/39/44 (15 August 2018).

State concerned,[63] the systematic and regular nature of the visits makes its procedure a periodic reporting mechanism.[64] Between 2000 and 2010 the CPT visited the militia detention centres and penitentiary institutions of Transnistria four times. In its procedure the CPT followed the same mechanism as it does with States: it examined the criminal and criminal procedural law applicable in the region, legal and administrative safeguards against the ill-treatment of persons deprived of their liberty, and the practice of local authorities.[65] On the model of the CPT, the UN Subcommittee on Prevention of Torture also interpreted its mandate as covering *de facto* regimes.[66]

The difficulty with such periodic reporting on *de facto* regimes is the highly-politicised nature of preparing each visit. The monitoring body has to obtain the authorisation of both the territorial State and the *de facto* authorities to effectuate the visit. Therefore, whenever there is a renewal of political tensions between the two sides, either side might revoke its authorisation, which happened during a CPT visit in Transnistria.[67] For similar reasons, since 2010 there have been no further visits effectuated in Transnsitria, although the secretariat of the CPT keeps regular communication with the *de facto* authorities.[68] Likewise, after the CPT could visit detention centres of Abkhazia in 2009[69] and the Georgian government unilaterally published the report, the Abkhazian and South-Ossetian *de facto* regimes decided to revoke their cooperation with the CPT.[70]

Ad hoc mechanisms such as UN special procedure mandate holders, working groups or fact-finding missions can extend their monitoring to *de facto* regimes more flexibly than periodic reporting mechanisms. Due to their informal procedure, these mechanisms may engage in a scrupulous analysis of the legal instruments and practice of *de facto* authorities and address the recommendations without the need to keep a certain

63 ECPT, Articles 1, 10–11. 64 ECPT, Article 7(1).

65 Report on the visit to the Transnistrian region of the Republic of Moldova, CPT/Inf (2002) 35, 12 December 2002. The visit was followed by other visits in 2003, 2006 and 2010 (interrupted).

66 CAT, UN Doc. CAT/C/SR.1531 (11 May 2017), para 11; Subcommittee on Prevention of Torture and Other Cruel, Inhuman or Degrading Treatment or Punishment, Visit to Ukraine, UN Doc. CAT/OP/UKR/3 (18 May 2017), para 8.

67 Report to the Government of the Republic of Moldova on the visit to Prison Establishment No. 8 in Bender, CPT/Inf (2008) 37 (4 December 2008), paras 4–5.

68 CPT/Inf (2011) 8, 3 March 2011, para 3.

69 Report on the visit to the region of Abkhazia, Georgia, CPT/Inf (2009) 38, 23 December 2009.

70 Interview with Dr. Haritini Dipla, Member of the CPT, Geneva, 12 December 2014.

regularity. For instance, the Working Group on Enforced or Involuntary Disappearances,[71] the Special Rapporteur on Freedom of Religion or Belief,[72] the Special Rapporteur on Torture and Other Cruel, Inhuman or Degrading Treatment or Punishment[73] and the Representative of the Secretary-General on the Human Rights of Internally Displaced Persons[74] all visited separatist areas and addressed recommendations to the *de facto* authorities. Others addressed written communications to *de facto* authorities.[75] Despite the flexibility of these *ad hoc* procedures, they lack follow-up and, thus, long-term dialogue.

In this regard, the dialogue instituted by UN Senior Expert Thomas Hammarberg with the Transnistrian *de facto* authorities is groundbreaking. He paid extensive visits to the region for fact-finding purposes in May, September and November 2012, and prepared a 50-page report with 38 observations on a wide range of rights-related issues and 38 recommendations.[76] His 2013 report covered all major issues of human rights, not limited to any specific domain that Special Rapporteurs usually are mandated to examine. The method followed by the Senior Expert is exemplary for any control mechanism: he conducted a transparent dialogue with the 'MRT', the Government of the Republic of Moldova and civil society organisations, and at the end of each visit there was a meeting with the Transnistrian leadership at which the Expert presented his preliminary observations. Due to the mutual confidence, *de facto* authorities cooperated with the Expert.[77] He organised a further visit

[71] Report of the Working Group on Enforced or Involuntary Disappearances on their visit to Ukraine, UN Doc. A/HRC/42/40/Add.2 (9 August 2019).

[72] Report of the Special Rapporteur on freedom of religion or belief, Heiner Bielefeldt, UN Doc. A/HRC/16/53/Add.1 (14 February 2011), paras 6–24 (Nagorno-Karabakh); Report of the Special Rapporteur on freedom of religion or belief, Heiner Bielefeldt, UN Doc. A/HRC/19/60/Add.2 (27 January 2012), paras 19, 59, 69, 87 (Transnistria).

[73] Report of the Special Rapporteur on torture and other cruel, inhuman or degrading treatment or punishment, Manfred Nowak, Mission to the Republic of Moldova, UN Doc. A/HRC/10/44/Add.3 (12 February 2009), e.g. paras 19–22, 60–61, 64, 71, 78 (Transnistria); Follow-up report of the Special Rapporteur on torture and other cruel, inhuman or degrading treatment or punishment, Juan E. Méndez, UN Doc. A/HRC/19/61/Add.3 (1 March 2012), 312, para 121, and 356–357, 398–399 (Transnistria).

[74] Report of the Representative of the Secretary-General on the human rights of internally displaced persons, Walter Kälin, Addendum, Mission to Georgia (21–24 December 2005), UN Doc. E/CN.4/2006/71/Add.7 (24 March 2006) (Abkhazia/South Ossetia).

[75] E.g. Letter of the Special Rapporteur on extrajudicial, summary or arbitrary executions, Case No. OTH 8/2012, UN Doc. A/HRC/22/67 (20 February 2013), 79 (addressing to Palestine and the Gaza authorities).

[76] 2013 Hammarberg Report (n 58).

[77] Ibid.

in 2018 in order to assess progress in the implementation process after five years, leading to a follow-up report.[78] In sum, transparency and full cooperation with all stakeholders made his *ad hoc* mission successful, as several positive developments and unilateral commitments of *de facto* authorities showed.[79]

These pragmatic procedures to a large extent treated *de facto* regimes as States since they analysed their laws and policies, identifying concerns about their human rights conformity. Transparent and status-neutral dialogue can ensure the consent of both the territorial (and outside) State and the *de facto* authorities, which are preconditions of any on-site visit.

8.3 Monitoring Multiple Actors

Unlike (quasi-)judicial mechanisms, the competence of non-judicial monitoring bodies is not limited to examining individual petitions but can follow a holistic approach about the territorial situation. Their flexible competence *ratione personae* allows the simultaneous examination of the conduct of all international law subjects implicated in the area. To effectively address the human rights situation, international monitoring bodies should examine the effectiveness of all possible international law subjects implicated, including the territorial State, *de facto* authorities or peace missions and any outside State controlling the area. Human rights monitoring bodies should remind them, depending on their effectiveness, of their concurrent international obligations and maintain a dialogue with all of them. As a welcome development, UN monitoring bodies have started to address recommendations to multiple actors.[80] In various regions, however, human rights monitoring bodies are not aware of the factual situation: to remedy this information gap, it is crucial that reporting States, individuals and civil societies provide credible information on the international law subjects implicated in the area and their effectiveness.

[78] Follow-up Report on Human Rights in the Transnistrian Region by Thomas Hammarberg, Senior UN Human Rights Expert, 2018.

[79] 2013 Hammarberg Report (n 58), 4 (releases of prisoners or reduction of their sentences), 6 (pledge to develop non-custodial punishments), 23 (pledge to develop non-custodial punishments).

[80] E.g. Report on the mission carried out by Mr. Roberto Garretón, Special Rapporteur on the situation of human rights in the Democratic Republic of the Congo, UN Doc. E/CN.4/2001/40/Add.1 (27 March 2001), para 90; UN Doc. A/HRC/42/40/Add.2 (n 71), paras 82–96; Case No. OTH 8/2012 (n 75).

8.4 Concluding Remarks

Non-judicial mechanisms should not be seen isolated from, but together with judicial human rights mechanisms. Their factual and legal conclusions can inspire judicial control mechanisms. Furthermore, they may provide support for the observance of judicial control mechanisms, especially if the given treaty body actively discusses the enforcement of international judgments.[81] Compared to judicial bodies, their advantage is that they can follow a holistic approach, monitoring the conduct of all international law subjects implicated in the area. Non-judicial control mechanisms could exert an influence on the addressee, States or a non-state actor controlling the 'grey zone', and on the international community. A constructive dialogue with those subjects might be more effective than decisions of (quasi-)judicial mechanisms.

[81] E.g. HRC, Concluding observations: Israel, UN Doc. CCPR/C/ISR/CO/4 (21 November 2014), para 17(d) (reference to the ICJ's *Wall* AO); UN Doc. CERD/C/SR.1861 (23 February 2010), para 61 (enforcement of *Ilascu*).

9 General Conclusions

The analysis of the applicability and implementation of international human rights law (IHRL) in areas beyond State territorial control shows that IHRL can normalise an imperfect, defective situation through pragmatic interpretation, as it imposes obligations both on the territorial State on account of its sovereign title and residual effectiveness, on the one hand, and on any subject of international law exercising territorial control over the area, on account of its effective control, on the other. These expected obligations vary according to the legal status of the subject (a State, a *de facto* regime or an international organisation (IO)) under international law and IHRL, and the factual circumstances that determine its effectiveness in the specific area. Therefore, the applicability of international human rights norms no longer is exclusively determined by formal sources of law because legal bindingness, it is argued, can be generated by effectiveness. By considering effectiveness beyond formal normative sources and titles of the subjects implicated in the territorial situation, IHRL is interpreted and applied in a manner that renders human rights practical and effective in matters of the applicability and scope of international human rights obligations, international responsibility for their breaches and international monitoring mechanisms.

This normalising role of IHRL has an important limit, the rights of States under general international law, and three hidden consequences: the effective use of the residual powers by the territorial State; the consolidation of the subject *de facto* controlling the area; and an activism required from multiple actors.

9.1 The Rights of States under General International Law

The normalising effect of IHRL is limited not only by the actual effectiveness of the duty-bearer subject, that is by facts, but also by general international law norms protecting the sovereign interests of States. Such norms are the principles of territorial integrity, the independence of States, non-interference, non-recognition of territorial acquisitions or special advantages obtained by force.

Several scenarios indicate the inherent tensions between those general international law norms and human rights in areas beyond State territorial control. First, the European Court of Human Rights (ECtHR)'s unqualified formulation on the territorial State's general obligation to take measures 'at its disposal to re-establish its control over' its territory might collude with the State's status settlement negotiations, defence and military strategies.[1] Second, territorial States and their citizens often argue that the obligation not to recognise as lawful situations resulting from the serious breach of peremptory norms excludes the exhaustion of domestic remedies rule.[2] The latter would otherwise impliedly legitimise acts and remedies available in a *de facto* regime. Third, territorial States and their citizens claim that the obligation of non-recognition equally excludes that settlers, that is, individuals who moved to the area through population transfers in breach of international humanitarian law (IHL), enjoy the protection of IHRL.[3] Fourth, they also invoke the territorial State's sovereign interests as a limit to its positive obligations to cooperate with *de facto* authorities in preventing or investigating human rights violations.[4] Fifth and finally, outside States controlling part of the territory of another State often restrict human rights in the area or deny cooperation with international human rights monitoring bodies for reasons of state security.[5]

Human rights monitoring bodies answered to these challenges by balancing human rights with general international norms protecting the sovereign interests of States, imposing positive obligations within those limits. In other words, human rights obligations shall be interpreted and applied in the triangle of IHRL-effectiveness-general

[1] *Supra*, Section 3.1.4.2.

[2] *Supra*, Section 7.2.2; another similar example is the tension between the general international law obligation of non-recognition and the protection of human rights in administrative acts and everyday transactions; *supra*, Section 3.1.4.1.

[3] *Supra*, Section 3.1.6.

[4] *Supra*, Section 3.1.5.4.

[5] *Supra*, Sections 3.2.3.4 and 8.2.2 (applicable to both *de facto* regimes and outside States controlling the territory of another State).

international law. The examples confirm that general international law norms protecting sovereign interests of States, rather than conflicting with or weakening IHRL, constitute legitimate thresholds as to the scope of human rights obligations. By balancing human rights with those general international norms protecting the sovereign interests of the State, IHRL ultimately promotes the 'rights of States'.

9.2 Reinforcement of the Territorial State

As contradictory as it seems, the bindingness of IHRL on the territorial State, often characterised as the 'failing State' on account of its lacking territorial control, contributes to the consolidation of that State. To a situation where subjects other than the territorial State control the area, international law answers by reiterating the territorial State's primary role: when monitoring bodies confirm the continued jurisdiction of the territorial State *vis-à-vis* individuals situated in a region beyond its control, they do so in order to reinforce the State's activism *vis-à-vis* the population of the territory. While requiring the State to take all appropriate measures in its power at the legal, political, economic and diplomatic level, IHRL contributes to the reconstitution of an ideal State, namely, a proactive State which protects individuals in its sovereign territory. The presumption of the State's jurisdiction over its entire territory is in harmony not only with the object and purpose of human rights conventions (the 'Convention legal space' and the elimination of 'vacuums' at the regional level, the principle of universality at the universal level) but also with the general international law obligation of due diligence or the concept 'responsibility to protect'. This ideal corresponds to the adage of Carl Schmitt that '[t]he *protego ergo obligo* is the *cogito ergo sum* of the state', changing the principle of Descartes.[6]

Two examples confirm the effect of IHRL on the reinforcement of the territorial State: the Republic of Moldova and Colombia. First, as a consequence of the *Ilaşcu* judgment, the Moldovan government took a series of structural measures to comply with its positive obligations. For instance, it allocated resources to the education of Moldovan pupils of Transnistria; the Moldovan diplomacy invoked questions of human rights in its foreign relations; national judges had to participate in countless training courses related to their obligations in conformity with

[6] Carl Schmitt, *The Concept of the Political* (Expanded ed, University of Chicago Press 2007) 52.

the *Ilaşcu* judgment; and so forth.[7] Second, in Colombia, thanks to the systematic application of Colombia's obligation of due diligence, the Colombian Council of State's case law guaranteed just satisfaction for a number of victims of the 'demilitarised enclave'.[8] Due to these positive actions, those territorial States have become more protective, if not stronger than before, *vis-à-vis* individuals situated in their 'grey zones'. The above-mentioned measures of national authorities satisfy IHRL and helped to remedy human rights violations at the national level.

9.3 Consolidation of Other Subjects

Beyond the territorial State, IHRL imposes obligations, on account of its effectiveness, on the subject *de facto* controlling the territory, be it an outside State or a non-state actor, a *de facto* regime or IO. The logic behind this pragmatism is that it is only the subject exercising territorial control that primarily is in the position to protect human rights on the spot. While doing so, IHRL normalises an imperfect situation, on the one hand, but also consolidates it, on the other. In other words, by binding subjects *de facto* controlling the territory, IHRL contributes to the persistence of 'frozen conflicts' with a view to making them more viable for the local population. The underlying rationale is that the stabilisation of an imperfect situation always is more favourable to the protection of human rights than the escalation of the conflict.

On the one hand, imposing human rights obligations on the subject administering the territory expresses no judgment on the territory's status or the lawfulness of the situation. Human rights monitoring bodies act under this principle called status neutrality. On the other hand, the respect for IHRL makes the territorial control by the given subject more acceptable in the eyes of the international community and, arguably, thus contributes to its legitimisation. This is particularly the case of non-state actors controlling the area: the local authorities under the administration of a peace operation or a *de facto* regime get closer to statehood, of which the ideal model is the democratic State respecting human rights.[9]

[7] *Supra*, Sections 2.2.2.3, 3.1.4.2, 3.1.5.1 and 3.1.5.2. [8] *Supra*, Section 5.2.2.3.

[9] It suffices to cite the political criteria of recognition in this sense, formulated by the member States of the EC: Declaration of the European Council on the Guidelines on the Recognition of New States in eastern Europe and in the Soviet Union, 16 December 1991, in: UN Doc. A/46/804 (18 December 1991), Annex.

Imposing obligations on international law subjects on account of their effectiveness can only normalise the situation if it is duly implemented in monitoring mechanisms. International monitoring bodies have also shown that pragmatism prevails over status questions: they have chosen the most suitable mechanism depending on the local relatities, irrespective of the legal title of the subject over the area. For instance, the dialogue between *de facto* authorities and human rights monitoring bodies is mainly informal, *ad hoc* and non-judicial, because of most States' preoccupation not to legitimise the territorial situation. As the visits of several human rights experts demonstrated, even such an *ad hoc* dialogue can produce positive effects.[10]

9.4 Activism Required from Multiple Actors

A consequence of taking into account the local realities is the concurrent obligations of multiple actors involved in the territorial situation who owe both negative and positive obligations towards individuals in the 'grey zone'.

At the heart of the territorial State's obligations, the obligation of due diligence expects an obligation of conduct, namely, the protection of human rights in the 'grey zone' as far as possible, against acts committed by third parties, including local authorities controlling the area. The limit of the State's positive obligations is its effectiveness or capabilities to prevent and mitigate the wrongful act: it is bound to take measures as far as possible, within the limits of its political, legal, diplomatic, military and economic capabilities.

The obligations of the outside State controlling the area are comparable to those binding it in its national territory, while their degree has to be interpreted functionally, according to the State's effectiveness in the area. The limitations of human rights that the outside State can apply must be understood narrowly: first, derogation may be applied under the strict conditions foreseen by the treaties. Second, IHRL must be 'accommodated, as far as possible', with applicable IHL as the recent case law does.[11]

Beyond States, IHRL is opposable towards non-state actors controlling the territory on account of their effectiveness and enshrined in various

[10] E.g. the positive developments and unilateral undertakings of *de facto* authorities after the visits of the Senior Expert in Transnistria, *supra*, Section 8.2.2.

[11] *Hassan* v. *United Kingdom* [GC], Appl. no. 29750/09, judgment of 16 September 2014, para 104.

alternative sources. Peace operations accepted such duties mainly in intrinsic legal sources. Their obligations present some specificity due to their jurisdictional immunity as a limitation of the right to remedy. Likewise, the international community increasingly recognises certain obligations of *de facto* regimes under IHRL, mainly derived from IHL, be it in the form of general international law, treaty obligations, acts of IOs or obligations voluntarily assumed by *de facto* regimes. Unlike peace operations, the specificity of their obligations results from their unrecognised status. Both non-state actors controlling territory have positive obligations to maintain public order and safety in the territory, comparable to the obligations of the occupying State which imply the same obligations of due diligence.

While the promotion of a 'direct horizontal effect' of obligations under IHRL might provide the States with an excuse for further human rights violations (the *tu quoque* argument), this threat is eliminated by the recognition of the parallel human rights obligations of subjects. In other words, the obligations imposed on non-state actors are parallel and complementary to the primary responsibility of States, and especially that of the territorial State.

The activism required from multiple subjects directly involved in the territorial situation has the consequence that individuals and human rights monitoring bodies also have to actively evaluate local relatities and engage concurrent responsibilities of those actors. Individuals and international monitoring bodies are encouraged to exploit the effectivenesss of the international law subjects implicated in the situation and establish their obligations and responsibility on that basis in all available international control mechanisms. In this regard, the case of lead-contaminated Roma camps in Kosovo is an instructive example.

Between 1999 and 2013 the Office of the United Nations High Commissioner for Refugees housed approximately 600 members of Roma, Ashkali and Egyptian families, displaced during the Kosovo conflict, in camps constructed on lead-contaminated toxic wasteland in the area of Mitrovica. Consequently, internally-displaced Roma were living in deplorable sanitary conditions and suffered from serious health problems due to their overexposure to heavy metals. After the United Nations Interim Administration Mission in Kosovo (UNMIK) administered the camps between 2001 and 2008, the Kosovo authorities took over the administration, and only closed down the camps between 2010 and 2013. In 2006 a non-governmental organisation (NGO) filed an application with the European Court of Human Rights (ECtHR) on behalf of the victims against UNMIK, as the *de facto* administration of Kosovo, which the Court rejected as inadmissible *ratione personae*, in line with *Behrami/ Saramati*.[12] Likewise, the UN Office of Legal Affairs rejected a third party claim against the UN, concluding that the request should be directed against UNMIK.[13] In 2016 the Human Rights Advisory Panel (Kosovo) (HRAP) found UNMIK responsible for the violation of various human rights of 138 members of three communities, recommending UNMIK to take appropriate steps towards payment of adequate individual compensation to the victims.[14] Meanwhile, the claimants also challenged the omission to initiate inquiries and to provide legal remedies by EULEX Kosovo; for its part, the Human Rights Review Panel (Kosovo) (HRRP) confirmed these violations and made some recommendations so that the head of mission could remedy them.[15] NGOs sent letters to several other human rights monitoring bodies such as the UN High Commissioner for Human Rights and various Special Rapporteurs whose mandate concerned the case,[16] whereas the UN Special Rapporteur on Toxics and Human Rights urged several organisations within the UN system to contribute to mobilising the necessary resources to provide the victims with effective remedies.[17] As a result, the UN Secretary-General in 2017 created a voluntary trust fund for community assistance projects to help the affected minority communities, although the received contribution falls short of the required resources to provide remedies to the victims.[18] While far from leading to effective remedies, the instigation of available international mechanisms helped to clarify the international obligations and responsibility of multiple subjects.

[12] European Court of Human Rights Has No Jurisdiction in Kosovo Lead Poisoning Case, European Roma Rights Centre, Press release, 3 April 2006, www.errc.org/article/european-court-of-human-rights-has-no-jurisdiction-in-kosovo-lead-poisoning-case/2568 (visited 9 July 2015).

[13] HRRP, *X. and 115 other complainants* v. *EULEX*, Case No. 2011-20, decision of 22 April 2015, para 36.

[14] HRAP, *N.M. and Others* v. *UNMIK*, Case No. 26/08, 26 February 2016, para 349.

[15] HRRP, *X. and 115 other complainants* v. *EULEX*, Case No. 2011-20, decision of 22 April 2015.

[16] European Roma Rights Centre, Press release (n 12).

[17] Letters addressed by the Special Rapporteur to the leaders of several organisations in the UN system, 13 March 2019, www.ohchr.org/EN/Issues/Environment/ToxicWastes/Pages/LeadContaminationKosovo.aspx (visited 10 February 2020).

[18] The UN Secretary General's reply, 4 October 2019, ibid.

It would be unrealistic to expect that IHRL eliminates the existence of 'grey zones'. The phenomenon will persist until a political deal settles the status of the area. Rather than extending the applicability of IHRL, lawyers should pragmatically interpret the existing legal framework within the limits of general international law. Within the triangle of IHRL-effectiveness-general international law, IHRL can normalise the situation and provide for viable legal solutions.

Bibliography

Abebe AM, 'Special Rapporteurs as Law Makers: The Developments and Evolution of the Normative Framework for Protecting and Assisting Internally Displaced Persons' (2011) 15 *The International Journal of Human Rights* 286.

Anzilotti D, 'La Responsabilité Internationale Des États à Raison Des Dommages Soufferts Par Des Étrangers' (1906) 13 *Revue générale de droit international public* 5.

Arai Y, *The Law of Occupation: Continuity and Change of International Humanitarian Law, and Its Interaction with International Human Rights Law* (Martinus Nijhoff Publishers 2009).

Ardila FM, 'La Responsabilidad Interacional Del Estado Por Actos de Particulares: Análisis Jurisprudencial Interamericano', in Comite Editorial Ministerios de Relaciones Exteriores, *Debate Interamericano* (Ministerio de Relaciones Exteriores 2009).

Baty T, 'Can an Anarchy Be a State' (1934) 28 *American Journal of International Law* 444.

Ben-Naftali O and Shany Y, 'Living in Denial: The Application of Human Rights in the Occupied Territories' (2004) 1 *Israel Law Review* 17.

Benvenisti E, 'Occupation, Pacific', in *Max Planck Encyclopedia of Public International Law* (Oxford University Press 2009).

'The Laws of Occupation and Commercial Law Reform in Occupied Territories: A Reply to Jose Alejandro Carballo Leyda' (2012) 23 *European Journal of International Law* 199.

Benzing M, 'Midwifing a New State: The United Nations in East Timor' (2005) 9 *Max Planck Yearbook of United Nations Law* 295.

'International Administration of Territories', in *Max Planck Encyclopedia of Public International Law* (Oxford University Press 2010).

Bianchi A, 'The Act of the State: The State of the Act Judicial Interpretation and Human Rights Enforcement', in MG Kohen (ed.), *Promoting Justice, Human Rights and Conflict Resolution through International Law: Liber Amicorum Lucius Caflisch* (Martinus Nijhoff Publishers 2007).

Binder C and Lachmayer K, 'Introduction. The Reception of Public International Law in the Jurisprudence of the European Court of Human Rights: Sign of Fragmentation or Unity?' in C Binder and K Lachmayer (eds.), *The European Court of Human Rights and Public International Law: Fragmentation or Unity?* (Nomos-Verl-Ges 2014).

Bjorge E, 'Human Rights, Treaties, Third-Party Effect', in *Max Planck Encyclopedia of Public International Law* (Oxford University Press 2011).

Bothe M, 'Peacekeeping Forces', in *Max Planck Encyclopedia of Public International Law* (Oxford University Press 2016).

Brand M, 'Effective Human Rights Protection When the UN "Becomes the State": Lessons from UNMIK', in ND White and D Klaasen (eds.), *The UN, Human Rights and Post-Conflict Situations* (Manchester University Press 2005).

Brems E, *Human Rights: Universality and Diversity*, vol 66 (Martinus Nijhoff Publishers 2001).

Brusa E, 'Responsabilité Des Etats à Raison Des Dommages Soufferts Par Des Étrangers En Cas d'emeute Ou de Guerre Civile' (1898) XVIII *Annuaire de l'Institut de Droit international* 96.

Cahin G, *La coutume internationale et les organisations internationales: l'incidence de la dimension institutionnelle sur le processus coutumier* (Pedone 2001).

'L'État défaillant en droit international: quel régime pour quelle notion?', in *Droit du pouvoir, pouvoir du droit: mélanges offerts à Jean Salmon* (Bruylant 2007).

Cameron L, 'Human Rights Accountability of International Civil Administrations to the People Subject to Administration' (2007) 2 *Human Rights & International Legal Discourse* 267.

Cassese A, 'The Status of Rebels under the 1977 Geneva Protocol on Non-International Armed Conflicts' (1981) 30 *International & Comparative Law Quarterly* 416.

'The Nicaragua and Tadić Tests Revisited in Light of the ICJ Judgment on Genocide in Bosnia' (2007) 18 *European Journal of International Law* 649.

Cerone J, 'Minding the Gap: Outlining KFOR Accountability in Post-Conflict Kosovo' (2001) 12 *European Journal of International Law* 469.

'Human Dignity in the Line of Fire: The Application of International Human Rights Law during Armed Conflict, Occupation, and Peace Operations' (2006) 39 *Vanderbilt Journal of Transnational Law* 1447.

Chesterman S, 'Unaccountable? The United Nations, Emergency Powers, and the Rule of Law' (2009) 42 *Vanderbildt Journal of Transnational Law* 1509.

Clapham A, *Human Rights Obligations of Non-State Actors* (Oxford University Press 2006).

'The Subject of Subject and the Attribution of Attribution', in LB de Chazournes and MG Kohen (eds.), *International Law and the Quest for Its Implementation: Liber Amicorum Vera Gowlland-Debbas* (Brill 2010).

Clunan AL and Trinkunas HA (eds.), *Ungoverned Spaces: Alternatives to State Authority in an Era of Softened Sovereignty* (Stanford Security Studies 2010).

Cogan JK, 'Stichting Mothers of Srebrenica v. Netherlands. Application No. 65542/12. Decision on Admissibility. At Http://Hudoc.Echr.Coe.Int. European

Court of Human Rights, June 11, 2013' (2013) 107 *American Journal of International Law* 884.

Cohen-Jonathan G, 'Responsabilité pour atteinte aux droits de l'homme', in Société française pour le droit international (ed.), *La responsabilité dans le système international. Société française pour le droit international, colloque du Mans, [31 mai–2 juin 1990]* (A Pedone 1991).

'La Territorialisation de La Juridiction de La Cour Européenne Des Droits de l'homme' (2002) 52 *Revue trimestrielle des droits de l'homme* 1069.

Cohen-Jonathan G and Flauss J-F, 'Cour Européenne Des Droits de l'homme et Droit International Général' (2004) 50 *Annuaire français de droit international* 778.

Condorelli L, 'L'imputation à l'Etat d'un Fait Internationalement Illicite: Solutions Classiques et Nouvelles Tendences' (1984) 189 *Recueil des Cours* 9.

Condorelli L and Kress C, 'The Rules of Attribution: General Considerations', in J Crawford, A Pellet and S Olleson (eds.), *The Law of International Responsibility* (Oxford University Press 2010).

Constantinides A, 'Human Rights Obligations and Accountability of Armed Opposition Groups: The Practice of the UN Security Council' (2010) 4 *Human Rights & International Legal Discourse* 89.

Corten O, 'Le Rapport de La Mission d'enquête Internationale Indépendante Sur Le Conflit En Géorgie' (2010) 114 *Revue générale de droit international public* 35.

Corten O and Klein P, 'Are Agreements between States and Non-State Entities Rooted in the International Legal Order?', in E Cannizzaro (ed.), *The Law of Treaties beyond the Vienna Convention* (Oxford University Press 2011).

Costa J-P, 'L'Etat, Le Territoire et La Convention Européenne Des Droits de l'homme', in *Promoting Justice, Human Rights and Conflict rResolution through International Law: liber amicorum Lucius Caflisch = La promotion de la justice, des droits de l'homme et du règlement des conflits* (Martinus Nijhoff Publishers 2007).

La Cour européenne des droits de l'homme: des juges pour la liberté (Dalloz 2013).

Cowan A, 'A New Watershed? Re-Evaluating Banković in Light of Al-Skeini' (2012) 1 *Cambridge Journal of International and Comparative Law* 213.

Crawford J, *State Responsibility: The General Part* (Cambridge University Press 2013).

Cullen A and Wheatley S, 'The Human Rights of Individuals in De Facto Regimes under the European Convention on Human Rights' (2013) 13 *Human Rights Law Review* 691.

Dannenbaum T, 'Translating the Standard of Effective Control into a System of Effective Accountability: How Liability Should Be Apportioned for Violations of Human Rights by Member State Troop Contingents Serving as United Nations Peacekeepers' (2010) 51 *Harvard International Law Journal* 113.

D'Argent P, *Les réparations de guerre en droit international public: la responsabilité internationale des États à l'épreuve de la guerre* (Bruylant 2002).

D'Aspremont J and De Hemptinne J, *Droit international humanitaire: thèmes choisis* (A Pedone 2012).

D'Aspremont J and Tranchez E, 'The Quest for a Non-Conflictual Coexistence of International Human Rights Law and Humanitarian Law: Which Role for the

Lex Specialis Principle?', in R Kolb and G Gaggioli (eds.), *Research Handbook on Human Rights and Humanitarian Law* (Edward Elgar 2013).

De Schutter O, 'Globalization and Jurisdiction: Lessons from the European Convention on Human Rights' (2006) 6 *Baltic Yearbook of International Law* 185.

De Schutter O, Eide A, Khalfan A, Orellana M, Salomon M and Seiderman I, 'Commentary to the Maastricht Principles on Extraterritorial Obligations of States in the Area of Economic, Social and Cultural Rights' (2012) 34 *Human Rights Quarterly* 1084.

De Visscher C, *Theory and Reality in Public International Law* (Percy Ellwood Corbett tr, Princeton University Press 1957).

Degan VD, *Sources of International Law* (Martinus Nijhoff Publishers 1997).

Dennis MJ, 'Application of Human Rights Treaties Extraterritorially in Times of Armed Conflict and Military Occupation' (2005) 99 *American Journal of International Law* 119.

'Non-Application of Civil and Political Rights Treaties Extraterritorially during Times of International Armed Conflict' (2007) 40 *Israel Law Review* 453.

Dinstein Y, *The International Law of Belligerent Occupation* (Cambridge University Press 2009).

Dopagne F, 'La Responsabilité de l'Etat Du Fait Des Particuliers: Les Causes d'imputation Revisitées Par Les Articles Sur La Responsabilité de l'Etat Pour Fait Internationalement Illicite' (2001) 34 *Revue Belge de Droit International* 492.

Dudai R, 'Closing the Gap: Symbolic Reparations and Armed Groups' (2011) 93 *International Review of the Red Cross* 783.

Dumberry P, 'New State Responsibility for Internationally Wrongful Acts by an Insurrectional Movement' (2006) 17 *European Journal of International Law* 605.

Eagleton C, *The Responsibility of States in International Law* (New York University Press 1928).

'Expert Meeting: Occupation and Other Forms of Administration of Foreign Territory' (International Committee of the Red Cross 2012). Available from: www.icrc.org/eng/assets/files/publications/icrc-002-4094.pdf (accessed 8 April 2021).

Ferraro T, 'Determining the Beginning and End of an Occupation under International Humanitarian Law' (2012) 94 *International Review of the Red Cross* 133.

'The Law of Occupation and Human Rights Law: Some Selected Issues' in R Kolb and G Gaggioli (eds.), *Research Handbook on Human Rights and Humanitarian Law* (Edward Elgar 2013).

Fitzmaurice M, 'The History of Article 38 of the Statute of the International Court of Jusice. The Journey from the Past to the Present', in J d'Aspremont, S Besson and S Knuchel (eds.), *The Oxford Handbook of the Sources of International Law* (Oxford University Press 2017).

Fleck D, 'The Law of Non-International Armed Conflicts', in D Fleck (ed.), *The Handbook of International Humanitarian Law* (Oxford University Press 2008).

Forteau M, 'Le droit applicable en matière des droits de l'homme aux administrations territoriales gérées par des organisations internationales', in H Ascensio and J-F Flauss (eds.), *La soumission des organisations internationales aux normes internationales relatives aux droits de l'homme* (Société française pour le droit international 2009).

'Organisations internationales et sources du droit', in É Lagrange and J-M Sorel (eds.), *Droit des organisations internationales* (LGDJ-Lextenso éditions 2013).

Fortin K, *The Accountability of Armed Groups under Human Rights Law* (Oxford University Press 2017).

Frouville O de, 'Ilaşcu et Autres c. Moldova et Russie' (2005) 109 *Journal du droit international* 472.

Frowein JA, *Das De facto-Regime im Völkerrecht: eine Untersuchung zur Rechtsstellung nichtanerkannter Staaten und ähnlicher Gebilde* (C Heymann 1968).

'De Facto Regime', in *Max Planck Encyclopedia of Public International Law* (Oxford University Press 2013).

García Amador y Rodríguez FV, Sohn LB and Baxter RR, *Recent Codification of the Law of State Responsibility for Injuries to Aliens* (Oceana Publications 1974).

Giustiniani FZ, 'New Hopes and Challenges for the Protection of IDPs in Africa: The Kampala Convention for the Protection and Assistance of Internally Displaced Persons in Africa' (2010) 39 *Denver Journal of International Law and Policy* 347.

Gottmann J, *The Significance of Territory* (University Press of Virginia 1973).

Gowlland-Debbas V, 'Is the UN Security Council Bound by Human Rights Law? Remarks' (2009) 103 *American Society of International Law Proceedings* 199.

Grant TD, 'EJIL: Talk! – Ukraine v. Russian Federation in Light of Ilaşcu: Two Short Points' (*EJIL: Talk!*, 22 May 2014). Available from: www.ejiltalk.org/ukraine-v-russian-federation-in-light-of-ilascu-two-short-points/ (accessed 15 January 2018).

Griebel J, *Die Zurechnungskategorie der De-facto-Organe im Recht der Staatenverantwortlichkeit* (Lit 2004).

Grotius H, *The Rights of War and Peace: Including the Law of Nature and Nations* (AC Campbell tr, MW Dunne 1901).

Hakimi M, 'State Bystander Responsibility' (2010) 21 *European Journal of International Law* 341.

Heijer M den and Lawson R, 'Extraterritorial Human Rights and the Concept of "Jurisdiction"', in M Langford, W Vandenhole and M Scheinin (eds.), *Global Justice, State Duties: the Extraterritorial Scope of Economic, Social, and Cultural Rights in International Law* (Cambridge University Press 2013).

Henckaerts J-M and Doswald-Beck L, *Customary International Humanitarian Law*, vol 1 (Rules) Comité international de la Croix-Rouge (ed.) (Cambridge University Press 2005).

Hessbruegge JA, 'Introductory Note to the European Court of Human Rights: Catan and Others v. Moldova and Russia' (2012) 52 *International Legal Materials* 217.

Hill-Cawthorne L, 'Humanitarian Law, Human Rights Law and the Bifurcation of Armed Conflict' (2015) 64 *International & Comparative Law Quarterly* 293.

Irmscher TH, 'The Legal Framework for the Activities of the United Nations Administration Mission in Kosovo: The Charter, Human Rights, and the Law of Occupation' (2001) 44 *German Yearbook of International Law* 353.

Istrefi K, 'Azemi v Serbia: Discontinuity of Serbia's de Jure Jurisdiction over Kosovo' (2014) 4 *European Human Rights Law Review* 388.

Jacob P, 'L'imputation d'un fait à l'Etat en droit international de la responsabilité' (Thèse de doctorat, Université de Rennes 2010).

Jashari J, 'U.N. Field Missions in the Context of Legal and Judicial Reform: The Kosovo Case' (2007) 1 *Columbia Journal of East European Law* 76.

Jorritsma R, 'Where General International Law Meets International Humanitarian Law: Attribution of Conduct and the Classification of Armed Conflicts' (2018) 23 *Journal of Conflict and Security Law* 405.

Kajtár G, *A Nem Állami Szereplők Elleni Önvédelem a Nemzetközi Jogban [Self-Defence against Non-State Actors in International Law]* (ELTE Eötvös Kiadó 2015).

Kalala T, *Les résolutions de l'ONU et les destinataires non étatiques* (Larcier 2009).

Karagiannis S, 'Le Territoire d'application de La Convention Européenne Des Droits de l'homme. Vetera et Nova' (2005) 61 *Revue trimestrielle des droits de l'homme* 33.

'Article 29', in O Corten and P Klein (eds.) *Les Conventions de Vienne sur le droit des traités: commentaire article par article*, vol 2 (Bruylant 2006).

Kelsen H, *Principles of International Law* (Rinehart 1952).

Khalfan A, 'Division of Responsibility amongst States', in M Langford, W Vandenhole and M Scheinin (eds.) *Global Justice, State Duties: The Extraterritorial Scope of Economic, Social, and Cultural Rights in International Law* (Cambridge University Press 2013).

Kidane W, 'Managing Displacement by Law in Africa: The Role of the New African Union IDPS Convention' (2011) 44 *Vanderbilt Journal of Transnational Law* 1.

King H, 'The Extraterritorial Human Rights Obligations of States' (2009) 9 *Human Rights Law Review* 521.

Kleffner JK, 'The Collective Accountability of Organised Armed Groups for System Crimes', in A Nollkaemper and H van der Wilt (eds.) *System Criminality in International Law* (Cambridge University Press 2009).

Klein P, 'Responsabilité Pour Les Faits Commis Dans Le Cadre d'opérations de Paix et Étendue Du Pouvoir de Contrôle de La Cour Européenne Des Droits de l'homme: Quelques Considérations Critiques Sur l'arrêt Behrami et Saramati' (2007) 53 *Annuaire français de droit international* 43.

'The Attribution of Acts to International Organizations', in J Crawford, A Pellet and S Olleson (eds.) *The Law of International Responsibility* (Oxford University Press 2010).

Koivurova T, 'Due Diligence', in *Max Planck Encyclopedia of Public International Law* (Oxford University Press 2010).

Kolb R, Porretto G and Vité S, *L'application du droit international humanitaire et des droits de l'homme aux organisations internationales: forces de paix et administrations civiles transitoires* (Bruylant 2005).

Koutroulis V, *Le début et la fin de l'application du droit de l'occupation* (Pedone 2010).

'The Application of International Humanitarian Law and International Human Rights Law in Situation of Prolonged Occupation: Only a Matter of Time?' (2012) 94 *International Review of the Red Cross* 165.

Kuijer M and Werner WG, 'The Paradoxical Place of Territory in International Law' (2016) *Netherlands Yearbook of International Law* 3.

Kulesza J, *Due Diligence in International Law* (Brill Nijhoff 2016).

Lagrange E, 'L'application de La Convention de Rome à Des Actes Accomplis Par Les Etats Parties En Dehors Du Territoire National' (2008) 112 *Revue générale de droit international public* 521.

Lagrange P, 'Responsabilité Des Etats Pour Actes Accomplis En Application Du Chapitre VII de La Charte Des Nations Unies – Observations à Propos de La Décision de La Cour Européenne Des Droits de l'homme (Grande Chambre) Sur La Recevabilité Des Requêtes Behrami et Behrami c. France et Saramati c. Allemagne, France et Norvège, 31 Mai 2007' (2008) 112 *Revue générale de droit international public* 85.

Lamb RD, *Ungoverned Areas and Threats from Safe Havens: Final Report of the Ungoverned Areas Project* (Office of the Under Secretary of Defense for Policy (OUSD(P)) 2008).

Larsen KM, 'Attribution of Conduct in Peace Operations: The "Ultimate Authority and Control" Test' (2008) 19 *European Journal of International Law* 509.

'Territorial Non-Application of the European Convention on Human Rights' (2009) 78 *Nordic Journal of International Law* 73.

The Human Rights Treaty Obligations of Peacekeepers (Cambridge University Press 2012).

Laval P-F, 'A Propos de La Juridiction Extraterritoriale de l'Etat. Observations Sur l'arrêt Al-Skeini de La Cour Européenne Des Droits de l'homme Du 7 Juillet 2011' (2012) 116 *Revue générale de droit international public* 61.

Leach P, Paraskeva C and Uzelac G, 'Human Rights Fact-Finding – The European Court of Human Rights at a Crossroads' (2010) 28 *Netherlands Quarterly of Human Rights* 41.

Leyda JAC, 'The Laws of Occupation and Commercial Law Reform in Occupied Territories: Clarifying a Widespread Misunderstanding' (2012) 23 *European Journal of International Law* 179.

Melzer N and International Committee of the Red Cross, *Interpretive Guidance on the Notion of Direct Participation in Hostilities under International Humanitarian Law* (International Committee of the Red Cross 2009).

Milanovic M, 'State Responsibility for Genocide' (2006) 17 *European Journal of International Law* 553.

Extraterritorial Application of Human Rights Treaties: Law, Principles, and Policy (Oxford University Press 2011).

'Al-Skeini and Al-Jedda in Strasbourg' (2012) 23 *European Journal of International Law* 121.

'Grand Chamber Judgment in Catan and Others' (*EJIL: Talk!*, 21 October 2012). Available from: www.ejiltalk.org/grand-chamber-judgment-in-catan-and-others/ (accessed 7 June 2013).

'The Spatial Dimension: Treaties and Territory' in CJ Tams, A Tzanakopoulos and A Zimmermann (eds.) *Research Handbook on the Law of Treaties* (Edward Elgar Publishing 2014).

Milanovic M and Papić T, 'The Applicability of the ECHR in Contested Territories' (2018) 67 *International and Comparative Law Quarterly* 779.

Miller S, 'Revisiting Extraterritorial Jurisdiction: A Territorial Justification for Extraterritorial Jurisdiction under the European Convention' (2009) 20 *European Journal of International Law* 1223.

Moir L, *The Law of Internal Armed Conflict* (Cambridge University Press 2002).

Moore JB, *History and Digest of the International Arbitrations to which the United States Has Been a Party*, vol 3 (Government Printing Office 1898).

Murphy R, *UN Peacekeeping in Lebanon, Somalia and Kosovo: Operational and Legal Issues in Practice* (Cambridge University Press 2007).

Murray D, *Human Rights Obligations of Non-State Armed Groups* (Hart Publishing 2016).

Murray R, *The African Charter on Human and Peoples' Rights: A Commentary* (Oxford University Press 2019).

Nollkaemper A, 'Universality', in *Max Planck Encyclopedia of Public International Law* (Oxford University Press 2011).

Nowicki M, Chinkin C and Tulkens F, 'Final Report of the Human Rights Advisory Panel' (2017) 28 *Criminal Law Forum* 77.

Ó Beacháin D, Comai G and Tsurtsumia-Zurabashvili A, 'The Secret Lives of Unrecognised States: Internal Dynamics, External Relations, and Counter-Recognition Strategies' (2016) 27 *Small Wars & Insurgencies* 440.

Oberleitner G, *Human Rights in Armed Conflict: Law, Practice, Policy* (Cambridge University Press 2015).

Oxman BH, 'Jurisdiction of States', in *Max Planck Encyclopedia of Public International Law* (Oxford University Press 2007).

Palchetti P, *L'organo di fatto dello Stato nell'illecito internazionale* (Giuffrè Editore 2007).

'Les Autorités Provisoires de Gouvernement (PISG) Du Kosovo, EULEX et ONU: Les Principes d'attribution à l'épreuve' (2013) 47 *Revue belge de droit international* 45.

Pasqualucci JM, *The Practice and Procedure of the Inter-American Court of Human Rights* (Cambridge University Press 2003).

Pellet A, 'L'imputabilité d'éventuels actes illicites - Responsabilité de l'OTAN ou des Etats membres?', in C Tomuschat (ed.), *Kosovo and the International Community: a Legal Assessment* (2002).

Petculescu I, 'La Contribution Du Droit International de La Responsabilité à La Protection Des Droits de l'homme. L'arrêt de La Cour Européenne Des Droits de l'homme Du 8 Juillet 2004 Dans l'affaire Ilascu et Autres c. La République de Moldova et La Fédération de Russie' (2005) 109 *Revue Générale de Droit International Public* 581.

Peters A, 'Extraterritorial Naturalizations: Between the Human Right to Nationality, State Sovereignty and Fair Principles of Jurisdiction' (2010) 53 *German Yearbook of International Law* 623.

'Article 25', in B Simma, D-E Khan, G Nolte and A Paulus (eds.), *The Charter of the United Nations: A Commentary* (3rd ed., Oxford University Press 2012).

Pictet J, *Le Droit Humanitaire et La Protection Des Victimes de La Guerre* (Sijthoff 1973).

Pictet J, Siordet F and International Committee of the Red Cross, *Geneva Convention for the Amelioration of the Condition of the Wounded and Sick in Armed Forces in the Field: Commentary* (International Committee of the Red Cross 1952).

Pisillo-Mazzeschi R, 'The Due Diligence Rule and the Nature of the International Responsibility of States' (1992) 35 *German Yearbook of International Law* 9.

'Responsabilité de l'Etat Pour Violation Des Obligations Positives Relatives Aux Droits de l'homme' (2008) 333 *Recueil des cours de l'Académie de droit international de La Haye* 175.

Polakiewicz J, 'Collective Responsibility and Reservations in a Common European Human Rights Area', in I Ziemele (ed.), *Reservations to Human Rights Treaties and the Vienna Convention Regime: Conflict, Harmony or Reconciliation* (2004).

Pound R, 'Standards in International Law' (1921) 34 *Harvard Law Review* 776.

Prezas I, *L'administration de collectivités territoriales par les Nations Unies: étude de la substitution de l'organisation internationale à l'État dans l'exercice des pouvoirs de gouvernement* (Anthemis 2012).

Rabasa A, Boraz S and Chalk P, *Ungoverned Territories: Understanding and Reducing Terrorism Risks* (RAND 2007).

Ratner SR, 'Foreign Occupation and International Territorial Administration: The Challenges of Convergence' (2005) 16 *European Journal of International Law* 695.

'Sources of International Humanitarian Law and International Criminal Law', in J d'Aspremont, S Besson and S Knuchel (eds.), *The Oxford Handbook of the Sources of International Law* (Oxford University Press 2017).

Reinold T, 'State Weakness, Irregular Warfare, and the Right to Self-Defense Post-9/11' (2011) 105 *American Journal of International Law* 244.

Reuter P, 'La responsabilité internationale. Problèmes choisis (1955-1956)', in *Le développement de l'ordre juridique international: écrits de droit international* (Économica 1995).

Reymond J, *L'attribution de comportements d'organes de facto et d'agents de l'Etat en droit international: étude sur la responsabilité internationale des Etats* (Schulthess 2013).

Röben V, 'Conference (Meeting) of States Parties', in *Max Planck Encyclopedia of Public International Law* (Oxford University Press 2010).

Rodenhäuser T, *Organizing Rebellion: Non-State Armed Groups under International Humanitarian Law, Human Rights Law, and International Criminal Law* (Oxford University Press 2018).

Rodley NS, 'Can Armed Opposition Groups Violate Human Rights?', in KE Mahoney and P Mahoney (eds.), *Human Rights in the Twenty-first Century: A Global Challenge* (Martinus Nijhoff Publishers 1993).

Ronchi P, 'The Borders of Human Rights' (2012) 128 *Law Quarterly Review* 20.

Ronen Y, 'Territory, Lease', in *Max Planck Encyclopedia of Public International Law* (Oxford University Press 2008).

'Human Rights Obligations of Territorial Non-State Actors' (2013) 46 *Cornell International Law Journal* 21.

Roxstrom E, Gibney M and Einarsen T, 'The NATO Bombing Case (Bankovic et al. v. Belgium et al.) and the Limits of Western Human Rights Protection' (2005) 23 *Boston University International Law Journal* 55.

Ryngaert C, 'Human Rights Obligations of Armed Groups' (2008) 41 *Revue belge de droit international* 355.

Salmon J, *Dictionnaire de droit international public* (Bruylant 2001).

Sandoz Y, Swinarski C and Zimmermann B (eds.), *Commentary on the Additional Protocols of 8 June 1977 to the Geneva Conventions of 12 August 1949* (Martinus Nijhoff Publishers 1987).

Sarooshi D, *The United Nations and the Development of Collective Security: The Delegation by the UN Security Council of its Chapter VII Powers* (Clarendon Press 1999).

Sassòli M, 'Article 43 of The Hague Regulations and Peace-Operations in the Twenty-First Century' (2004) Background Paper prepared for Informal High-Level Expert Meeting on Current Challenges to International Humanitarian Law. Available at: www.hpcrresearch.org/sites/default/files/publications/sassoli.pdf (accessed 25 August 2013).

'Legislation and Maintenance of Public Order and Civil Life by Occupying Powers' (2005) 16 *European Journal of International Law* 661.

'The Approach of the Eritrea-Ethiopia Claims Commission towards the Treatment of Protected Persons in International Humanitarian Law', in A De Guttry, HHG Post and G Venturini (eds), *The 1998–2000 War between Eritrea and Ethiopia. An International Law Perspective* (TMC Asser Press 2009).

'Taking Armed Groups Seriously: Ways to Improve Their Compliance with International Humanitarian Law' (2010) 1 *International Humanitarian Legal Studies* 5.

Schaefer M, 'Al-Skeini and the Elusive Parameters of Extraterritorial Jurisdiction' (2011) 5 *European Human Rights Law Review* 566.

Schindler D, 'Human Rights and Humanitarian Law' (1981) 31 *American University Law Review* 935.

Schmitt C, *The Concept of the Political* (expanded ed., University of Chicago Press 2007).

Schoiswohl M, 'De Facto Regimes and Human Rights Obligations - The Twilight Zone of Public International Law' (2001) 6 *Austrian Review of International and European Law* 45.

Schwelb E, 'Civil and Political Rights: The International Measures of Implementation' (1968) 62 *American Journal of International Law* 827.

Sicilianos L-A, 'L'(ir)responsabilité des forces multinationales?', in LB de Chazournes and MG Kohen (eds.), *International Law and the Quest for Its Implementation: Liber Amicorum Vera Gowlland-Debbas* (Brill 2010).

Silvanie H, 'Responsibility of States for Acts of Insurgent Governments' (1939) 33 *American Journal of International Law* 78.

Sivakumaran S, 'Re-Envisaging the International Law of Internal Armed Conflict' (2011) 22 *European Journal of International Law* 219.

The Law of Non-International Armed Conflict (Oxford University Press 2012).

Soldati A, *La responsabilité des États dans le droit international* (Libr de Jurisprudence ancienne et moderne E Duchemin 1934).

Sorathia SR, 'Behrami v. France: An Unfortunate Step Backwards in the Protection of Human Rights' (2011) 26 *Maryland Journal of International Law* 271.

Sperotto F, 'The International Security Presence in Kosovo and the Protection of Human Rights' (2008) 48 *Human Rights & Human Welfare Working Papers* 1.

Stahn C, 'The United Nations Transitional Administrations in Kosovo and East Timor: A First Analysis' (2001) 5 *Max Planck Yearbook of United Nations Law* 105.

Talmon S, *Kollektive Nichtanerkennung illegaler Staaten: Grundlagen und Rechtsfolgen einer international koordinierten Sanktion dargestellt am Beispiel der Türkischen Republik Nord-Zypern* (Mohr Siebeck 2006).

'The Responsibility of Outside Powers for Acts of Secessionist Entities' (2009) 58 *International & Comparative Law Quarterly* 493.

Tanzi A, 'Necessity, State Of', in *Max Planck Encyclopedia of Public International Law* (Oxford University Press 2013).

Thienel T, 'Georgian Conflict, Racial Discrimination and the ICJ: The Order on Provisional Measures of 15 October 2008' (2009) 9 *Human Rights Law Review* 465.

Tomuschat C, 'The Applicability of Human Rights Law to Insurgent Movements', in *Krisensicherung und humanitärer Schutz: Festschrift für Dieter Fleck* (Berliner Wissenschatfs-Verlag 2004).

Tsagourias N, 'Non-State Actors, Ungoverned Spaces and International Responsibility for Cyber Acts' (2016) 21 *Journal of Conflict and Security Law* 455.

Tzevelekos VP, 'The Use of Article 31(3)(C) of the VCLT in the Case Law of the ECtHR: An Effective Anti-Fragmentation Tool or a Selective Loophole for the Reinforcement of Human Rights Teleology – Between Evolution and Systemic Integration' (2009) 31 *Michigan Journal of International Law* 621.

'Reconstructing the Effective Control Criterion in Extraterritorial Human Rights Breaches: Direct Attribution of Wrongfulness, Due Diligence, and Concurrent Responsibility' (2014) 36 *Michigan Journal of International Law* 129.

Ulfstein G, 'Les activités normatives de l'organisation internationale' in É Lagrange and J-M Sorel (eds.), *Droit des organisations internationales* (LGDJ-Lextenso éditions 2013).

UNOHCHR, *International Legal Protection of Human Rights in Armed Conflict* (United Nations 2011).

Vandewiele T, *Optional Protocol: The Involvement of Children in Armed Conflicts* (Martinus Nijhoff Publishers 2006).

Vanneste F, *General International Law before Human Rights Courts: Assessing the Speciality Claims of International Human Rights Law* (Intersentia 2010).

Verhoeven SI, 'International Responsibility of Armed Opposition Groups: Lessons from State Responsibility for Actions of Armed Opposition Groups', in N Gal-Or, M Noortmann and C Ryngaert (eds.), *Responsibilities of the Non-State Actor in Armed Conflict and the Market Place* (Brill 2015).

Villiger ME, *Commentary on the 1969 Vienna Convention on the Law of Treaties* (Brill 2009).

Vité S, 'L'applicabilité Du Droit International de l'occupation Militaire Aux Activités Des Organisations Internationales' (2004) 86 *International Review of the Red Cross* 9.

Vitzthum W and Proelß A (eds.), *Völkerrecht* (6. Auflage, De Gruyter Lehrbuch 2013).

Walter C, 'Subjects of International Law', in *Max Planck Encyclopedia of Public International Law* (Oxford University Press 2007).

Waters C, 'Law in Places That Don't Exist' (2006) 34 *Denver Journal of International Law and Policy* 401.

Watkin K, 'Use of Force during Occupation: Law Enforcement and Conduct of Hostilities' (2012) 94 *International Review of the Red Cross* 267.

Wilde R, 'The Extraterritorial Application of International Human Rights Law on Civil and Political Rights', in S Sheeran and Sir N Rodley (eds.) *Routledge Handbook of International Human Rights Law* (1st ed., Routledge 2013).

Yudkivska G, 'Territorial Jurisdiction and Positive Obligations of an Occupied State: Some Reflections on Evolving Issues Under Article 1 of the European Convention', in A van Aaken and I Motoc (eds.) *The European Convention on Human Rights and General International Law* (Oxford University Press 2018).

Zegveld L, *Accountability of Armed Opposition Groups in International Law* (Cambridge University Press 2002).

Zwanenburg M, Bothe M and Sassòli M, 'Is the Law of Occupation Applicable to the Invasion Phase?' (2012) 94 *International Review of the Red Cross* 29.

Index

CAMBRIDGE STUDIES IN INTERNATIONAL AND COMPARATIVE LAW: 156

Books in the Series

156 *International Human Rights Law Beyond State Territorial Control*
Antal Berkes

155 *The Crime of Aggression under the Rome Statute of the International Criminal Court*
Carrie McDougall

154 *Minorities and the Making of Postcolonial States in International Law*
Mohammad Shahabuddin

153 *Preclassical Conflict of Laws*
Nikitas E. Hatzimihail

152 *International Law and History: Modern Interfaces*
Ignacio de la Rasilla del Moral

151 *Marketing Global Justice: The Political Economy of International Criminal Law*
Christine Schwöbel-Patel

150 *International Status in the Shadow of Empire*
Cait Storr

149 *Treaties in Motion: The Evolution of Treaties from Formation to Termination*
Edited by Malgosia Fitzmaurice and Panos Merkouris

148 *Humanitarian Disarmament: An Historical Enquiry*
Treasa Dunworth

147 *Complementarity, Catalysts, Compliance: The International Criminal Court in Uganda, Kenya, and the Democratic Republic of Congo*
Christian M. De Vos

146 *Cyber Operations and International Law*
François Delerue

145 *Comparative Reasoning in International Courts and Tribunals*
Daniel Peat

144 *Maritime Delimitation as a Judicial Process*
Massimo Lando

143 *Prosecuting Sexual and Gender-Based Crimes at the International Criminal Court: Practice, Progress and Potential*
Rosemary Grey

142 *Capitalism as Civilisation: A History of International Law*
Ntina Tzouvala

141 *Sovereignty in China: A Genealogy of a Concept Since 1840*
Adele Carrai

140 *Narratives of Hunger in International Law: Feeding the World in Times of Climate Change*
Anne Saab

139 *Victim Reparation under the Ius Post Bellum: An Historical and Normative Perspective*
Shavana Musa
138 *The Analogy between States and International Organizations*
Fernando Lusa Bordin
137 *The Process of International Legal Reproduction: Inequality, Historiography, Resistance*
Rose Parfitt
136 *State Responsibility for Breaches of Investment Contracts*
Jean Ho
135 *Coalitions of the Willing and International Law: The Interplay between Formality and Informality*
Alejandro Rodiles
134 *Self-Determination in Disputed Colonial Territories*
Jamie Trinidad
133 *International Law as a Belief System*
Jean d'Aspremont
132 *Legal Consequences of Peremptory Norms in International Law*
Daniel Costelloe
131 *Third-Party Countermeasures in International Law*
Martin Dawidowicz
130 *Justification and Excuse in International Law: Concept and Theory of General Defences*
Federica Paddeu
129 *Exclusion from Public Space: A Comparative Constitutional Analysis*
Daniel Moeckli
128 *Provisional Measures before International Courts and Tribunals*
Cameron A. Miles
127 *Humanity at Sea: Maritime Migration and the Foundations of International Law*
Itamar Mann
126 *Beyond Human Rights: The Legal Status of the Individual in International Law*
Anne Peters
125 *The Doctrine of Odious Debt in International Law: A Restatement*
Jeff King
124 *Static and Evolutive Treaty Interpretation: A Functional Reconstruction*
Christian Djeffal
123 *Civil Liability in Europe for Terrorism-Related Risk*
Lucas Bergkamp, Michael Faure, Monika Hinteregger and Niels Philipsen
122 *Proportionality and Deference in Investor-State Arbitration: Balancing Investment Protection and Regulatory Autonomy*
Caroline Henckels
121 *International Law and Governance of Natural Resources in Conflict and Post-Conflict Situations*
Daniëlla Dam-de Jong
120 *Proof of Causation in Tort Law*
Sandy Steel

119 *The Formation and Identification of Rules of Customary International Law in International Investment Law*
Patrick Dumberry

118 *Religious Hatred and International Law: The Prohibition of Incitement to Violence or Discrimination*
Jeroen Temperman

117 *Taking Economic, Social and Cultural Rights Seriously in International Criminal Law*
Evelyne Schmid

116 *Climate Change Litigation: Regulatory Pathways to Cleaner Energy*
Jacqueline Peel and Hari M. Osofsky

115 *Mestizo International Law: A Global Intellectual History 1842–1933*
Arnulf Becker Lorca

114 *Sugar and the Making of International Trade Law*
Michael Fakhri

113 *Strategically Created Treaty Conflicts and the Politics of International Law*
Surabhi Ranganathan

112 *Investment Treaty Arbitration As Public International Law: Procedural Aspects and Implications*
Eric De Brabandere

111 *The New Entrants Problem in International Fisheries Law*
Andrew Serdy

110 *Substantive Protection under Investment Treaties: A Legal and Economic Analysis*
Jonathan Bonnitcha

109 *Popular Governance of Post-Conflict Reconstruction: The Role of International Law*
Matthew Saul

108 *Evolution of International Environmental Regimes: The Case of Climate Change*
Simone Schiele

107 *Judges, Law and War: The Judicial Development of International Humanitarian Law*
Shane Darcy

106 *Religious Offence and Human Rights: The Implications of Defamation of Religions*
Lorenz Langer

105 *Forum Shopping in International Adjudication: The Role of Preliminary Objections*
Luiz Eduardo Salles

104 *Domestic Politics and International Human Rights Tribunals: The Problem of Compliance*
Courtney Hillebrecht

103 *International Law and the Arctic*
Michael Byers

102 *Cooperation in the Law of Transboundary Water Resources*
Christina Leb

101 *Underwater Cultural Heritage and International Law*
Sarah Dromgoole

100 *State Responsibility: The General Part*
James Crawford

99 *The Origins of International Investment Law: Empire, Environment and the Safeguarding of Capital*
Kate Miles
98 *The Crime of Aggression under the Rome Statute of the International Criminal Court*
Carrie McDougall
97 *'Crimes against Peace' and International Law*
Kirsten Sellars
96 *Non-Legality in International Law: Unruly Law*
Fleur Johns
95 *Armed Conflict and Displacement: The Protection of Refugees and Displaced Persons under International Humanitarian Law*
Mélanie Jacques
94 *Foreign Investment and the Environment in International Law*
Jorge E. Viñuales
93 *The Human Rights Treaty Obligations of Peacekeepers*
Kjetil Mujezinović Larsen
92 *Cyber Warfare and the Laws of War*
Heather Harrison Dinniss
91 *The Right to Reparation in International Law for Victims of Armed Conflict*
Christine Evans
90 *Global Public Interest in International Investment Law*
Andreas Kulick
89 *State Immunity in International Law*
Xiaodong Yang
88 *Reparations and Victim Support in the International Criminal Court*
Conor McCarthy
87 *Reducing Genocide to Law: Definition, Meaning, and the Ultimate Crime*
Payam Akhavan
86 *Decolonising International Law: Development, Economic Growth and the Politics of Universality*
Sundhya Pahuja
85 *Complicity and the Law of State Responsibility*
Helmut Philipp Aust
84 *State Control over Private Military and Security Companies in Armed Conflict*
Hannah Tonkin
83 *'Fair and Equitable Treatment' in International Investment Law*
Roland Kläger
82 *The UN and Human Rights: Who Guards the Guardians?*
Guglielmo Verdirame
81 *Sovereign Defaults before International Courts and Tribunals*
Michael Waibel
80 *Making the Law of the Sea: A Study in the Development of International Law*
James Harrison

79 *Science and the Precautionary Principle in International Courts and Tribunals: Expert Evidence, Burden of Proof and Finality*
Caroline E. Foster
78 *Transition from Illegal Regimes under International Law*
Yaël Ronen
77 *Access to Asylum: International Refugee Law and the Globalisation of Migration Control*
Thomas Gammeltoft-Hansen
76 *Trading Fish, Saving Fish: The Interaction between Regimes in International Law*
Margaret A. Young
75 *The Individual in the International Legal System: Continuity and Change in International Law*
Kate Parlett
74 *'Armed Attack' and Article 51 of the UN Charter: Evolutions in Customary Law and Practice*
Tom Ruys
73 *Theatre of the Rule of Law: Transnational Legal Intervention in Theory and Practice*
Stephen Humphreys
72 *Science and Risk Regulation in International Law*
Jacqueline Peel
71 *The Participation of States in International Organisations: The Role of Human Rights and Democracy*
Alison Duxbury
70 *Legal Personality in International Law*
Roland Portmann
69 *Vicarious Liability in Tort: A Comparative Perspective*
Paula Giliker
68 *The Public International Law Theory of Hans Kelsen: Believing in Universal Law*
Jochen von Bernstorff
67 *Legitimacy and Legality in International Law: An Interactional Account*
Jutta Brunnée and Stephen J. Toope
66 *The Concept of Non-International Armed Conflict in International Humanitarian Law*
Anthony Cullen
65 *The Principle of Legality in International and Comparative Criminal Law*
Kenneth S. Gallant
64 *The Challenge of Child Labour in International Law*
Franziska Humbert
63 *Shipping Interdiction and the Law of the Sea*
Douglas Guilfoyle
62 *International Courts and Environmental Protection*
Tim Stephens
61 *Legal Principles in WTO Disputes*
Andrew D. Mitchell
60 *War Crimes in Internal Armed Conflicts*
Eve La Haye

59 *Humanitarian Occupation*
Gregory H. Fox

58 *The International Law of Environmental Impact Assessment: Process, Substance and Integration*
Neil Craik

57 *The Law and Practice of International Territorial Administration: Versailles to Iraq and Beyond*
Carsten Stahn

56 *United Nations Sanctions and the Rule of Law*
Jeremy Matam Farrall

55 *National Law in WTO Law: Effectiveness and Good Governance in the World Trading System*
Sharif Bhuiyan

54 *Cultural Products and the World Trade Organization*
Tania Voon

53 *The Threat of Force in International Law*
Nikolas Stürchler

52 *Indigenous Rights and United Nations Standards: Self-Determination, Culture and Land*
Alexandra Xanthaki

51 *International Refugee Law and Socio-Economic Rights: Refuge from Deprivation*
Michelle Foster

50 *The Protection of Cultural Property in Armed Conflict*
Roger O'Keefe

49 *Interpretation and Revision of International Boundary Decisions*
Kaiyan Homi Kaikobad

48 *Multinationals and Corporate Social Responsibility: Limitations and Opportunities in International Law*
Jennifer A. Zerk

47 *Judiciaries within Europe: A Comparative Review*
John Bell

46 *Law in Times of Crisis: Emergency Powers in Theory and Practice*
Oren Gross and Fionnuala Ní Aoláin

45 *Vessel-Source Marine Pollution: The Law and Politics of International Regulation*
Alan Khee-Jin Tan

44 *Enforcing Obligations Erga Omnes in International Law*
Christian J. Tams

43 *Non-Governmental Organisations in International Law*
Anna-Karin Lindblom

42 *Democracy, Minorities and International Law*
Steven Wheatley

41 *Prosecuting International Crimes: Selectivity and the International Criminal Law Regime*
Robert Cryer

40 *Compensation for Personal Injury in English, German and Italian Law: A Comparative Outline*
Basil Markesinis, Michael Coester, Guido Alpa and Augustus Ullstein

39 *Dispute Settlement in the UN Convention on the Law of the Sea*
Natalie Klein

38 *The International Protection of Internally Displaced Persons*
Catherine Phuong

37 *Imperialism, Sovereignty and the Making of International Law*
Antony Anghie

35 *Necessity, Proportionality and the Use of Force by States*
Judith Gardam

34 *International Legal Argument in the Permanent Court of International Justice: The Rise of the International Judiciary*
Ole Spiermann

32 *Great Powers and Outlaw States: Unequal Sovereigns in the International Legal Order*
Gerry Simpson

31 *Local Remedies in International Law (second edition)*
Chittharanjan Felix Amerasinghe

30 *Reading Humanitarian Intervention: Human Rights and the Use of Force in International Law*
Anne Orford

29 *Conflict of Norms in Public International Law: How WTO Law Relates to Other Rules of International Law*
Joost Pauwelyn

27 *Transboundary Damage in International Law*
Hanqin Xue

25 *European Criminal Procedures*
Edited by Mireille Delmas-Marty and J. R. Spencer

24 *Accountability of Armed Opposition Groups in International Law*
Liesbeth Zegveld

23 *Sharing Transboundary Resources: International Law and Optimal Resource Use*
Eyal Benvenisti

22 *International Human Rights and Humanitarian Law*
René Provost

21 *Remedies against International Organisations*
Karel Wellens

20 *Diversity and Self-Determination in International Law*
Karen Knop

19 *The Law of Internal Armed Conflict*
Lindsay Moir

18 *International Commercial Arbitration and African States: Practice, Participation and Institutional Development*
Amazu A. Asouzu

17 *The Enforceability of Promises in European Contract Law*
James Gordley

16 *International Law in Antiquity*
David J. Bederman

15 *Money Laundering: A New International Law Enforcement Model*
Guy Stessens

14 *Good Faith in European Contract Law*
Reinhard Zimmermann and Simon Whittaker

13 *On Civil Procedure*
J. A. Jolowicz

12 *Trusts: A Comparative Study*
Maurizio Lupoi and Simon Dix

11 *The Right to Property in Commonwealth Constitutions*
Tom Allen

10 *International Organizations before National Courts*
August Reinisch

9 *The Changing International Law of High Seas Fisheries*
Francisco Orrego Vicuña

8 *Trade and the Environment: A Comparative Study of EC and US Law*
Damien Geradin

7 *Unjust Enrichment: A Study of Private Law and Public Values*
Hanoch Dagan

6 *Religious Liberty and International Law in Europe*
Malcolm D. Evans

5 *Ethics and Authority in International Law*
Alfred P. Rubin

4 *Sovereignty over Natural Resources: Balancing Rights and Duties*
Nico Schrijver

3 *The Polar Regions and the Development of International Law*
Donald R. Rothwell

2 *Fragmentation and the International Relations of Micro-States: Self-Determination and Statehood*
Jorri C. Duursma

1 *Principles of the Institutional Law of International Organizations*
C. F. Amerasinghe